Culture and Economic Transformation

ICSSR

Culture and Economic Transformation

Perspectives from India and China

Editors
Surjit Singh
Surinder S. Jodhka

Indian Council of Social Science Research
New Delhi

RAWAT PUBLICATIONS
Jaipur • New Delhi • Bangalore • Hyderabad • Guwahati • Kolkata

ISBN 978-81-316-0584-4

Published in association with ICSSR, New Delhi

Published by
Prem Rawat for **Rawat Publications**
Satyam Apartments, Sector 3, Jawahar Nagar, Jaipur 302 004 (India)
Phone: 0141 265 1748 / 7006 Fax: 0141 265 1748
E-mail: info@rawatbooks.com
Website: www.rawatbooks.com

New Delhi Office
4858/24, Ansari Road, Daryaganj, New Delhi 110 002
Phone: 011 2326 3290

Also at *Bangalore, Hyderabad, Guwahati* and *Kolkata*

Typeset by Rawat Computers, Jaipur
Printed at Chaman Enterprises, New Delhi

Contents

Part II
Changing Culture and Society

Foreword

The Indian Council of Social Science Research (ICSSR), New Delhi, through its International Collaboration Programme, invests significant time and energy in developing collaborative links with social scientists, scientists, social science organizations and academic institutions in India and the overseas. Over the years, it has established strong international links with several countries across continents through research collaborations and exchange of academia. The global focus and presence of ICSSR broadens the international opportunities available to Indian social scientists. The ICSSR and the Chinese Academy of Social Sciences (CASS), Beijing, for example, have been collaborating and promoting understanding and cooperation among the social scientists of the two countries. A major component of the understanding is to provide a platform to scholars of both the countries to share their research through organizing joint seminars.

Keeping above in view, a two-day ICSSR-CASS seminar on 'Meanings of Change: Culture and Economic Transformation in India and China' was held in association with the Institute of Development Studies, Jaipur during 9–10 April 2011. The presentations in the seminar were organized around the themes of city and the country, emerging middle classes, pattern of consumption, cultures of exclusions, caste, community, migrant labour, gender and society, civil society, national minorities, etc.

Professor Surinder S. Jodhka of Jawaharlal Nehru University, New Delhi was the leader of the Indian delegation while Professor Du Zhixiong, Senior Research Fellow and Deputy Director General of the Institute of Rural Development, CASS, Beijing and Professor Zhang Youyun, Deputy

Director General, International Cooperation Bureau, CASS led the Chinese side. Dr K.N. Jehangir, former Director and M.A. Jawaid, Deputy Director, ICSSR coordinated the organization of the seminar in association with Professor Surjit Singh, Director, Institute of Development Studies, Jaipur. ICSSR puts on record its appreciation for Professor Singh and Professor Jodhka for taking the responsibility of editing the papers and preparing a final manuscript for publication. The Council is also grateful to Rawat Publications, Jaipur for bringing out the volume.

We hope that this volume will be of immense use to both the teachers and students interested in the study of social and cultural life in the two great countries. It will also be of benefit to the policy makers as well as general readers who are interested in understanding the contemporary and emerging social realities in India and China.

Sukhadeo Thorat
Chairman, Indian Council of Social Science Research
New Delhi

Acknowledgements

The Indian Council of Social Science Research (ICSSR), New Delhi and the Chinese Academy of Social Science (CASS), Beijing jointly organized a seminar at Jaipur that brought together scholars from both the countries to discuss culture and economic transformation in their respective countries. A variety of papers were presented by these scholars that touched upon such important aspects as migration, the emerging middle classes, gender, preference for sons, income inequalities, rural-urban differences, urban housing, labour market, small and medium enterprises, and the minority question among others. The present volume is a collection of these papers in a somewhat revised form. We owe our gratitude to all the contributors who spared their valuable time to participate in the seminar and revise their papers for the volume.

We are grateful to the ICSSR for entrusting us with the onerous task of editing the volume. A wide range of experts participated in the seminar as chairpersons of different sessions, discussants and rapporteurs. We thank them all. Special mention must be made of Prof. M.M. Salunkhe, Vice Chancellor, Central University of Rajasthan, who took time off from his busy schedule to inaugurate the seminar. We owe our gratitude to Prof. Javeed Alam and Dr. Ranjit Sinha, the then Chairman and member-secretary of the ICSSR for their support and active participation in the seminar. Prof. K.L. Sharma, Vice Chancellor, Jaipur National University also extended his unstinting support and we are thankful to him. We are also grateful to Prof. Du Zhixiong, Senior Research Fellow and Deputy Director General of the Institute of Rural Development, CASS, Beijing and Prof. Zhang Youyun, Deputy Director General, International

Cooperation Bureau, CASS who led the Chinese delegation to the seminar besides a few other Chinese scholars like Zhang Juwei, Wu Xiaoping, He Rong, Zhang Liping, Chen Guangjin, Wang Zhiyong among others for participating in the seminar. We are equally grateful to the Indian scholars who came from different parts of the country to participate in the seminar. Dr K.N. Jehangir, former Director, Dr M.A. Jawaid, Deputy Director and Dr Sobin George, Assistant Director of ICSSR worked hard in doing preparatory work for the seminar.

We express our gratitude to the ICSSR for giving us the opportunity to bring together scholars from the two countries. Finally, we are also grateful to Rawat Publications for publishing this volume in a nice and timely manner.

Surjit Singh
Surinder S. Jodhka

Contributors

Jayanti Alam, formerly Senior Fellow, ICSSR New Delhi, now based in Hyderabad as an independent scholar.

Surinder S. Jodhka, Professor, Centre for Study of Social Systems, Jawaharlal Nehru University, New Delhi.

Zhang Juwei, Deputy Director and Professor, Institute of Population and Labour Economics, Chinese Academy of Social Sciences, Beijing.

Zhang Liping, Associate Research Fellow, Institute of Sociology, Chinese Academy of Social Sciences, Beijing.

Darshini Mahadevia, Professor, Faculty of Planning and Public Policy, CEPT University, Ahmedabad.

R.K. Mishra, Director, Institute of Public Enterprises, Hyderabad.

Aseem Prakash, Assistant Professor, Jindal School of Government and Public Policy, O.P. Jindal Global University, Sonepat.

N. Rajaram, Professor, Central University of Gujarat, Gandhinagar.

He Rong, Associate Research Fellow, Institute of Sociology, Chinese Academy of Social Sciences, Beijing.

Surjit Singh, Professor and Director, Institute of Development Studies, Jaipur.

Wu Xiaoying, Associate Research Fellow, Institute of Sociology, Chinese Academy of Social Sciences, Beijing.

Wang Zhiyong, Associate Professor, Institute of Population and Labour Economics, Chinese Academy of Social Sciences, Beijing.

Introduction

SURJIT SINGH AND SURINDER S. JODHKA

India and China are the two rapidly growing economies of the world today. The pace of economic growth in the two countries has been particularly rapid over the past two or three decades. Simple calculations by economists would suggest that China would soon overtake the United States of America as the largest economy of the world. Similarly, India is also fast emerging as an economic giant. With their growing integration in the global economy and increasing circulation of their populations, their role in the shaping of future world is going to be very critical. Apart from their growing economic might, the demographics of India and China are also going to be extremely significant. These two Asian countries are home to nearly one-third of the entire humanity. Compared to the western developed nations, their population is also relatively younger and potentially more productive and mobile. With growing emphasis on education and human resource development, the new middle classes of the two countries have the potential of producing leadership in different fields of activity in the world of tomorrow. From two great civilisations of the past, China and India are fast emerging as two important nation-states of the 21st century.

While the world at large is faced with the challenge of re-negotiating its self-image, which has for long been West-centric, these two developing nations also face some critical challenges internally and in relation to each other. The two great civilisations of Asia have for long been culturally interacting with each other. In the recent decades, this interaction has again grown through increasing economic trade. However, the growing economic exchange between the two countries is only beginning of the story. More important areas of interaction are political, social and cultural, which have to be shaped as much by common people of the countries as by the political elite. How could these relations be shaped and what could the two countries learn from each other's experience?

The two countries also face common problems of cultural change. Development and global integration have been very uneven processes in both the countries. Over the past twenty or thirty years social and economic inequalities have grown significantly in both the countries. Their origins and forms are complex and need to be understood and addressed politically. How could we comparatively understand the new 'cultures of exclusions' and help each other in dealing with them?

Given the vastness of their populations and geographical areas, the two countries also encounter internal cultural differences of communities and regions. While these diversities have been age-old and some of them have over the years become less significant, with growth of cities and internal migrations, one also witnesses newer forms of diversities. How could the two countries comparatively understand and engage with these 'old' and 'new' cultures of diversity?

Economic growth in the two countries, rising purchasing powers, particularly of their middle classes, and rapid growth of markets, have transformed patterns of consumption and also produced a new 'culture of consumption'. This new culture indeed helps the two countries to integrate in the global market, but this also creates tensions and conflicts between old values and new attitudes, between older generations and younger people, and between the city and the countryside. How could the two countries learn from each other's experiences in dealing with these complicated cultural challenges?

While the challenges and opportunities confronting the two countries have many similarities, communication across them is rather limited. In absence of direct interaction, understandings about each other invariably happen through the West, mediated by western categories and western scholarship. Interestingly, even when rest of the world is actively speculating about the possible impact of the rise of China and India on the global economy and its social, cultural and political imaginations, the two countries have not yet begun to invest in learning about each other as they ought to be doing.

Such an engagement is critical for the emerging world because of the historical context in which the two countries are rising is very different. Even when they appear to be pursuing a path of economic development which has similarities with the Western experience of industrialization and urbanization, their experience of development is not the same. For example, the social and political framework in which the Chinese manufacturing is organized today is very different from what has been the case with the European capitalist development in the past or in the present. Similarly, notwithstanding its institutional similarities, the democratic politics in India has followed a very different historical trajectory when compared to any country of the West.

The present book is a collection of papers presented in an India-China seminar held in April 2011 wherein scholars from both the countries got together to discuss the issues raised above. A few papers have also been invited later to add wealth to the understanding of the issues.

Issues in Economic Transformation

The book is divided into two sections. The first section deals with China's policies, migration, housing problems and policies. The discussion also throws light on the labour market in China and the changes taking place therein besides the role of trade, self-employed enterprises and labour restrictions.

Surjit Singh is his paper on labour markets in China tries to look at relationship of trade with employment, examines the role of private sector and self-employment enterprises in Chinese economy and then draws some lessons for the labour market. China has observed significant improvement in its gross domestic product per person employed since 1978. Chinese economy has grown at 10 per cent during the reform era and, as a consequence, its labour market has observed wide-ranging changes. Structural change in employment pattern has also occurred and the tertiary sector is now a significant sector in China. As China's population has increased significantly and large numbers of people have entered the labour market over the last two decades or so, during which employment creation has been weak, the country finds itself confronted with a giant problem of unemployment. Over time, more and more sacked workers have become permanently unemployed with limited scope of re-employment due to increasing oversupply of labour. The role of private and self-employment enterprises is thus increasing in creating employment. Jiang Zemin's theory of the 'Three Represents' said the party must embody the changed society, allowing private businessmen to join the party. Inequalities have increased and pushed the efforts to improve poverty situation backward. China increasingly is loosing the advantage of low productivity and low wage. The main reason for low productivity was the lack of technologies in China's manufacturing Industry. But missing educational and skill-enhancing investment in the labour force also has been a contributing factor. International experience shows that the short-term gains that *sweatshop* conditions might give to producers are more than those lost in comparison with the long-term productivity gains that a healthy, motivated and increasingly competent staff can provide. The second largest economy in the South East Asia would require gigantic efforts to absorb rural surplus labour. The changing laws would encourage rural-urban migration and distort labour market. Social insurance system also requires modifications, especially in rural areas. In case of rural workers, entirely voluntary savings, possibly with some support from communities and benefits according to the accumulation on individual accounts, are the social securities. The issue of migrant workers is posing serious problems for Chinese economy and not all are covered by social security measures. The housing policy is also mainly urban-oriented. Labour supply may affect the development of rural industries through two mechanisms – availability of cheap labour and unemployment pressure – the paper argues. Like any other developing country, increasingly self-employment is a significant mode of employment in China. This is the result of poor employment effect of growth, which is explained by both the process of shedding of labour in the state-owned enterprises (SOEs) and rapid technological change. There is lack of consistent and regular monitoring of labour standards throughout China due to insufficient allocation of financial and personnel resources. Both collusion at the local level and widespread corruption are exacerbating the problem. Many localities turn a blind eye to problems or are part of the management or ownership of the enterprise in question. The paper also argues that if the Chinese strategy for further growth, employment creation and poverty eradication is based only on securing a larger share in global trade, it may not lead to the desired success. Unemployment will continue to rise, poverty eradication will slow down and inequality will rise significantly. Moreover, the Chinese experience – which by many is seen as a success story of the virtues of international trade liberalisation – pays testimony to the critique that free trade alone does not ensure jobs, development and poverty eradication.

R.K. Mishra, in his paper on 'Small and Medium Enterprise Clusters in India', points out that the SME sector is expanding. Micro-enterprises, which have been growing at rapid pace and are providing institutional support to the disadvantaged people, are joining the SME sector. This new development, he argues, would change the SME cluster horizon and call for new approaches and strategies for both financial institutions and the governments. The facilitating and supporting environment by the financial institutions and government authorities through better financing patterns, minimum financing constraints, good governance policies, low inflation, minimum entry level regulation and processing time, good skilled manpower, coupled with transparent processing procedures, least supervisory hurdles, can make SMEs prosper. Since, from the government point of view, the development and growth of SMEs is important for economic growth, social development, poverty alleviation, employment generation and technological innovation, there is need for paradigm shift in financial services for SMEs. The shift includes change of mindset of bankers, shift from product focus to customer focus, and from just lending to package of financial services.

Juwei and Zhiyong, in their paper 'Rural Migrant Workers in China', try to estimate the scale and structure of rural migrant workers. They attempt to describe some important characteristics of rural migrant workers, especially their working and living status in urban areas. The paper reports that though the wages are rising for rural migrant workers, their earnings are still very low in comparison to local resident workers. Most rural migrant workers earn minimum wage during the regular working time, but they can earn double the wage by working overtime. The overtime income contributes more than half the regular income. The economic recession did contribute to reduction in production by firms thereby leading to reduction in overtime incomes of rural migrant workers. Rural migrant workers do struggle to earn higher incomes. They are eager to work overtime in practice. As most rural migrant workers are aware of the fact that they would not be able to stay in urban area for a long time, so they try to earn as much as possible. Most rural migrant workers invariably do not have social security and social insurance. Injury insurance is the only insurance for most. The paper also reveals that as firms have to pay insurance cost for workers under the contract law, they invariably try to pay as less as possible in order to lower the cost. In the face of lack of strict inspection from the local social security authority, firms do manage cost cutting for social insurances. Injury incidences are much higher for rural migrant workers than for urban workers as for the former, working conditions are rather poor. It is, therefore, beneficial for firms to pay injury insurance cost for rural migrant workers as for pension and housing insurance, firms and workers have to share the cost of subscription. The authors report that from the perspective of rural migrant workers, it is better to give up these insurances and social securities as most do not plan to stay in urban area for a long. If they have to return to rural areas, then, they cannot get these insurances. In some urban areas such as Kunshan of Jiangsu province, firms are strictly required to pay all the insurances for rural migrant workers. There is no doubt that legally rural migrant workers can have all the required insurances and social securities in urban areas. Living conditions for rural migrant workers are also poor. Most rural migrant workers live in the suburbs of the cities, or what are called villages in the cities. Many rural migrant workers live in the dormitories or barrack-type shelters provided by firms. Others live in rented houses/apartments having poor living conditions. As the costs are rising, rural migrant workers tend to live far away from the city centre. But, without rural migrant workers' settling down in urban areas, China's urbanisation and industrialisation process would be much slower. The paper calls for government to take effective measures either to increase income of rural migrant workers or provide subsidies for their comfortable settlement in city such as for housing, education and medical care. Hu Jintao's push for the 'scientific-development outlook' and 'harmonious development' to deal with the disharmony created by the yawning wealth gap have apparently not worked.

Jayanti Alam in her paper looks at the migration from gender perspective and raises a host of issues concerning migrating women in India and China. In 2001 there were 314 million migrants in India constituting 31 per cent of the total population and 70 per cent of them were females (221 million). Most women migrate because of marriage and movement of the family for one or other reason. In tribal areas, young unmarried daughters/sisters migrate to cities to work as domestic workers and the males stay back to cultivate the little land the family has. A large number of the migrants are forced to leave the place of their birth due to the forcible grabbing of their land by the government or the big industrial houses. In China, the migration of a large number of rural labourers, especially young and middle-aged farmers, to the cities has led to the emergence of new problems both for the migrant workers and the development of agriculture/rural areas. For example, skills and the other qualifications of the migrant workers are unable to meet the needs of development in the secondary and the tertiary sectors, and agricultural work thus is shouldered by the old and the women. Similarly, a big majority, like in case of India, may return to their lands for harvesting even if the earnings in the cities are higher than in agriculture. The author cites other reasons for women migration (in both the countries) like (i) they want to earn more or/and independently of men, (ii) escape the fear/torture of sexual abuse and violence, (iii) single women, divorcees and widows desiring to escape from the social rules and stigma, and (iv) escape pressures of marriage and/or to remain chaste. Women are increasingly moving as job seekers, independent of their men, neither as 'associational' nor as 'forced' or 'tied up'. The migrants in China are, unlike in India again, have been brought under the urban social security systems, but it is also argued that they do not get the minimum living allowances. Though the government provides free training to migrant workers nationwide, the poor and the needy still can hardly avail it because of lack of information. It is also argued that women's work and studies are always looked down upon and devalued. This results in discrimination of women in terms of low wages and hardships in promotion. The paper also notes that compared to single or unmarried women, married women have lower chance of gainful employment. This shows how unabashedly patriarchal the society and the world of finance market is and how the females are regarded as mere sex objects and reproductive machines! It is also believed that single women do not have the burden of a family to take care of and, therefore, they can devote more time to work better.

Darshini Mahadevia in her paper states that both India and China have resorted to very different urban policy regimes, land ownership regimes and migration policies, resulting in very different outcomes for migrants in the urban areas. The paper deals with housing policies in general and for the migrants in particular in these two countries. It first discusses urbanisation, migration and urban poverty and then the institutional settings and housing policies in both the countries drawing implications of these on the housing of the migrants. The housing conditions of the urban migrants in both the countries are then described. The author notes that low-income migrants are the most vulnerable and discriminated against the native population in both the countries although the national economic growth is very much dependent on the contribution of the migrants. None of them have any strong policy for facilitating or ensuring decent housing conditions for the migrant workers. While *hukou* determine the fate of migrants in China's urban areas, availability of affordable housing, employment and income, and restrictive state level policies on defining urban citizenship determine the fate of migrants in India's urban areas. In both countries, housing for the migrants has been tagged on to the overall urban housing policy and there are institutional restrictions in migrants' access to subsidised public housing. If migrants can afford to buy, they can procure a house from the private housing market in both the countries. In China, the pace of urban transformation is much faster than India. This has resulted in massive demolitions: in India of the slums and squatter settlements and in China of the migrant enclaves. In India, the recent migrants, without residency proof, lose out and do not get any alternative accommodation. It seems that even in China the migrants lose out, even though there is now some compensation mechanism put in place through the pressure of the migrant communities themselves and academics and activists in the cities. Besides, rural migrants in urban areas of China are among the poorest of the rural residents. In India, economically better off rural population migrates to the cities. Hence, the low-income rural migrants start from very different positions in the urban settings. The reforms with regard to migrants in China in recent years have helped these migrants accessing relatively better housing than before. In India, no such reforms have been witnessed and the urban areas in general and metropolitan cities in particular remain overwhelmingly hostile to the low-income migrants. In fact, this hostility, manifesting in numerous ways such as elitist land policy, complex and bureaucratised citizenship criteria and chauvinist political environment, has reduced rural-urban migration since 1990s. The recent housing policies in India, ironically based on market paradigm, are being offered to the migrants which have been failed by both the state and the market. The low-income migrants continue to live in Indian cities through subversions of existing legislation, seeking support from caste and religious political affiliations (clientalism) and if none else then protests and resistance movements. Migrants in Chinese cities also circumvent the regulatory mechanisms to survive but do not subvert them.

The author argues that the rhetoric of putting growth, rather than equitable growth, at the centre stage of the development processes has led to perverse outcomes. A human-centred housing policy does not exist that is inclusive of concerns of the low-income migrants. Indian state has weak ability in welfare distribution in favour of the vulnerable sections, including the urban poor, while Chinese socialist market economy displays higher order of equity transfers compared to India. China does have a better policy environment as well as better implementation practices of the policies for the low-income migrants compared to India. Both the countries can learn from each other's experience with regard to policies for incremental housing. Finally, both the countries have to go a long way to ensure a decent housing to the low-income migrant population in their cities, in view of rapid urbanisation in the coming decades.

Changing Culture and Society

The papers in section two address the issues concerning changing culture and society. Some papers deal with changing role of the middle class while others confront changing consumption behaviour and rising inequalities in these two countries. The issue of religious monetary giving at individual level in contemporary China is also discussed. A paper also explores the impact of globalisation on the construction and transformation of gender discourse, and also the influence of this transformation on the situation of working women. The preference for son and related issues are browsed in another paper.

Aseem Prakash in his paper 'Towards Understanding the Nature of Indian State and the Role of Middle Class' indicates that the state is not a homogenous organic whole. It is not only divided administratively into macro, meso and micro levels but is segmented by differing economic interests, caste, religion, ethnicity and religion. State is not autonomous, though its autonomy at each level is constrained by different sets of socio-economic groups. The interests of these groups, present at different levels of polity, do not necessarily complement each other. The unevenness of economic reforms is the best testimony of this fact. The fact is that the middle class articulates dominant interests at all levels. At the macro level, it has acquired the legitimacy to speak on behalf of the society. It provides an ideological articulation and legitimacy to the present face of capitalist development under the overall domination of corporate capital in alliance with international capital. At the sub-national level, the situation is complex. This very middle class articulates their interests with the help of their social identity – be it religion, caste or ethnicity. The use of social identity ruptures the boundaries between state and market and allows the permeation of dominant interests in the rank and file of the state. The argument the paper puts forth is that the middle class identity is predominantly an upper caste identity. There is relatively more middle class amongst the other backward classes but its presence amongst the Dalits, Adivasis and Muslims is very little. In a scenario of segmented state, the role of middle class becomes crucial in preserving the status quo.

N. Rajaram in his paper examines the continuities and discontinuities in the emerging middle class of India. The paper finds that the old middle class exhibited probity in public and showed concern for others, but the new middle class is brash in lifestyle exhibiting self-centred consumerism. This increasing consumerism has accompanied increasing insecurity in the conditions of employment and insecurity. This ambivalence in attitude is clearly visible in the increasing consumerism. The author reports that there is increasing religiosity of the middle class, especially among the Hindus. It is not only the increase in religiosity, but there is also an attempt to reinvent it and women have been given greater roles in rituals and practices. The middle class has become global in taste, lifestyle and consumption. Women belonging to the middle class have greater opportunities to take up new occupations emerging in the new economy, like business process outsourcing (BPO) sector. However, in the north and western states of India, there is also a worrying phenomenon of declining sex ratio of females amongst the middle classes – indicating still a strong 'son preference' in spite of increase in wealth and education. The paper concludes that all this portends to a difficult future for the middle class, and shows that while consumerism has become the status marker of having arrived to show off rank and status, the reinventing of religion and the declining sex ratio in the states in which the middle class is growing seems to reflect the continuance of traditional hierarchical normative structure.

Surjit Singh's paper on 'Emerging Patterns of Income and Consumption in China' tries to analyse the emerging patterns in income and consumption in the background of emerging inequalities in China. The paper reveals that since the initiation of reforms and especially after 1990 not only China has witnessed high growth rates but it has also observed rising inequalities and significant changes in per capita income, its sources and consumption levels and its structure. Rural China too has witnessed an upward improvement in per capita income and consumption patterns. The two major sources of rural income are farming and animal husbandry activities, the paper notes. The importance of food in total consumption expenditure is going down, as expected, with increasing incomes across areas and regions. There are still laggard regions and even within coastal regions some provinces are performing better than others. Rural areas lag behind urban areas in terms of educational achievements and vocational training. Quality of life has improved in urban areas with increasing per capita floor area. There are four types of dualities found in China, viz., dual household registration system, dual employment system, dual system of income distribution and dual education system. The common notion that households are increasingly using savings to incur expenditure is not witnessed as in both rural and urban areas households are borrowing for housing and business. The paper shows that there are various factors fuelling the income and consumption gaps in China, ranging from policy restrictions, taxation regime, international trade and the reform process itself, and have also led to development of urban real estate interests and corruption, education, health and social security development problems. However, growth has led to poverty reduction across areas and states with varying effects. Rural growth reduces inequality in both urban and rural areas, and also between them. Not only the wages are lagging behind profits in recent times, the entire population is also not covered by social security system.

Given the above scenario, the Chinese government needs to protect the property rights of low-income people and create equal opportunities for smaller companies to enter all sectors. It is articulated that greater urbanisation may help ease the income gap. China needs to boost economic transformation and improve social security. China's poor have acquiesced in an iniquitous system because their income is also rising; if that stops, they might not be so tolerant of entrenched privilege. The state has to address its consumption-light growth model. The government's efforts have been focused on extending public health, education and pension services to reduce the need for household precautionary savings and to free up income to enhance expenditure, but it may not be enough. The reason the mass of China's households are not spending is not because they save too much, but because the incomes are too low. The reason the rich are saving is not because they want to, but because they have too much money to spend all of it. The best way to boost consumption in China is not through extending public services but through a more equitable distribution of income. A high Gini coefficient is not disastrous and is commonly seen in the process of rapid economic growth. In the short term, the government can narrow the wealth gap through transfer payments, including welfare, social security and government subsidies, and in the long term, better education can effectively equalise opportunity. Tax increases are not necessary to increase social security and welfare. Increased consumption and the retained profits of state-owned enterprises can provide the means for income redistribution, and transfer payments can help ease the widening income gap while expanding domestic demand. The need is to restructure expenditures to focus on increasing social welfare instead of building roads and bridges alone.

He Rong in her paper focuses on religious monetary giving at individual level in contemporary China. It attempts to find the determinants of religious giving based on the research done by western scholars and goes on to test the connections using the data of empirical study of values in China. The paper is helpful in getting the basis of religious giving and also an overview of religious life in China. It is observed that in both urban and rural China, religious giving has significant link with religious involvement, participation and belief. However, the only exception is belief in the existence of 'karma' held by rural people. In both urban and rural China, however, religious giving has no strong link with the demographic variables, though the education is an exception; countrymen with more education do tend to give more. The paper says that since belief in 'karma' focuses more on this-world effect, and good deed-good effect causation, in some way a self-made ideal, it has no significant effect on religious giving in rural areas. Demonstrating the basic pattern of religious involvement and giving, compared to the more institutionalised and continual religious giving in Christian tradition, the paper articulates that in China religious giving is small in amount, situational and discretionary than being a fixed part of the household expenditure. It also shows that religious giving is strongly related to religiosity, whether or not there has been a congregational religious life. From policy perspective, the results show that religious activity will encourage voluntary giving and can be a way to foster altruism, cooperation and other civic virtues in contemporary Chinese society.

Surinder S. Jodhka in his paper on 'Religious Diversity and Nation-State' argues that after independence, India, unlike the nation-states of Western Europe, had not evolved as a homogenous 'political community'. For him the experience of participation in the freedom movement against colonial rule had brought people from different walks of life together. The new institutions of governance and communication introduced by colonial rulers made Indian nationalism possible. However, India basically is still characterised by a large number of diversities. The political elite that acquired power after 1947 had a rather narrow social base and were mostly from the traditional upper castes of Indian society with Western education in schools and colleges opened by the colonial rulers. Some returned after studying further in British universities to join modern professions in colonial India. It is argued that from the days of colonial censuses, caste groups had started to consolidate themselves into regional blocks and were to play an important role in democratic politics in the coming days. However, the most challenging was the diversity of religions. Mobilisation of communities around religious passion has produced immense amount of violence in the 20th century in India and in other parts of the subcontinent. Among the followers of Islam in India, at the levels of cultural mores, social/kinship networks and language, there have always been diverse communities. Christians and Sikhs too were important minority groups in independent India, with several other religious communities, like Buddhists, Jains, Zoroastrians and Jews, showing their presence. Besides this, India was confronted with several material/economic difficulties. Due to colonial policies and the historically evolved structures of social hierarchy and dependency, the prevailing state of affairs in rural India was rather dismal.

The paper also deals with nation, development and secularism. India adopted the path of mixed economy for its economic development. The state was not only to regulate the economy and markets to bring growth and prosperity, but to invest in building economic infrastructure and industrial production. The paper also looks at religious diversity and the challenges it poses to development. It is pointed out that development and modernisation of a country with a stagnant economy, and divided culturally and socially, was indeed a difficult task. Besides, India also faced historical and demographic compulsions that made its new leadership to choose the path of secularism. To the author, all sections of social scientists recognised the centrality of religion though it did not acquire centrality in the research agenda of any of the social science disciplines. It is argued that despite varied criticisms of the grand theses on modernisation and development, religion, or even culture, rarely became a serious topic for public policy debate until the 1980s. Though scholars, for academic reasons, did study religious communities and traditions, the planners and those engaged with the implementation of development projects seldom took the question of ethnic minorities and their socio-economic status seriously. The designed programmes were mainly based on economic criteria. This approach to religion and secularism had many problems. It was rarely seen as a political process or an ideological system. The continued presence of religion just meant distortion and it could not become a part of the development discourse in India, but was seen as hindrance to development.

The paper also deals with the crisis of development and the cultural turn. The 1980s saw some interesting new trends, including the rise of several 'new' social movements. A variety of actors critiqued the dominant development paradigms. Also popular mobilisations on religious and communal lines produced an acute sense of anxiety among the 'secular' elite of India. The question of ethnic identity acquired a new dimension with old Nehruvian secularism becoming a contentious issue. The question of community identities and their place in building a democratic national society was raised as a core issue in this debate. The ideas of development and modernity were criticised on moral grounds as well. Also religious movements addressed the globalisation of production and consumption, including flexibility and mobility of their labour, and became a major element in their politics of belonging. India too witnessed the rise of several 'new' social and political movements around questions of environment, ethnicity, gender, urban bias in development, and human rights, during the decades of 1980s and 1990s. Finally, the paper deals with the question of minority getting centre stage in the development. The question of citizenship has begun to take priority over the questions of identity and cultural distinctiveness. The paper argues that though not everyone will swallow with relegation of the identity question, the shift is certainly going to have an appeal for the large mass of Indian Muslims for whom struggles of everyday life have always been paramount. Questions of cultural identity are indeed very critical, but they will have to be articulated through the language of citizenship and democratic rights.

Wu Xiaoying's paper explores the impact of globalisation on the construction and transformation of gender discourse, and also the influence of this transformation on the situation of working women. A comparative analysis of the related state policies and gender events or discussions in media in Maoist and post-Maoist eras is attempted based on the categorisation and analysis of the oral narrative data of 21 working women from different occupations, ages, strata and marital statuses. The paper concludes that the construction of gender discourse in Chinese society has an obvious transformation from Maoist to post-Maoist period. This transformation is not simply from a state discourse to another market discourse, but from a gender discourse of state-dominant 'pan-politicalisation' to a market-oriented 'pan-marketism'. Further, the gender discourse in Maoist time has elements of the state discourse and the traditional discourse, which are respectively bound in the two poles of a spring. Through exclusion and rebound it establishes the authoritative position of the state discourse, and also determines the existing space of the traditional discourse. This kind of gender equality as the base of the state will has a very strong rallying point and practical consequence. But, since it is limited in the equality of gender obligations and ignores the demands of women, they gain half the world, but they lose the freedom of choice under the double burden of the reality. The gender discourse in post-Maoist era has elements of dominant market discourse aside from the state discourse and traditional discourse. They overlap each other, forming a dynamic balance and collaboration. Among them the state discourse to a large extent relies on the market discourse, and the market discourse gets support from the traditional discourse. Facing the complicated state of overlapping of the three discourses, women have various opportunities and freedom of choice, but simultaneously they often lose the direction of choice in contradictory gender discourses. The market discourse in globalised era is just a quality discourse, which is divided into two aspects, viz., the modern competitive ability based on the principle of individualism and the symbol of body consumption based on the orientation of women's special role in the relationship of gender. The first aspect gets the strong mobilisation and support from the state, whereas the second aspect gains assistance from the traditional discourse and becomes a part of consumptive fashion. The core of the market discourse is the relationship of alternative between 'doing well' and 'marrying well' for women. Besides, the paper argues that on the one hand, globalisation has changed the narrative content and way of the state discourse, on the other hand, it has led to the alliance of the market and the traditional discourse. The discourse combining marketism and sexism is the main characteristic of gender discourse in the present era of globalisation. It represents no longer a myth of gender equality ideologically constructed by the state and discounted in reality, but a calculated negotiating strategy of utilising the balance of various forces among the state, market and traditional culture to make subject choice in the process of pursuing the modernity and individual freedom. The feminist thoughts and consciousness of human rights entering into China along with the globalisation will destroy to some extent the characteristics of the gender discourse. In the risky society of globalisation, there exists a universal crisis sense among Chinese working women. The different understandings and evaluations on the state of gender equality and the situation of women themselves indicate that the transformation of gender discourse has varied impact on the working women with different ages and strata in extent and direction. On the contrary, their negotiating strategies facing the crisis are respectively different. Women today hold the nominal chances to pursue overall possibilities and opportunities: yet in the masculinity culture, many of this kind of paths are closed actually. Furthermore, for getting the existing possibilities and opportunities, women have to abandon the old stereotyped identity in a more thorough way than men. In other words, they experience the arrival of the late modernity in a way which is more perfect and contradictory.

The last paper by Zhang Liping puts forward a vital question of raising son or daughter and preference for son in southwest China. It analyses that the gender preference has been the cause of increased sex ratio at birth. The author argues that from the cultural point of view, the existence of the patrilineal inheritance system ensures the continuation of a descent. A son and a daughter is thus a very good model. Another perspective is what the family resources permit. Limited resources hinder the replacement level of children, as woman has to maintain the level of per capita resources. As an ideal model, not every family can achieve the premise of natural birth and an artificially altered natural reproductive choice, is bound to change the law of nature, thereby changing the natural distribution of sex ratio at birth. The paper reports that there are disputes arising due the remarriage of the woman after the death of her husband because of limited property of the family. The skills are also inherited and not allowed to go outside the family. In the families with no son, clan elders together protect the inheritance and family's wealth. In the study area, non-sub-family within the family members gets the endowment. Childless families also adopt child and generally a son of the brother is adopted. Nephew of the family gets the family pension and fields as inheritance. The paper states that as daughters do not inherit property, the dowry is increasing hugely, which has become heavy economic burden on poor families. In some cases, the dowry brought in by the daughter-in-law is passed on to the daughter. In the village studies, majority wanted two children and that too the boys. Thus, from cultural viewpoint, the existence of the patrilineal inheritance system ensures the continuation of a family. It is also reported that resources of the family limit the size of the family. Under the China's current one-child norm, families can afford to have daughters because of interest-oriented mechanism. Such families can get state subsidies or subsistence allowances. This means economic advantage results in birth of females. Family with two girls gets subsidies from the state, which is envy of many. In the study village, the promotion of daughter for old age has emerged among the villagers. It would break the male line of succession in case of real estate and land inheritance.

Thus, the book, as a whole, gives a broad overview of the issues involved in the economic and socio-cultural transformations of the two societies, viz., China and India. There are many cultural similarities between the two, though economic transformation is trying to break the traditional modes of functioning of the societies. If on the one hand economic inequalities are increasing in both the countries, on the other hand gender rights and cultural shifts are taking place. The volume has simply discussed the bare issues, which gives better understanding of two countries. Knowing each other better holds promise for future.

Part I

Issues in Economic Transformation

1

Labour Market Experiences in China

Some Insights

SURJIT SINGH

Large numbers of Asians still live in poverty and this poverty is widespread across Asia. This is despite the fact that Asian economies have made significant strides in last few decades. How can Asia help its poor get out of poverty? There are many causes of poverty. The major reason is that the poor earn too little from the work that they do. Most Asians sustain themselves and their families by using labour. Most Chinese work as self-employed workers, especially in rural areas. They work on family farms/enterprises in kind or for a wage. This means improvement in labour market opportunities can help enhance incomes, reduction in poverty and improve living standards. The challenge thus is not merely to create jobs for the unemployed and the new entrants to the labour force, but also to improve the productivity and earnings of the available jobs. China has done fairly well since the onset of reforms in 1978, especially in the rural areas. However, in the recent years, China too is facing challenges of poverty, unemployment and raising productivity of workers. China's labour market is exceptional as it has huge labour force that is concentrated in agriculture. Above all, China is an economy in transition with enormous rural-urban disparity (ADB, 2005). However, the economic reforms since 1978 served China very well as it increasingly became market-oriented with Chinese characteristics. Along with the importance of state-owned enterprises (SOEs) and township and village enterprises (TVEs), private sector also has developed significantly in recent years. Private sector especially has now an added role in the labour market. Self-employed enterprises too have been emerging importantly. Self-employment in both rural and urban areas is increasing fast due to distress situation and also as a consequence of dislocations due to the development strategy. Of late trade is also having wide-ranging ramifications in Chinese economy with regard to employment. Against this backdrop the paper analyses the Chinese labour market and issues related to it. It also looks at relation of trade with employment, and the role of private sector and self-employment enterprises in Chinese economy in recent times. In the end, it also tries to draw some lessons for the labour market.

Economic Performance: A Backdrop

China initiated modernisation process with a modest economic base.[1] In 1979, its gross domestic product (GDP) was $177 billion (at 2002 prices) and per capita income was $183. This GDP largely came from agriculture and stark poverty stared at it. The World Bank estimates that in the more than two decades since reforms started, average income per capita in China has quadrupled, while more than 270 million people have been lifted out of poverty (Chen and Wang, 2001). From 1978 to 2004, GDP growth in China averaged nearly 10 per cent, the highest rate of any country in the world for the same period (Qin et al., 2006; Yusuf, Nabeshima and Perkins, 2006). Deng Xiaoping's vision put the economy on a different path in 1978 (Singh, 1995, 1998, 2007). By the end of 2004, China's GDP was $1.65 trillion with $1,268 per capita income. It is now the second largest economy after Japan in South East Asia.

China is perhaps one-sixth as large as the United States in current dollars, and that India is one-sixteenth as large (Winters and Yusuf, 2007). Any economic shock arising from Germany or Japan will have higher impact compared to one emanating from China and the least from India. Looking at growth of output and income, China and India have performed very strongly since 1995 in comparison to other large economies of the world (Table 1). China accounted for 13 per cent of the world growth in output over 1995–2004 when India merely accounted for 3 per cent. USA accounted for 33 per cent when its much higher starting share in 1995 offsets its slower growth rate. The 2020 projections put China second only to the USA in terms of contribution to world growth. India is projected to have a slower growth rate during 2005–2020 compared to 1995–2004, but marginally higher contribution to world growth. Amongst the two Asian giants, China outscores. It may be noted here that these two countries are projected to account for 10.3 per cent of world GDP in 2020 – a significant increase from 6.4 per cent contribution. However, emerging economies' growth rates are typically more volatile than industrial countries' rates and as these countries become bigger, volatility would affect others strongly (ibid.).

Table 1

Gross Domestic Products (%)

Economy	*Share of world GDP (2004 $ and exchange rates)*		*Average annual real growth rates*		*Average contribution to world growth*	
	2004	*2020*	*1995–2004*	*2005–2020*	*1995–2004*	*2005–2020*
China	4.7	7.9	9.1	6.6	12.8	15.8
India	1.7	2.4	6.1	5.5	3.2	4.1
USA	28.4	28.5	3.3	3.2	33.1	28.1
Japan	11.2	8.8	1.2	1.6	5.3	4.6
Germany	6.6	5.4	1.5	1.9	3.0	3.3
Brazil	1.5	1.5	2.4	3.6	1.5	1.7
World	100	100	3.0	3.2	100	100

Source: World Bank (2005), *World Bank Indicators.*

Labour Market: Some Concerns

Labour Force Structure

Significant changes have occurred in China's labour force structure since 1978. One marked change in 2005 compared to 1978 is that the China's labour force is not young now (see Appendix 1). In 1978, 55.5 per cent of the labour force was below 34 years of age while in 2005, this proportion stood at 39.6 per cent. The labour force in the age group 15–19 observed a dramatic decline from 13.82 per cent in 1978 to just 1.58 per cent in 2005. This decline has been continuous over the period. Similar fall is observed in case of labour in age group 19–24 where the proportion declined from 15.28 per cent in 1978 to 8.60 per cent by 2005. Labour force in the age group 25–29 increased since 1978 till 1991, to decline thereafter. In most other age groups, the labour has observed increases. Labour in 55-plus age group is 8.7 per cent in 2005 compared to 8.9 per cent in 1978. Some of these changes are driven by population policy that China enforced, i.e., single child norm. Education is another factor that has pulled down share of younger people from the labour force.

What is the employment situation in China? Data shows that in 1978, 401.52 million persons were employed of the 406.82 million economically active populations in China (98.7%) (see Appendix 2). The economically active population increased to 785.79 million by 2011 – a 1.93 times increase. The percentage of employed persons in economically active population stood at 97.3 per cent in 2011, down from 98.7 per cent in 1978. The employed persons increased 1.90 times. The structure of employment has undergone significant change since 1978. For instance, primary sector employed 70.53 per cent of all employed persons in China in 1978 and this proportion continuously fell to 34.8 per cent in 2011. On the other hand, the share of industry in employment was 17.3 per cent in 1978 which increased to 29.5 per cent by 2011 – a 12.2 percentage point increase. The tertiary sector has become the second most important employer in China with 35.7 per cent persons employed in it in 2011 compared to 12.18 per cent in 1978. The importance of primary industry has declined remarkably as China observed significant growth rates in manufacturing sector. However, primary industry employed the largest number of persons in absolute terms. In 1978, it employed 283.18 million persons and touched the peak in 1991 when 390.98 million persons were employed. Since then the number of employed had fluctuated to touch 265.94 million in 2011. The number of employed in secondary industry rose by 3.25 times between 1978 and 2011 when the increase in tertiary industry share in employment was to the extent of 5.58 times. The employment in secondary industry has more or less stagnated around 160 million in the mid-nineties and first half of the present century. Tertiary industry was the second most important employer in terms of absolute numbers in 2011 and growth of services has been phenomenal (9%) since 1990 (Qin, 2004).[2] This appears to be the result of government strategy of promoting tertiary industries to alleviate the acute labour supply pressure at relatively low expenses of material and capital resources. Moreover, growing service industries would help strengthen the non-state-owned business sector, though pricing in the services sector is going to pose a risk of cost disease to the whole economy (ibid.).

The rural population in China increased from 803.2 million in 1978 to 942.54 million in 2004. The rural labour stood at 306.38 million, i.e., labour force participation rate of 38.14 per cent in 1978 and this rate went up to 52.73 per cent in 2004 when rural labour force was 496.95 million (see Appendix 3). In rural areas labour force is dominated by males in China. At the province level, in 2004, top provinces, namely, Henan, Shangdong, Hunan, Guangdong and Sichuan accounted for 36.5 per cent all rural labour in China (Appendix 4). Also, especially in rural China, the importance of farming, forestry, animal husbandry and fisheries has gone down as almost all rural labour was engaged in these activities in 1978, but by 2004, the share of these activities in rural labour declined to 61.6 per cent (Appendix 5). This decline is compensated by rising share of industry to 10.9 per cent in 2004 from 2.9 per cent in 1980. The share of construction activities in rural labour more than doubled during 1980 and 2004 while other non-farm agricultural trades improved their share in rural labour from 5.3 per cent in 1980 to 12.3 per cent in 2004. Thus, rural China has observed significant structural change during the reform era. It also seems that tertiary sector now accounts for one-fifth of rural labour force. At the province level, in 2004, the highest proportion of rural labour was 85.9 per cent in Xinjiang and the lowest 26.3 per cent in Shanghai in farming, forestry, animal husbandry and fisheries activities (Appendix 6). Thus, there are inter-province variations in rural labour engaged in farming, forestry, animal husbandry and fisheries activities. This is reflected in the development level of provinces. The share of rural labour in industry is the highest in Shanghai (45.9%) and the lowest (1.9 %) in Tibet. This shows wide disparity in rural industrialisation across provinces in China. The inter-province variations are not that significant in case of other rural activities as regards the rural labour. Of course, other non-farm agricultural trades have marked differences across provinces.

Economic reforms thus from all perspectives have served Chinese economy very well. It has been among the fastest growing economy in the world till date. China's economic expansion has been led by industry. For instance, the production of manufactured goods increased annually at the rate of 12 per cent during 1990–2002. Moreover, the Chinese economy has also become increasingly more integrated into the global economy. China is more integrated in the world trading system compared to other large economies like Brazil, India, or the United States. Exports and imports are about 25 per cent of GDP in the case of these three countries. However, in case of China, trade represents 70 per cent of its GDP.

There is no doubt that the rapid expansion of Chinese economy has meant improved labour market outcomes for many of its workers, especially those in urban centres and the coastal provinces. However, the economy faces severe challenges in the labour market. First, there exists considerable underemployment in the rural sector, which employed about 490 million workers in 2002 having low productivity.[3] The state enterprises that employed almost 40 million workers in 2001 took care of surplus labour of the economy (Brooks and Tao, 2003). Though employment in state enterprises has contracted considerably since the mid-1990s, falling by almost 37 million between 1995 and 2001, the labour productivity continues to be much lower than in the non-state sector. Research studies suggest that an improvement of labour productivity in state enterprises to non-state levels would render 10 to 11 million workers in these enterprises redundant (ADB, 2005). State enterprises laid off large number of workers in the 1990s. However, jobs did increase annually by 3 per cent since the early 1990s in urban areas. This expansion of jobs took place in the formal private sector that includes foreign-funded enterprises. This sector created 17.5 million jobs between 1995 and 2001. On the other side, labour force surveys report that a far larger number of jobs, around 75 million, were created in the informal sector (Brooks and Tao, 2003). As many jobs in the informal sector are low-productivity and low-paying ones, underemployment is a problem in urban China.

As regards the employment prospects, urban areas fared better than the rural areas. This is largely reflected in the large rural-urban income disparity. This did not lead to large-scale permanent rural to urban migration because of a range of imperfections in the labour market. China's traditional emphasis on heavy industry-based industrialisation caused segmentation between areas. On the one hand, an excessive concentration of capital in urban areas took place and on the other hand, concentration of labour in rural areas. This also created enormous distortions in factor markets. While China initiated reforms in its product markets culminating to World Trade Organisation (WTO) accession, the same vigour was lacking in factor market reforms.

The labour code governing the operation of private enterprises in China does not present obstacles for firms to adjust their employment levels and/or their wages. Instead, rigidities in the labour market are external to the labour code. There are two main restrictions in the labour market – one is the system of official registration used for controlling rural to urban migration. The authorities require households to have a *hukou* (household registration system) card to legally reside in any given place. Like any developing country, even in China there are wide differences between the provisioning of services in rural and urban areas. The *hukou* card ensures access to the amenities that cities provide, such as housing and education, which otherwise are limited and expensive. This restrains legal migration from rural to urban areas and migration between cities. Highly skilled workers and investors are permitted to buy a permit called a 'blue stamp' *hukou* card that enables them to reside in the place of their choice (Chan and Zhang, 1999). This section even if does not buy one they have adequate incomes to pay for the higher fees for services they obtain in the social sector. However, majority of rural workers cannot afford blue stamp *hukou* card. The restrictions on rural-urban migration, however, are gradually being relaxed, though still being important.[4]

Migration in China is thus a transitory phenomenon. However, many workers endure to take advantage of the very significant wage differential. Zhao (1999) for Sichuan province finds that rural labourers earn much higher incomes as migrants than they do as workers in local non-farm and farm sectors and in 1995 there was an annual wage gap between rural and urban work of 2,388 yuan for unskilled workers of comparable background and ability. There is considerable evidence that temporary migrants prefer to stay at home in rural areas and engage in non-farm work if it is available. A less than a third of the difference is accounted for by explicit costs of migration such as transportation and urban housing. Most of the wage gap is due to the social costs associated with migration.[5] These include the disutility of being away from the family, poor quality of housing, limited social services for migrants, danger of being robbed during the trip, and uncertainty associated with not having a *hukou* card.

This has led to an enormous number of floating workers – an estimate puts them at 90 million which is 19 per cent of the total rural labour force (excluding commuters) (Hertel and Zhai, 2004). These workers live and work in one place but do not have a *hukou* card and thus have very limited access to the urban amenities. The other restriction in the labour market in China relates to off-farm labour mobility in the absence of a fully functioning land market that would permit existing land owners to lease out their land to others and migrate to the city to earn higher wages. The result is that the existing land tenure system has raised the opportunity cost of leaving the farm. The fear is that if they do not farm the land they may lose the rights to it. This acts as a strong incentive to continue some level of agricultural activity at a very low profitability level.

Self-employment

One of the most significant employment trends in rural China is the rise of off-farm self-employment in recent years. There has been a veritable explosion of traders, merchants and small- and medium-scale, individual- and household-run businesses (Entwisle et al., 1995). During 1988–95, up to 30 million self-employed workers emerged in rural China, and the self-employment sector was the fastest growing off-farm sector in rural China (Rozelle, Guo and Minggao, 1999). During this period, almost 40 per cent of all new off-farm jobs belonged to the newly self-employed. Self-employment grew fastest in the rich coastal provinces but rural residents began working for themselves in other provinces as well. Among many reasons for this increasing trend in self-employment is argued to the increase in earnings from self-employed work that in turn increased the China's rural incomes in the late 1980a and 1990s (Parish, Zhe and Li, 1995). One view in the development literature is that the emergence of a strong self-employment sector in an economy plays an important role in the overall development process besides being a source of income and employment for rural residents. de Soto in his *The Other Path* (2002) described the emergence of self-employed workers as the foundation of development. Transition economists argue that the rise of self-employment is a sign of the growing importance of markets relative to the state. It is felt that self-employment opens up opportunities for workers that improve incomes, increase capital assets and the overall standard of living of the rural community as new enterprises grow into medium and large size businesses. But this appears to a minority view. Not all scholars agree that the rise of self-employment is a sign of a healthy labour market (Singh and Singh, 1989). Most downplay its importance in the process of economic development. This latter view is based on the premise that the emergence of self-employment often parallels the rise of informal forms of employment in developing economies. In some countries growth in inefficient forms of self-employment has caused conflict with poverty alleviation programmes (World Bank, 2000). Across the world – from India to Brazil and Kenya to

South Africa – informal sector self-employment is empirically shown to be unproductive and lacks social security measures. It is also pointed out that self-employment may play a negative role in the economy by distorting labour market incentives, decreasing official output, reducing government tax revenues and constraining the growth of the private sector. Compared to workers with wage earning jobs, those who are self-employed in rural China earn more on an hourly basis but also assume higher risks (Zhang, Rozelle and Boucher, 2005).

However, education of the participants in informal self-employment could change the perception as is articulated in some circles (see Mohapatra, Rozelle and Goodhue, 2006). It is possible that superior education is more valuable in starting and running self-employed businesses relative to wage work in state and non-state enterprises.[6] The dominant view of informal sector does argue that there is an upward labour mobility from a low productivity activity to high productivity activities. Self-employment in rural China is predominantly a way to step up the employment ladder. The probability of switching to the low productivity sector is low in contrast to the high probability of switching into the high productivity sector. By far the largest share of those that switch out of wage employment is moving towards the high productivity sector. There are still some households that do move into the low productivity sector (ibid.). Self-employment can also/and is a refuge even in a rapidly developing country as China. It is possible that a larger fraction of the labour force might be shifting to the low productive sector in an economic distress situation. In China, there are individuals who are moving from wage employment to the low productivity sector, the main direction of mobility is from wage employment to the high productivity self-employment sector.

There are of course gender aspects to self-employment. It has been shown that women are less likely than men to move out of farming to enter either self-employment or wage employment. Women who have managed to break into the wage sector are also more likely than men to move back into farming. This is very true of China and many studies of rural China reveal an increasing concentration of women in farm work. There is limited number of women in self-employment in rural China. In the developed world, however, women have been the fastest growing segment (in relation to men) among the self-employed.[7] Age of an individual is another factor that determines mobility at the lower end of labour market. Younger workers are more likely to move out of farming to go into self-employment and wage employment; older people in post-reform economies are less mobile due to the accumulation of sector-specific capital.

What exactly is the situation as regards the self-employment in China? In 2004, China had 23.50 million self-employed enterprises (see

Appendix 7), which provided employment to 45.87 million persons. This means, on an average, a self-employed enterprise employed 1.95 persons. The maximum number of self-employed enterprises is located in Guangdong (8.34%) while the least number are in Tibet (0.24%). The top five provinces with self-employed enterprises are Jiangsu, Zhejiang, Shangdong, Guangdong and Sichuan (35.72% of all enterprises) and have 29.02 per cent of all self-employed. Thus, one observes wide variations in self-employment across provinces. The self-employment in urban areas is slight higher than rural areas; 54.96 per cent self-employed are in urban areas. This proportion is the highest in Jilin (85.89%) and the lowest in Hebei (34.14%). Therefore, there is uniform pattern in self-employment across provinces. The reasons for this are amply pointed out in the above discussion. However, in 2010, 25.4 million self-employed individuals were there in rural China itself (see Appendix 8) and this number increased from 14.91 million in 1990 – a 70.4 per cent increase over the years. The number of self-employed in rural employment has almost doubled during 1990 and 2010, though still TVEs is the major employer. It appears that the self-employment in China is going to increase with WTO deepening and other changes taking place in the economy like property rights, etc.

Private Enterprises

From a slow start in the 1980s, the pace of privatisation moved very fast during the 1990s. In China, household responsibility system facilitated the growth of private enterprises. Starting with dismantling of rural collectives and the creation of four special economic zones in Guangdong province initiated the whole process of privatisation.[8] In 2004, there were 36.51 million private enterprises in China employing 50.17 million workers (see Appendix 9). There are three provinces, viz., Shanghai, Jiangsu and Guangdong, accounting for 33 per cent of all private enterprises in China. But Jiangsu and Guangdong together employ one-fifth of all private enterprise persons. And, per enterprise employment varies between 25.2 persons in Hunan and 9.7 persons in Hubei.

Also, about 18.91 per cent of persons employed in private enterprises are employers themselves. This proportion varies from a low of 8.9 per cent in Jilin to a high of 33.31 per cent in Shaanxi. This means that Jilin has created more wage employment in private enterprises. Further, 59.7 per cent employees in private enterprises are in urban areas while the other 40.3 per cent are in rural enterprises. Thus greater private enterprise employment is in urban areas. There are of course inter-province variations; from 28.2 per cent in Hebei to 91.93 per cent in Jilin.

It may also be mentioned here that in 1990, there were 1.13 million private enterprise employed persons in rural areas (see Appendix 8). This employment went up to 33.47 million in 2010, which is 29.6 times increase over these years. As regards the share of private rural enterprises in employment is concerned, it improved from 0.24 per cent in 1990 to 8.1 per cent in 2010.

Influence of Trade

One of the biggest uncertainties for the labour market concerns the impact of opening the Chinese economy as a consequence of WTO accession on rural-urban inequality and income distribution. Labour regulations identified with inefficient functioning of the labour market, such as minimum wage laws and restrictions on hiring and firing, are found to place few serious constraints on the operation of firms. This may either be because the regulations are not particularly binding on closer scrutiny of the labour code, or because compliance with the regulations is weak. Put differently, the factors underlying weak labour market outcomes are to be found elsewhere, and not in cumbersome labour regulations. Also, where labour regulations are constraining the efficient and fair functioning of the labour market, there will typically be only a few elements of the labour code that are a problem. Reforms should focus on these. Even where elements of the labour code need reforms, these elements are by no means the only factors in weak labour market outcomes. Thus improving labour market outcomes will require reforms and interventions in many other areas. Studies show that the factors behind weak labour market outcomes are to be found outside the realm of labour market policies.

Hertel and Zhai (2004) simulate the impact of two key labour market reforms, viz., the *hukou* household registration system and the lack of off-farm mobility on rural-urban inequality and income distribution. It explores how these factor market reforms interact with product market reforms being made as part of China's WTO accession. If *hukou* system is relaxed, it is argued that the labour market distortion caused by this system will amount to tax on rural wages of nearly 81 per cent. The labour market reforms also lead to an increase in migration from the rural to the urban sector. The study shows that 10.1 million additional workers can leave agriculture if they are permitted to lease out land as opposed to simply leaving it behind. Further, if these workers migrate to the off-farm rural labour market, it may in turn induce an additional 7.9 million temporary migrants to the urban sector in order to equalise rural and urban wages. Most of these workers (5 million) are semi-skilled. The release of these workers from agriculture would depress unskilled and semi-skilled wages in the rural non-farming economy by 8.9 per cent and 3.2 per cent respectively. If this happens, skilled wages in the rural non-farming economy would rise by 1.1 per cent. In case of unskilled workers urban wages would decline by 8.4 per cent and for the semi-skilled workers by 2.7 per cent. However, the urban wages for the skilled group would increase by 1.1 per cent. If we reduce the transaction costs associated with temporary migration due to the elimination of the *hukou* system, rural-urban migration would expand by 26.8 million workers, of which 67 per cent would be semi-skilled workers. This whole process would increase the supply of rural labour to the urban economy leading to increase in rural wages and consequently depressing urban wages. Moreover, the reform of the *hukou* system may also draw additional 3.1 million workers labour out of agriculture. The relaxation of the *hukou* system can improve income distribution from 2.59 to 2.42, if measured in terms of the urban-rural income ratio. The combined effect would be much more; it will increase GDP by 2.1 per cent. The urban unskilled wages decline by 17.3 per cent compared to 7.1 per cent fall in urban semi-skilled. When the impact of WTO accession is considered, the skilled wages rise more than semi-skilled wages, which in turn rise more than unskilled wages. The decline in agricultural profitability and the consequent expansion of urban activity not only leads to additional out-migration for agriculture, but also increases temporary migration of 1.2 million workers in the absence of labour market reforms.[9] When labour market reforms are affected, the migration response would be to the tune of 1.3 million workers due to the higher degree of labour mobility out of agriculture. The study finds that the effect of the WTO accession is similar to a second-best result, which appears moderated when labour market reforms precede WTO accession. In the context of WTO accession, GDP increases without labour market reforms by 0.6 per cent and with labour market reforms by 0.5 per cent. This is because the productivity differential across sectors is smaller with the labour market reforms. The reduction in trade barriers gives a substantial boost to trade in China with both exports and imports rising by 15 per cent.

However, what has been the real impact of WTO entry of China on employment in China. Studies have argued that greater market access created a surge in the export of Chinese products. From 2002 to 2007, net exports as a share of GDP in China increased from 2.6 per cent to 7.7 per cent (Chen, 2009). By 2010, China's current account balance was $305 billion. China's exports have primarily been labour- intensive manufactured goods due to China's abundance of inexpensive labour. This focus on labour-intensive manufacturing shifted workers away from the primary sector towards the secondary sector (Martí, Puertas and Fernández, 2011). The percentage of workers employed in agriculture declined from 50 per cent in 2001 to 11.2 per cent in 2010 (World Bank, 2011) when the per cent of GDP attributed to the primary sector declined from 23.5 per cent in 1994 to 11.7 per cent in 2006. As more labour- intensive products are manufactured, there is a greater demand for labour to continue production, which resulted in rising real wages in China across industries. From 2001 to 2006 real annual wages across industries doubled from 12000 yuan to 24000 yuan, in terms of 2007 yuan (Yuan, 2010). This jump in real wages was not limited to the Chinese upper class; it included typically low-wage industries like manufactured and retail. Further, WTO accession helped in greater inflow of foreign direct investment (FDI) into China due to relaxation in restrictions. The FDI actually used increased from US$ 46,878 million in 2001 to US$ 1,16,011 million in 2006 – a jump of 148 per cent. Not only FDI increased, it led to export growth. The foreign invested firms (FIFs) are some of the largest exporters in China with processed exports touching 45 per cent of Chinese exports. Between 2001 and 2006, FIFs provided employment to additional 11 million persons (Chen, 2009). China was able to avoid *maquiladoras* type problem of Mexico due to the gradual decreases in FDI limitations. Maquiladoras are well-known for underpaid overworked employees. China enacted Trade Union Law in 2001, which allowed for collective negotiations (Fung et al. 2006). This helped Chinese workers to form labour unions, granting employees more power to negotiate wages and working conditions. However, the role of SOEs in the economy declined that led greater role of private enterprises. It is also argued that difference in the labour productivity of domestic firms and FIFs declined after WTO accession. In 2001, the labour productivity of FIFs across industries was 1.6 times that of domestically invested firms, which by 2006 reduced to 1.02 times (Chen, 2009a). FIFs have lost the advantage of higher labour productivity they had initially. It is also pointed out that revaluation of yuan is leading to reduction in exports recently resulting in massive unemployment especially in sectors like textiles, clothing, shoemaking, toys, motorcycles and agricultural sectors. Any appreciation in the range of 5 to 10 per cent in yuan would cause a loss of 3.5 million non-agricultural jobs in China (Zhang, 2009). A slow revaluation process would have less intense negative repercussions. However, the yuan appreciated 18 per cent during January 2006 and June 2008 itself (ibid.). Moreover, trade-rate-quotas (TQRs) restricted structural unemployment in the agricultural sector (Zhou and Kang, 2009). Situation has got complicated after 2008 financial meltdown that reduced over all economic growth and affected employment.

But may be it is good for Chinese economy to rely more on domestic market and dependence on export- and investment-led growth to an economic structure that draws greater support from domestic private consumption. By drawing increased support from services-led consumer demand, China's model could embrace a more labour intensive growth recipe. It is estimated that China's model could embrace a more labour-intensive growth recipe. It is estimated that China's services sector requires about 35 per cent more jobs per unit of GDP than do manufacturing and construction – the primary drivers of the old model. This implies China could grow at an annual rate of 7–8 per cent and still achieve its objectives with respect to employment and poverty reduction which was not possible with any thing less than 10 per cent growth because China's old model was not generating enough jobs per unit of output. Services-led growth is, in many ways, the antidote to the 'unstable, unbalanced, uncoordinated, and ultimately unsustainable' growth model. Current indications are positive on services-led growth process this count, but more time would be needed to firm it up. China has to avoid the middle-income-trap that many high-growth emerging economies faced at the juncture that China has reached now. The criticism of former Primier Wen Jiabao (of 2007) has to be taken seriously to save growth and employment.

Village and Township Enterprises

Village and township-run enterprises in China are latching on to WTO to seek faster development. After 40 years of evolution, China's village and township businesses have become a key force driving the country's market economy. They are adept at adapting to market changes. More than 20.8 million such enterprises employed 128 million rural residents in 2001, generating a combined export value of 940 billion yuan. With China's entry into the WTO, township enterprises are expected to encounter unprecedented challenges in terms of fierce competition and a more rigid market environment. Rural firms may fare well given the fact that they have flexible operational mechanisms and many of them are engaged in intensive sectors. Most of China's township enterprises have grown in the market economy system and have withstood its tests. The rules of the WTO are based on the market economy, so the rules with regard to rural businesses match those of the WTO. The non-discrimination provisions of the WTO will help rural firms unleash their advantages in sectors including farm product processing, textile and household electrical appliances. Their export volume is expected to expand. For one thing, they will find it easier to obtain the power to engage in export trade. Less than 10,000 township enterprises were given this privilege at the end of 2000, according to Lui Zengsheng, Director Ministry of TVEs. Accession to the WTO will enable rural firms to compete with other types of businesses in the country on an equal footing. Township enterprises will be able to expand the scale of using foreign funds through their advantages in resources, operational mechanisms and labour force. The development of township enterprises has been bottlenecked by a lack of funds, partly because it is difficult for them to obtain bank loans, as compared with state-owned enterprises (Singh, 1996). On the other hand, they can also tap the overseas market by launching more joint ventures outside China. By end of 2000, China's village and township-run companies had invested 1.5 billion yuan to run as many as 1,886 businesses abroad (*China Daily,* 21 January 2002).

While China's economy has benefited from the country's economic reforms in the last decades and a certain measure of development and social progress has occurred, the benefit of China's WTO membership can certainly be debated. China's accession to the WTO has had negative employment consequences. It has been profoundly involved in stalling the country's poverty eradication. It has left the majority of its people – its peasants – worse off. The incidence of extreme poverty in rural China declined from 29.2 per cent in 1990 to 13.8 per cent in 1996, but then stopped declining. In urban China, incidence of extreme poverty declined from 2.5 per cent in 1990 to 0.6 per cent in 1996 but then it too stopped declining. As regards the employment, a similar picture appears: employment conditions showed significant improvement in both rural and urban areas from 1990 to 1996 while in the subsequent period from 1996 to 2002, rural employment conditions continued to improve but urban employment conditions worsened substantially. This highlights the flaws in the model of trade liberalisation advocated and facilitated by the WTO. It leaves no space for social and developmental concerns and does nothing to alleviate the externalities it creates. There is no doubt that China achieved a measure of success in exports because of its WTO membership, the negative aspects of WTO accession on employment are also a reality. This is coming through import competition and the resulting in closure of inefficient domestic firms, especially those in the state sector. However, this impact will not be evenly spread across industries. It will hit hardest the sectors of agriculture, automobiles and machinery. Estimates by the World Bank suggested that employment in the agricultural sector will be reduced by 9.6 million (3.6% of the current total), automobiles by 5 million (14.5% of the total), and machinery by 5.8 million (2.5% of the total) by 2008. Though effects differ across industries, the overall employment situation following WTO accession is very challenging. China's labour force was expected to grow by about 80 million by 2010, from approximately 742 million in 2000 to more or less 822 million in 2010. Considering these new entrants to the labour market and the continuing employment losses in agriculture and in state-owned enterprises, China will have to create 10 to 20 or 30 million new jobs each year. This is much higher than China's current job-creation capacity. Thus, in the coming few years, high technology and advanced manufacturing sectors are not expected to be able to add more than one-tenth of that. The main source of job creation will therefore have to continue to be labour-intensive industries, such as textiles and services. Though WTO membership has brought advantages, the negative employment impact of the accession stands to be greater than its positive effect, especially in the short run. Those benefiting straight away are primarily qualified white-collar employees and private capitalists, the people who have already gained most over the last ten years of reforms, while those who are losing are mainly blue-collar workers, farmers and unskilled office workers, whose income has remained more or less stagnant for the last ten years.[10]

Inequalities and Poverty

Just as WTO membership does not appear to have had a positive influence on employment in China, it does not appear to have changed the trend of rising inequality or help reduce poverty.[11] The recent Chinese history shows no positive correlation between poverty eradication, the opening up of markets and participation in international trade. China experienced a dramatic decline in poverty in the first few years of the 1980s, with the rural poverty rate falling from 76 per cent in 1980 to 23 per cent in 1985 (also see Lui, 2006). The late 1980s and early 1990s were more difficult periods for China's poor, with poverty actually rising in some years. Progress was restored around the middle of the 1990s, when rural poverty dropped to 11.5 per cent (in 1998). The late 1990s, however, saw a slowdown in poverty elimination again, and in 2001 the rural poverty rate stood at 12.5 per cent. The early 1980s saw high growth in agricultural output and rapid rural poverty reduction in the wake of the de-collectivisation and the privatisation of land rights under the *household responsibility system*.[12] Organised brigades previously did farming on agricultural land, in which all members shared the output equally. These reforms were without doubt important in stimulating rural economic growth at the early stages of China's transition. Overall, there are strong reasons to be sceptical of any positive correlation between trade liberalisation and poverty eradication. The bulk of trade reforms did not occur in the early 1980s, when poverty was falling most rapidly, but later, notably with the extension of the special economic zone principle to the entire country in 1986, and from 1995 and up to China's accession to the WTO. Average tariff rates fell only slightly in the 1980s and non-tariff barriers actually increased. And, some of the trade policies of this early period were unlikely to have been good for either equity or efficiency. Arguably, the bulk of China's trade reforms has been after the times of most rapid poverty reduction, and indeed in times of relatively stagnant poverty eradication.

As China had begun to adapt to the expected change well in advance to its official WTO accession in 2001, another way of looking at the question of trade and poverty eradication is by dividing the time around accession to the WTO into two periods – from 1995 to 2001 (in which tariffs started to fall in anticipation of accession) and the period from 2001 onwards. From 1995 to 2001 an overall gain of about 1.5 per cent in mean income took place in China. In the next period, 2001–07, the development in mean income was neutral and was also expected to continue to be so. From 2001 to 2007, poverty was projected to increase slightly as a result of the price changes most probably taking place after the remaining tariff changes.

The above narration suggests that trade openness in China has had a negligible effect on total poverty – in fact halting poverty eradication rather than enhancing it. Moreover, WTO membership is expected to negatively influence inequality: about three quarters of rural households are predicted to lose real income in the period 2001–07. This scenario is true for only one in ten urban households. This loss for rural households, which still make up two-thirds of the Chinese population, is due to a combination of falling rural wages and increases in the prices of the main consumption goods of this group. These developments in the rural areas, mainly because of liberalisation in the agricultural sector, increase the incentives for rural workers to leave the farmlands and look for work in the cities. Thus, as predicted, 28 million agricultural workers would leave agriculture sector to look for manufacturing work.[13] This shift would put downward pressure on unskilled wages in urban areas, one that is forecasted to reduce by up to 5 per cent.

In fact, rural poverty is still a major problem in China – one that might be exacerbated in the near future[14] and one that is intrinsically linked to the country's WTO membership. In 2004, China's State Statistics Bureau acknowledged that the number of rural people living in extreme poverty actually increased from 28.2 million in 2002 to 29 million in 2003, despite rapid GDP growth. And, even more significantly, from 2000 to 2002, 42 per cent of rural households experienced decreased income in absolute terms. Most analysts see this rise in poverty as an effect of trade liberalisation in the form of increased agricultural imports, and expect Chinese small farmers to face even greater hardship as they struggle to compete against the highly subsidised global agribusiness that is now entering China.[15] In sum, trade liberalisation is no panacea for country's economic problems. Therefore, if the Chinese strategy for further growth, employment creation and poverty eradication is based only on securing a larger share of global trade, it may not achieve the desired success. Unemployment will continue to rise, poverty eradication will slow down and inequality will rise significantly. Moreover, the Chinese experience – which by many is seen as a success story of the virtues of international trade liberalisation – pays testimony to the critique that free trade alone does not ensure jobs, development and poverty eradication.

Leap Forward or Backward?

Within the last few decades China has emerged as the world's manufacturing powerhouse and as one of the world's leading exporter. It is considered as the winner *per se* in and of international trade. But winning in this game has not been a joyful experience for its huge population that is left exploited and without a decent share in the country's recent prosperity. China is still *sweatshopping* its way to success, basing its competitiveness on unnaturally low wages. China might have as many newly unemployed people as the rest of the world together. It is experiencing a surge in inequality as discussed above (and in chapter 8) and finds half of its people entrenched in poverty. China's main comparative advantage is its cheap labour. Low pay, excessive hours, poor working conditions and minimal other costs have been its road to success. It is a road that China is mastering, foreign enterprises appear to appreciate, and the Chinese authorities appear to continue with. But it is a road based on eliminating and minimising obstacles and hindrances rather than constructively building competence and opportunities. It is also based on downsizing the public sector, exploiting the environment, abandoning welfare, pressurizing the workforce, creating flexibility at the price of security, and constantly reducing prices and lowering labour costs. It adds only a minimum of value at each stage of production mainly relying on the low wages paid to local workers.

Productivity in the country is still very low. In fact, in the booming manufacturing industry, measured by GDP per person employed in the sector, China is up to 30 times less productive than countries like the US and Japan. And, Germany and Finland are 20 times more productive than China. Even in comparison with countries that China is defeating in the export markets, its productivity per employee is low: Brazil is 6.71 times as productive, Malaysia 4.58 times and Thailand 2.87 times (IMD, 2000). The main reason for this low productivity is the lack of technologies in China's manufacturing industry as pointed out earlier. But missing educational and skill-enhancing investment in the labour force is also a contributing factor. International experience shows that the short-term gains that *sweatshop* conditions might give to producers are more than lost in comparison with the long-term productivity gains that a healthy, motivated and increasingly competent staff provides.

In spite of its low productivity, China has seen an explosion in private companies and corporations since the inception of its economic transformation. Chinese have set some of these companies up while others by foreign investors. But only a fraction of them have delivered decent work enabling a decent life to their employees. The majority of them exploit and abuse their workers on an unimaginable scale. Thus, the people who produce the goods that are flooding most of the world have 60–70 hour working weeks, live in dormitories with 8–16 people in each room, earn less than the minimum wages which go as low as US$ 44, and the only prospect of injury at work is unemployment. A study showed that only 33.4 per cent of private enterprises provided their staff with medical insurance, only 8.7 per cent offered pension plans and just 16.6 per cent had unemployment insurance. The insured staff members were mostly those in senior management positions or high-level technical staff. Most of the rank and file generally did not receive any of these benefits, the survey showed. In sum, only 14.5 per cent of the workers interviewed were covered by medical insurance, while only 22.7 per cent and 6 per cent of the workers had pension and unemployment insurance respectively (*China Labour Bulletin*, 2005).

Working in the many old and new factories in China poses a serious threat to health, well-being and safety. Statistics from the Chinese Centre for Disease Control and Prevention show that 83 per cent of township enterprises have work environments with varying degrees of occupational hazards. Harmful levels of dust and toxic substances affect nearly 34 per cent of the workers in these enterprises. As a result, about 15 per cent of workers in township enterprises develop or are suspected of developing various occupational illnesses. About 37 per cent of the foreign-invested factories were shown to have hazardous conditions with 34.7 per cent of workers employed in these plants in danger of developing occupational illnesses. Once again, it is the workers who work the most, are paid the least and have the least insurance that are most vulnerable at work. Thus, there is a clear correlation between being economically exploited and being at risk of losing a limb. And, contrary to widespread conjecture, no evidence suggests that work injuries are less frequent in the factories that are foreign-owned or produce for exports. Also, the limited regulatory efforts to avoid accidents give little hope for better times as such regulation reportedly is easily avoidable. This implies that China's workers should be able to avoid accidents just by demanding that their employers follow the law. The law in itself is not that bad, however, the implementation of it surely is. Hence, it does not appear that the right to stoppages over health and safety issues is very often respected.[16] Rather, the numerous examples of employees being forced to continue working in unsafe conditions show that workers in practice have little confidence in using their rights to work stoppages under the Labour Law, the Trade Union Law and the Occupational Safety and Health Law. In sum, there is a lack of consistent and regular monitoring of standards throughout China due to insufficient allocation of financial and personnel resources. Both collusion at the local level and widespread corruption are exacerbating the problem. Many localities turn a blind eye to problems or are part of the management or ownership of the enterprise in question.

Jobs Hard to Find

In spite of China's impressive growth and its success as an exporter, most Chinese have to look hard to see the signs of progress in their personal lives. Indeed, many of them would end up looking in vain. Around 250 million Chinese people, or 16.6 per cent of the population, still survive on less than US$ 1 a day and close to 700 million, or 47 per cent of the population, live on less than US$ 2 a day. Inequality has been rising sharply and China is now among the most unequal countries. There may be as many newly unemployed former industrial workers in the country as in the rest of the world put together. And, most workers struggle to get by and risk losing their lives and limbs every day. China's economic rise and emergence as a labour-intensive, leading manufacturer of cheap products for the whole world has resulted in a minimal number of new jobs. Thus, according to estimates by the World Bank, in the 1980s, when China's economic growth was at 9.3 per cent a year, net employment growth was only 3 per cent. Similarly, in the 1990s, when economic growth was about 10.4 per cent, net employment growth was as low as 1.1 per cent per year. In sum, between 1996 and 2001, the number of urban workers fell from 149 million to 108 million – a fall of 41 million or 28 per cent. Besides, the new jobs created are of lower quality than the ones that were shed, since they are mainly of the informal and self-employed kind. As a consequence, this group climbed by 13.3 million, a 57 per cent increase, in the urban areas from 1996 to 2001 (Zeng, 2005).

As China's population has increased significantly and large numbers of people have entered the labour market over the last two decades or so, during which employment creation has been weak, the country finds itself confronted with a giant problem of unemployment. Over time, more and more sacked workers become permanently unemployed who have limited scope of re-employment due to increasing oversupply of labour.

The Unemployment Scenario

Official Chinese statistics do not present a true situation on unemployment. China keeps most of its central statistics secret – not least the ones on employment and other associated issues such as protests and strikes. Employment, along with other labour-related areas such as protests, strikes and structural reform, is the subject of two main regulations issued jointly by the State Secrets Protection Bureau. The State Secrets Bureau and the Ministry of Ministry of Labour and Social Security (MOLSS) issued the first regulation in 2000, while the All China Federation of Trade Unions (ACFTU) and the State Secrets Bureau in 1996 issued the second regulation. There are three main areas of state secrets, viz., top secret (*juemi*), highly secret (*jimi*) and secret (*mimi*). Finally, there is internal secret (*neibu*) which, although is not strictly a state secret, constitutes internal material that should not be disclosed without approval of the relevant agency. The two regulations dealing with labour related-state secrets include highly secret, secret and internal classification. In this secrecy regime, in 2005, the International Labour Organisation (ILO) released a significant study of the recent trends and future challenges of employment in China (Ghose, 2005). The study analysed employment creation from 1990 to 2002, and identified two quite different trends during this period. Throughout the period of 1990 to 2002, aggregate employment in the Chinese economy grew at an average annual rate of 1 per cent. This growth was fully accounted for by China's cities. Thus, urban employment growth was at 3.5 per cent annually, while rural employment showed zero growth. In spite of the cities' industrialisation in the period, the urban employment growth covers only irregular employment – that is, migrant workers and urban laid-off workers who, for example, hold casual wage employment in construction or services or are self-employed in activities such as street vending, repair services, etc. Thus overall employment conditions in urban areas actually deteriorated during this period. In contrast, employment conditions in the rural areas have improved since regular employment grew while irregular employment declined. However, from 1996 to 2002, employment growth was due entirely to a dramatic growth of irregular employment in the urban areas (Table 2). Formal employment in urban areas showed a steep decline and the growth of informal employment was not sufficient to prevent a rapid decline in regular employment. Such a decline is a negative sign in terms of labour market sustainability and social well-being: growth of regular employment is a true indicator of growth of labour demand while growth of irregular employment is a symptom of growing excess supply of labour.

Table 2

Annual Employment Growth, 1990–2002 (%)

Type of employment	*Rural*	*Urban*	*Total*
Formal	3.3	–3.0	–0.6
Regular	1.1	–0.4	0.8
Irregular	–2.3	18.5	3.2
Total	0.1	3.5	1.0

Source: Ghose (2005).

As we know the mass lay-offs in state-owned enterprises began in 1995 and more than 50 million workers lost jobs by 2000. Thus, the unfavourable employment trends in urban China during 1996–2002 are mainly attributable to the elimination of workers in the state sector. In sum, some of the urban job losers did find new jobs in the emerging informal sector, some became unemployed and some withdrew from the labour force, with the latter part being so big that the labour force participation rate of urban residents fell from 72.9 per cent in 1996 to 66.5 per cent in 2002. The loss of jobs in China went hand in hand with gains in productivity. From 1996 to 2002, when manufacturing employment declined at a rate of more than 3 per cent annually, the growth of labour productivity was nearly 12 per cent (Table 3). This suggests that the poor employment effect of growth in this period is explained by both the process of shedding of labour in the SOEs and rapid technological change. Thus, employment conditions did worsen in this period, though economic miracle much talked about in China.

Table 3

Output and Employment, 1990–2002

Output	*Average annual rate of growth in per cent*		
	1990–96	*1996–2002*	*1990–2002*
GDP	11.3	7.5	9.3
Agriculture	4.1	2.7	3.6
Manufacturing	14.6	8.7	11.2
Other industries	20.0	8.3	14.0
Services			
Employment			
Total	1.6	0.1	0.8
Agriculture	–0.9	–0.2	–0.4
Manufacturing	2.1	–3.1	–1.1
Other industries	3.5	0.4	1.5
Services	7.2	2.4	4.6

Source: Ghose (2005).

Like any other developing country, self-employment is a significant mode of employment in China. Despite China's recent industrialisation and strong economic results, the relative importance of self-employment has remained stable. On the other hand, formal wage employment has declined and informal wage employment has risen in importance (Table 4) which, a negative sign for the people trying to live decent lives. Most remarkably, though, the change in the structure of employment was healthier in the rural than in the urban economy. In the latter, in contrast, self-employment, informal wage employment and irregular employment have all grown in importance while the relative importance of formal wage employment has declined.

Rural Surplus Labour

De-collectivisation of agriculture turned rural surplus labour force into potential wage labourers. Under collective farming, the production team was the basic unit of accounting. Peasants got work points for their work on the collective farm and would be paid partly in kind (grain, cotton, etc.) and partly in cash for their accumulated work points at the end of a harvest season. Individual peasants got their work assignments each day and were not free to be engaged in non-agricultural activities on their own. A craftsman had to have permission from team leader to work his trade. He had to remit his earnings to his team for redistribution and got work points in return. The household responsibility system broke down the collective big rice-pot. Freed from collective farms, peasants become independent commodity producers. They can choose what to do and keep for them what they earn from agricultural and non-agricultural activities. They are free to become industrial wage labourers.

Table 4

Structure of Employment by Status

Type of employment	*1990*		*1996*		*2002*	
	No.	*%*	*No.*	*%*	*No.*	*%*
Total						
Self-employment	56.1	64.0	56.3	61.9	54.5	63.1
Regular wage employment	31.5	36.0	34.7	38.1	31.9	36.9
Formal sector	31.2	35.6	33.0	36.2	27.3	31.6
Informal sector	0.3	0.4	1.7	1.9	4.6	5.3
Irregular employment	12.4		9.0		13.6	
Rural						
Self-employment	73.7	85.1	75.3	81.5	76.9	77.6
Regular wage employment	12.9	14.9	17.1	18.5	22.2	22.4
Formal sector	12.6	14.5	16.0	17.3	19.3	19.5
Informal sector	0.3	0.4	1.1	1.2	2.9	2.9
Irregular employment	13.4	7.6	0.9			
Urban						
Self-employment	3.7	4.1	8.9	10.1	9.6	15.7
Regular wage employment	86.8	95.9	78.9	89.9	51.4	84.3
Formal sector	86.5	95.6	75.8	86.4	43.2	70.9
Informal sector	0.3	0.3	3.1	3.5	8.2	13.4
Irregular employment	9.5		12.2		39.0	

Source: Ghose (2005).

China has an acute shortage of farmland and a huge surplus of peasants. The size of China's rural labour force (without urban registration) was about 431 million in 1991 and 444 million in 1993, which accounted for over 70 per cent of the total labour force. Nationally, the average land-labour ratio is about 3*mu* (one-fifth of a hectare) per peasant. On the basis of the current rate of agricultural productivity in China, it is estimated that no more than 150 million are needed for agricultural employment. Therefore, roughly two-thirds of the officially classified peasants are surplus labourers and require non-agricultural work. China's rural enterprises employed 52 million peasant workers in 1984, 96 million in 1991, and 112.8 million or about 25 per cent of the rural labour force by 1993. Likewise, 331 million people were classified as agricultural labourers in 1993 but over half of them were actually unemployed. On the basis of the current rate of expansion of rural enterprises, the projected growth of labour force size, and given the amount of arable land as in 2000, there will be approximately 150 million surplus labourers in China.

Labour supply may affect the development of rural industries through two mechanisms: availability of cheap labour and unemployment pressure (Peng, 1995). Although there is each year a large army of *floating labourers* roaming the country in search of jobs, the household registration system still restricts formal migration and adds friction to the geographic flow of labour. Therefore, local abundance of cheap labour itself may be an advantage for local development of rural industries. More importantly, surplus labour exerts unemployment pressure on local community. Community governments play an active role in rural industrialisation. They are concerned with the social goal of increasing employment as well as the economic goal of enriching their collective coffers. Even though in the few developed regions (Zhejiang, Southern Jiangsu and Guangdong), employment goal comes secondary to profits in the priority list by local cadres, it is the foremost motivation for the industrialisation drive for cadres in less developed regions.

Social Insurance System

As per the household registration system, Chinese citizens must carry a household register card, called *hukou,* issued in the locality of residence. There are two main categories, viz., agricultural (rural) *hukou,* giving a right to a small piece of land and a duty to cultivate it, and non-agricultural (urban) *hukou,* giving a right to urban public services in the locality concerned. Migrants can apply for temporary registration where they live. But permanent *hukou* changes are accorded only under specific conditions that can be difficult to fulfil, especially for low-skilled and poor persons. In practice, over 20 per cent of most big cities' inhabitants have rural *hukou,* and so do not enjoy full rights to public services. For example, their children's education often takes place in special schools that are less attractive than other schools in urban areas.

The reforms initiated were in the form of regional pilot experiments that began in the 1990s and encompassed several provinces since 2001, principally the eastern coastal area but also Sichuan and Anhui. In these provinces, rural citizens can obtain *hukou* in a city if they have permanent work and residence there. Some localities are particularly liberal, while others, including most big cities, are partly exempted. From October 2001, all towns and cities with up to about 1,00,000 inhabitants give urban *hukou* to residents with fixed jobs and homes (State Council Circular No. 6). In January 2003, the State Council's notice on the management of and services for rural people coming to work in cities gave many new instructions to public officials: (1) Abolish administrative controls (notably by labour bureaus) of enterprises hiring rural workers. Remove restrictions concerning the job categories in which rural workers can be hired. Simplify procedures. Abolish procedures and fees that have been imposed only on rural workers. (2) Enterprises must sign labour contracts with rural workers and give them all rights stipulated by the Labour Law. On dismissal, employers should pay them lump-sum compensation. Labour bureaus should reinforce their inspection of rural workers' labour contracts. (3) Rural workers should have work injury insurance. If conditions permit, local governments can set up health care insurance for them. Training of rural workers should be organised. Rural workers' children should be guaranteed education at no extra fees, and poor families should be exempted from part of the fees (Reutersward, 2005). In June 2003, the State Council issued the notice on the administrative measures on assistance and administration of poor urban vagrants and beggars. This replaced a previous regulation from 1982 about arresting and evicting the same groups, which had been considered to justify frequent identity checks by police. According to the new regulation, beggars and other poor rural citizens in cities should no longer be arrested and evicted, but advised to visit help centres. These centres, to be set up by city authorities other than the police, should provide food, accommodation and assistance, including tickets home or to find jobs.

The public pension system for urban workers is three-tiered. Two tiers are mandatory for employees in all enterprises and the third is voluntary for the self-employed. There is a provision through transitional rules for those who had contributed before 1997. *First tier:* A pay-as-you-go defined-benefit programme. As regards the funding, employer contributions vary around a national standard of 20 per cent, of which 17 percentage points is for the first tier. Pooling mostly at prefecture (city) level, sometimes by province or by county, the benefits accrue after at least 15 years of work and it is 20 per cent of the local average wage. The pension age is 60 (men) and 50 (most women). However, no first-tier benefits accrue if the contribution is for fewer than 10 years. *Second tier:* A defined-contribution programme with individual saving accounts. In this case employee contributes 7 per cent of the wage and it has been raised to 8 per cent. In addition, 3 percentage points of the employer contribution go to the individual accounts. The government administers it. The government can either invest the money, mostly in bank accounts and bonds, or use it on a pay-as-you-go basis. In the latter case, which is most common, the government pays a certain rate of interest to the notional accounts. As regards the benefits per month, 1/120 of the fund is accumulated on retirement. Thus, the programme assumes an average life expectancy of 10 years on retirement, but pensions are paid until death. Workers who stop contributing after less than ten years in a locality (pooling unit) can withdraw the individual accounts. But they receive no first-tier pensions. *Third tier:* A voluntary pension saving, which is mostly enterprise pension for employees.

In case of rural workers, entire voluntary savings, possibly with some support from communities and benefits according to the accumulation on individual accounts, are the social securities.

Social Insurance for Rural Migrants

In this regard two experiments are worth noting. *Chengdu, Sichuan* introduced an optional low-cost insurance package for migrants in March 2003, covering second-tier pension insurance, work injury insurance and basic medical insurance (hospitalisation). Flexible contributions calculated on a *base wage*, defined as the previous year's average wage in the city times one of the following multiples: 60 per cent, 70 per cent, 80 per cent, 90 per cent, 100 per cent, 120 per cent, 150 per cent. The employer chooses a multiple for each worker, with effects on benefits as well as on contributions. The contribution rate, applicable to the chosen base wage, is 14.5 per cent for the employer and 5.5 per cent for the employee. For the self-employed, it is 20 per cent. At the end of 2003, this scheme covered 84,000 workers, or 10 per cent of the rural migrants in Chengdu. For urban workers in Chengdu, the standard contribution rates for pension, work injury and medical insurance are, respectively, 20 per cent, 0.6 to 2 per cent and 7.5 per cent for employers and 8 per cent, 0 per cent and 2 per cent for workers. In other words, rural migrants and their employers contribute at about half of the rates that apply to urban workers. Chengdu also gives employers in the urban private sector a 3 percentage point rebate on their pension contributions, down to 17 per cent. This affects the city's revenues to the pay-as-you-go first tier, not the individual accounts. Such workers get the full insurance package despite the rebate. *Xiamen, Fujian* offers reduced contributions to rural migrants and their employers in the standard social insurance. Contributions are then calculated on the basis of the city's minimum wage, and employers are offered an 8 percentage point rebate on the pension contribution rate, down to 6 per cent compared with Xiamen's standard rate of 14 per cent. The employee contribution rate (for second-tier pensions) is the same as for urban workers: 8 per cent. The rebate only affects the city's revenues in the first-tier pay-as-you-go pension scheme.

Conclusions

China has observed significant improvement in GDP per person employed since 1978, i.e., from US$ 2,041 (1990 prices) to US$ 6,181 in 1998 and employment as percentage of population went up from 41.1 to 50.4 in 1998. The economy has grown at 10 per cent during the reform era. China's labour market has observed wide-ranging changes. Structural change in employment pattern has occurred during the reform period. Tertiary sector is now significant sector in China. The role of private and self-employment enterprises is increasing in creating employment. However, WTO accession has had adverse impact on employment creation. Inequalities have increased and pushed the efforts to improve poverty situation backward. China may not have now low productivity low wage advantage. The second largest economy in the South East Asia would require gigantic efforts to absorb rural surplus labour. The changing laws would encourage rural-urban migration and distort labour market. Social insurance system also requires modifications especially in rural areas. China plans to locate about 40 per cent of township enterprises in small towns.

Notes

1. About 36 per cent of global GDP accrued in China in the early 19th century. After 1820, China rapidly lost ground because of various domestic reasons (Maddison 1998).
2. The output share of the services sector in nominal terms rises significantly from about one-fifth in 1980 to one-third in 2004, but the output share in real terms remains almost stagnant. It is also noted that real-unit labour cost in the services sector has reached about twice that of manufacturing sector in developed provinces, whereas it has exceeded twice and even reached three times in some inland and poor provinces (Qin 2004).
3. Low agricultural labour productivity is well known in China (see, Yang and Zhou 1999).
4. China's new leaders are planning a system of national residence permits to replace the household registration or *hukou* regime, a vital reform that will boost its urbanisation campaign and drive consumption-led growth. The *hukou* system, which dates to 1958, has split China's 1.3 billion people along urban-rural lines, preventing many of the roughly 800 million Chinese who are registered as rural residents from settling in cities and enjoying basic urban welfare and services. Critics have called for changes for years and possibly a 'unified national residence permit system' would be adopted as policy as part of a 10-year urbanisation plan. Benefits and entitlement under the new system would be 'basically equal'; it is pointed out, although the changes would be eased in slowly. It may take some to be true. The trend is to dilute the urban-rural household registration divide. Previous administrations have experimented with reform on the fringes of *hukou* for years but have not delivered on calls to overhaul the system, which affords different welfare and civic services to urban and rural citizens. In a speech to parliament (NPC) on March 5th 2103 that laid out the blueprint of the new leaders, outgoing Premier Wen Jiabao had stated that *hukou* reforms should be accelerated to drive an urbanisation effort that would underpin economic development. Zhang Ping, head of the National Development and Reform Commission, China's main economic

planning agency, had reported that on March 6th 2013 that guideline for the urbanisation plan would be launched in the first half of 2013. 'Urbanisation is the biggest potential force driving China's domestic demand in the years ahead' Zhang reported. plans to spend 40 trillion ($6.4 trillion) to bring 400 million people to cities over the next decade as the new leadership of president-in-waiting Xi Jinping and premier-designate Li Keqiang seeks to turn China into a wealthy world power with economic growth generated by affluent consumers. Premier Wen Jiabao stated that consumption was the key to unlocking the full potential of domestic demand in the and would reduce excess, inefficiency and inequality. It would also help deliver growth of 7.5 percent in 2013 - a level China barely beat in 2012 when growth eased to 7.8 percent, its slowest pace in 13 years. *Hukou* reform can also unlock the funds of about 200 million rural residents who work in cities as migrants and spend much of their incomes on benefits like medical services and education their children, which are given free to urban dwellers. If policymakers successfully harness this demographic shift, China will enjoy continued economic strength. If not, it could lead to social and political instability. However, the critics point out that if they don't get it right, instead of growing a middle class, they are going to grow a huge underclass in the city, and that's very scary. Without granting urban *hukou* to rural urban migrants it is very hard to turn them into the middle class. They will always be second class. One of the main reasons the reform has been delayed is money. Local city governments have dragged their feet on plans to give migrants equal welfare, saying they lack the fiscal means to foot the bill. If the central government is serious they have got to talk about how to this.

The urbanisation plan would broadly put the burden of funding on central and local governments, enterprises that employ migrants and individuals, it is argued. In doing so it can be ensured that some people can transition from being rural to urban citizens and ensure basic public services for this segment of people. Another key reform needed in the urbanisation plan would be new rural land management rules. Peasants now do not have the freedom to sell their land at market prices, which has exacerbated China's wide rich-poor gap and made many reluctant to fully abandon their rural plots. Official like Chen Xiwen, the head of the Central Committee's rural working group, have cautioned against urbanisation, saying it could lead to a shrinking of farms as land is converted to other uses. Migrant workers have for years lamented inequalities in the *hukou* system, like the lack of local medical coverage or equal access to higher education. In the countryside, people generally want to change their rural *hukou* for city *hukous.* It's just better if one has a city *hukou* (if you live in a city), it is pointed out (source: http://www.reuters.com/article/2013/03/06/us-china-parliament-urbanisation-idUSBRE92509020130306)

5. Various studies ascribe rural-urban wage differentials to *hukou* system.

6. Data on China show that off-farm participation rates have grown steadily between 1981 and 2004. In fact, it appears that the trend of off-farm sector growth is almost linear if not accelerating.
7. In the United States, self-employment rate among women increased from 4.1 per cent in 1975 to 6.7 per cent in 1990 (Devine 1994).
8. For detailed processes of privatisation in China see, Yusuf, Nabeshima and Perkins (2006).
9. Also see, Anderson, Huang and Ianchovichina (2003) for impact of WTO accession on farmers' incomes and on rural poverty, and Chen and Ravallion (2004) for welfare impact.
10. Ibid.
11. Income inequality had remained fairly mild and stable under an egalitarian regime prior to economic reforms that started in 1978 (Qin et al. 2006).
12. The household responsibility system initially resulted in rural income growth surpassing urban income growth as farms achieved greater productivity, but this trend was soon reversed as agricultural productivity hit the ceiling and rural income fell further behind urban income (Qin et al. 2006). Also see appendix 10 for rural income that shows large regional inequality. At one end is Shanghai (16053.79 yuan per capita income) and at the other end is Gansu (3909.37 yuan per capita income) in 2011. This amounts to 1: 4.1 differences. In 1990, this difference had stood at 1: 4.43. In 2011, of the 30 provinces, 17 share lower per capita income then the national average.
13. National People's Congress (NPC) on 16 March 2007 approved a new corporate tax law that abolished preferential rates for foreign companies. The property bill that comes into effect on 1 October 2007 stipulates that law protects the property of the state, the collective and the individual, and no units or individuals may infringe upon it. This bill, in a sense, gives importance to private sector. The contribution of private sector to GDP is 65 per cent and about 70 per cent of tax revenue accrues from private sector. This would also give a push to urban middle class. Urban home ownership rate is more than 80 per cent now (*The Hindu*, 17 March 2007: 15).
14. During 2001 and 2005, 24,000 kms of new highways were built as per the Chinese Transport Planning and Research Institute (*The Hindu*, 2007) believing that this would help in poverty reduction. It could play a role in reducing discontent in rural China. In this process, China's National Reform and Development Commission had planned to invest 18 billion yuan on 23,000 kms of rural roads.
15. For instance, in Guangxi, this link between trade and poverty is very clear. The province once had a thriving sugarcane economy but when China became a member of the WTO, cheap and highly subsidised sugarcane flooded its market and millions of Chinese sugarcane farmers were pushed into poverty (most farmers in this region owned less than

one hectare of land). Thus, before China entered the WTO, the price for raw sugarcane was around 250 yuan per ton. After China entered the global agriculture market, sugarcane prices plummeted to 190 yuan per ton between 2002 and 2003, and then further to 170 yuan per ton between 2003 and 2004.

16. Overall, preliminary figures on safety in the workplace in 2004 reveal that there were 9,864 industrial accidents in privately-owned mines and factories in which 11,278 workers were killed. These figures represented 67 per cent and 68 per cent of all accidents and fatalities nationwide that is a significant increase over 2003 figures. Statistics show that China reported 3,341 coal mine accidents in 2005, which killed a total of 5,938 people.

References

ADB (2001). *Asian Development Outlook 2001*, Manila.

—— (2003). *Private Sector Assessment in the People's Republic of China*, Manila.

—— (2005). *Key Indicators 2005: Labour Markets in Asia: Promoting Full, Productive, and Decent Employment*, Manila.

Aziz, Jahangir, Steven Dunaway and Eswar Prasad (2006). *China and India Learning from Each Other: Reforms and Policies for Sustained Growth*, Washington, DC: IMF.

Banister, Judith (2005). 'Manufacturing Employment and Compensation in China' (http: www.bls.gov/opub/mlr/2005/07).

Banister, Judith and Jeffrey R. Taylor (1990). 'China: Surplus Labour and Migration', *Asia-Pacific Population Journal*, 4 (4).

Brooks, Ray and Ran Tao (2003). 'China's Labour Market Performance and Challenges', IMF Working Paper (WP/03/210) (www/imf.org/external/ft/wp/2003).

Chan, K.W. and L. Zhang (1999). 'The Hukou System and Rural-Urban Migration in China: Processes and Changes', *China Quarterly*, 160 (1): 818–55.

Chen, Chunlai, ed. (2009). *China's Integration with the Global Economy: WTO Accession, Foreign Direct Investment, and International Trade* (Advances in Chinese Economic Studies), Cheltenham, UK: Edward Elgar Publishing Limited.

Chen, Chunlai (2009a). 'Characteristics of FDI Firms in China After WTO Accession', in Chunlai Chen, ed. (2009): Chapter 6.

Chen, Shaohua and Martin Ravallion (2004). 'Household Welfare Impacts of WTO Accession in China', *World Bank Economic Review*, 18 (1): 29–58.

Chen, Shaohua and Y. Wang (2001). 'China's Growth and Poverty Reduction: Recent Trends between 1990 and 1999', World Bank Policy Research Working Paper No. 2651, Washington, DC.

China Labour Bulletin (2005). China News Services, February 3.

Devine, Theresa J. (1994). 'Changes in Wage-and-Salary Returns to Skill and the Recent Rise in Self-Employment', *American Economic Review*, 84 (2): 108–13.

Entwisle, B., G.E. Henderson, S. Short, J. Bouma and Z. Fengying (1995). 'Gender and Family Businesses in Rural China', *American Sociological Review*, 60 (1): 36–57.

Fung, Hung-gay, Changhong Pei, Kevin H. Zhang, eds. (2006). *China and the Challenge of Economic Globalization: The Impact of WTO Membership*, Armonk, NY: M. E. Sharpe.

Gale, Fred and Hongguo Dai (2002). 'Small Town Development in China: A 21st Century Challenge', *Rural America*, 17 (1), Spring.

Ghose, Ajit K. (2005). 'Employment in China: Recent Trends and Future Challenges', Employment Strategy Papers, Geneva: ILO.

Hertel, Thomas and Fan Zhai (2004). 'Labour Market Distortions, Rural-Urban Inequality and the Opening of People's Republic of China's Economy', ERD Working Paper No. 59, ADB, Manila, November (www.adb.org/documents/ERD/Working_papers/WP059.pdf) accessed on 9 March 2011.

IMD (2000). *The World Competitiveness Yearbook 2000*, Lousanne, Switzerland: International Institute for Management and Development.

Jefferson, Gary H. and Inderjit Singh (1999). *Enterprise Reform in China: Ownership, Transition, and Performance*, Oxford: Oxford University Press.

Li, Kunwang and Xiaosong Wang (2009). 'China's Foreign Trade: Trends and Issues after WTO Accession' in Chunlai Chen, ed. (2009), chapter 2: 19–26.

Lui, Hui (2006). 'Changing Regional Rural Inequality in China 1980–2002', *Area*, 38 (4): 377–89.

Maddison, Angus (1998). *Chinese Economic Performance in the Long Run*, Paris: OECD.

—— (2001). *The World Economy: A Millennial Perspective*, Paris: OECD.

Martí, Luisa, Rosa Puertas and J. Ismael Fernández (2011). 'Industrial Productivity and Convergence in Chinese Regions: The Effects of Entering the World Trade Organisation', *Journal of Asian Economics*, 22 (2): 128–141.

Mohapatra, Sandeep, Scott Rozelle and Rachael Goodhue (2006). 'The Rise of Self-employment in Rural China: Development or Distress', *World Development*, 35 (1): 163–81.

Parish, W.L., L. Zhe and F. Li (1995). 'Non-farm Work and Marketization of the Chinese Countryside', *China Quarterly*, 143: 697–730.

Peng, Yusheng (1995). 'China's Rural Enterprises: Effects of Agriculture, Surplus Labour, and Human Capital', Institute of Social Science Research, University of California (http://respositories.cdlib.org/issr/volume6/7).

Qin, Duo (2004). 'Is Rising Services Sector in the People's Republic of China Leading to Cost Disease', ERD Working Paper Series No. 50, ADB, Manila,

April (www.adb.org/documents/ERD/Working_papers/WP050.pdf) accessed on 9 March 2011.

Qin, Duo et al. (2006). 'Income Disparity and Economic Growth: Evidence from People's Republic of China', ERD Working Paper Series No. 84, ADB, Manila, October (www.adb.org/documents/ERD/Working_papers/WP084.pdf) accessed on 13 March 2011.

Ravaillion, Martin (2004). 'Looking Beyond Averages in the Trade and Poverty Debate', Policy Research Working Paper 3461, Washington, DC: World Bank.

Reutersward, Anders (2005). 'Labour Protection in China: Challenges Facing Labour Offices and Social Insurance', Social, Employment and Migration Working Paper 30, Paris: OECD (www.oecd.org/dataoecd).

Rozelle, S., L. Guo and S. Minggao (1999). 'Leaving China's Farms: Survey Results of New Paths and Remaining Hurdles to Rural Migration', *The China Quarterly*, 158: 367–93.

Singh, Surjit (1995). 'Trends in Chinese Economy', *China Report*, October–December, 31 (4): 429–46.

—— (1996). 'Rural Industries in Contemporary China', *China Report*, July–September, 32 (3): 269–94.

—— (1998). 'Economic Reforms and State Enterprises in China', *China Report*, April–June, 34 (2): 199–212.

—— (2007). 'Financial Sector in China: Issues and Challenges', in Sudhakar Reddy (ed.), *Economic Reforms in India and China: Emerging Issues and Challenges*, Delhi: Sage Publications.

Singh, Surjit and Arvinder Singh (1989). 'The Urban Informal Sector: Some Issues', *IASSI Quarterly*, December.

Wang, Huijiong (2001). 'Sustainable Industrial Overview of China: Current and Future Perspective', Development Research Centre, The State Council, PRC, July.

Winters, L. Alan and Shahid Yusuf (eds) (2007). *Dancing with Giants: China, India and the Global Economy*, Washington, DC: World Bank and Institute of Policy Studies.

World Bank (2000). *Making Transition Work for Everyone: Poverty and Inequality in Europe and Central Asia*, Washington, DC.

World Bank (2011). *'Employment in Agriculture (% of Total Employment)'* (http://data.worldbank.org/indicators/SL.AGR.EMPL.ZS) data tables accessed on 28 November 2012.

WTO (2011). *Understanding the WTO: Principles of the Trading System*, accessed on 28 November 2012.

Yang, D.T. and H. Zhou (1999). 'Rural Urban Disparity and Sectoral Labor Allocation in China', *Journal of Development Studies*, 35 (3): 105–33.

Yang, Dennis Tao, Vivian Chen and Ryan Monarch (2010). 'Rising Wages: Has China Lost Its Global Labor Advantage?', IZA Discussion Papers 5008,

Institute for the Study of Labor (IZA) (http://ftp.iza.org/dp5008.pdf). accessed on November 2012.

Yusuf, Shahid, Kaoru Nabeshima and Dwight H. Perkins (2006). *Under New Ownership: Privatizing China's State-owned Enterprises*, California: Stanford University Press.

Zeng, Douglas Zhihua (2005). 'China's Employment Challenges and Strategies after the WTO Accession', World Bank Policy Research Working Paper 3522, February.

Zhang, James Xiaohe (2009). 'The Impact of RMB Revaluation on China and the World Economy', in Chunlai Chen, ed. (2009): chapter 8: 141–160.

Zhao, Yaohui (1999). 'Labor Migration and Earnings Differences: The Case of Rural China', *Economic Development and Cultural Change*, 47 (4): 767–82.

Zhou, Zhangyue and Xia Kang (2009). 'China's Grain TRQs: Five Years Since WTO Accession', in Chunlai Chen, ed. (2009), chapter 9: 161–182.

Appendix 1

Distribution of Labour Force by Age

Year	*Labour force by age (years)*										
	15–19	*20–24*	*25–29*	*30–34*	*35–39*	*40–44*	*45–49*	*50–54*	*55–59*	*60–64*	*65+*
1978	13.82	15.28	16.19	10.19	10.32	9.22	8.63	7.46	5.05	2.86	0.99
1979	13.32	14.83	16.67	10.59	10.28	9.15	8.46	7.66	5.25	2.79	1.00
1980	12.26	14.71	17.32	11.09	10.27	9.26	8.33	7.75	5.33	2.75	0.95
1981	11.50	14.58	17.46	12.26	9.85	9.28	8.09	7.67	5.47	2.85	0.99
1982	10.68	14.46	17.42	14.01	9.20	9.33	7.98	8.92	5.56	2.92	0.98
1983	9.85	14.35	17.42	15.02	9.43	9.23	7.83	7.16	5.66	3.00	1.05
1984	8.96	14.20	17.54	15.57	9.88	9.18	7.85	6.96	5.75	3.04	1.07
1985	8.27	13.82	17.53	16.02	10.78	8.86	7.89	6.73	5.75	3.14	1.20
1986	7.80	13.63	17.41	16.22	10.75	8.43	7.97	6.48	5.63	3.10	1.33
1987	7.17	13.39	17.37	16.28	13.04	8.29	7.94	6.35	5.55	3.26	1.37
1988	6.37	12.83	17.57	16.35	13.82	8.50	7.99	6.38	5.51	3.38	1.31
1989	5.86	12.47	17.53	16.35	14.29	8.94	7.89	6.38	5.34	3.49	1.44
1990	5.13	12.06	17.55	16.57	14.86	9.59	7.76	6.42	5.12	3.49	1.42
1991	4.73	11.73	17.29	16.41	15.12	10.85	7.31	6.55	4.96	3.56	1.51
1992	4.30	11.40	16.93	16.47	15.31	11.84	7.27	6.57	4.89	3.50	1.51
1993	4.02	11.09	16.41	16.55	15.40	12.65	7.43	6.55	4.87	3.44	1.60
1994	4.20	10.78	15.97	16.43	15.41	13.29	7.77	6.48	4.79	3.25	1.62
1995	4.10	10.29	15.70	16.25	15.49	13.71	8.51	6.19	4.83	3.20	1.69
1996	3.92	9.97	15.47	16.17	15.55	14.08	9.53	5.84	4.84	3.04	1.60
1997	3.70	9.89	15.15	15.88	15.60	14.13	10.46	5.75	4.82	3.02	1.59
1998	3.27	9.92	15.00	15.64	15.72	14.22	11.04	6.02	4.70	2.90	1.58
1999	3.13	10.19	14.71	15.34	15.61	14.29	11.46	6.43	4.49	2.85	1.49
2000	2.86	10.25	14.53	15.14	15.54	14.41	11.90	6.86	4.28	2.76	1.48
2001	2.50	10.18	14.36	15.00	15.57	14.44	12.32	7.45	4.03	2.70	1.45
2002	2.24	9.95	14.57	14.81	15.24	14.53	12.26	8.23	3.96	2.69	1.55
2003	1.91	9.45	14.71	14.58	14.98	14.67	12.50	8.88	4.04	2.71	1.59
2004	1.71	9.12	15.02	14.24	14.75	14.66	12.72	9.33	4.29	2.65	1.52
2005	1.58	8.60	15.38	14.00	14.54	14.57	12.90	9.74	4.68	2.49	1.52

Source: China Statistical Yearbook, 2006.

Appendix 2

Number of Persons Employed by Industry (10,000 persons)

Year	Economically active population	Total persons employed	Primary industry	Secondary industry	Tertiary industry	% employed of active population	% share primary industry	% share secondary industry	% share tertiary industry
1978	40682	40152	28318	6945	4890	98.70	70.53	17.30	12.18
1979	41592	41024	28634	7214	5177	98.63	69.80	17.58	12.62
1980	42903	42361	29122	7707	5532	98.74	68.75	18.19	13.06
1981	44165	43725	29777	8003	5945	99.00	68.10	18.30	13.60
1982	45674	45295	30859	8346	6090	99.17	68.13	18.43	13.45
1983	46707	46436	31151	8679	6606	99.42	67.08	18.69	14.23
1984	48433	48197	30868	9590	7739	99.51	64.05	19.90	16.06
1985	50112	49873	31130	10384	8359	99.52	62.42	20.82	16.76
1986	51546	51282	31254	11216	8811	99.49	60.95	21.87	17.18
1987	53060	52783	31663	11726	9395	99.48	59.99	22.22	17.80
1988	54630	54334	32249	12152	9933	99.46	59.35	22.37	18.28
1989	55707	55329	33225	11976	10129	99.32	60.05	21.65	18.31
1990	65323	64749	38914	13856	11979	99.12	60.10	21.40	18.50
1991	66091	65491	39098	14015	12378	99.09	59.70	21.40	18.90
1992	66782	66152	38699	14355	13098	99.06	58.50	21.70	19.80
1993	67468	66808	37680	14965	14163	99.02	56.40	22.40	21.20
1994	68135	67455	36628	15312	15515	99.00	54.30	22.70	23.00
1995	68855	68065	35530	15655	16880	98.85	52.20	23.00	24.80
1996	69765	68950	34820	16203	17927	98.83	50.50	23.50	26.00
1997	70800	68920	34840	16547	18432	97.34	50.55	24.01	26.74
1998	72087	70637	35177	16600	18860	97.99	49.80	23.50	26.70
1999	72791	71394	35768	16421	19205	98.08	50.10	23.00	26.90
2000	73992	72085	36043	16219	19823	97.42	50.00	22.50	27.50
2001	73884	72797	36399	16234	20165	98.53	50.00	22.30	27.70
2002	74492	73280	36640	15682	20958	98.37	50.00	21.40	28.60
2003	74911	73736	36204	15927	21605	98.43	49.10	21.60	29.30
2004	75290	74264	34830	16709	22725	98.64	46.90	22.50	30.60
2005	76120	74647	33442	17766	23439	98.06	44.80	23.80	31.40
2006	76315	74978	31941	18894	24143	98.25	42.60	25.20	32.20
2007	76315	74978	31941	18894	24143	98.25	42.60	25.20	32.20
2008	77046	75564	29923	20553	25087	98.08	39.60	27.20	33.20
2009	77510	75828	28890	21080	25857	97.83	38.10	27.80	34.10
2010	78388	76105	27931	21842	26332	97.09	36.70	28.70	34.60
2011	78579	76420	26594	22544	27282	97.25	34.80	29.50	35.70

Source: China Statistical Yearbook, 2006 and 2012.

Appendix 3

Rural Population and Labour (0000 persons)

Provinces	*Rural*		*Rural labour*		*% share in labour*		*% share of*
	population	*labour*	*male*	*female*	*male*	*female*	*labour in population*
1978	80320.0	30637.8	16548.4	14089.4	54.01	45.99	38.14
1980	81096.0	31835.9	17379.7	14456.2	54.59	45.41	39.26
1985	84419.7	37065.1	20153.2	16911.9	54.37	45.63	43.91
1989	87831.0	40938.8	22218.0	18720.8	54.27	45.73	46.61
1990	89590.3	42009.5	22551.8	19457.7	53.68	46.32	46.89
1991	90525.1	43092.5	23121.9	19970.6	53.66	46.34	47.60
1992	91154.4	43801.6	23449.9	20351.7	53.54	46.46	48.05
1993	91333.5	44255.7	23653.1	20602.6	53.45	46.55	48.46
1994	91526.2	44654.1	23854.1	20800.0	53.42	46.58	48.79
1995	91674.6	45041.8	24037.4	21004.4	53.37	46.63	49.13
1996	91941.0	45288.0	24154.9	21133.1	53.34	46.66	49.26
1997	91524.7	46234.3	24633.4	21600.9	53.28	46.72	50.52
1998	91960.1	46432.3	24733.1	21699.2	53.27	46.73	50.49
1999	92216.3	46896.5	24995.7	21900.8	53.30	46.70	50.85
2000	92819.7	47962.1	25517.8	22444.3	53.20	46.80	51.67
2001	93382.9	48228.9	25685.4	22543.5	53.26	46.74	51.65
2002	93502.5	48526.9	25850.1	22676.8	53.27	46.73	51.90
2003	93750.6	48971.0	26121.0	22850.0	53.34	46.66	52.24
2004	94253.7	49695.3	26525.8	23169.5	53.38	46.62	52.73

Source: China Statistical Yearbook, 2006.

Appendix 4

Rural Population and Labour by Provinces, 2004 (0000 persons)

Provinces	Rural		Rural labour		Share in labour		% share of
	population	labour	male	female	male	female	labour in population
Beijing	359.9	171.4	89.2	82.2	52.04	47.96	47.62
Tianjin	395.2	175.7	95.9	79.8	54.58	45.42	44.46
Hebei	5389.9	2772.0	1484.1	1287.9	53.54	46.46	51.43
Shanxi	2344.5	1021.5	565.1	456.4	55.32	44.68	43.57
Inner Mangolia	1352.3	675.8	381.6	294.2	56.47	43.53	49.97
Liaoning	2338.9	1083.9	602.9	481.0	55.62	44.38	46.34
Jilin	1440.1	670.9	383.0	287.9	57.09	42.91	46.59
Heilongjiang	1899.3	943.3	540.5	402.8	57.30	42.70	49.67
Shanghai	347.9	248.1	128.4	119.7	51.75	48.25	71.31
Jiangsu	5248.0	2664.8	1380.4	1284.4	51.80	48.20	50.78
Zhejiang	3734.8	2252.3	1203.0	1049.3	53.41	46.59	60.31
Anhui	5198.2	2910.8	1554.7	1356.1	53.41	46.59	56.00
Fujian	2686.3	1311.5	706.5	605.0	53.87	46.13	48.82
Jiangxi	3266.6	1605.4	843.1	762.3	52.52	47.48	49.15
Shandong	7042.5	3754.2	1995.4	1758.8	53.15	46.85	53.31
Henan	7968.8	4718.0	2498.8	2219.2	52.96	47.04	59.21
Hubei	3965.3	1877.0	995.4	881.6	53.03	46.97	47.34
Hunan	5455.8	2951.6	1604.7	1346.9	54.37	45.63	54.10
Guangdong	6254.5	2944.6	1539.9	1404.7	52.30	47.70	47.08
Guangxi	4123.4	2245.4	1187.0	1058.4	52.86	47.14	54.46
Hainan	519.6	250.1	129.0	121.1	51.58	48.42	48.13
Chongqing	2425.3	1361.5	730.5	631.0	53.65	46.35	56.14
Sichuan	6885.7	3774.0	2003.3	1770.7	53.08	46.92	54.81
Guizhou	3253.6	1903.0	1012.4	890.6	53.20	46.80	58.49
Yunnan	3537.9	2030.0	1056.7	973.3	52.05	47.95	57.38
Tibet	223.6	105.7	53.5	52.2	50.61	49.39	47.27
Shaanxi	2790.8	1425.5	778.4	647.1	54.61	45.39	51.08
Gansu	2063.6	1057.9	557.6	500.3	52.71	47.29	51.26
Qinghai	354.1	184.6	97.5	87.1	52.82	47.18	52.13
Ningxia	412.1	209.9	109.9	100.0	52.36	47.64	50.93
Xinjiang	975.5	395.1	217.6	177.5	55.07	44.93	40.50

Source: Same as Appendix 3.

Appendix 5

Distribution of Rural Labour by Activities

Years	*Farming, forestry, animal husbandry and fishery*	*Industry*	*Construction*	*Transport, storage, post and communication services*	*Wholesale, retail trade and catering services*	*Other non-agricultural trades*
1978	100.00					
1980	97.02	2.98				
1985	81.89	7.40	3.05	1.17	1.25	5.25
1989	79.24	7.95	3.67	1.50	1.59	6.04
1990	79.35	7.69	3.62	1.51	1.65	6.17
1991	79.33	7.58	3.56	1.52	1.68	6.33
1992	77.71	7.92	3.79	1.61	1.86	7.12
1993	75.15	8.27	4.26	1.81	2.14	8.37
1994	73.21	8.62	4.61	2.03	2.43	9.10
1995	71.79	8.82	4.89	2.18	2.60	9.72
1996	71.23	8.87	5.09	2.27	2.79	9.75
1997	70.68	8.72	5.13	2.29	3.00	10.18
1998	70.27	8.46	5.28	2.34	3.15	10.50
1999	70.18	8.43	5.40	2.38	3.38	10.23
2000	68.38	8.57	5.61	2.44	3.65	11.35
2001	67.29	8.91	5.80	2.50	3.87	11.64
2002	65.92	9.28	6.10	2.59	4.11	11.98
2003	63.83	10.08	6.54	2.71	4.20	12.63
2004	61.57	10.94	6.80	2.97	5.44	12.28

Source: Same as Appendix 3.

Appendix 6

Distribution of Rural Labour by Activities, 2004

Provinces	*Farming, forestry, animal husbandry and fishery*	*Industry*	*Constru- ction*	*Transport, storage, post and communi- cation services*	*Wholesale, retail trade and catering services*	*Other non- agricultural trades*
Beijing	33.76	18.78	9.85	10.09	11.25	16.27
Tianjin	45.79	26.62	7.17	6.71	8.13	5.57
Hebei	57.73	17.37	9.36	4.10	6.63	4.81
Shanxi	62.68	13.19	5.83	5.98	5.80	6.52
Inner Mangolia	77.51	3.42	4.14	2.01	3.91	9.01
Liaoning	63.27	8.76	6.57	3.99	6.36	11.06
Jilin	74.03	4.25	5.05	2.82	5.13	8.72
Heilongjiang	74.85	5.08	5.00	2.60	6.01	6.46
Shanghai	26.29	45.89	4.92	3.67	6.33	12.90
Jiangsu	42.59	20.85	11.30	3.76	5.30	16.20
Zhejiang	36.70	31.11	6.14	3.99	9.04	13.02
Anhui	61.65	9.00	8.73	2.89	6.32	11.41
Fujian	55.10	14.70	6.47	3.21	6.20	14.33
Jiangxi	59.86	10.78	5.68	2.17	4.13	17.38
Shandong	58.07	12.67	9.14	4.02	6.67	9.44
Henan	68.57	10.04	7.40	3.08	5.48	5.43
Hubei	58.90	6.14	6.18	2.63	4.78	21.37
Hunan	66.94	8.23	5.29	2.56	5.35	11.63
Guangdong	51.79	18.49	6.84	2.94	7.34	12.61
Guangxi	67.52	3.51	4.24	1.83	3.23	19.67
Hainan	76.29	3.44	3.24	2.72	6.88	7.44
Chongqing	58.82	6.96	8.23	1.73	4.14	20.12
Sichuan	62.72	6.25	7.50	1.92	4.72	16.89
Guizhou	67.71	4.01	2.38	1.35	2.90	21.66
Yunnan	83.44	2.77	2.96	1.94	2.63	6.27
Tibet	80.61	1.89	5.68	2.37	2.46	7.00
Shaanxi	67.14	5.39	6.82	2.90	4.54	13.22
Gansu	72.14	3.34	5.48	2.30	3.37	13.38
Qinghai	71.45	5.25	7.20	3.03	5.15	7.91
Ningxia	68.57	6.71	9.10	4.57	6.00	5.05
Xinjiang	85.92	2.68	1.95	3.01	4.15	2.28

Source: Same as Appendix 3.

Appendix 7

Number of Self-employed Individuals across Provinces, 2004

Provinces	*Number of*		*Persons employed*		*Share in employed persons*		*Per unit*	*Distribution of*		*Distribution of*	
	Enterprises	*Employed*	*Urban*	*Rural*	*Urban*	*Rural*	*Employment*	*Enterprises*	*Employed*	*Urban*	*Rural*
China	2350.5	4587.1	2521.2	2065.9	54.96	45.04	1.95	100	100	100	100
Beijing	52.7	69.3	45.6	23.7	65.80	34.20	1.31	2.24	1.51	1.81	1.15
Tianjin	17.8	25.2	10.3	14.9	40.87	59.13	1.42	0.76	0.55	0.41	0.72
Hebei	101.9	255.4	87.2	168.2	34.14	65.86	2.51	4.34	5.57	3.46	8.14
Shanxi	43.9	85.4	38.5	47.0	45.08	55.04	1.95	1.87	1.86	1.53	2.28
Inner Mangolia	44.4	78.0	56.1	21.8	71.92	27.95	1.76	1.89	1.70	2.23	1.06
Liaoning	126.4	285.0	188.1	97.0	66.00	34.04	2.25	5.38	6.21	7.46	4.70
Jilin	42.4	80.1	68.8	11.3	85.89	14.11	1.89	1.80	1.75	2.73	0.55
Heilongjiang	69.8	147.7	105.6	42.1	71.50	28.50	2.12	2.97	3.22	4.19	2.04
Shanghai	27.5	33.4	22.0	11.4	65.87	34.13	1.21	1.17	0.73	0.87	0.55
Jiangsu	164.5	249.8	147.1	102.6	58.89	41.07	1.52	7.00	5.45	5.83	4.97
Zhejiang	168.4	312.8	146.7	166.1	46.90	53.10	1.86	7.16	6.82	5.82	8.04
Anhui	106.7	256.2	118.6	137.7	46.29	53.75	2.40	4.54	5.59	4.70	6.67
Fujian	46.8	85.8	52.9	32.9	61.66	38.34	1.83	1.99	1.87	2.10	1.59
Jiangxi	60.9	149.5	87.3	62.3	58.39	41.67	2.45	2.59	3.26	3.46	3.02
Shandong	166.0	344.5	164.5	180.1	47.75	52.28	2.08	7.06	7.51	6.52	8.72
Henan	123.1	258.0	116.7	141.3	45.23	54.77	2.10	5.24	5.62	4.63	6.84
Hubei	99.1	214.4	128.7	85.7	60.03	39.97	2.16	4.22	4.67	5.10	4.15
Hunan	94.5	196.3	121.4	75.0	61.84	38.21	2.08	4.02	4.28	4.82	3.63
Guangdong	196.0	423.7	229.4	194.2	54.14	45.83	2.16	8.34	9.24	9.10	9.40
Guangxi	98.5	152.9	78.2	74.7	51.14	48.86	1.55	4.19	3.33	3.10	3.62
Hainan	12.4	24.8	16.5	8.3	66.53	33.47	2.00	0.53	0.54	0.65	0.40
Chongqing	45.6	91.5	48.1	43.4	52.57	47.43	2.01	1.94	1.99	1.91	2.10
Sichuan	144.7	230.7	121.0	109.7	52.45	47.55	1.59	6.16	5.03	4.80	5.31
Guizhou	43.3	63.1	38.0	25.1	60.22	39.78	1.46	1.84	1.38	1.51	1.21
Yunnan	69.5	125.9	78.1	47.8	62.03	37.97	1.81	2.96	2.74	3.10	2.31
Tibet	5.7	9.8	7.8	2.0	79.59	20.41	1.72	0.24	0.21	0.31	0.10
Shaanxi	74.2	156.3	73.8	82.5	47.22	52.78	2.11	3.16	3.41	2.93	3.99
Gansu	34.2	63.4	38.7	24.7	61.04	38.96	1.85	1.46	1.38	1.53	1.20
Qinghai	13.1	27.1	18.5	8.6	68.27	31.73	2.07	0.56	0.59	0.73	0.42
Ningxia	9.8	16.7	11.9	4.8	71.26	28.74	1.70	0.42	0.36	0.47	0.23
Xinjiang	46.7	74.2	55.2	19.0	74.39	25.61	1.59	1.99	1.62	2.19	0.92

Source: Same as Appendix 3.

Appendix 8

Employed Persons in Rural Areas (10,000)

		Persons employed			% share of persons employed		
Year	*Persons employed*	*TVEs*	*Private enterprises*	*Self-employed*	*TVEs*	*Private enterprises*	*Self-employed*
1978	30638	2827			9.23		
1980	31836	3000			9.42		
1985	37065	6979			18.83		
1990	47708	9265	113	1491	19.42	0.24	3.13
1991	48026	9609	116	1616	20.01	0.24	3.36
1992	48291	10625	134	1728	22.00	0.28	3.58
1993	48546	12345	187	2010	25.43	0.39	4.14
1994	48802	12017	316	2551	24.62	0.65	5.23
1995	49025	12862	471	3054	26.24	0.96	6.23
1996	49028	13508	551	3308	27.55	1.12	6.75
1997	49039	13050	600	3522	26.61	1.22	7.18
1998	49021	12537	737	3855	25.57	1.50	7.86
1999	48982	12704	969	3827	25.94	1.98	7.81
2000	48934	12820	1139	2934	26.20	2.33	6.00
2001	48674	13086	1187	2929	26.88	2.44	5.40
2002	48121	13288	1411	2474	27.61	2.93	5.14
2003	47506	13573	1754	2260	28.57	3.69	4.76
2004	46971	13866	2024	2066	29.52	4.31	4.40
2005	46258	14272	2366	2123	30.85	5.11	4.59
2006	45348	14680	2632	2147	32.37	5.80	4.73
2007	44368	15090	2672	2187	34.01	6.02	4.93
2008	43461	15451	2780	2167	35.55	6.40	4.99
2009	42506	15588	3063	2341	36.67	7.21	5.51
2010	41418	15893	3347	2540	38.37	8.08	6.13

Note: Number of registered unemployed person in urban areas stood at 8.30 million which increased to 9.22 million in 2011; an increase of 0.92 million. The unemployment rate has been between 4.1 and 4.3 percent since 2007.

Source: China Statistical Yearbook, various years.

Appendix 9

Distribution of Employed Persons in Private Enterprises (2004) (in 10,000)

Provinces	Per unit	Share of (%) in total employment			Share of (%) employers in employment		Percentage distribution (%) across provinces						
	employment	employers	urban employed	rural employed	urban	rural	No. of enterprises	No. of employed persons	employers	No. of urban employed persons	No. of urban employed persons	No. of rural employed persons	No. of rural employers
China	13.7	18.91	59.67	40.33	20.39	16.71	100	100	100	100	100	100	100
Beijing	12.1	20.93	64.22	35.78	23.40	16.60	6.16	5.44	6.02	5.85	6.72	4.82	4.79
Tianjin	11.0	22.43	54.76	45.24	23.81	21.04	1.92	1.53	1.81	1.40	1.64	1.71	2.16
Hebei	20.7	13.35	28.17	71.83	18.54	11.37	2.96	4.46	3.15	2.11	1.92	7.95	5.41
Shanxi	17.0	14.15	55.24	44.76	16.32	11.48	1.53	1.90	1.42	1.76	1.41	2.11	1.45
Inner Mangolia	14.2	19.44	72.22	27.78	20.81	15.88	1.18	1.22	1.25	1.48	1.51	0.84	0.80
Liaoning	16.5	14.66	78.39	21.57	16.10	9.45	3.75	4.50	3.49	5.91	4.67	2.41	1.36
Jilin	19.4	8.88	91.93	8.07	8.12	17.50	1.40	1.98	0.93	3.04	1.21	0.40	0.41
Heilongjiang	14.5	19.88	81.19	18.81	20.53	17.09	1.59	1.67	1.76	2.28	2.29	0.78	0.80
Shanghai	10.5	20.40	52.14	47.84	21.51	19.20	10.55	8.07	8.71	7.05	7.44	9.57	11.00
Jiangsu	13.4	17.36	53.53	46.47	17.12	17.50	11.45	11.20	10.29	10.05	8.44	12.91	13.51
Zhejiang	15.5	14.73	45.70	54.32	18.32	11.71	9.12	10.31	8.03	7.90	7.09	13.89	9.73
Anhui	15.9	16.21	58.32	41.68	17.60	14.09	2.44	2.82	2.41	2.75	2.38	2.91	2.45

Cont'd...

Cont'd...

Fujian	10.1	20.84	67.74	32.26	24.27	13.65	3.01	2.22	2.45	2.52	3.00	1.77	1.45
Jiangxi	18.7	13.75	66.37	33.54	14.91	11.49	1.67	2.28	1.66	2.53	1.85	1.89	1.30
Shandong	14.1	20.04	58.66	41.31	23.11	15.69	7.56	7.78	8.24	7.65	8.67	7.97	7.48
Henan	11.1	24.27	47.62	52.38	26.19	22.52	2.96	2.38	3.06	1.90	2.44	3.09	4.17
Hubei	9.7	26.84	66.09	33.91	33.06	14.71	3.12	2.20	3.12	2.44	3.95	1.85	1.63
Hunan	25.2	17.24	76.49	23.51	14.12	27.38	1.89	3.47	3.16	4.45	3.08	2.02	3.31
Guangdong	11.1	22.74	71.62	28.38	25.32	16.22	10.68	8.66	10.42	10.40	12.91	6.09	5.91
Guangxi	15.4	17.92	74.25	25.75	18.66	15.20	1.18	1.32	1.25	1.65	1.51	0.85	0.77
Hainan	11.6	21.03	87.59	12.41	20.87	22.22	0.68	0.58	0.64	0.85	0.87	0.18	0.24
Chongqing	14.6	18.69	66.53	33.37	19.49	17.47	1.86	1.98	1.96	2.21	2.11	1.64	1.71
Sichuan	13.9	19.43	57.48	42.52	21.05	17.23	3.73	3.76	3.86	3.62	3.74	3.96	4.08
Guizhou	10.2	25.00	68.75	31.25	26.09	22.61	0.99	0.73	0.97	0.85	1.08	0.57	0.77
Yunnan	14.8	18.75	61.72	38.28	24.05	10.20	1.42	1.53	1.52	1.58	1.87	1.45	0.89
Tibet	21.5	11.63	88.37	11.63	13.16	0.00	0.05	0.09	0.05	0.13	0.08	0.02	0.00
Shaanxi	17.5	33.31	35.35	64.59	23.05	38.96	2.38	3.03	5.34	1.80	2.03	4.86	11.32
Gansu	12.8	20.05	74.29	25.71	21.90	13.76	0.90	0.85	0.90	1.05	1.13	0.54	0.44
Qinghai	24.5	11.02	71.43	28.57	12.57	5.71	0.27	0.49	0.28	0.58	0.36	0.35	0.12
Ningxia	12.5	22.54	74.18	25.82	24.68	14.55	0.47	0.42	0.51	0.53	0.64	0.27	0.24
Xinjiang	13.3	22.69	88.66	11.34	23.82	13.85	1.18	1.14	1.37	1.70	1.98	0.32	0.27

Source: Same as Appendix 3.

Appendix 10

Per Capita Net Income of Rural Households by Region (yuan)

Provinces	*1990*	*2000*	*2011*	*% change in 2000 over 1990*	*% change in 2011 over 2000*	*% change in 2011 over 1990*	*Times change in 2000 over 1990*	*Times change in 2011 over 2000*	*Times change in 2011 over 1990*
China	686.31	2253.42	6977.29	228.3	209.6	916.6	3.28	3.10	10.17
Beijing	1297.05	4604.55	14735.68	255.0	220.0	1036.1	3.55	3.20	11.36
Tianjin	1069.04	3622.39	12321.22	238.8	240.1	1052.5	3.39	3.40	11.53
Hebei	621.67	2478.86	7119.69	298.7	187.2	1045.3	3.99	2.87	11.45
Shanxi	603.51	1905.61	5601.40	215.8	193.9	828.1	3.16	2.94	9.28
Inner Mongolia	607.15	2038.21	6641.56	235.7	225.9	993.9	3.36	3.26	10.94
Liaoning	836.17	2355.58	8296.54	181.7	252.2	892.2	2.82	3.52	9.92
Jilin	803.52	2022.50	7509.95	151.7	271.3	834.6	2.52	3.71	9.35
Heilong-jiang	759.86	2148.22	7590.68	182.7	253.3	899.0	2.83	3.53	9.99
Shanghai	1907.32	5596.37	16053.79	193.4	186.9	741.7	2.93	2.87	8.42
Jiangsu	959.06	3595.09	10804.95	274.9	200.5	1026.6	3.75	3.01	11.27
Zhejiang	1099.04	4253.67	13070.69	287.0	207.3	1089.3	3.87	3.07	11.89
Anhui	539.16	1934.57	6232.21	258.8	222.1	1055.9	3.59	3.22	11.56
Fujian	764.41	3230.49	8778.55	322.6	171.7	1048.4	4.23	2.72	11.48
Jiangxi	669.90	2135.30	6891.63	218.7	222.7	928.8	3.19	3.23	10.29
Shandong	680.18	2659.20	8342.13	291.0	213.7	1126.5	3.91	3.14	12.26
Henan	526.95	1985.82	6604.03	276.9	232.6	1153.3	3.77	3.33	12.53
Hubei	670.80	2268.59	6897.92	238.2	204.1	928.3	3.38	3.04	10.28
Hunan	664.24	2197.16	6567.06	230.8	198.9	888.7	3.31	2.99	9.89
Guang-dong	1043.03	3654.48	9371.73	250.4	156.4	798.5	3.50	2.56	8.99
Guangxi	639.45	1864.51	5231.33	191.6	180.6	718.1	2.92	2.81	8.18
Hainan	696.22	2182.26	6446.01	213.4	195.4	825.9	3.13	2.95	9.26
Chong-qing	—	1892.44	6480.41	—	242.4	—	—	3.42	—
Sichuan	557.76	1903.60	6128.55	241.3	221.9	998.8	3.41	3.22	10.99
Guizhou	435.14	1374.16	4145.35	215.8	201.7	852.6	3.16	3.02	9.53
Yunnan	540.86	1478.60	4721.99	173.4	219.4	773.1	2.73	3.19	8.73
Shaanxi	530.80	1443.86	5027.87	172.0	248.2	847.2	2.72	3.48	9.47
Gansu	430.98	1428.68	3909.37	231.5	173.6	807.1	3.31	2.74	9.07
Qinghai	559.78	1490.49	4608.46	166.3	209.2	723.3	2.66	3.09	8.23
Ningxia	578.13	1724.30	5409.95	198.3	213.7	835.8	2.98	3.14	9.36
Xinjiang	683.47	1618.08	5442.15	136.7	236.3	696.3	2.37	3.36	7.96

Source: Same as Appendex 8.

2

Small and Medium Enterprise Clusters in India

R.K. MISHRA

Nowadays, economic activities are moving toward knowledge-intensive business, accompanied by rapid development of technology in globalised economy era. This condition has impact on the tight competition, and rapid change in business environment. Domestic manufacturing products are directly competing with foreign products and business world must accept this reality that technology advancement has become a reason on the absolvent production facilities, short product life-cycle and lower profit margin. Clusters are geographic concentrations of interconnected companies, specialised suppliers, service providers, and associated institutions in a particular field that are present in a nation or region. Clusters arise because they increase the productivity with which companies can compete. The development and upgrading of clusters is an important agenda for governments, companies and other institutions. Cluster development initiatives are an important new direction in economic policy, building on earlier efforts in macro-economic stabilisation, privatisation and market opening, and reducing the costs of doing business.

Small and medium enterprise (SME) clusters have always been the engine of growth and job creation for every country, be it in developed, developing or transition economies. The cluster building creates a sound industrial base amongst developing countries. They, along with micro-enterprises, have been identified as high potential sector for employment generation and source of livelihood to millions of people in Asia, Africa and Latin America. The SME clusters dominated the economies of the most developed countries. SMEs are spring boards for technological innovation and entrepreneurship. They also play vital role in engagement of poor skilled manpower. Many developed countries are on their way of industrialisation through SME clusters. Japan's SME clusters contribute 55 million jobs and 52 per cent exports.

A thriving SME cluster is vital to economic growth of India as well. The importance of an SME cluster as a pillar of Indian economy cannot be overlooked. We cannot depend only on a few large industrial houses for driving our industrialisation process. The employment-intensive nature and the greater regional spread of SMEs make them attractive option for industrial growth. India has nearly three million SMEs that account for nearly 50 per cent of India's industrial output and contribute over 30 per cent of exports. They constitute 80 per cent of the total number of industrial enterprises and over 50 per cent of private sector employment. It is the micro-enterprises and SMEs that discover the dynamic comparative advantages of a country. Since the SMEs are an important constituent of the supply chain, it is indeed quite intriguing to know what holds them back from realising their potential in the international markets. Indeed, they have the potential to become leading business conglomerates of tomorrow. Gaining access to global markets is the key to realising this potential for high growth. In order to access the international markets, they must learn to manufacture quality products and at the same time be cost competitive. China has become the workshop of the world precisely because of its cost competitiveness.

SMEs and Industrial Policies in India

In any country, the domestic policy environment consists of three parts:

- *The macro-economic environment:* Any macro-economic instability in a country leads to balance of payments crisis, high inflation and current account deficits and appreciation in exchange rates. Given their small size and limited resources, SMEs have fewer options to defend against such instability compared to large firms. Therefore, ensuring macro-economic stability is an important way to help SMEs emerge, grow and prosper. This might be the best support a government could give to SMEs.
- *Incentive policies*: The most important task the policy makers have to perform is creating a level playing environment for SMEs through various incentive policies, competitiveness and succeed internationally.
- *Institutions*: Building institutions and a responsive support structure for SMEs is no less important. The existence of a good legal system and faster dispute settlement mechanism is also of equal importance.

The strategic objective of Indian policy makers, immediately after achieving independence, was creation of a self-reliant economy and reduction in the high levels of poverty that existed, all within a democratic political framework. In order to achieve these objectives, the authorities steadfastly followed a socialist strategy of state-directed, heavy industry-oriented and capital-intensive industrialisation, complemented by an across-the-board import substitution policy and complex industrial and statutory requirements. Notwithstanding some notable successes, the highly state-centric and interventionist development policies adhered to during the period of insulation, led to a severely distorted production structure.

The six industrial policy resolutions adopted by the successive governments at the Centre aimed at promoting industrial growth and determined a pattern of state intervention and assistance. They have set out the guidelines for the country's industrial development. The basic framework for industrialisation is provided in the Industries Development and Regulation Act of 1951. Small-scale industries were given due importance under the provisions of the Act. The Act determined the licensing policies for the sector and the reservation of products for exclusive manufacture by the sector. Promotion of small-scale sector has always been an important thrust of India's industrial policy since independence though the priorities changed with each five-year plan.

Cluster Development in India

The concept of cluster is not new to India. Clusters have been in existence in India for decades, perhaps centuries, in some cases. According to a survey conducted by UNIDO in 1996, there were about 350 small sector industry (SSI) clusters and approximately 2,000 rural artisan-based clusters in India. Some of these clusters are so big that they contribute about 70–80 per cent of Indian output in that particular product. It is estimated that these clusters contribute about 60 per cent of the finished goods exports from India. Notable among these clusters are:

- Panipat in Haryana accounting for 75 per cent of the total blankets produced in India.
- Thirupur, a small township in Coimbatore district of Tamil Nadu, accounting for 80 per cent of the cotton hosiery exports.
- Agra in Uttar Pradesh virtually a Footwear City with 800 registered and 6,000 unregistered small and cottage footwear production units, making 0.15 million pairs of shoes per day with a production value of 1.3 million dollars per day and exporting shoes worth US$ 57.14 million per year (see special feature on 'Leather and Leather Goods', *Economic Times*, New Delhi, 21 October 1996).
- Ludhiana, also known as Manchester of India, contributes 95 per cent of the country's woollen knit wear, 85 per cent of the country's

sewing machines and 60 per cent of the nation's bicycle and bicycle parts.

- The city of Bangalore deserves an explicit reference in its contribution to software sector.

Indian Initiatives

In India, the small-scale industries (SSI) sector has been accorded a distinct place and plays a crucial role in the process of economic development by value addition, employment generation, equitable distribution of national income, removal of regional disparities, wide dispersion of industries, mobilisation of capital, upgradation of entrepreneurial skills and substantial contribution by way of export earnings. The small-scale industries in India present a wide spectrum consisting of tiny, cottage and village industries and modern sunrise industries, i.e., from traditional sector to sophisticated state-of-the-art technology. The enactment of the Small and Medium Enterprises (Development) Act, 2006 and the policy on credit announced in 2005 have triggered a change in the mindset of small and medium entrepreneurs in India. The new thrust is towards upscaling the size, finances and technological upgradation. After due consultation with the stakeholders and on the recommendation of the Advisory Committee, the Ministry of Small Scale Industries of Government of India has identified 180 items for de-reservation. In order to give a fresh impetus to lending following new initiatives have been envisaged by the Small Industries Development Bank of India (SIDBI): (i) recognise SMEs in the services sector, and treat the small-scale enterprises in the services sector at par with the small-scale enterprises in the manufacturing sector; (ii) raise the corpus of the Credit Guarantee Fund from ₹ 11,320 million at end of March 2006 to ₹ 25,000 million in five years. In 2006–07, a sum of ₹ 1,180 million was proposed; (iii) advise Credit Guarantee Trust for Small Industries (CGTSI) to reduce the one-time guarantee fee from 2.5 per cent to 1.5 per cent for all loans; and (iv) extend insurance cover to approximately 30,000 borrowers, identified as chief promoters, under the CGTSI. The sum insured would be ₹ 2,00,000 per beneficiary and the premium will be paid by CGTSI.

The National Common Minimum Programme (NCMP) of the present UPA government draws attention to the fact that in the past few years, the most employment-intensive segment of small-scale industry has suffered extensive neglect. This also states that the SSI sector will be freed from 'Inspector Raj' and will be given improved access to credit, technological and marketing support. It also assures small businesses that infrastructure upgradation in major industrial clusters will receive adequate attention. The Government of India has proposed to increase the financial assistance to existing clusters of micro, small and medium enterprises up to 80 per cent of their financial requirements during the Eleventh Plan

(2007–2012). Financing SMEs linked to large corporate, covering suppliers, ancillary units, dealers, etc., would enhance competitiveness of the corporates as well as the SME participants. There are 25–30 very active and successful NGOs in South India and some other states, which have outstanding record of successful micro-credit management. They provide ideal role models for training and development of groups and individuals in other parts of the country. Besides NGOs, there are other successful micro-credit institutions who serve small, tiny and individual entrepreneurs in Tamil Nadu, Andhra Pradesh and Karnataka.

Growth of SMEs would be the key to significant growth in GDP as well as in creating employment over time. SMEs are an integral part of the national economy. While globalisation is creating new opportunities for them, they are also faced with many difficult challenges. Recognising the challenges that technology, globalisation and market changes will create for SMEs, the following need to be focused:

(i) Entire Business Development
(ii) Problem-solving Techniques for SMEs
(iii) Outsourcing Strategies for SMEs
(iv) Incubators for SMEs
(v) Supply Chain Management for SMEs
(vi) Cluster Approach for Industrial Development
(vii) Quality Management for SMEs
(viii) Strategic Alliances among SMEs through Technology Fusion

Government and quasi-government agencies need to do much more to act as facilitators, so as to make SMEs more competitive. While years of liberalisation in India have given big businesses much more freedom to operate, still there exist problems for small businesses. While the big can still afford to deal with a myriad of rules and regulations, those whose whole business often comprises only a dozen people (or less) cannot afford to have even one of them tied down in filling forms and 'managing' the governmental system.

Micro, Small and Medium Enterprises

At present, a small-scale industrial unit is an undertaking in which investment in plant and machinery, does not exceed ₹ 10 million, except in respect of certain specified items under hosiery, hand tools, drugs and pharmaceuticals, stationery items and sports goods, where this investment limit has been enhanced to ₹ 50 million. Units with investment in plant and machinery in excess of SSI limit and up to ₹ 100 million are treated as medium enterprise. The Government of India has since enacted the Micro, Small and Medium Enterprises Development (MSMED) Act, 2006 which was notified on 2 October 2006. So much so, the Government of India has changed the name of Department of Small Scale Industries to Department of Small and Medium Enterprises. Consistent with the said notification the definition of micro, small and medium enterprises engaged in manufacturing or production and in providing or rendering of services is being modified and is required to be implemented by the banks along with other policy measures.

(a) Enterprises engaged in the manufacture or production, processing or preservation of goods as specified below:

  (i) A micro-enterprise is an enterprise where investment in plant and machinery (original cost excluding land and building and the items specified by the Ministry of Small Scale Industries vide its notification dated 5 October 2006) does not exceed ₹ 2.5 million.

  (ii) A small enterprise is an enterprise where the investment in plant and machinery (original cost excluding land and building and the items specified by the Ministry of Small Scale Industries vide its notification dated 5 October 2006) is more than ₹ 2.5 million but does not exceed ₹ 50 million.

  (iii) A medium enterprise is an enterprise where the investment in plant and machinery (original cost excluding land and building and the items specified by the Ministry of Small Scale Industries vide its notification dated 5 October 2006) is more than ₹ 50 million but does not exceed ₹ 100 million.

(b) Enterprises engaged in providing or rendering of services and whose investment in equipment (original cost excluding land and building and furniture, fittings, and other items not directly related to the service rendered or as may be notified under the MSMED Act, 2006) are specified below. These will include small road and water transport operators (owning a fleet of vehicles not exceeding ten vehicles), retail trade (with credit limits not exceeding ₹ 1 million), small business (whose original cost price of the equipment used for the purpose of business does not exceed ₹ 2 million) and professional and self-employed persons (whose borrowing limits do not exceed ₹ 1 million of which not more than ₹ 2 million should be for working capital requirements except in case of professionally qualified medical practitioners setting up of practice in semi-urban and rural areas, the borrowing limits should not exceed ₹ 1.5 million with a sub-ceiling of ₹ 0.3 million for working capital requirements).

  (i) A micro-enterprise is an enterprise where the investment in equipment does not exceed ₹ 1 million.

  (ii) A small enterprise is an enterprise where the investment in equipment is more than ₹ 1 million but does not exceed ₹ 20 million.

  (iii) A medium enterprise is an enterprise where the investment in equipment is more than ₹ 20 million but does not exceed ₹ 50 million.

SME Clusters in India

The SME clusters for the following analysis have been chosen and categorised mostly based upon the secondary data available such as write-ups and studies by researchers, judgements of informed persons, each one cross-checked and reconfirmed from several possible sources to improve the reliability of information. There may be some limitations or differences in viewpoint. Due to the scarcity of research studies available for most of these clusters, this improvised method of data collection is entirely the responsibility of the researcher with a few possible limitations or differences in viewpoint.

Size and heterogeneity in the cluster network: It has been estimated that there exist about 350 SME clusters in India. These clusters are overwhelmingly predominant with small industries and the share of medium and large industries in the sales turnover, production and employment is nominal. The size in terms of the number of units and the quantum of output of clusters may vary significantly. Some of them are so big that they produce up to 70 to 80 per cent of the total volume of that particular product produced in India. For example, the township of Panipat produces 75 per cent of the total blankets produced in the country. Similarly, Tirupur, a small township in the Coimbatore district of Tamil Nadu, contributes 80 per cent of the country's cotton hosiery exports. Yet another example would be of the city of Agra, virtually a Footwear City with 800 registered and 6,000 unregistered small and cottage footwear production units, making 0.15 million pairs of shoes per day with a production value of 1.3 million dollars per day and exporting shoes worth US$ 57.14 million per year.

State-wise distribution of SME clusters: It would be interesting to note that the industrially developed states of Maharashtra, Gujarat, Punjab, Rajasthan, Tamil nadu and Haryana have the maximum number of clusters. The top six industrially developed states account for about 54 per cent of the SSI units and 71 per cent of the clusters are located in them. The common states among them are Gujarat, Punjab, Uttar Pradesh and West Bengal. Surprisingly, the state of Madhya Pradesh, which has the maximum number of small-scale enterprises (12.7%) as per the Second All India Survey of SSIs, seems to have very few clusters (1.4%).

Table 1

State-wise Distribution of Clusters

State	*No. of Clusters*	*State*	*No. of Clusters*
Maharashtra	25	Haryana	12
Gujarat	20	West Bengal	9
Punjab	15	Tamil Nadu	8
Rajasthan	14	Himachal Pradesh	5
Uttar Pradesh	13		

Source: Second All India Survey of SSIs.

Region-wise distribution of clusters: Out of 138 clusters, the largest concentration of clusters is in Western India with 58 clusters and which is closely followed by Northern India with 52 clusters. The concentration of clusters in these two parts of the country can be attributed to the fact that these are rich in entrepreneurial talent and are industrially well developed. Also, since these parts are agriculturally better developed, they provide a rich base for consumption of goods produced in SSIs.

Table 2

Distribution of Clusters

Industry Group	*NIC Code*	*No. of Clusters*
Machinery and parts except electrical	35	20
Cotton textiles	23	15
Chemical and chemical products	31	14
Metal products	34	13
Hosiery and garments	26	10
Food products	21, 20	9
Non-metallic mineral products	32	9
Electrical machinery and parts	36	8
Wool, silk and synthetic fibre textiles	24	8
Transport equipment and parts	37	7
Others eight categories	Several	25
Total		138

Source: Second All India Survey of SSIs.

Rural clusters: Cluster formation in rural areas has taken place for the products with less need for infrastructure and supply of raw material. According to the Second All India Census, the number of modern SME clusters that exist in rural areas or small towns is much lesser. One possible reason for this variation can be attributed to the units that have come up in rural areas and are small firms catering to limited local markets that are not significant enough to induce formation of a cluster. The clusters in metropolitan cities are either demand-based arising from large population or they cater to export markets or to the large mother units as ancillaries to them. The detailed break-up of the locations of these clusters is given as under (see Table 3):

The induced clusters are those where government takes a decision and makes a conscious effort resulting in the concentration of similar units in that area. On a close examination, we could classify 125 clusters out of 138 as natural. This means 90.57 per cent of the clusters that exist in the country have come up on their own. This seems to be in line with the pattern of cluster development at the international level.

Table 3

Location-wise Distribution of Clusters

Location	*No. of Clusters*
City	50
Metro	14
Town	61
Small town/rural	13
Total	138

Table 4

Cluster Formation: Induced and Natural

Type of Cluster	*No. of Clusters*
Natural	125
Induced	13
Total	138

SME Clusters: Challenges and Opportunities

Globalisation of the financial services industry: Globalisation and technology are fundamentally changing the financial services industry worldwide. Competition has accelerated and is fierce for best credits/corporates in most countries as new competitors entered the market. Margins and fees are narrowing significantly. Development of securities markets is dis-intermediating banks. Impact on the domestic financial intermediaries has been great due to deregulations, mergers, acquisitions, consolidations, global networks/alliances. Financial institutions (FIs) have the interest to tap new markets but the enabling environment is not friendly for SME finance and FIs lack strategies and skills to tackle impediments associated with SMEs and micro-enterprises.

SMEs and economic development: SMEs are expected to boost efficiency and growth and lead to economic development because of being engine of job creation, seedbed for innovation and entrepreneurship. SMEs play an important role in promoting growth and development for the poor. These are more likely to be able to play important role in economic development in countries with better financial development and low financing constraints, good policies and good institutions like control of corruption, rule of law, property rights, etc.

Financial Institutions facing the choice: In many transition and developing countries, deposit-taking FIs are awash with deposits. For many governments, the development of SMEs is crucial for economic and social development, but SMEs are perceived as high risk and high cost entities.

Constraints Faced by Indian SME Clusters

The financial constraints faced by Indian SMEs are attributable to a combination of factors that are rooted in:

(a) legal/regulatory framework that makes recovery of bad loans to SMEs, bankruptcy and contract enforcement difficult for creditors;

(b) institutional weaknesses such as the absence of good credit appraisal and risk management/monitoring tools, that increase banks' transaction costs in dealing with SMEs;

(c) absence of reliable credit information on SMEs, and the lack of sufficient market credibility of the SME sector. This has made a difficult for lenders to assess risk premiums properly, creating differences in the perceived versus real risk profiles of SMEs and resulting in untapped lending opportunities to SMEs.

Support of Government of India

In recent years, the Indian government has taken several steps to support SME financing and development to overcome this situation.

- There has been a welcome shift in focus from 'SS' to 'SME' as Government of India announced ₹ 100 billion (US$ 2.3 billion) SME Fund operated by the Small Industries Development Bank of India (SIDBI), which is the apex bank for SMEs in India.
- To strengthen the framework for tackling loan defaults and contract enforcement, the Government of India has enacted the Securitisation and Reconstruction of Financial Assets and Enforcement of Security Interest (SARFAESI) Act. The Act empowers secured creditors to foreclose and enforce securities in case of default, without intervention of a court or tribunal, and has also created an enabling framework for asset reconstruction companies and securitisation in general. New bankruptcy legislation was enacted in 2003 and Sick Industrial Companies Act (SICA) has been repealed. The challenge is now to ensure the efficient implementation/enforcement of these laws as they apply to SMEs.
- RBI has issued a directive requiring all banks to introduce standardised credit appraisal systems and guidelines. Most public sector banks require upgradation of credit scoring tools for SME loans. The latest scoring tools would help banks better understand, appreciate, and mitigate SME credit risk, making them more confident in lending to the sector.
- Efforts have also been made in recent years by SIDBI and others to improve business development services for SMEs and enhance market linkages, which are critical to ensuring the long-term commercial viability and bankability of SMEs.

Conclusions

SME sector is expanding. Micro-enterprises, which have been growing at rapid pace and providing institutional support to the disadvantaged people, are joining the SME sector. This new development will change the SME cluster horizon and call for new approaches and strategies for both financial institutions and the governments. The facilitating and supporting environment by the financial institutions and government authorities through better financing patterns, minimum financing constraints, good governance policies, low inflation, minimum entry level regulation and processing time, good skilled manpower, coupled with transparent processing procedures, least supervisory hurdles, can make SMEs prosper. As from the government point of view, the development and growth of SMEs is important for economic growth, social development, poverty alleviation, employment generation and technological innovation, there is need for paradigm shift in financial services for SMEs. The shift includes change of mindset of bankers, shift from product focus to customer focus, and also from just lending to package of financial services.

3

Rural Migrant Workers in China

ZHANG JUWEI AND WANG ZHIYONG

Migration process in China mainly refers to farming labour migrating to industry sector or to urban areas. Rural migrant workers are the mainstream of the migrant workers as well as of the migration in China. It is very hard trying to escape from understanding the structure, allocation, and characteristics of rural migrant workers while understanding migration process in China. Every year, usually between the middle of January and the early of February, there are a huge amount of rural migrant workers going home, or put another way, from urban areas to rural areas. Thus, understanding the scale, structure and tendency of rural migrant workers in China is very crucial for understanding migration process in China. Based on the above understanding, we need to estimate the scale and structure of rural migrant workers. Moreover, using specific survey data by Institute of Population and Labour Economics, Chinese Academy of Social Sciences (IPLE, CASS), we can also describe some important characteristics of rural migrant workers, especially their working and living status in urban areas.

Number and Location of Rural Migrant Workers

The financial crisis in 2008 had a great impact on rural migrant workers. We need to know the number of rural migrants and where they are before figuring out the specific employment impact on them (i.e., which industries and regions are hardest hit). Given their scattered locations and mobility, it is difficult to count the total population of rural migrant workers. A more feasible approach is to estimate their total number. But with different informations and methods, the results vary greatly. Table 1 lists several estimate results that are the most representative until now. Drafted by the Research Office of the State Council, *Report on the Survey of China's Rural Migrant Workers* puts the figure at 200 million (of 2004) in reference to the following estimates. This figure includes the rural migrants who work at local township and village enterprises.

Table 1

Several Estimate Results on the Total Number of Rural Migrants

Information Source		*Rural migrant workers working out of their hometown in 2004*	*Total number of rural migrant workers*
Population and Family Planning Commission	Survey on rural migrant population	100 million *	
National Bureau of Statistics	Survey on 68,000 rural households in 31 provinces	118 million	
Ministry of Agriculture	Follow-up survey on 10,000 rural households	100 million	
(Former) Ministry of Labour and Social Security	Statistical account of incoming rural migrants above prefecture level	90 million **	
Research Office of the State Council	Reference to the above estimates	120 million	200 million

Notes: *Size of nation-wide mobile employment in 2003.
**Number of mobile employment of rural migrants is estimated to be 120 million.

Estimate using census data is a more reliable way to know the total number of rural migrants. Based on the national 1 per cent population sampling survey conducted in 2005, the proportion of rural migrants across various industries can be estimated. Presuming this proportion to be constant for several years, the sector-wise number of rural migrants can be calculated using the latest overall employment figures. The total number of rural migrants can then be reached by adding up sector-wise figures.

According to the statistical yearbook abstract (2010), national non-agricultural employment was 482.87 million (persons) by the end of 2009. Over the past six years, China's non-agricultural employment grew by 17.34 million on an annual basis. Of which, employment growth in 2009 was 14.61 million. Presuming that non-agricultural employment grew by 14 million in 2010, total non-agricultural employment stood at 496.87 million (Juwei, 2008).[1] According to the national 1 per cent population sampling survey conducted in 2005, rural migrant workers accounted for 50.5 per cent of total non-agricultural employment. It can be thus calculated that there were 250 million rural migrant workers in 2010. It should be noted that the proportion of rural migrant workers in non-agricultural employment keeps on rising every year. Therefore, the actual number might be higher than 250 million in 2010. According to the estimate, in 2010, rural migrant workers accounted for 65 per cent in total employment of secondary industry and 39 per cent in tertiary industry. According to the fifth census of China in 2000, the proportion of rural migrant workers in secondary and tertiary industries was 58 per cent and 52 per cent respectively. This trend shows that secondary industry is attracting a greater number of rural migrant workers.

From a sector-wise perspective, there were 104.95 million rural migrant workers in manufacturing sector, accounting for 41.8 per cent of total rural migrant workers: 42.23 million in wholesale and retail services, or 16.83 per cent; 29.52 million in construction sector[2], or 11.77 per cent; 19.41 million in transportation, warehouse and postal services, or 7.74 per cent; 14.44 million in hotel and catering industry, or 5.76 per cent; and 14.02 million in community and other services, or 5.59 per cent.

As the figures suggest, the number of rural migrants is uneven across various sectors. Most of them are employed in manufacturing, construction, hotel and catering, community and other services, mining and the like, which do not require a highly skilled or well-educated workforce. Other industries, however, are not major sources of employment for rural migrant workers. They include: scientific research, technical services and geological surveying, education, finance, public administration and social organisations. These sectors have higher requirements on educational backgrounds and skills of the workforce, which rural migrant workers often cannot meet.

Regional Distribution and Cross-provincial Migration

According to China's household registration system, rural migrant workers are still regarded as 'rural population', although they work and live in urban areas. Their flow is characterised by the seasonal migration between the countryside and cities (Taskforce of Research Office of the State Council, 2006). Research on the regional distribution of rural migrants, particularly the source and destination areas, as well as regional and sector-wise differences, will help provide policy guidance. Given the massive flows, rural migrant workers may bring about tremendous employment pressures whenever they go.

From a regional perspective, the number of rural migrants is uneven. Obviously, the eastern region is a major source of jobs for rural migrant workers coming from the central and western regions. In 2004, the mobile employment of rural migrant workers from central and western regions accounted for 67 per cent of national total (ibid.). According to figures released by the Agricultural Survey Team of the National Bureau of Statistics, after 2005, more than 70 per cent of rural migrant workers work in the

Table 2

Sector-wise Estimates of Numbers of Rural Migrant Workers in 2010

(unit: 10,000 persons, %)

Sectors	*Number of Employment*	*Number of Rural Migrant Workers*	*Proportion to Total Number of Rural Migrant Workers*
Mining	1318.29	671.48	2.68
Manufacturing	15788.39	10495.27	41.83
Electric power, gas and water production and supply	871.82	174.20	0.69
Construction	4011.43	2952.02	11.77
Transportation, storage and postal services	3955.03	1941.02	7.74
Information transmission, computer services and software	524.24	106.13	0.42
Wholesale and retail	8162.03	4223.03	16.83
Hotel and catering	2418.81	1444.06	5.76
Financial sector	745.29	73.98	0.29
Real estate	508.29	116.65	0.46
Rental and business services	675.10	183.33	0.73
Scientific research, technical services and geologic surveying	377.25	35.43	0.14
Water conservancy, environmental and public facilities management	414.32	110.40	0.44
Community services and others	2277.91	1402.23	5.59
Education	2779.95	332.78	1.33
Healthcare, social security and social welfare	1319.27	264.05	1.05
Mining	1318.29	671.48	2.68
Manufacturing	15788.39	10495.27	41.83
Electric power, gas and water production and supply	871.82	174.20	0.69
Total	49687.00	25090.66	100.00

Source: Estimated based on *Abstract of China Statistical Yearbook* (2010) and the national 1 per cent population sample survey conducted in 2005.

eastern region (see Table 3). However, the concept of 'rural migrant workers' refers not only to those working in other towns and cities, but also those working at local township and village enterprises. According to the brief survey conducted by the Ministry of Labour and Social Security in 2005, the proportions of rural migrant workers working in eastern, central and western regions are 62 per cent, 20 per cent and 18 per cent respectively (ibid.). This result includes the number of locally employed rural migrant workers and provides an estimate of the regional distribution of all rural migrant workers.

Table 3

Regional Distribution of Rural Migrants Working in Other Towns and Cities

Region	*Regional Distribution (%)*		
	2003	*2004*	*2005*
Eastern	67.84	69.81	70.54
Central	14.88	14.40	14.44
Western	17.28	15.79	15.02

Source: Department of Countryside Social and Economic Survey, National Bureau of Statistics, *Yearbook of Surveys on China's Rural Households, 2004–2006*, Beijing, China Statistics Press.

Table 4

Sector-wise Distribution of Rural Migrant Workers

Sectors	*Eastern Region*	*Central Region*	*Western Region*
Mining	1.08	6.09	5.43
Manufacturing	50.74	27.11	21.97
Electric power, gas and water production and supply	0.58	0.89	0.94
Construction	10.43	13.83	14.88
Transport, storage and postal services	6.09	11.62	10.20
Information transmission, computer services and software	0.38	0.51	0.52
Wholesale and retail	14.97	19.45	21.47
Hotel and catering	4.83	6.58	8.56
Financial services	0.26	0.37	0.34
Real estate	0.58	0.14	0.35
Rental and business services	0.80	0.55	0.63
Scientific research, technical services and geological surveying	0.15	0.12	0.14
Water conservancy, environmental and public facilities management	0.44	0.38	0.50
Community services and others	4.92	6.66	7.09
Education	0.93	2.04	2.17
Healthcare, social security and welfare	0.75	1.58	1.71
Culture, sports and entertainment	0.56	0.46	0.64
Public administration and social organisations	1.52	1.61	2.44
International organisations	0.00	0.00	0.00

Source: Estimated according to *China Statistical Yearbook (2008)* and the national 1 per cent population sample survey conducted in 2005.

Subject to limited statistics, we employ the figures of 2007 in conducting regional estimates. According to the results, in 2007, about 110 million rural migrants worked in the eastern region, or 55.3 per cent, and 50.98 million and 41.46 million[3] rural migrants worked in the central and western regions, accounting for 24.65 per cent and 20.05 per cent respectively. In comparison to the estimates of the Ministry of Labour and Social Security on the regional distribution of rural migrants conducted in 2005, the employment of rural migrants in the central and western regions keeps on the rise in recent years, as the regions have become an alternative to the eastern region for many rural migrant workers. This may come as a result of the industrial relocation from the eastern region to the central and western regions, or the national go-west campaign that stimulated non-agricultural development in these regions.

Sector-wise distribution of rural migrant workers varies greatly from region to region. In the eastern region, most of rural migrant workers are employed in manufacturing, accounting for more than half. However, although the majority of rural migrant workers are also employed in manufacturing sector in the central and western regions, a great number of them are engaged in construction, wholesale, retail and others. In the western region, construction, wholesale and retail sectors have similar numbers of rural migrant workers.

In terms of province, most of rural migrant workers are in provinces like Henan (15.95 million), Guangdong (14.28 million), Jiangsu (13.78 million), Shandong (13.41 million) and Sichuan (12.96 million). Henan and Sichuan are populous provinces where there are a great number of rural migrant workers. This has a lot to do with local industrial structure and already large population. In addition, coastal provinces in the east like Hebei, Liaoning, Zhejiang and Fujian also have significant numbers of rural migrant workers, partly due to the large local populations there. But, in relatively backward provinces and regions in the western part, like Ningxia (1.11 million), Qinghai (1.07 million) and Tibet (260,000), the number of rural migrant workers is much smaller due to backward development of non-agricultural sectors and smaller local populations.

As mentioned before, the differences in regional numbers have a lot do to with disparate regional industrial structures. Take manufacturing for example, the industry has employed the greatest number of rural migrant workers, who are primarily located in Guangdong, Shandong, Jiangsu and Henan. In contrast, the number of rural migrants employed in manufacturing sector is much smaller in Xinjiang, Qinghai, Ningxia and Tibet. A comparison on the distribution of rural migrant workers in Figure 1 and Figure 2 reveals a high degree of similarities in the distribution of rural migrant workers in various provinces.

Figure 1

Distribution of Rural Migrant Workers in Various Provinces and Regions (2007)

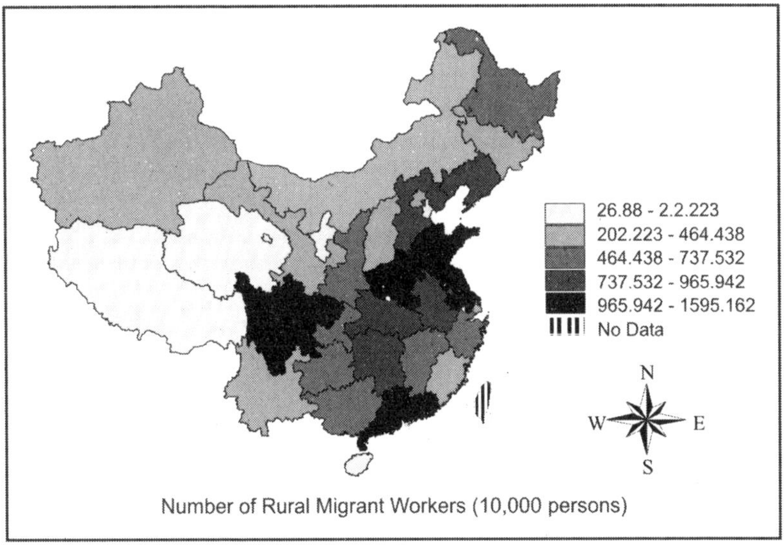

Figure 2

Distribution of Rural Migrants Employed in Manufacturing in Various Provinces (2007)

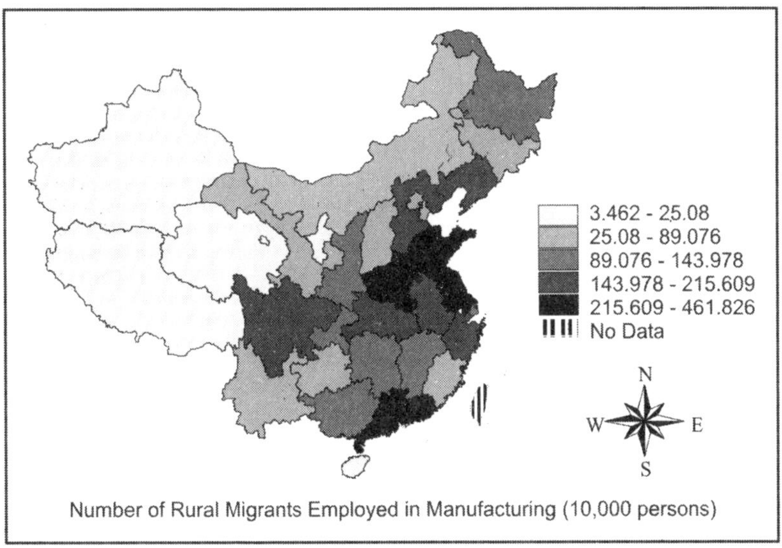

Over the past few years, the number of rural migrant workers has been increasing year by year, with the size of cross-provincial employment expanding as well. According to the *Report on the Survey of China's Migrant Workers,* which estimates that there were 200 million rural migrant workers in 2004, 60 per cent are rural migrants working in other cities, and about half (60 million) left their hometown for other provinces. According to this structure, there were about 71.4 million rural migrant workers of cross-provincial employment in 2008.

Most of the cross-provincial rural migrants work in coastal regions in the east, especially the Pearl River Delta and Yangtze River Delta regions. Prosperous regions (where rural migrant workers are in urgent demand) will first attract rural migrant workers from neighbouring provinces before trying to employ those from non-neighbouring provinces. Take Guangdong for example, most of non-local migrant workers are from Guangxi, Hunan, Jiangxi, Hubei, Henan and Sichuan, and those from remote regions like Xinjiang, Inner Mongolia and Heilongjiang are far less in number (Figure 3).

Figure 3

Regional Distribution of Non-local Rural migrant workers in Guangdong

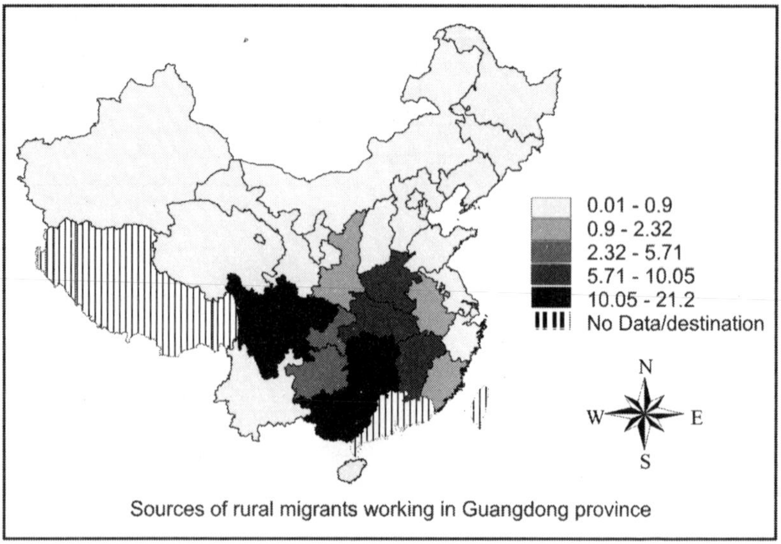

Characteristics of Rural Migrant Workers in China

Although wages are rising for rural migrant workers, their earning is still very low, especially compared with those of local resident workers. Most rural migrant workers earn minimum wage during the regular working time. But they can earn doubled wage for the overtime working. Over one-half of their income comes from their overtime working. During the economic recession due to financial crisis, firms reduced their production thus reduced the overtime working, causing the distinctive income decreasing of rural migrant workers. From the point of view of rural migrant workers, they struggle to earn as much as they can. Thus, rural migrant workers are eager to work overtime in practice. Most rural migrant workers know from the very beginning of their entering into the urban area that they are not able to stay in urban area for a long time. Thus, earning as much as possible becomes one of their most important goals.

Most rural migrant workers have few social security and social insurance. Injury insurance is the only insurance for most rural migrant workers. Since firms have to pay insurance cost for workers as required by law, especially the newly enforced contract law, they usually try to pay as less as possible in order to save the cost. Without the strict inspection from the local social security authority, firms can attain their goal of saving cost for social insurances. Injury incidence is much higher for rural migrant workers than for urban workers as the former working condition is rather poor. It is beneficial for firms to pay injury insurance cost for rural migrant workers. As for some other insurance such as pension and housing insurance, firms and workers share the payments. Thus, from the point of view of rural migrant workers, they would rather to give up these insurances and social securities since most of them do not plan to stay in urban area for a long time due to their incapacity of settling down in cities and they may not be able to get these insurances in the end. However, in some urban areas such as Kunshan of Jiangsu Province, firms are strictly required to pay all the insurances for rural migrant workers by local labour and social security authority. Thus, rural migrant workers can have all the required insurances and social securities in these urban areas.

Living condition for rural migrant workers is rather poor. Although wages for rural migrant workers have been rising over the past few years, rural migrant workers still earn a low wage rate as compared with urban workers. Most rural migrant workers live in suburb areas of city, or so called villages in city. Many rural migrant workers live in dormitories or barrack-type shelters provided by firms. Others live in rented simple houses or apartments, with very bad living conditions. With the rising housing prices, rural migrant workers have to live far way from the city centre if they still want to live in urban areas. As housing cost is the most expensive cost for living in a city, it is unthinkable that rural migrant workers will settle down in city with the rising high cost of housing. But, without rural migrant workers' settling down in urban area, China's urbanisation and industrialisation process will be much slower. Governments have to take some effective measures either to increase rural migrant workers' income or to provide subsidies for their settlement in city such as housing, education and medical care.

Future Outlook

As expected in the early of 2009, in the second half of 2009, demand for rural migrant workers increased gradually in some areas dramatically. In the end of 2009, shortage of rural migrant workers had become one of the biggest obstacles, especially in the Pearl River and Yangtze River Delta areas. Practically, the situation happened as we expected in the early of 2009. Besides, more and more rural migrant workers got jobs in the central and western China instead of eastern China. Basically, governments played a key role in promoting employment, especially of rural migrant workers. Governments' investment in the field of infrastructure such as high-speed railway not only increased the demand for rural migrant workers directly, but also pushed relative firms to enlarge their output, thus increasing labour demand indirectly. In order to deal with the financial crisis, China had a huge investment plan, namely, the 4,000 billion RMB investments for 2009 and 2010. Most of the investments were used infrastructure and people's livelihood.

In future the demand for rural migrant workers will continue if the government's investment continues. However, the prospect of China's economy is not definitely optimistic. Bubbles in real estate will have a comprehensive effect on China's economy growth. After a rapid increase in housing price from 2007 to 2010, more and more people are deeply involved in bubbles of real estate. Most of those having bought apartments in past two or three years will have to cut their consumption in order to save enough money for mortgage. Thus, on one side, China's economy growth will mainly depend on investment and export. Facing the pressure of high housing price, the central government of China had taken some rigid measures to curb the price growth of real estate at the end of 2009, even more rigid measures in the early of 2011. One of the important measures is to have real estate firm speed up their house constructing procedure. Moreover, governments are prompting to build more subsidised houses. Thus, on the other side, we might expect that the construction industry will increase their demand for rural migrant workers. However, the performance of China's economy in the next few years is still hard to forecast. Bubbles in real estate may be burst soon, which may trigger a recession in many industries, causing lay-off of rural migrant workers. Moreover, China's economy cannot heavily depend on intensive investment. Measures have to be taken to encourage consumption and speed up the growth of small and median sized firms. In that way, employment of rural migrant workers can increase steadily.

Notes

1. The financial crisis began to take its toll on the employment of rural migrants in the second half of 2008. But, the total size of annual employment and additional employment was calculated at the beginning of the year. Therefore, it is reasonable to presume that employment grew in 2008 by a similar degree as in previous years.
2. According to the Ministry of Construction, there are 32 million rural migrants engaged in construction sector (Taskforce of Research Office of the State Council 2006). Our estimated result is similar to the figure of the Ministry of Construction which proves that our method is correct.
3. The sum of rural migrants in the eastern, central and western regions does not equal the national total (according to our estimate, there were 229 million rural migrants in 2007). The reason is that the figures do not add up (the sum of non-agricultural employment figures of various provinces does not equal the national total).

References

Huang, Zhuhui and Liu Yaping (2008). 'Study on Generation Difference of Rural Migrant Workers' Employment', *Issues of Agriculture Economics*, 10: 51–59.

Taskforce of Research Office of the State Council (2006). *Survey Report on China's Rural Migrant Workers*, Beijing: China Yanshi Press.

Xiao, Yun and Xu Yan (2005). 'Study on Mechanism Formation and Improvement of Unemployment and Social Security for Rural Migrant Workers: A Case in Chongqing', *Journal of Northwest University*.

Xianping, Bi and Yang Ming (2008). 'Study on Characteristic of Employment Mobility of China's Youth Rural Migrant Workers and its Affect', *Study on Modern Youth*, 4: 44–50.

4

Migration in China and India

A Gender Angle

JAYANTI ALAM

According to 2001 Census of India, the total number of migrants in India, based on the place of last residence criterion, was 314 million, forming around 31 per cent of the total population. Females counted were 221 million, about 70 per cent of the total migrants. But, according to National Sample Survey (NSS) data, women constituted as high as 77 per cent of the total migrants – 80 per cent of the intra-state migrants, 56 per cent of the inter-state migrants and 81 per cent of migrants due to marriage. Alarming, isn't it if we believe that no non-nomadic human likes to migrate unless for better opportunities or love for a new land. Humans, by nature, are gregarious and like to stay close to one's family or friends or cultural belt. Indians may suffer from the lure of 'luxurious' life and much higher income in the West or West Asia, but a deeper study shows that a great majority of the migrants are forced to leave the place of their birth due to the forcible grabbing of their land and forest by the governments or the big industrial houses (with active support of the government – the State or the Union); in case of women, of course, a majority of migrations take place due to marriage or due to the migration of her family or husband. There are cases, particularly in the tribal areas, when young, unmarried daughters/sisters migrate to big cities to mainly work as domestic workers and the males stay back to cultivate the little land left behind after the 'SEZisation'. That is why, the number of female migrants is much higher – more than double – of the total number of migrants. Women comprise 73 per cent of the 'intra-state' migrants, thus indicating that a lion's share of those are due to marriage; inter-state female migrants, on the other hand, comprise 54 per cent, thus indicating migration more due to 'development-induced displacements' than due to marriage or choice.

In China, the transfer of a large number of rural labour, especially young and middle-aged farmers, to the cities has led to the emergence of new problems both for the migrant (to urban areas) workers and the development of agriculture/rural areas. These are:

1. Skills and the other qualifications of the migrant workers are unable to meet the needs of developments in the secondary and the tertiary sectors.
2. Agricultural work thus is mainly shouldered by the old and the women; a big majority, like in case of India, may return to their lands for harvesting even if the earnings in the cities are quite a bit higher than in agriculture, which is not done by the best of the hands because those have got attracted more to the cities.

This becomes quite a vicious cycle – higher the incomes in the cities (in spite of being in the unorganised/not preferred sector), the greater is the urge to migrate and thus lower is agricultural productivity; and the lower the productivity in the rural areas, greater is the urge to migrate. The situation in India is exactly the same ever since 'Liberalisation-Privatisation-Globalisation' (LPG) has been adopted as the economic policy.

China's population is unevenly distributed – 96 per cent living on 46 per cent of the total land mass (in 2006). There were 230 million farmer-turned-workers of which 150 million went to cities as migrant workers in 2009. At first they had migrated to the nearby townships; but, from 1990 onwards, when China had entered the era of rapid economic growth, the migrants started going farther and farther to the big cities, with the flow being maximum towards the highly developed and modernised south-east, concentrating on the export-oriented enterprises. The income gap between the city workers/dwellers and the rural workers kept on widening (quite like in India). In 1978, the income of the city dwellers was 2.4 times more than that of the farm dwellers; by 2008, the disparity went up to 3.13 times. Quality farmland, with sufficient water and heat (in India, 'heat', on the contrary, is a problem, being between the equatorial and the tropical regions) accounts for only one-third of the total cultivated land in China. Besides, the industrial wastes, the acid rains and the application of chemical fertilizers over a long period have polluted 6.7 million hectares of land. More than 60 per cent of farmland is located in areas of water scarcity and abysmally low forest cover, which is only 18.21 per cent or less than two-thirds of the world average!

It is becoming increasingly difficult to maintain ecological balance in China, especially in the north-west. The 1997 World Bank Report says that the losses caused by air and water pollution account for 3 to 8 per cent of

China's GDP. Over 20 million farmers have lost land and, thus, China's rural areas have over 150 million. redundant labour, who need to find jobs in the urban/non-agricultural sectors; and there is an annual increase of more than 15 million 'newcomers' to the labour market of the urban China. But, they possess a low level of skills, required for employment in the industries; they never got the opportunity to develop their skills in a totally different field or arena. Yet, industries are facing a 'structural' shortage of labour. The migrants or the new labour force may be good at carpentry, painting (buildings), plastering and placing tiles at the most. The industrialists and the urban development bodies never thought of or think of putting this labour force to development of their abilities in a totally different field. Discouragement, instead of encouragement, reigns supreme; payment of wages get delayed more often than not and even amounts are deducted without any reason being furnished, apart from intense work schedules and long working hours. In the construction sector, they have to work for unspecified number of hours and even through the night in the summer months. Most of these conditions are akin to those prevalent in India. They do not have a proper residence and very often 5–6 members of a family have to live huddled up in a 10 square metre room – rather, a shack.

At the end of 2007, the number of total employed people of China was 769.9 million, 5.9 million more than in the preceding year; 293.5 million were employed in urban areas, of which 12.04 million were 'newly-increased labour' or, in other words, 'migrants', who were/are mostly employed in labour-intensive industries or small and/or medium-sized enterprises. By 2030, it is estimated, China's urban population will rise to 900 million to one billion due to never-stoppable migration from the rural/agricultural areas. Thus, enhancing job opportunities of the migrants from the rural areas and safeguarding their rights by solving their problems has become an urgent task of the governments now.

According to All China Federation of Trade Unions, the new-generation migrants are much better off than their parents were. They do not suffer from hunger and/or cold. They have strong appetite for advanced learning; the highest craze is for technological know-how, the next group for legal studies and the third for enhancing knowledge about their own culture. Although the major motive/cause behind migration is to earn more and more money, quite a few others want 'to develop' himself/herself after graduation, or to learn a skill, etc., but, there are a few who have migrated for the lure of the glamour of city life; they say 'we want to have fun' and 'the village life is too dull'.

It is clearly prescribed in China that compensation to the farmers, whose lands have been taken away for industrial purposes or Special Economic Zones (SEZs), should be raised depending on the particular local situation. And, vocational training is imparted on them so that they can properly utilise the newly earned money (viz., the compensation) and not waste those on the lure of luxury goods and luxurious life or paying up the unduly huge loan they had taken from the most oppressive moneylenders. The migrants are, brought under the urban social security systems though, according to another account (*China Today*, May 2008), they do not enjoy the minimum living allowances. Government-funded free training of migrant workers has been systematically implemented nationwide but, the poor and the needy can hardly avail of that since such information is given on the electronic and the print media and they neither have a TV, nor read newspapers. Here, again conditions are similar to India.

Back in 1958, when the emphasis of the Chinese governmental policies was on development of farming and village life, a temporary permit of merely three days to live in a city used to be given, thus totally discouraging rural-urban migration. In 1984, on the contrary, with the adoption of the new economic model, as high as 80 per cent of the rural population or 230 million surged into the cities seeking new means of livelihood. In order to discourage this trend, the migrants were not allowed any socio-economic benefits, which the city dwellers were enjoying. Slowly and slowly, the migrants became an inevitable part of city life (as mentioned elsewhere) and thus, they started getting medicare, education, labour insurance, employment and social security. In return, they had to pay the taxes.

Unlike in India, the governments in China have a 'will', but are unaware of the 'way'; they have not thought of door-to-door campaign (which is rather common in India particularly because of the presence of an unwieldy large number of NGOs). Before 1990 or the beginning of the open market economy the Peoples' Republic of China (PRC) government used to give 180 tons of food grain each year to each citizen (similar was the situation in India; there was the public distribution system, popularly known as 'ration' or 'fair price' shops). The villagers and even the migrants have also been elected as Deputies to the National Peoples' Congress, thus getting political power even. But, those are the ideal situations (like the much-hyped NREGA in India) and the reality depends on enforcement of the laws. Interestingly totally contradictory reports about the condition and the acceptability of the rural-urban migrants are also prevalent.

A scholar of the Labour Science Studies Institute (China) made an interesting observation that 'China's demographic structure does not match its industrial structure and that its rate of urbanisation is far behind its rate of industrialisation'. A Professor at the Graduate School of Chinese Academy of Social Sciences (CASS), who is also the Director of the National Economic Research Institute, wrote: 'How to encourage the migrant workers to settle down permanently in the cities should be the top concern of the policy-makers in the years leading up to 2015'. One suggestion was that the schooling of the migrant children – the nine-year free and compulsory education – has to be effectively enforced as a minimum a migrant is entitled to. The experimental primary schools for the migrants' children are being run, though.

Women are smarter in and keener for earning and, thus, making a living, than men; they adjust better in the new – may be even adverse and/or hostile – situations than their menfolk who, quite often than not, get way led and misguided by the glamour of city life. In fact, they quite often take to the life of drinking and gambling (perhaps to make easy money). Women's 'workforce' data reveal that women become more active after migration and the percentage of 'self-employed' women increase from 1 per cent before migration to 8 per cent after. Their share in casual wage labour improved from 9 to 16 per cent though the percentage of unpaid family worker rose from 6 to 18 per cent after migration. Thus, the percentage of women as a 'home-maker' only has gone down to 35 per cent from 59 per cent (before migration). Observations show that there are only 2 per cent unemployed women among the non-migrants, whereas only 0.4 per cent among the migrants; they get positive economic returns from migration. Women in the higher age group (25–59) have twice the chances of becoming gainfully employed. Can we, in that case, assume that the women are better valued after migration since they show better resilience and ability to adjust to a completely new situation geographically and culturally? Yet, migration of men are regarded as 'economic', whereas the migration of women as 'social' (because they are 'forced' to migrate due to marriage or accompanying her marital or parental family).

Women are, by nature and by their bringing up, trained in adjusting to any situation; they have to adjust to the whims of her in-laws and ill-treatment by them. Yet, even if much more and steadily women earn (having settled down in the urban slums), they or their income remain invisible in the official data (both in China and India) because of the way the concepts are defined and the data are collected.

Educated women are the worst affected in the employment market; the higher the education and the higher the caste (in case of India only) and class of a particular woman, proportionately lower is the chance of getting gainful employment. Even the school-passed girl/woman has 48 per cent lesser chance of being employed and as high as 83 per cent of women who have studied beyond school level and may have become graduates do not have any probability of getting a job appropriately suitable! Exactly the opposite happens in case of men.

This explains so starkly the eternal truth that women's work and studies are always looked down upon and devalued. How can otherwise, men try to prove inferiority of women and justify the low wages, low salaries and difficult promotions for women?

The next striking observation is that compared to single or unmarried women, married women have 75 per cent less chances of being gainfully employed. This shows how unabashedly patriarchal the society and the world of finance market is and how the females are regarded as mere sex objects and reproductive machines! It is also believed that single women do not have the burden of a family to take care of and, therefore, they can devote to work better.

The other reasons valid for women who want to migrate (in both the countries) are or may be that they

(i) want to earn more or independently of men,
(ii) escape the fear/torture of sexual abuse and violence,
(iii) single women, divorcees and widows desiring to escape from the social rules and stigma, and
(iv) escape pressures of marriage and/or to remain 'chaste'.

Men May Migrate to Avoid Conscription

Migration is regarded, in general, as a labour market process that redistributes labour resources to areas where they can be utilised effectively. People move in response to spatial differences in wage rates and unemployment – a process that tends to augment earnings and employment prospects. Migrant households are 33 per thousand in the urban and 13 per thousand in the rural areas and they are defined as 'those for whom the last usual place of residence (UPR) is different from the present place of enumeration'. Similarly, 'return migrants' are those, who had reported that the present place of enumeration was the UPR any time in the past. Apart from the women mentioned above, there may be married/unmarried women in search of employment, induced to migrate by perceived urban-rural differentials. The economic maximisation model of migration presumes that anticipated changes in family earnings, including those of women, figure strongly in cost-benefit calculations made prior to decision-making on family migration. 'Associational' migration takes place even when the women experience personal losses or something unsuitable for their life or work situation. They become kind of 'tied movers'. Apart from the gender and residence identity, caste/social group as well as income class have a bearing on migrant identity.

Longer duration or permanent residence has a positive effect on the employment status of migrant women; those, who are residing in a place for more than 10 years, have 1.7 times higher chances of being employed. Being known to the employer or to the 'go-between' gives the impression that the work seeker is 'dependable'. And, those, who have been employed before migration have 8.9 times greater chance of being employed in a suitable job than those who had remained unemployed before migration and had migrated in search of employment or some income.

In India, there was a high rise in the urban-to-urban migration between the states in 1991–2001 along with a high rise in inter-state rural-to-urban migration. The states of Punjab, Haryana, Delhi, Maharashtra, Gujarat and Karnataka are the in-migrating states whereas the states in the Hindi belt (Bihar, Uttar Pradesh, Madhya Pradesh and Rajasthan) or the so-called 'Bimaru' (sick) states (the above-mentioned plus Odisha and Assam), along with those in the neglected Northeast, are the out-migrating ones. The so-called saviours (in the garb of 'economic liberalisation' and 'economic reforms') have not been able to reduce the regional inequality and imbalances; those have become more and more formidable.

Sixty-two per cent of the rural migration in India is not to urban, but to more prosperous rural, like from Bihar to Punjab. Let me also mention that brides are 'imported' by the prosperous and 'anti-female' states of Punjab, Haryana and Rajasthan, thus raising the proportion of marital migration very high. The states with textiles and garments industries experience pull factor in a big way particularly, or may be exclusively, for women; women and children are in great demand in labour-intensive, low-paying sectors. And, who does not know that the sex trade is the largest exporter and importer of women and children in the underdeveloped countries as well as in the underdeveloped regions of the developing countries. Women export themselves as childcare-givers, leaving their own children to be uncared for; how much substitutes can the father or the grandmother become? Can we in that case say that migration influences gender relations by either entrenching inequalities and traditional roles or challenging and changing them? There are 25 million internally displaced persons in more than 50 countries and half of these are in eternally war-torn Africa.

The low level of education and skill of the rural population is one of the most important reasons why push factors are not effective in accelerating rural-urban migration; combined with these are high cost of living in the cities and hostile city governments and the judiciary prohibiting 'squatting'. They or their slums are blamed for all the woes of city life, including deteriorating transport system and environment. Thus, one school believes that it is not the poor and uneducated, but the educated and with capital (to start a business) migrates to the cities.

This view is quite contrary to what we have discussed in the earlier paragraphs. The seasonal and temporary migrants work for short duration in activities like construction, brick-making, stone quarrying, fisheries, plantations, rice mills, paddy cultivation and harvesting, etc. This can be both rural-urban and urban-rural, like workers returning home for paddy cultivation and harvesting. There are schools and colleges in Himachal Pradesh in India, for example, which close during the paddy transplanting and harvesting seasons.

The city-rich of China complain about the 'filth' and the lack of 'hygiene' among the migrant poor and in the clusters/slums they have to live in (the same is true of India). But, now the same group finds it difficult to live without the help of the domestic labour from the 'scum-of-the-earth'! The former find them in a soup when the migrant villagers go home for a family re-union during the spring festival. There is nobody to dispose of the garbage even. The pressure from the rich has thus made the local/city governments do things for the betterment of the migrants' lives in their new environments though, 100,000 people live on the collection and sorting of the garbage (akin to India). They are the poorest of the poor, not being able to acquire any skill whatsoever or rather, not being offered any training or opportunity for skill development. Some of them open barber shops, small stores or small restaurants and their income is low due to the fact that their customers are their fellow migrant workers only.

Some of them have picked up the required skills well and in a short time and have thus done well and have become project contractors/ employers and/or businessmen and earned enough to buy apartments and live like the original prosperous city dwellers. Yet, rarely do they enjoy the 'permanent household registration' so as to benefit from all the urban welfare systems. Second generation migrants have higher educational and skill levels. So, in China it becomes difficult, like educated Indians, to get a suitable job or an opportunity for earning.

That the so-called economic reform has been a big failure and that the so-called 'growth rate' is a myth are proven by the stark reality that rural-urban or even rural-rural migration has arisen and is continuing to rise. Migration is usually due to 'expected' rather than real income differences in the rural and urban centres because the 'push' factors are agricultural failure, drought, other natural calamities, debts and low wages. But, mass migration has often caused clashes between the 'pushed' (migrants) and the local or indigenous people (though a big majority of the Adivasis or the indigenous people are themselves victims of the 'push' factors). The real problem arises if the migrants become more successful like it has happened in the Kangra district of Himachal Pradesh; the locals are perennially resenting the flourishing of the Tibetan 'refugees' in McLeodgunj (Dharamshala). In the Jharkhand area the opposite has happened; the Marwaris, North Biharis and the Bengalis (known as 'Dikus' or the 'Satans') have pushed the Adivasis out of their forests, lands and eco-political power. They become wary of losing their employment/income opportunities and cultural identities. A few vested interests and the political parties often take advantage of this jealousy and deep fear and try to gain the confidence of the earlier inhabitants in driving the migrants out.

The best examples are Shiv Sena driving away the South Indians, and the Maharashtra Navnirman Sena (MNS) driving out the Hindi-speaking North Indians, particularly Biharis. Similar attacks have taken place in Goa, Assam (against the kind of 'colonising' Bengalis) and Meghalaya (once again against the 'colonising' non-tribals, particularly against those who were marrying the tribal girls because in a 'matrilineal' society the girl gets all the property). Ultimately, the patriarchal non-tribal husband manages to get a hold of his wife's property. In Assam the protests were from the tribes, which were not deriving the benefits of being scheduled tribes. In which category can we put the 'cleansing' of Gujarat from the Muslims? The latter definitely were not migrants and as much residents of Gujarat as the Hindus.

Let us, at the end, bring in the type of migration, which is popularly known as 'brain-drain' or the staying back of the Indians (or from other developing countries) with plush jobs after the completion of their studies for which they originally migrate. There is great demand for the Indian doctors and the software experts in USA and UK especially. Quite a few of them take up the citizenship of the country they have chosen to live in and quite a few Indian aspirants to citizenships marry an Indian, who is a citizen of the 'migrated' country. In such situations usually there are no conflicts and only the 'pull' factor works, never the 'push' factor.

In 2000 there were 175 million international migrants – one out of every 35 persons! The refugees accounted for 17 million or 9.7 per cent of the total migrants. The number of international migrants has more than doubled since 1960, i.e., ever since the disintegration of Czechoslovakia, Yugoslavia and the USSR. The Philippines is the largest exporter of migrant labour, women being in majority, in the world. Yet, a greater number of men are asylum seekers. Women are increasingly moving as job seekers, independent of their men – neither as 'associational', nor as forced or 'tied up'. Combined international migration of China and India exceeds the total migration worldwide.

Finally, migration is on an increase in both India and China. Migrants face severe hardships when they move to urban areas in these countries because of poor housing, poor living conditions and apathy of the urban communities. Women face greater challenges as migrants, especially those moving for employment. There is urgent need for social security for migrants and more so for women.

5

Housing for Low Income Urban Migrants in India and China

DARSHINI MAHADEVIA

A study of housing for the urban migrants lays out before us the whole gamut of policies on urbanisation as well as well-being of the most vulnerable in a society. This paper presents a comparative perspective on housing for the urban migrants in the two largest and currently the economically fastest growing developing countries of this century, India and People's Republic of China (PRC), referred to as China henceforth. These are the only two billion plus economies in the world. Incidentally, both are Asian countries, are neighbours, have a long history of relationship with each other and have emerged as a nation-state at the same time, China in 1949, as a Socialist Republic and India in 1947 as Secular, Democratic, Socialist[1] Republic. Both, begin almost on a clean slate, the former ravaged by the war, mired in poverty and social backwardness and with more than 90 per cent population living in the rural areas, the latter ravaged by the British colonialism, also mired in poverty and social backwardness, more than 90 per cent population living in the rural areas, and uniquely, a multi-religious, multi-caste and non-negotiable hierarchy-based social structure. But these similarities end here and take off on very different development trajectories.

India pronounced itself as a socialist republic but in essence pursued capitalism as the main development path. The public sector dominated basic infrastructure sector industries, some alleging that it was to serve the private corporate sector under what was called 'Bombay Plan'. The consequence of such a path is nation's inability to progress on human development front, and the country now severely criticised internally as well as externally for not being able to improve human development even under the so-called 'socialist path'. China indeed moved on socialist path, experimenting with different production systems till it opened up for economic reforms in a gradual way, from 1978. Till then, the nation had progressed significantly on human development and had institutionalised some 'human-centred' policies. Its continuation in the current period is also observed in the housing policies, as we would see later in this article. India embarked on economic reforms from 1991 onwards, however, with dilution of whatever social policies it had. This is also reflected in the housing policies as we would also see in this article.

China's current urbanisation level is 45 per cent, whereas that of India's is much lower, just 30 per cent. However, both are expecting high rate of rural-urban migration as a consequence of expected high economic growth rates. Hence, challenge before both the countries is welfare policies for their migrant populations. Among these, housing policies for the migrants is of great importance because shelter is considered next only to food and clothing in terms of human priorities (Oberlander, 1985). Shelter and shelter security assume more importance in countries such as India, where, there is no other institutional regime to give citizenship right to an individual other than a residential address, unlike China, where citizenship right is tied to *hukou*, or residential registration. While *hukou* in China ensures a number of entitlements, a residential address in India does not ensure but at the least opens up access to entitlements, in absence of weak social policies and weaker implementation of these social policies. Independently, shelter ensures protection against elements of nature, violence of society, emotional security, privacy, dignity, a risk-hedging asset, secure environment for children to study, hygienic living and hence good health, and above all wellness of being. Hence, housing security of migrants becomes much more than improvement in basic living conditions in both the countries.

Both countries have resorted to very different urban policy regimes, land ownership regimes and migration policies, resulting in very different outcomes for migrants in the urban areas. This paper is a comparative research on housing policies in general and for the migrants in particular in the two countries. The paper firstly gives the brief information on urbanisation, migration and urban poverty. It then moves on to discussing the institutional settings and housing policies in both the countries drawing implications of these on the housing of the migrants. The housing conditions of the urban migrants in both the countries are then described. Finally, it draws conclusions on the implications of the study on urban studies in both the countries and also for policy purposes in both the countries.

Urbanisation, Migration and Poverty

With urbanisation level of about 45 per cent in mid-2000 and an urbanisation rate of 4.3 per cent per annum during 1990–2000 (China National Bureau of Statistics, 2006), there are about 600 million people living in the urban areas and another 300 million expected to move to the cities in the next two decades or so in China.[2] It is also argued that if the *hukou* did not control migration, there would have been 300–400 million[3] more urban residents in China than they are now. The decade of 1980s too registered a very high urbanisation rate of 4.5 per cent per annum. In contrast, the natural growth rate of population in China has been just 1.04 per cent per annum during 1990–2000 (calculated from China National Bureau of Statistics, 2006). Roughly, the net rural to urban migration rate is therefore 3.24 per cent per annum. Thus, urbanisation is primarily due to migration in China and since the economic reforms in 1978, migration restraints have loosened permitting migrants to move to manufacturing centres, largely located within the eastern coastal provinces. There is a strong recognition in China that migrants contribute greatly to the city and national economy.

In contrast, the urbanisation rate in India has been very low, just 2.75 per cent per annum during 1991–2001 period. In the previous decade, the rate of urbanisation was 3.09 per cent per annum, indicating that urbanisation has slowed down in India since 1980s, in spite of economic growth picking up. In contrast to China, natural population growth rate has contributed more to urbanisation process than migration; the natural increase of population has ranged from 51 per cent to about 65 per cent during 1961–2001 (Sivaramakrishnan et al., 2005). Urbanisation rate and levels are low in India in spite of no official controls on migration but dictated through large many discouraging policies, like in most countries in the world (United Nations Population Fund, 2007), no distributive urban policies, exclusionary urban planning and chauvinistic politics. Nonetheless, as per the population census of 2001, there were total 315 million migrants in the country,[4] not necessarily all being in the urban areas.

Migrants are considered as 'underclass'[5] in China. They come from poor agriculture population from less developed provinces of Anhui, Henan and Sichuan, with low level of education. There are estimated 150–200 million migrants in the cities of China.[6] A more recent estimate by the Office of Migrant Workers in the State Council and the Vice Ministry of Labour and Social Security has estimated 210 million migrant workers in China in 2007.[7] They are registered as temporary residents in the city they work and they are also known as *floating population*. Besides the temporary residents, there are a section of migrants who do not even have temporary registration and may be prone to deportation by the authorities on being detected in the city.

According to a survey conducted by the labour and social security department, within 2,600 enterprises in 26 Chinese cities, including Beijing, Tianjin and Shenzhen, migrant workers earn an average 660 yuan per month. This is lower by about 300 yuan than that earned by urban industrial workers.[8] A survey of 243 migrants in Fujian province also found that the migrants have low income. The survey showed that nearly 80 per cent of the respondents had monthly income below 1,000 yuan, and 40.7 per cent of them had monthly income of only 500–800 yuan (Zhu, 2007: 71). On an average, Head Count Ratio (HCR) (incidence of poverty) among the migrants is 1.5 times that among the local urban population (ADB, 2001). In larger cities, the incidence of poverty among the migrants is far higher than the locals, i.e., 2.3 times in Beijing, 3.1 times in Shanghai, 3.4 times in Tianjin, 2.4 times in Wuhan and 3.1 times in Nanjing, than the local population, whereas in Dalian it was 1, and in Harbin and Hangzhou 1.1 times (ibid.: 93). In only some cities such as Changsha, Xian, Chongqing, Xiamen, etc., the ratio was less than 1, indicating that the incidence of poverty was higher among the locals than the migrants (ibid.). In a recent field visit to Huaxian, Henan province, one of the local officials mentioned that the rural households with less land have a tendency to migrate to the cities and in the end they tend to be better off than the households with large land parcel.

This is in contrast to situation in India where the poor rural population does not migrate to the cities. Based on 1999–00 National Sample Survey (NSS) data, Kundu and Sarangi (2007) show that the rural poor in India do not migrate easily because of their low capability or inability to overcome institutional barriers. Migrants into urban areas are from the top two quintiles of the rural population being 26.1 per cent and 22.9 per cent of the total migrants respectively. The bottom-most quintile's share in the total migrants was only 14.2 per cent and that of second quintile from the bottom's share was 17.5 per cent. There are two types of rural-urban migrants in the urban areas of India – permanent and seasonal – and in both types, individuals from the top quintiles were more likely to out-migrate from the rural areas than from the bottom quintiles. In other words, poverty is not a key factor behind seasonal migration or to put it other way, the rural poor do not have capabilities for even short-term mobility, leave aside long-term mobility. This lays to rest the arguments made in context of urban poverty that it is an outcome of migration of rural poor to urban areas. Hence, the rural population that migrates to urban areas is better endowed in terms of economic resources as well as educational capabilities. This is truer for the long-term migrants than seasonal migrants. Kundu and Sarangi (2007) also shows that all migrant households are not poor: just 5.6 per cent among them are poor.

In India, three types of rural-urban migrants can be observed: (i) long-term or permanent migrants with the intention of settling down in the urban areas, many getting into regular employment but keeping strong links with the native village/town; (ii) seasonal migrants, defined as those who stay in the urban areas for more than 60 days in a year but returning back for some period, mainly during monsoon and going to cities to tide over lean agricultural seasons; and (iii) migrants tied to the employers, who move from one place of employment to other, and about whom no estimates are available. But, in general, if migrants are able to assimilate in the urban economy, they do not return back to the rural areas. Srivastava and Sasikumar (2003) have classified migrants in India into three categories, viz., 'permanent', 'semi-permanent' and 'temporary' migrants, based on how long they are away from their place of origin, the links they maintain, and the likelihood that they will return home.

The three types of migrants in urban India, discussed above, face different types of challenges in urban areas. The permanent migrants, those who eventually get integrated with the urban settings, tend to enter the urban labour market at the lower end as temporary workers, eventually working their way up into the system. Many a permanent migrant come to the urban areas as single male migrants, at young age, and then call their families, once they are reasonably financially, socially and shelter-wise secure. Migrants from some states, in particular from the North Indian states of Uttar Pradesh and Bihar, do not settle down and would like to return back to their native villages and hence do not bring their spouse or family to the cities. In these communities, female spouses tend not to work. Since female members do not work, it is sometimes not possible to support a family in urban area and hence they do not bring them to the city. The chances of most migrants returning back to their native villages is rare except under specific circumstances such as urban violence emanating from communal polity and regional chauvinism and also slum demolition (Mahadevia and Narayanan, 2008a).

Institutional Settings and Housing Policies

Institutional Settings

Both the countries have very different institutional settings as far as migrants are concerned and so do both countries have very different approach to urban housing policies. In China, migration is controlled through *hukou*. *Hukou* is a residential permit system that classifies Chinese residents into urban and rural, with those having urban *hukou* or residential permit, entitled to live and work in cities and access benefits of employment programmes, subsidised housing, public education and healthcare system, social security and all other programmes that urban local governments finance. Besides, in cities such as Beijing, there are special entitlements such as licence to own and drive a taxi. Those with rural *hukou* are entitled to agricultural lands, which those with urban *hukou* are not entitled to. It is not easy to get an urban *hukou* and much more difficult to get *hukou* of large cities such as Beijing. However, some provinces, such as Guangdong, dependent on the migrant labour for their economic growth, have relaxed the *hukou* provisions for sometimes and made availability of temporary *hukou* easier than before. Zhu (2007) has argued that the system of *hukou* alone does not explain temporary nature of the floating population in the cities and there are many other reasons why the floating population does not wish to settle down in the cities.

In India, migration is free; any Indian citizen, whether a rural resident or an urban resident is free to migrate to any part of the country as many times as s/he wants to. Male migration is largely for the reasons of employment and female migration on account of marriage. The citizenship of a place is defined through various documents that a person or a household holds: (i) a ration card[9] – a Below Poverty Line (BPL) card or an Above Poverty Line (APL) card, which has the permanent address of the person/household; (ii) an election card, that is a Voter's Identity Card issued to all those above age of 18 for the purpose of voting in elections held for the three tiers of government – local, state and national; (iii) for those having access to electricity and having electricity metres in their house, and getting an electricity bill; (iv) an identity (ID) card issued by the urban local government for those living in slums, based on a cut-off date declared by it from time to time;[10] (v) a property tax payment receipt, and (vi) a letter of identity issued by the local elected representative. Thus, urban citizenship notion and definition is fluid and amorphous, prone to negotiations and political pressures from below in cases where there are local social movements.

A few interesting examples of political pressure from the below are:

(i) In 2004–05, the local government demolished about 90,000 slum dwellings across Mumbai and the residents in them not just lost their homes and assets but also all the documents that established their urban citizenship. Through the help of the housing and human rights activists, slum dwellers put up a strong resistance to demolitions and finally caught attention of not just media but also the national leadership of the political party in power in the state[11] of Maharashtra (in which Mumbai is located). The national leadership asked the state government to allocate two sites in the city for the rehabilitation of these households and asked the intermediating organisation, the National Alliance of People's Movement and its local affiliate named Shelter Security Movement, to carry out a survey and prepare a list of households to be allocated a plot of land on the new sites. The process was also carried out to give these households new identity card.[12] A large proportion of these dwellers were long-term migrants to Mumbai.

(ii) In Ahmedabad, about 30,000 households have been displaced since 2006 for various urban infrastructure projects. A section of these households were overnight dumped on an undeveloped and poorly connected land on the city's periphery. People struggled to live and a few committed suicide, as they were unable to bear the shock of displacement and also of other shocks such as major illness, etc. A human rights group, Action Aid stepped in to support the households and file legal cases, an academic institution carried out research on the impacts of displacement on the lives of households, and finally concerned citizens of the city stood up and held public hearing of displacements in the city. The local government in response came up with the idea of issuing ration cards to these households, which in essence meant, giving these households entitlements vis-à-vis the local government. These too were long-term migrants and had lost their citizenship because they had lost their shelter security. Conversely, such citizenship documents are necessary to access public housing or any other local government's development programmes.

In India, there is no structured way of accessing urban citizenship, as in case of China. The low-income migrants just come to a city in case the person has contact and is expecting to get some employment. Then, foothold in urban settings and an entry to climb up the ladder of urban citizenship begins with gaining access to rental housing in an established low income settlement or squatting on a piece of land, mainly public land and then negotiate to get name registered in the urban voting list through getting an urban patron. Then onwards, is the gradual and patient marching up the ladder to gain full citizenship through possessing a few of the above-mentioned documents.

One important institutional mechanism that assists the poor migrants in the upward housing mobility is the democratic space created by electoral politics. It is true that there is fair amount of convergence against the poor in most cities aspiring to renew their image through infrastructure and beautification projects. But, at some point, there is also a fear of losing the vote bank as a consequence of demolitions. There is also a flip-flop on giving citizenship to the recent migrants.

For example, in case of Mumbai, before the 2004–05 demolitions, a coalition of the centrist political parties came to power in state of Maharashtra after 2004 state elections. Incidentally, the same coalition had come to power in May 2004 at the national level. The most important promise made by the winning coalition to the urban poor of the state was to extend the cut-off date for legitimising slum dwellers from 1995 to 2000. This meant that those slum dwellers who could establish that they had migrated to Mumbai up to 2000 would be given an identity card, which would then entitle the dwellers to legal residency in the city and in case their dwelling had to be demolished, they would be given an alternative accommodation. This was an election promise and not a law. Thus, the state government was not technically wrong when it ordered demolition of slums in Mumbai. The elected representatives did not help in gaining them rehabilitation but the slum dwellers' own resistance did. But, electoral politics was the cause of the promise to the Mumbai slum dwellers that they would be legalised. Thus, institutional context is of democratic space offered by an electoral democracy.

Housing Policies

Housing policies in both the countries are at the provincial/state level, while the national government sets broad directions. In spite of differences in the political systems in the two countries, in both, the housing policies are somehow targeted towards the legal residents of the cities. In China, subsidised public housing is accessible to only those with urban *hukou*. Temporary residents can however purchase a house in a city in the private market, called commercial housing, in case the household can afford it. Thus, only better off temporary residents of urban areas are able to purchase a house in the cities. In India, the state governments have begun making their own policies after the National Urban Housing and Habitat Policy, 2007 was accepted at the national level. But, the states' emphasis is on the households having 'domicile' in the state defined through possession of number of identity cards. Hence, in both the countries, the migrants have to find their own housing unless the employers are providing housing.

In China, recently, there have been some changes in housing policies related to migrants. To begin with, the highest national policy making body, the National Development and Reform Commission (NDRC), together with other departments, have begun to re-look at the urbanisation policies with the view of assisting the rural migrants settling down in the cities. There are 140 million migrant workers nationwide, and that figure can increase to 300 million, taking their families into account. If these people can afford to buy or rent an apartment to settle down in cities, the potential for expanding consumption is huge, eventually leading to expanding overall consumption in the economy.[13] The NDRC has also realised that average urbanisation rate for a country with a per capita income of $3,000 should be around 55 per cent,[14] which is only 45 per cent, indicating under-urbanisation because of migration controls.

With the signal coming from the NDRC to introduce new urban policies inclusive of migrants, provinces and cities have begun reforms on *hukou* and welfare of the migrants. For example:

(i) The Construction Department of Henan province has issued new rules directing construction companies implementing projects in the province to buy insurance for their respective workers, including housing insurance scheme through which the workers could contribute to a house reservation fund and in doing so for five years be eligible for a housing loan at low interest rate and be able to buy a house in the city of the province.[15]

ii) A professor of Tsinghua University, Beijing, has urged the city of Shenzhen to build a housing project for the rural migrant workers on the city's periphery arguing that the migrants contribute greatly to the city's economy but get nothing in return from the city and on the contrary they are driven out by the city once their contribution to the city cease. Migrants being the poorest of the urban residents forced to live in temporary factory dormitories[16] and not having a permanent residence (either rental or ownership) inside the metropolitan areas, are unable to live a normal family life. This was not fair and if the government was unable to afford houses for them, the migrants themselves should be facilitated to do so through ensuring availability of affordable housing.[17] This argument is very similar to that being made for the urban poor in India.

iii) It has also been realised that in spite of massive urban economic growth and prosperity, there was a need of small, low-cost and affordable housing, to be supported through tax measures, credit policy and land supply increase. Premier Wen Jiabao therefore had announced that efforts would be made to improve the living conditions of the migrants in the cities, one among these to be low-rent housing.[18]

iv) For the first time, the national government issued a document in March 2006 stipulating improvement in the living conditions of the migrant workers. It also asked the related government departments to intensify supervision to ensure that housing for migrant workers met all hygiene and safety standards. Since then, many local governments have begun exploring ways to improve low-rent housing for migrant workers. For example, Chongqing municipality has built 36 apartment buildings, which provide low-rent housing for 13,000 migrant workers in Chongqing city proper. Changsha, which had 400,000 migrant workers before the 2008 earthquake, had its municipal government investing in building 618 sets of low-rent apartments, with a cafeteria, library, reading rooms, video rooms, public baths, warehouse rooms for workers to store their tools, personal lockers and steel anti-theft doors at the rent varying from 50 yuan to 70 yuan per month.[19]

In short, there were no particular national housing policies for the low-income migrants in the cities before 2007 in China. Generally, the employers build dormitories for them near or in their work premises. The living conditions and facilities were basic and simple. But, following the policy of harmonious development and recognition of important role of the migrants in Chinese economy, researchers, policy makers and government officials have begun to notice the poor living conditions of this group of population and have therefore reacted to rectify the situation through national and local policies of reaching out to the migrants.

Following this, some regulations have been enacted. These are: (i) provision of housing by the employers to the migrant workers in accordance with the safety standards and accepted sanitation conditions, (ii) building of dormitories for the low-income migrants in the developing zones and industrial garden areas, (iii) creation of a special fund for housing this section of the migrants and contribution of the employers to this fund and ensuring that the employers comply through entering into contract with the workers, (iv) drawing up of housing security plan at the city level and including low-income migrants in the plan, and (v) issuance of a national government plan to include the low-income migrants in necessary preparation of a city level housing security plan.

In India, there has not been much of policy discussion on the shelter security of the low-income migrants but this issue is subsumed under the discussion on shelter security for the urban poor. Many draft national housing policies have been framed in the past. However, the recent one – the National Urban Housing and Habitat Policy (NUHHP, 2007) – has been accepted by the national government and the state governments have been asked to make their own policies.

The NUHHP (2007) has nothing specific for the migrant workers, except that there is discussion on increasing supply of rental housing, which could be for the recent migrants. There is mention of temporary accommodation with appropriate toilet facilities on the construction sites, to be provided by the construction companies and the public authorities. There is also mention of need for employer housing. For each of these suggestions some actionable agenda has been suggested. However, there is no mention of the transit accommodation or anything special for the recent migrants. In general, housing for the migrants has been left upon the market. The NUHHP (2007) is a market-driven policy and there are questions as to whether it is going to serve the purpose of reducing housing gap. Two large national housing programmes, Basic Services for the Urban Poor (BSUP) under the largest national level urban development programme called Jawaharlal Nehru National Urban Renewal Mission (JNNURM) launched in 2005 and Rajiv Awaas Yojana (RAY), a slum re-development and affordable housing programme, launched in 2009, are expected to increase housing supply for low-income households through private sector participation. The basic idea of these two programmes is to give funding to the tune of 80 per cent to the state governments for the purpose and let the state governments bring in private sector to construct new housing for the urban poor. There is no mention of the special provisions for the low-income recent migrants and no schemes to fund their housing.

But, all these housing programmes are for what are termed as 'eligible' slum dwellers. Most cities and state governments are against the low-income migrants, more so if they are from other Indian states. There are tensions in the developed states as they have attracted migrants from the less developed states. These tensions are articulated in terms of regional nationalism.[20] A regional chauvinism wave and ensuing violence then hits out at the low-income population from other states. The contemporary political history of India is full of these instances, which flare up just before the local elections.

The anti-migrant bias can be seen in case of slum policies of some states. For example, the state of Gujarat (a state in Western India and one of the most industrialised states) has announced its own slum policy in March 2010, named Regulations for the Rehabilitation and Redevelopment of the Slums, 2010, wherein, those to be covered by it are called the 'beneficiaries', defined as one who is eligible slum dweller or any project affected person. An eligible slum dweller is one who is 'not a foreign national and is the occupant of hutment for a period of minimum 10 years and has a domicile of Gujarat for 25 years or his descendant' (p. 4).[21] For proof of occupancy, any two of the following documents are required: (i) copy of ration card, (ii) copy of electricity bills, (iii) proof of being included in the electoral rolls, and (iv) any other proof as decided by the prescribed authority (p. 4). Then, the proposed rehabilitation is through a high-rise building constructed by a developer. In fact, the regulations are only for the rehabilitation of displaced slum dwellers. Hence, this is not a slum policy.

The comparison of the institutional and policy environments in both the countries shows that both have realised that there was a specific need to address the housing requirements of the migrant workers. However, in case of China, this need has been directly addressed by firstly the policies and then regulations in favour of the migrants. In India, the housing markets have failed the urban poor and tragically the policy response has been to address the market failure through more of market-oriented policies! This is reflected in the living conditions of migrants in the two countries.

Housing Conditions of Low-income Urban Migrants

China

Migrants in China live in several different types of housing: (i) employer housing on factory premises or construction sites that is largely dormitory type, (ii) rental housing in urban villages, largely located in the urban periphery, (iii) rental housing in private housing (private housing increases as one moves towards smaller cities and towns as compared to metropolitan cities where there is more of *danwei* housing of the state-owned enterprises (SOEs), (iv) rental housing market in former *danwei* housing and public housing, (v) dormitory employer housing provided by now large many service enterprises such as restaurants, hotels, etc., and (vi) living with the employers in case of those engaged as household help. Type four of rental housing is not legally acknowledged or allowed, but exists. Except that last type of housing is shared by a group of migrants of the same sex. The rents being as high as the monthly income of the migrant worker working as wage labour they share a room (Wang, 2004: 70). Housing in urban villages is for families.

Zhejiangcun area on the south periphery of Beijing, with estimated 100,000 migrants in 1995 (Liu and Liang, 1997; Wang, 2004: 70), was a typical example of migrant housing. But, that housed migrants from Wenzhou, who are businessmen and hence many of them could afford to rent a room for them alone. Zhang (2001) describes the housing as rural lands sub-divided by the farmers and *siheyuan* type housing constructed on them and each migrant, if able to afford, renting a tiny cubicle. Those with families had some family members working out of the home. These were therefore work units as well. Finally, the entire village was demolished.

Another example of this is Xiao Jia He community, in Haidian district. It is located between the 5th and the 6th ring road. It is a large community. The settlement had drainage and sewerage lines, had tarred roads in the inner lanes, and houses were of brick with a sloping roof when we visited it in June 2008. There were community baths. There were garbage collection points and also a solid waste transfer station. The streets were clean, quite unlike a slum in Indian city. Some houses also had individual water supply and some were using community taps. The housing by the migrants was rental: some rooms shared by single male migrants and some rented by families. The discussions with some individuals indicated that they were working in private sector units in Beijing city. In this community, there are 4,000 native inhabitants and nearly 30,000 migrant workers.[22] Many suburban farmers rent their houses to migrant workers, living on the proceeds.[23] A section of waste collectors and recyclers of the city also live in settlements such as Picun and Xiaojiahe. The rate for a 15 square metre room in 2008 was 120 yuan per month, and had seen a 100 per cent increase from 60 yuan a few years back. The rent comes to about 12 per cent to 15 per cent of their monthly income. Thus, migrant workers tend to share a room.[24]

Construction workers live near construction sites in dormitory type housing. In Beijing, 20 per cent of the migrants lived on construction sites (Wang, 2004: 70) – a figure that would have gone up subsequently on account of construction work related to 2008 Beijing Olympics. The description of construction worker housing has been given in Chan (2006:

26): 'Originally from Sichuan province, Wei Zhang is one of the hundreds of construction workers who arrived in May 2006 to handle the job of expanding Beijing's subway in preparation for the 2008 Olympics. He works a 12–hour shift most days and lives with his colleagues in a dormitory at the construction site, taking his meals in the canteen, and sleeping on his plywood bed along with eight other males in one room. Despite his hard work and tolerance for these conditions, his employer refuses to pay him until the project is completed. When his job is done, Zhang does not know whether he will stay in Beijing. Like many of his colleagues, he will have to leave his temporary home and find another job to sustain himself.'

The example of migrants renting former state owned enterprise (SOE) housing has been mentioned in Zhang (2001), which states that the displaced households from Zhejiangcun eventually shifted to renting in the SOE housing in the neighbourhood (ibid.).

There are many single woman migrants engaged in housework in large cities. Some are also employed for taking care of elderly. They tend to live with the families they are working for. Their employment is through the employment agencies that ensure their safety and security and also regular payment to them from their employers. In exchange they give a percentage of their income to this agency.

Chan (2006) indicates that occupation of the migrant workers determined their dwelling unit condition depending on the type of job and income of the worker. In some jobs, husband and wife could not stay together and they would live in their sex's dormitory. Some employers offered housing as a part of the job benefits. Large prestigious work units were more likely to have more resources to house their employees as compared to the self-employed. Self-employed had almost no access to any job benefits including housing and therefore they had to live in housing paying their own rents. Some jobs required workers to be on site and hence are provided housing close by, for example, security guard. In many cities including Beijing, their respective employers also offered the restaurant worker's jobs and shared accommodation. Such workers were found to be living farther away from their jobs in Beijing. It is not mandatory for private employers like restaurant owners to give housing but they did more out of custom and tradition than functional need. Construction workers always lived on the site and were not allowed to keep their family members with them in such housing. For example, a construction worker from Anhui province had brought his wife to Beijing, but she works as a domestic help and lives on her own while the husband lives on construction site and there is a family reunion once a week if that is feasible. Self-employed workers are more likely to live with their family members and relatives.

Chan (2006: 37–38) gives results of a study by Fei Guo and Cai Fang of 'Shanty Towns in Chinese Cities: A Five City Study of Migration and Urban Poverty' (quoted in Chan, 2006) that included Beijing, with a sample of 2,351 individuals including the migrants as well as permanent residents and found that majority of migrants (42.7%) only had access to outdoor public toilets while most local residents had indoor toilets for family use (71.4%). Conversely, only 31.1 per cent of migrants have this luxury. Similarly, 78.6 per cent migrant workers occupied one-bedroom house compared to 19.9 per cent of the local residents living in this small house. Migrants are likely to live in a single-story house (41.4%) or rented accommodation (33.8%), while most local residents lived in multi-storey building (31.8%) or a privately owned apartment unit (26.8%). This survey indicates relatively poor living conditions of the temporary urban residents as compared to permanent urban residents.

Table 1 shows the difference in living conditions between the permanent residents in Beijing vis-à-vis the temporary residents, i.e., the migrants. The living conditions of permanent residents are far better as compared to the temporary residents. A large proportion of migrants tend to live in single room dormitory type of dwelling units. Only one in three lives in a house with two or three rooms, whereas only 8 per cent of permanent residents live in one room house. It need to be mentioned that the living conditions of permanent residents in city like Beijing have improved substantially over time. Further, many migrants living in dormitory type of housing did not have a kitchen and bathing facility and toilets were communal. In some instances, the migrants had to pay minimal fees for the communal bathing facility and flush toilets.

There is some housing mobility observed among the migrant workers. Wang (2004) illustrates that they first come as floating population or temporary migrants and live in rental accommodation and can be equated with 'bridge headers' as in Turner's concept. Then, they seek special residency permits, the blue cards that give them some level of formal status in the cities, a move observed in many manufacturing cities/SEZs such as Shenzhen, etc., which brings them in Turner's category of 'consolidators'. The third stage is that of 'status seekers' where they get permanent migrant status that integrates them with the other urban residents. Wang's (2004) study of Shenyang and Chongqing and Liu and Liyang's (1997) of Zhejiangcun of Beijing show that only those who are able to get permanent residency attain the 'status seeker' position and these are mainly those in business. The wage labour, whose incomes are low, are not able to attain permanent status and hence do not move into permanent housing.

Table 1

Beijing: Comparing Living Conditions of Permanent Residents vs Migrants

Indicator	*Permanent residents**	*Migrants***
Average per capita useable area (sq. m.)	19.45	—
Sharing dwelling of 10 sq. m. (%)		10.8
Sharing dwelling of 20 sq. m. (%)		11.8
Sharing dwelling of 34 sq. m. (%)		8.8
Households occupying one room (%)	8.3	68.7
Households occupying two rooms (%)	59.0	16.7
Households occupying three rooms (%)	19.5	14.7
Households occupying four rooms (%)	2.1	—
Households with private tap water access (%)	92.6	—
Households with public tap water for access (%)	7.4	—
Households having bathroom + flush toilet (%)	75.2	—
Households having bathroom and no flush toilet (%)	16.1	—

Source: * Beijing Municipal Bureau of Statistics (2000). ** Chan (2006).

Numerous scholars have also investigated the *hukou* as a decisive factor in housing provision. As temporary residents, migrant workers cannot access the subsidised public housing reserved for permanent urban residents or obtain home mortgages (Wu, 2003). Because they cannot rent affordable housing, they often have no choice but to resort to employer-supplied housing or rental apartments located on the urban fringe. Migrant workers' housing conditions are generally inferior to those of local registered residents with the urban *hukou*. In addition, Huang (2003) conducted fieldwork in five Chinese cities and found that migrant workers face many problems like overcrowding, lack of kitchen and bathroom facilities and structural instability.

Though *hukou* has acted as an institutional barrier for accessing urban housing, recent studies have shown that the migrant workers have used informal channels to bypass *hukou* for social mobility. Such studies have not directly addressed the question of housing provision. But, Zhang, Zhao and Tian (2003) have examined the rise of migrant enclaves (*chengzhongcun*) on the urban fringe of Beijing as example of how migrants have bypassed the institutional barriers to access housing. The migrant enclaves have taken advantage of the institutional limitation, wherein the local governments cannot regulate the land beyond their city boundaries, and hence, the peasants on the urban fringe with rural *hukou* have converted their collectively owned land to finance private housing constructed for renting purposes. These enclaves have survived in spite of the city governments viewing them as 'unregulated housing' fit for cleansing out through various ingenious methods. In particular the migrants from Wenzhou, considered to have smart business acumen, survived the 'cleansing campaigns' of the local government of Beijing (He, 2005).

India

In India, the low-income migrants find place in the slum settlements or they squat on the vacant land on the urban periphery or on the pavements. The migrants who stay back in the cities then begin a gradual process of consolidation in the city through first consolidating their shelter situation and then employment. This is called *incremental housing process,* which is described below.

The migrants when they first come to the city, squat on a public land or stay on rental basis in some existing settlement or stay with a friend/family member paying some rent to them. They move to then purchasing a plot of land in an informal settlement. There is no regular legal document of such purchase. They would erect a temporary roof over temporary walls. And then on, when the money is available, they would carry out incremental improvements: walls constructed of temporary materials are made permanent; temporary roofs are made permanent and so on. The shelter upgrading priorities in low-income settlements are: (i) repairing a leaking roof; (ii) converting mud walls into brick walls with cement mortar; (iii) making tiling floors; (iv) connecting to water supply; (v) building individual toilets; (vi) connecting to electricity supply; (vii) extending the house; and (viii) buying a new house or hut. The benefits of each of these improvements are: (i) a water connection saves time; (ii) roof repairing saves or protects the quality of goods, especially for home-based producers; (iii) electricity facilitates longer working hours, which in turn increases productivity and thus income; (iv) clean drinking water reduces illness and saves expense on healthcare and by that makes income available for other purposes such as education, income-generation, buying durable assets, etc.; (v) tiled floors also improve productivity for home-based workers; (vi) brick walls with cement mortar save recurring expenses of repairing walls after intense rains or flooding; and (viii) house extension is useful for expanding home-based production activities, renting out for earning additional income and keeping the extended family together.

In recent times, migrants come and squat on urban periphery. In the earlier times, they tended to get adjusted in the rental housing in the existing slum and low-income settlements. These getting overcrowded and lands not being available in the central parts of the city, they began occupying lands on the city periphery, largely in the city parts where there are industrial areas (Mahadevia, 2002; Mahadevia and Narayanan, 2008b).

In absence of a pro-active shelter policy for the poor, at least one generation of low-income migrants spent their life in a slum. Our research on slums in Ahmedabad and Surat[25] shows that, in fact, slum dwellers have been living in the same slum for more than 20 years. This is an outcome of lack of land tenure regularisation policy, slum upgradation policy and affordable housing policy. The recent policies, the NUHHP (2007) and RAY (2009), are less likely to address this problem as these are based on the principles of market, which have excluded than included the urban poor. This indicates that not just the recent migrants but even long-term migrants would continue to live in slums.

As per the population census of 2001, 15 per cent or 42.58 million of the total urban population in India live in slums (Office of the Registrar General and Census Commissioner, India, 2005: 21). In the metropolitan cities, this proportion was much higher: at 24.1 per cent accounting to 17.70 million population living in slums (ibid.: 22). In individual cities too, the proportion is much higher: Mumbai, 60 per cent, Ahmedabad 26 per cent, Surat 19 per cent and so on (Mahadevia, 2009).

There are no separate studies to document/analyse living conditions of the migrant workers in urban India. But, there is large number of them documenting life and living of slum dwellers (D'Costa and Das, 2002; Narayanan et al., 2008). We have not presented these here. But, it might be worthwhile describing the conditions of living in slums from the national level survey of housing carried out in 2002. This National Sample Survey (NSS) gives the following description of living conditions in slums in India (National Sample Survey Organisation, 2004):

1. A slum was a compact area with a collection of poorly built tenements, mostly of temporary nature, crowded together usually with inadequate sanitary and drinking water facilities in unhygienic conditions (p. 11).
2. 67 per cent of the dwelling units were permanent in nature and the rest were semi-permanent or temporary structures.
3. Only 20 per cent of dwelling units in a slum had a plinth area of more than 50 square metres.
4. Per capita floor area available in the slums was 4.6 square metres.
5. 66 per cent of the slum dwellers built their own house and could be classified as 'illegal' as far as the urban laws are concerned.
6. 15 per cent dwelling units in urban slums had all the three facilities, viz., drinking water, electricity for lighting and a toilet, and 11 per cent had none of these facilities. For other types of dwelling units, these figures were 63 per cent (for all facilities) and 4 per cent (for no facilities) (p. 47).

7. Only 40 per cent of the slum households had water supply access within their house, whereas this figure for all other households was 74 per cent (p. 51).
8. 32 per cent households in slums did not have access to any toilet facility, and this figure for all other households was 16 per cent (p. 51).

There are also micro studies of living and working conditions of the recent or temporary migrants. A study of the migrants in the destination area indicates that the migrants work long hours and often live in accommodation provided by the employer. But, because of the same reason, it is difficult to contact the migrant workers in their destination area for organising them for anything. In a sense, these workers are completely disenfranchised.[26] A DISHA (2002: 45) study also states the same:

> By whatever route they get there, at work sites migrants experience long hours, hard work, harsh conditions, injuries (with inadequate medical help or compensation), and social isolation and humiliation. Water is scarce at work places and encampments and migrants have to negotiate access to it from construction sites or private houses rather than the municipality. ... Security is another major problem. Most *adivasi* (tribal[27]) migrants sleep in the open or bivouac under makeshift structures.' This study describes the living conditions of tribal migrants in the cities of Gujarat state. Mosse, Gupta and Shah (2005: 3027) write: 'Staying in urban spaces, migrants face harassment, abuse, theft, forcible eviction by the police, or the demolition of their dwellings by urban authorities. The abuse of *adivasi* migrants is closely related to their lack of identity or dwellings in urban places. Here they stand out as marginal, transitional people. They are subject to prejudice, stigmatised and criminalised, falsely accused of theft or looting, and detained and beaten by police. ... Migrant women describe fear at night and fitful sleep in exposed places.

For the tribal migrants shelter is a priority (Mosse, Gupta and Shah, 2005). If the workers are organised or have any institutional support, then they get access to shelter. One such group, studied by these authors, was organised by the *Bandhkam Mazdoor Sangathan* (BMS) (Construction Workers Association), and the latter got them access to municipal land under a flyover for the construction of night shelter. The tribal migrants generally get work in the construction sector, in which, as per Mosse, Gupta and Shah the work availability was intermittent and the workers remained underemployed. But, going back to the villages not being a desired option by them, they tend to live in the most miserable conditions and are exposed to harassment in the city. They also show that the worksites of the tribal migrants are dispersed over the city and have no basic services. Their children cannot go to school, and many of them do come with their families. They do not have access to health centres. The biggest problem these migrants face is harassment, from the local anti-social elements as well as municipal authorities. Sometimes, the municipal authorities may get involved to set up a 'permanent' shelter for the migrants to control and regulate these moving populations so that they do not litter the pavements, create other troubles, do not throng the railway station and so on. But, there is equally or more strong resistance to giving them any temporary shelter with the fear that such shelter clusters could become permanent settlements in the city.

DISHA's study in Ahmedabad found that 54 per cent of the migrants slept in the open and 41 per cent in huts built from tarpaulins or jute bags. Factors influencing the choice of dwelling place included availability of open ground free from harassment, water and fuel availability and remaining with members from the same village in order to share news, and send remittances (DISHA, 2002: 6 in Mosse, Gupta and Shah, 2005). Most other studies (Gramin Vikas Trust, 2002; Rani and Shylendra, 2001; Srivastava and Sasikumar, 2003) also have similar observation of the deplorable living conditions of the migrant labour in the cities: many living on the footpaths and city parks, without provision of safe drinking water, without basic services, exposed to vagaries of nature, subject to all types of harassment and women in particular subjected to lack of privacy and sexual harassment.

In general, housing conditions of the migrants in India are closely related to the type of migrants. The long-term migrants prefer to follow the path of incremental housing, as described above. But, some of them employed in manufacturing may also get employee housing. Employee housing in the manufacturing depends on whether the industry is in the organised or unorganised sector. Organised sector manufacturing is generally large-scale manufacturing and employee housing here could vary between semi-permanent to permanent type with adequate basic facilities. But, employee housing in unorganised manufacturing sector is like a slum devoid of adequate basic facilities. The disadvantage of employee housing in the unorganised sector is that the workers may be under the control of the employers and they may lose bargaining power given that they have no choice but to live on the premises of the employers. This situation is similar to what could be found in China in some instances. The latter type of employee housing also found in the construction sector. But, given the nature of construction sector, this is not permanent arrangement. There are also construction workers who are permanently living in the cities and they tend to live in incremental housing. In fact, the construction workers put in their sweat equity in their housing. Lastly, some regions of India send only male migrants to the cities to work and they tend to live in shared rental room for long years. They do not invest in housing in urban areas and all the savings are remitted back to the rural areas for consumption in rural areas as well improvement in housing conditions in the rural areas.

The short-term migrants choose options depending on the type of their employment. These are:

(i) On-site housing in temporary shelter, made of brick walls and corrugated tin sheet roof or even made of corrugated tin sheet walls and roofs, mainly found on large construction sites. Typically, there are no sanitation facilities and there is open defecation, and water supply for construction purposes is used by the workers living on the site for drinking, bathing and other domestic purposes. There is no electricity in the dwelling units but there is electricity connection on the construction site for the work. The migrant workers living on the site however do not benefit from this electricity connection.

(ii) Off-site housing in existing slums, however, shared by more than one worker or workers' families. In such a case the contractor transports the workers to and from the construction site every day. The migrants then may or may not have access to basic services depending on the slum they live in.

(iii) On the pavement, along the roads and on open plots (wherever the open lands are available), temporary shelters constructed of bamboo poles and plastic sheet. Two bamboo poles are erected and a plastic sheet is tied to it in tent-like structure and the single migrant or migrant with family crouch inside it in hot sun and rains; otherwise sleeping in open in the night. There is no water and no sanitation and the occupants get free water from any nearby public tap or private tap if the owner of the latter allows. In some instances, the owner of a private tap may charge them for water. There is no electricity and no protection against anything.

(iv) Single male migrants share a room in the existing slum settlements. There is a rotation of occupants of the unit.

(v) There are seasonal migrants to the city who come for some specific jobs in specific seasons and tend to stay on the work site in temporary shelter units provided by the employers or erected by them in case the employer does not provide.

(vi) Very short-term migrants also live on footpaths in the business areas of the cities, which are near the railway station. Some cities have arrangement of night shelters but these are either in short supply or non-livable on account of crime infestation in these shelters. If night shelters are not available or the migrants chose not to use them, they live on footpath in open for months together, even in winter months when they take on rent quilts to protect against winter chill. Many of them are employed in para-transport sector or in retail trade, working in small shops or themselves are street vendors.

Conclusions

Low-income migrants are the most vulnerable and discriminated against population in both the countries although the national economic growth is very much impingent on the contribution of the migrants. None of them have any strong policy for facilitating or ensuring decent housing conditions for the migrant workers. While *hukou* determines the fate of migrants in China's urban areas, availability of affordable housing, employment and income, restrictive state level policies on defining urban citizenship determine the fate of migrants in India's urban areas. In both countries, housing for the migrants has been tagged on to the overall urban housing policy and there are institutional barriers in migrants' access to subsidised public housing. If migrants can afford to buy, they can procure a house from the private housing market in both the countries.

Globalisation thrusts upon the large cities; in other words, in quest to make 'world class cities', both countries have begun rapid transformation of their cities. In China, the pace of urban transformation is much faster than India. In fact, there is no comparison between the urban transformation processes of two countries. But, in both the countries, this has resulted in massive demolitions: in India of the slums and squatter settlements and in China of the migrant enclaves. In India, the recent migrants, without residency proof, lose out and do not get any alternative accommodation. It seems that even in China the migrants lose out, even though there is now some compensation mechanisms put in place through the pressure of the migrant communities themselves and academics and activists in the cities.

The similarities between the two countries end here. Rural migrants in urban areas of China are among the poorest of the rural residents. In India, economically better-off rural population migrate to the cities. Hence, the low-income rural migrants start from very different positions in the urban settings. The reforms with regard to migrants in China in the recent years have helped these migrants accessing relatively better housing than before. In India, no such reforms have been witnessed and the urban areas in general and metropolitan cities in particular remain overwhelmingly hostile to the low-income migrants. In fact, this hostility, manifesting in numerous ways such as elitist land policy, complex and bureaucratised citizenship criteria and chauvinist political environment, has reduced rural-urban migration since 1990s. The recent housing policies in India, ironically based on market paradigm, are being offered to the migrants who have been failed by both the state and the market! The low-income migrants continue to live in Indian cities through subversions of existing legislation, seeking support from caste and religious political affiliations (clientalism) and if none else then protests and resistance movements. Migrants in Chinese cities also circumvent the regulatory mechanisms to survive but do not subvert them.

India is a capitalist economy, following the neo-liberal development route, in spite of the current policy rhetoric of 'inclusive growth'. This rhetoric puts growth, rather than equitable growth, at the centre of the development processes and hence we observe very perverse outcomes of a growth process followed at any cost. Thus, we do not find any human-centred housing policy, which would include the concerns of the low-income migrants. Indian state is called 'instrumental' and has displayed very weak ability in welfare distribution in favour of the vulnerable sections, including the urban poor (Nolan, 2004). In contrast, the 'socialist market economy' of China has displayed higher order of equity transfers as compared to India (ibid.). Hence, we do observe a better policy environment as well as better implementation practices of the policies for the low-income migrants in China as compared to India.

India can learn from China with regard to employer housing for certain segments of urban labour force. China can learn from India with regard to policies for incremental housing. But, both the countries have to go a long way with regard to ensuring a decent housing to the low-income migrant population in their cities, given that both would continue to urbanise rapidly in the coming decades.

Notes

Part of the paper has appeared in Mahadevia, Liu and Yuan (2012).

1. Socialist term gets added to the Indian Constitution in 1975.
2. (http://www.chinadaily.com.cn/bizchina/200908/27/content_8622023.htm), accessed on 12 October 2009.
3. See article by Wuzhou Li, *China Today* (http://www.chinatoday.com.cn/English/e2004/e200404/p26.htm), accessed on 16 October 2009.
4. (http://www.imfmetal.org/files/08102914241866/Migrant_workers_in_India.pdf), accessed on 18 October 2009.
5. See article by Wuzhou Li, op. cit.
6. Ibid.
7. Dated 4 March 2008 (http://english.peopledaily.com.cn/90001/90776/90882/6365964.html), accessed on 16 October 2009.
8. See article by Wuzhou Li, op. cit.
9. This card entitles a household to food entitlements at subsidized rates in case of a household holding a Below Poverty Line (BPL) Card.
10. A cut-off date is declared in each city to give citizenship right to a slum household. Each city has a different cut-off date.
11. A state in India is equivalent to a province in China.

12. For details of the demolitions and resistance by the slum dwellers, see Mahadevia and Narayanan (2008a) and Bhide (2008).
13. (http://www.chinadaily.com.cn/bizchina/200907/09/content_8402814.htm), accessed on 18 October 2009.
14. Ibid.
15. (http://www.chinacsr.com/2006/06/28/572–henan-province-issues-preferential-housing-policies-for-migrant-workers), accessed on 13 June 2008.
16. The discussions with researchers at Tsinghua University, in May 2008, suggested that the migrants were under the control of the employers when they lived in dormitory housing, much in the same way that Friedrich Engels had argued way back in 1872 in *The Housing Question*.
17. (http://www.china.org.cn/china/local/2008–04/14/content_14949824.htm), accessed on 13 June 2008.
18. (http://english.gov.cn/2008–03/05/content_909973.htm), accessed on 13 June 2008.
19. Feng Jianhua (2008). 'Rural Roots, City Shoots', *Beijing Review*, April 3 (http://www.bjreview.com.cn/quotes/txt/2008–04/01/content_108292.htm), accessed on 13 June 2008.
20. States in India are organised on the basis of a particular language and there is often political mobilisation around regional language. Thus, it is easy to identify migrants by their language and then whether they are long-term residents or not is not seen closely.
21. (http://www.udd.gujarat.gov.in/udd/smPolicy.pdf), accessed on 22 June 2010.
22. The author of this paper has visited this site.
23. (http://www.chinatoday.com.cn/English/e2008/e200805/p17.htm), accessed on 18 October 2009.
24. Ibid.
25. Two cities in the western Indian state of Gujarat.
26. This is from an unpublished report of lessons of nearly two years of work carried out in an action research project by Prayas under the aegis of Dakshini Rajasthan Majdoor Union and Gujarat Ginning and Mill Majdoor Union. The project has been supported by Aga Khan Foundation and Action Aid India.
27. Term used for indigenous people, and are called Scheduled Tribes as they have special status in the Indian Constitution.

References

ADB (2001). *Poverty in People's Republic of China*, Manila.

Beijing Municipal Bureau of Statistics (2000). *Beijing Statistical Yearbook 2000*, Beijing: China Statistics Press.

Bhide, A. (2008). 'Dynamics and Contours of Resisting Displacement in Mumbai', in Darshini Mahadevia (ed.), *Inside the Transforming Urban Asia: Processes, Policies and Public Actions*, New Delhi: Concept Publishers, pp. 590–600.

Chan, D. (2006). 'How Migrant Workers Find Housing in Beijing: The Role of Individual Agency in Differential Housing Access and Outcomes', Unpublished Master's Thesis, Programme in Urban Studies, Stanford University (http://urbanstudies.stanford.edu/programs/documents/ChanThesis.pdf), accessed on 21 October 2009.

China National Bureau of Statistics (2006). *China Statistical Yearbook 2006*, Beijing: China Statistics Press.

D'Costa, W. and B. Das (2002). 'Life and Living of the Vulnerable in Ahmedabad City', in Amitabh Kundu and Darshini Mahadevia (eds), *Poverty and Vulnerability in a Globalising Metropolis: Ahmedabad*, Delhi: Manak Publishers, pp. 179–206.

DISHA (2002). *The Migrant Tribal Construction Labourers in Ahmedabad: A Study* (originally in Gujarati, 1994, translated 2002), Himmatnagar: DISHA.

Gramin Vikas Trust (2002). *Migration: An Essential Component of Rural Livelihoods*, Ratlam: Gramin Vikas Trust.

He, X. (2005). 'Why Do They Not Comply with the Law: Illegality and Semi-Legality among Rural-Urban, Migrant Entrepreneurs in Beijing', *Law and Society Review*, 39: 527–62.

Huang, Y. (2003). 'Renters' Housing Behaviour in Transitional Urban China', *Housing Studies*, 18: 103–26.

Kundu, Amitabh and N. Sarangi (2007). 'Migration, Employment Status and Poverty: An Analysis across Urban Centres', *Economic and Political Weekly*, January 27: 299–306.

Liu, X. and W. Liang (1997). 'Zhejiangcun: Social and Spatial Implications of Informal Urbanization on the Periphery of Beijing', *Cities*, 14 (20): 95–108.

Mahadevia, Darshini (1998). 'State Supported Segmentation of Mumbai: Policy Options in the Global Economy', *Review of Development and Change*, 3 (1): 12–41.

—— (2002). 'Interventions in Development: A Shift towards a Model of Exclusion', in Amitabh Kundu and Darshini Mahadevia (eds), *Poverty and Vulnerability in a Globalising Metropolis: Ahmedabad*, Delhi: Manak Publishers, pp. 80–132.

—— (2009). 'Urban Land Market and Access of the Poor' in India, Ministry of Housing and Urban Poverty Alleviation (ed.), *India: Urban Poverty Report 2009*, New Delhi: Oxford University Press, pp. 199–221.

Mahadevia, Darshini and H. Narayanan (2008a). 'Shanghaing Mumbai: Politics of Evictions and Resistance in Slum Settlements', in Darshini Mahadevia (ed.), *Inside the Transforming Urban Asia: Processes, Policies and Public Actions*, New Delhi: Concept Publishers, pp. 549–89.

—— (2008b). 'Slumbay to Shanghai: Envisioning Renewal or Take Over?', in Darshini Mahadevia (ed.), *Inside the Transforming Urban Asia: Processes, Policies and Public Actions*, New Delhi: Concept Publishers, pp. 94–131.

Mahadevia, Darshini, Zhiyan Liu and Xiuming Yuan (2012). 'Housing of Urban Migrants in India and China', *Environment and Urbanization ASIA*, 3(1): 143–163.

Mosse, D., S. Gupta and V. Shah (2005). 'On the Margins in the City: Adivasi Seasonal Labour Migration in Western India', *Economic and Political Weekly*, 40 (28): 3025–38.

Narayanan, H., Darshini Mahadevia and R. Mathews (2008). 'Demolition of Lives and Livelihoods: Mumbai', in Darshini Mahadevia (ed.), *Inside the Transforming Urban Asia: Processes, Policies and Public Actions*, New Delhi: Concept Publishers, pp. 415–50.

National Sample Survey Organization (NSSO) (2004). *Housing Condition in India: Housing Stock and Constructions* (NSS 558th Round, July–December 2002), Report No. 488 (58/1.2/1), Ministry of Statistics and Programme Implementation, New Delhi: Government of India.

Nolan, Peter (2004). *Transforming China: Globalization, Transition and Development*, London: Anthem Press.

Oberlander, P. (1985). *Land: The Central Human Settlement Issue*, Vancouver: University of British Columbia Press.

Office of the Registrar General and Census Commissioner, India (2005). *Slum Population, Series-1, Census of India, 2001*, New Delhi, India: Office of the Registrar General and Census Commissioner.

Rani, U. and H.S. Shylendra (2001). 'Seasonal Migration and Rural-Urban Interface in Semi-Arid Tropics of Gujarat: Study of a Tribal Village', *Journal of Rural Development*, 20: 187–217.

Sivaramakrishnan, K.C., Amitabh Kundu and B.N. Singh (2005). *Handbook of Urbanization in India: An Analysis of Trends and Processes*, New Delhi and New York: Oxford University Press.

Srivastava, Ravi and S.K. Sasikumar (2003). 'An Overview of Migration in India: Its Impacts and Key Issues', paper presented at the Regional Conference on Migration, Development and Pro-Poor Policy Choices in Asia jointly organised by the Refugee and Migratory Movements Research Unit, Bangladesh, and the Department for International Development, UK, 22–24 June, Dhaka (http://www.eldis.org/vfile/upload/1/document/0903/Dhaka_CP_2.pdf), accessed on 20 October 2009.

United Nations Population Fund (2007). *State of World Population, 2007: Unleashing the Potential of Urban Growth*, New York: UNFPA (from the website).

Wang, Y.P. (2004). *Urban Poverty, Housing and Social Change in China*, Abingdon: Routledge.

Wu, W. (2003). 'Sources of Migrant Housing Disadvantage in Urban China', *Environment and Planning*, 36: 1285–304.

Zax, J. (1997). 'Latent Demand for Urban Housing in the People's Republic of China', *Journal of Urban Economics*, 42: 377–401.

Zhang, L., S. Zhao and J. Tian (2003). 'Self-Help in Housing and Chengzhongcun in China's Urbanization', *International Journal of Urban and Regional Research*, 27: 912–37.

Zhang, Li (2001). *Strangers in the City: Reconfigurations of Space, Power, and Social Networks within China's Floating Population*, Palo Alto, CA: Stanford University Press.

Zhu, Yu (2007). 'China's Floating Population and Their Settlement Intention in the Cities: Beyond the Hukou Reform', *Habitat International*, 31: 65–76.

Part II

Changing Culture and Society

6

Towards Understanding the Nature of Indian State and the Role of Middle Class

ASEEM PRAKASH

While studying the state, Philip Abrams suggests that states can be studied analytically by dividing them into the state system and the state idea. The former refers to a 'palpable nexus of practice and institutional structure centred in government' and the latter explains the idea about the state, projected, purveyed and variously believed in different societies and different time' (Abrams, 1988: 82). The latter can be understood as the ideological grounding of the state giving legitimacy to the practice of state power (state system). In other words, the functional institutions of the state governing everyday practice cannot be divorced from its ideological structure. The latter not only gives birth to the former, but both of them continuously shape each other. Together they shape and define the character of the state.

It is in this context that it is enormously challenging as well as exciting to unravel the character of the Indian state. It is an enormous challenge because the Indian polity is home to a multitude of socio-economic and political patterns, which disallow easy generalisation. It is also exciting because of the inherent dynamism in the polity, which quickly unsettles known socio-economic and political patterns and leaves behind a feeling that the existing understanding about the state may be lacking. But why do we study the nature or character of the state? An understanding of the character of the state on the part of the students studying it enables them to comment on its vision, institutions and processes (as reflected in the laws, policies, and programmes and other executive actions). More importantly, it allows them to understand how they are shaped and affected by the existing socio-economic and political formations.

A Synoptic View of the Indian State

The coming of independence also saw the foundation of the modern Indian state based on secular principles and a written constitution, having a discernable socio-economic and political programme for the country and its citizens. The state as an institution was seen as both state system and state idea – in the context referred to earlier. Ashis Nandy argues that it was expected that the state would usher in the ideology of modernisation that would become the basis of a more coherent form of Indianness, overriding the enormous diversity. Secondly, it was also expected that over a period of time, 'state would give way to its working conditions to the universal principles of statecraft and able to persuade, mobilise or coerce the society to adjust to the state's ideology' (Nandy, 2000: 67). The ideology of the new nation-state was formally enshrined in the Constitution of India promising to its citizens a sovereign, democratic, secular and socialist republic. The various aspects of the state idea were delineated in the bulky Constitution, which in turn mandated an array of administrative, political and legal institutions, including specialised institutions of coercion to implement this vision in practice. The Constitution reflected the state idea but it was further and more eloquently articulated in the Directive Principles of State Policy.

It is in this context that the state as an institution was also seen as a source of remedies for all problems. In Khilnani's words, the state 'etched itself into the imagination of India in a way that no previous political agency had ever done' (Khilnani, 1998: 41). However, the 65-year journey of the Indian state can be seen as a story of failures, marginal successes as well as a source of tremendous hope.

Various scholars have interpreted this story differently. The foremost among them are the scholars who emphasise the state system rather than the state idea. There are three sets of scholars who understand the character of the state through the study of state systems. The first group can be broadly clubbed as the scholars who took a state-centric view. Kohli, Bardhan, Rudolphs and Vanaik all see the state as having a sort of autonomous existence, albeit also constrained by dominant interests of various types. Kohli (1987) makes a distinction between the state and political regimes and shows the possibility of a political regime having an ideology that is left-of-centre remaining substantially autonomous from vested interests while executing pro-poor policies. Bardhan's eloquent thesis points to the possibility of the state 'neither acting at behest nor on the behalf of the proprietary classes' (1987: 38). This unique condition is achieved because the three dominant proprietary classes – rich farmers, industrial capitalists and professionals (both civil and military including white-collared workers) – are not able to command hegemony over each other, thereby allowing the state to acquire a certain kind of autonomy. However, this autonomy is reflected in a regulatory role (and hence patronage-dispensing role) rather than a developmental role. Vanaik (1990) also broadly endorsed the thesis. However, Vanaik also stressed the relative political strength of the agrarian bourgeoisie in the dominant coalition – a thesis also supported by Rudolphs (1987) and Varshney (1995). Rudolphs' story of the career of the state is also stated in terms of conflicts between demand polity (when societal demands expressed as electoral pressures dominate over the state) and command polity (when state hegemony dominates over society). In the course of the conflict, the state is seen as a 'self-determining third actor' and by far the most powerful organisational entity, when seen in relation with organised capital and organised labour.

The second set of scholars study the state system from the society-centric perspective. The society-centric perspective seeks to analyse and reflect on the crises in the Indian state. Rajni Kothari, a renowned political scientist, sees the crisis in the centralisation and monopolisation of political parties and state institutions by political elite thereby undermining essential features of liberal democracy. He further argues that the role of political parties to channelise the demands of the people in the political system has degraded to the extent that democracy as a system is neither functional nor procedural. The state increasingly does not curb violence of the powerful against the weak. Moreover, the state itself resorts to illegitimate violence against the people. In Kothari's view, state itself has turned against democracy. Kohli (1990) argues that the failure of the state to live up to its declared agenda is attributed to the logic of democracy. Kohli's view the deepening of democracy has led to enhanced political participation, which in turn has multiplied demands on the state that the latter is not able to meet. Saberwal (1996) argues that the crisis of the Indian state stems from the chasm between formal institutions of modernity based on the rational principle of impersonality and the logic of the traditional order, which upholds segmentation along the social identity. The logic of segmentation, in his view, frustrates the modernist aspirations of impersonality required for the functioning of a modern secular state. Roy (2006) through the story of the Narmada dam explains that the development initiatives favouring the rich and entrenched groups are invariably identified as national development. Any opposition to it is seen as anti-national. The brunt of national development (read elite-centric development) is borne by the poor, especially those who belong to the historically deprived social groups.

The third set of scholars study the state system anthropologically. The anthropological approach has meant that they painstakingly document the interaction of the local level state with the mass of citizenry for whom the (non)-actions of the state matter the most. The very characteristic of the local state also implies that they do not study the character of the state through the nature of its policies, but how they are implemented or not implemented and often changed beyond recognition during execution. In these writings, the character of the state is understood through the proxy analysis of political mobilisation, corruption affecting citizens, especially the poor, and role of social identity affecting the outcome of state policies.

Gupta (1995) analyses corruption and the local state ethnographically and argues that corruption 'draws attention to powerful cultural practices by which the state is symbolically represented to its employees and to the citizens' (p. 385). He further explains: 'The discourse of corruption is central to our understanding of the relationship between the state and social groups precisely because it plays this dual role of enabling the people to construct the state symbolically and to define themselves as citizens. For it is through such representation, and through the public practices of various government agencies, that the state comes to be marked and delineated from other organisations and institutions in social life' (p. 389). Thus, corruption appears to be the central idiom through which the citizens' relationship with the state is structured.

Often, but not always, the (non)-action of the state and how it is executed vis-à-vis the poor is explained from the lens of caste, religion, ethnicity and other social identity. Bailey's (1963) important contribution in the early 1960s told us about the role of factional leaders (often inspired by social identity) as brokers between local and state levels. In effect, Bailey indicated how faction leaders, often identified through particular social groups, seek and get favours through the patronage-dispensing machinery of the state, in return for their political support to the political regime. For Harriss-White (2003), the present gradual withdrawal of the state does not alter the character of the state for the poor. In her account, the state was never present for the poor since it was always captured by the elites in their vested interests. She further argues that the outcomes in the economy are shaped at the intersection of caste, gender, religion and ethnicity. She terms this the social structure of accumulation. Violence against the lower castes and class is an integral part of the social structure of accumulation regime. That the decline of traditional authority is questionable is also shown by Lerche's (1995) work on western Uttar Pradesh. He convincingly shows the capture of the state system by the *jat* landowners to their advantage.

There are other influential accounts, which discuss the character of the state from the vantage point of state idea. Chatterjee (1993), for example, put forth a thesis that Indian nationalism created a division between the spiritual and material domains. The spiritual domain was believed and upheld as autonomous, one, which cannot be affected by any foreign thought. The nation considered itself culturally superior to the colonizers. However, the West was taken as superior in the material domain (the domain of economy and of the state craft, of science and technology) and hence the experience of the western nations was to be replicated. The Constitution of India itself provides the best example of the acceptance of the western thought and practice (enlightened thought), which is most eloquently articulated in it. The key institutions of modern state – liberal democracy, universal adult franchise, an independent judiciary, citizenship, secularism, institutions of governance – were all put in place in the formative year (Austin, 2000). Given the framework for the new republic, the institution of planning was expected to carve out a modern nation-state. In other words, the all-powerful, all-knowing state, taking the help of a body of experts, was to set the development agenda and its governance arm was to execute the agenda (Chatterjee, 2000). In its operational form, the character of the state was interpreted as one which is ushering in a passive revolution in the Gramscian sense of the term, that is, 'where an emergent bourgeoisie lacks the social conditions for establishing the complete hegemony over the new nations, it resorts to a "passive revolution", by attempting a molecular transformation of the old dominant classes into partners in a new historical block and only a partial appropriation of the popular masses' (Chatterjee, 1986: 30). Kaviraj (1989) also substantiates this thesis of the passive revolution of capital through provision of an overview of the political history of independent India. He shows how power has to be shared between various dominant classes because no one class had the ability to exercise hegemony on its own. His political history elaborates on the dominance and decline of the industrial capitalists, the rural elites and the bureaucratic managerial elite in various phases of political history. The ascendance of one class was always at the expense of other. Chatterjee (2008) argues that the present phase of passive revolution has substantially altered. He argues that there is a clear-cut ascendance of corporate capital in the present market-friendly India. Corporate capital still acquires surplus through primitive accumulation (disassociation of labour from the means labour). However, the passive revolution of capital, under the conditions of a vibrant electoral democracy, makes it 'unacceptable and illegitimate for the government to leave these marginalised populations without the means of labour to simply fend (for) themselves' (p. 62). Hence, the state launches a battery of development schemes perceived to be pro-poor to reverse the effect of primitive accumulation, albeit their ability to absorb the peasant society in the corporate economy is minimal.

Other authors introduce a critique of the 'original' state idea. For example, Madan (1997) and Nandy (1997) see the roots of crisis in the state due to alien western institutions imposed by the westernised elite on the ordinary masses. Western democracy for the masses was alien and religion was 'the' principle for governing the social conduct. The people are not ready to accept that beliefs cherished by them hold no or minimal value in the public domain. According to them, this is the source of crisis in the Indian state often reflected on the question of secularism.

These informed debates about the character of the Indian state help us build on these insights for a possibly new thinking on the state. In all these accounts of the character of the state, the argument, which comes out quite forcefully, suggests that the boundaries between state and civil society are quite porous. These more often than not act detrimental to the interest of the poor. What makes the boundaries of the state porous? Is it only the corporate interest or rent-seeking endeavours of the state? How do we relate the macro interpretation of the character of the state with micro (anthropological literature on state) socio-political patterns? The influential writings of Chatterjee (2004; 2008) try and answer this puzzle by invoking the concept of political society. Political society is the realm where strategic negotiations of the marginalised communities take place with the state and help in reversing the adverse effect of primitive accumulation by corporate capital. This begs other questions: Is political society homogenous? Is the relationship of all social groups in the realm of political society on equal terms with the state? Is there no domination and subordination within the realm of political society? If there is, how is it affected? How is the relationship of the macro-level state carved out with the micro-level political society? How does the relationship acquire apparent stability?

These are the few questions we will explore in our attempt to understand the nature of Indian state. While doing so, we also try to understand the ascendance of the middle class and their relationship with their caste identity.

Nature of Indian State: Role of Middle Class and Upper Caste

The Indian state, as ever, is still a bundle of contradictions. Some important contradictions present in the Indian state are discussed below:

Contradiction of the Economics of Markets and the Politics of Democracy

The contradictory movements of markets and democracy shape the present Indian state. The contradiction emanates from an ideological commitment to market-led development, which has failed to include the asset-less and capability-less while the institutions of democracy promise equitable inclusion. In other words, the contradiction in the Indian state is between the economics of markets and the politics of democracy. The former indicates economic policies directed towards a market-friendly regime. The economics of markets is supported by the hitherto national bourgeoisie in alliance with international capital and also finds empowering support and encouragement from the neo-liberal mandarins and urban-based middle and upper middle classes. Politics of democracy is represented by the electoral compulsions of the political parties to be perceived as working for the large mass of the impoverished citizenry. Economics of markets excludes people lacking in assets and capabilities, while political formations try to include them through the politics of democracy. The politics of democracy is no longer limited to the perception of political empowerment but its very nature requires concrete policy demands for inclusion in the economic process (the latest avtar being MGNREGA). The general election of 2009 and the past few state level elections are testimony to this fact. One of the crucial reasons for the political regimes successfully negotiating the anti-incumbency factor was due to fact that they were seen as pro-poor. The election results in fact were the reinforcement of the trajectory of the Indian state to weld itself more strongly in the new liberal regime presided over by the international capital. The institutions, which support these contradictory trends, are shown in Tables 1–4 and Appendix 1.

Nature of Contradictory Institutions

The institutions formed to regulate the market are believed to be efficient.

- The recommendations of these institutions are mostly accepted.
- Perhaps it can be said that institutions do not shape the policy idea but pre-conceived ideas give birth to the market regulating and promoting institutions.
- A broad consensus already exists among the political elites over the policy ideas, and the institutions are constituted to put them in practice.
- This broad consensus allows a convergence of efforts between all concerned government departments.

On the other hand, the institutions supported by the political democracy are mostly conceived because of the constant pressure from below:

(i) Many of the institutions demanded from below invariably go against the interests of the markets.

(ii) There is neither a similar ideological commitment (as seen for institutions governing the markets) nor a political will to translate the work of these institutions (created by the demand of political democracy) into policy outcomes.

(iii) The fact is best reflected in recent years in the toned down version of the unorganised sector bill and the limping implementation of MGNREGA. On the other hand, one can marvel at the ease with which the Jawaharlal Nehru Urban Renewable Mission (JNURM), special economic zones (SEZs) and public-private partnership, which have already acquired the necessary political will and are giving excellent results from the standpoint of their given political mandate.

These institutions governing the markets reflect the priority of merely 9–15 per cent of the Indian population. In this sense, the dominant coalition of Bardhan (2003) has been substantially reworked. The coalition comprises of industrial capitalists (in partnership with foreign capital), agro-mercantile capitalists (owning large farms in countryside but also having economic stakes in the nearby urban areas), and politico-administrative elite having a firm faith in the trajectory of market-based development and the burgeoning middle class benefiting from the new-found purchasing power to enjoy the 'modern' market-based consumerism. The middle class in the present context can be described as a powerful social group, not necessarily located in big metros, and who have acquired the legitimacy to speak on behalf of the society.

The second contradiction is between the dominant capitalist class at the national level and the similar dominant class at the state level. The nature of economic growth is perhaps contingent on the convergence of priorities between the national and state level dominant social groups. The more the convergence, the better is the possibility of states reflecting the national priorities. The more the divergence, the more different the trajectories would be in pursuit of economic growth. This is best reflected in the unevenness of the reforms between national and state levels as well as between states; the official explanation given for this failure being the incapacity to conceive policy measures to open up markets and failure to provide adequate infrastructure. This is not a plausible reason because this logic has been given for almost two decades. It is more likely that there was no political will to open up. There seem to be several reasons for this:

(a) The first reason can be located in the recent history. The regions, which were able to throw up stronger sub-national capitalists based on regional identity, took the lead in developing industry-based economies (Tamil Nadu, Maharashtra, Gujarat, Karnataka, Andhra Pradesh, etc.). These regions were early to integrate themselves in the national economic reforms. Other regions, which have the political presence of dominant agriculture landlords, never wanted to be open up their economy (Uttar Pradesh, Madhya Pradesh, Rajasthan etc.).

(b) At many times, the interests of the national capitalists do not coincide with the dominant/entrenched regional/state capitalists. Hence, any market-oriented reforms are not easily possible. For instance, market reforms in the leather goods industry and mining sector were substantially delayed in several states for this reason. On the other hand, despite the serious and intense protests by the local poor affected by the projects, the mining sector reforms in Orissa (having substantial stake of state level capitalists) were never rolled back.[1]

(c) The dominance at the state level is again through a coalition of regional agro/industrial capitalists (regulating their interests and influencing the state apparatus through a combination of caste, religion, region and language), politico-social elites and the middle class (which also includes substantial rural-based middle class). A combination of social identities (religion, caste, ethnicity, etc.) is used to regulate the economy and shape up accumulation.

The third contradiction is at the local level where the fruits of democratic struggle and market expansion are captured by the entrenched/dominant caste/class/religion. This results in a variety of conflicts. The dominant social groups capture most of the government programmes. Dominant caste groups, local bureaucracy/politicians and the muscle power of the politicians and dominant groups constitute the local dominant coalition at the local groups. The accumulation at the local level is shaped by state pilferage and caste domination where all or most of the dominant groups are the stakeholders.

Outcomes of Contradictions

There has been a proactive measure taken by the state to open up the economy to private capital, both national and international, through 'efficient' governance. This has resulted in exceptionally high and sustained economic growth. But it has also resulted in extreme social inequality. The manifestation of the extreme social inequality can be captured through the following facts:

- The growth, as a result of the integration with the globalisation, has bypassed the majority of Indian population. About 77 per cent of the population continue to live below less than $2 per day (the internationally accepted poverty line) of daily per capita consumption expenditure. In terms of total population, the poor and vulnerable were 836 million out of a total population of 1,090 million in 2004–05, compared to 732 million out of 894 million in 1993–94. If we disaggregate this data in terms of social groups, 87 per cent of scheduled castes (SCs)/scheduled tribes (STs) survive with earnings below $2 per day, nearly 85 per cent of Muslims also earn around or below $2 (Sengupta et al., 2009).
- The middle and high income groups, which have been disproportionately benefited by growth, constitute nearly 24 per cent of the population. Out of this, middle income groups that earn around $4 per day constitute 19.3 per cent. The high income group with an

income bracket of $10.2 or more is comprised of merely 4 per cent of the population (ibid.).

- The high-middle and high income groups are mostly concentrated in upper caste Hindus. There is a thin layer among the minorities, Dalits and Adivasis (see Appendix 2).

It is this fraction of population, ranging anything between 8–15 per cent (taking the average), which constitutes the middle class in India. This is the socio-economic group that has acquired the legitimacy to speak on behalf of the society and is the most ardent supporters of globalisation (neo-liberal policies). This group is not only economically prosperous but also commands social dominance in the society. A high proportion of the members of this group are upper caste Hindus.

Thus, the main question which arises is what gives the Indian state an apparent stability in face of such massive social inequality? We explore this question through the help of three interrelated explorations. The first comment is made on the nature of party system, followed by two case studies.

Nature of Party System

The Indian party system has moved from a one party-dominant system to a competitive multiparty system – with existence of two parties at the state level, the diversity of which gives the appearance of a multiparty system at the national level (Yadav, 1996). At the present juncture, this theorisation only empowers us to know about the existence of several political parties. In other words, the emergence of various political parties was expected to represent the agenda of the social groups, which were the original cause of their electoral empowerment. The presence of numerous political parties was also to reflect the existing social cleavage in the society. But, the political plurality (increase in number of political parties) has not necessarily translated into social plurality. In fact, the political and socio-economic agenda of all political parties have almost converged, except some token articulation of the core issues affecting their core constituency, as revealed by an analysis of the manifestos of all major national and regional parties. Moreover, in practice, the dominant left parties have also failed to exhibit a different vision for the economic development of the country. The apparent stability is in fact also (among other factors) a manifestation of the lack of genuine articulation of pro-poor voices in the political system.

Social Collectives, Political Mobilisation and the Local State

This section explores the emergence and role of select civil, social and religious collectives in political mobilisation, i.e., ethno-religious groups, caste collectives, religious social orders and petty business and trade associations, the surfacing of new political and social elites at the local level and their relationship with the local state apparatus. The discussion is based on field surveys conducted in two urban centres of India, viz., Lucknow and Ahmedabad. Here, we document the social collectives, which are open and draw membership from a cross-section of the population (Tables 1–4).

In an urban electoral setting, social collectives present themselves as an important medium through which political support is mobilised. In this

Table 1

Ethno-religious Groups

Name of social collective	*City*	*Agenda*	*Nature of membership*	*Political party to which they are ideologically/functionally close*
Rashtriya Swamsewak Sangh (National Volunteer Crop)	Ahmedabad, Lucknow	Inculcates Hindutva ideology	Open	BJP
Vishwa Hindu Parishad (World Hindu Council)	Ahmedabad, Lucknow	Performs aggressive and agitational role for promoting Hindutva	Open	BJP
Bajrang Dal	Ahmedabad, Lucknow	Militant wing of VHP and was started to provide muscle and manpower to VHP's agitation	Open	BJP
Sewa Vibhag (a) Sewa International (b) Sewa Bharti (c) Vanwasi Kalyan Aashram (d) Ekal Vidayalaya Foundation (e) Vikas Bharti	Ahmedabad	Formed apparently to carry out social service to the community. In practice, provide entry point for carrying out core ideological work by ideological volunteers	Open	BJP
Durga Vahini (Women's Front)	Ahmedabad, Lucknow	Organise Hindu women and inculcate religiosity, also provide entry point to ideological volunteers	Open	BJP
Hindu Jagran Manch (HJM)	Ahmedabad, Lucknow	Organise Hindu women and men, also provide entry point to ideological volunteers	Open	BJP

Note: BJP: Bharatiya Janata Party.

regard, it is crucial to understand how they mobilise people and discipline individuals' minds towards the social and political agenda of the collectives.

The ethno-religious groups seek consent for their agenda through the trajectory of 'discipline, hatred and punishment'. Discipline implies enlisting the support of the Hindus, activating them in campaigns and organising them under their leadership. In other words, Hindutvising the popular consciousness by constructing a social profile of minorities, especially Muslims, as culturally polluting, anti-national, pro-Pakistan, favoured at the expense of Hindus, driving a wedge between Christian Adivasis and Hindu Adivasis, etc.[2] Vishwa Hindu Parishad (VHP) works dextrously for developing unity between upper and lower castes by propagating that exploitation of Dalits by Brahmins is not the fault of the Hindu religion but the fault of individual(s). This has resulted in Dalits entering into the social constituency of Hindutva in large numbers, specifically in Ahmedabad. This nature of cultural and political disciplining has varied implications. It tries to create a consolidated Hindu social block vis-à-vis minorities while also attempting to obscure the socio-economic and

Table 2

Caste Collectives

Name of social collective	*City*	*Agenda*	*Nature of membership*	*Political party to which they are ideologically/ functionally close*
Patel Panchayat	Ahmedabad	Promotes caste solidarity and acts as an interest group	Restricted	BJP
Gujarat Kshatriya Sabha	Ahmedabad	-do- and influential in electoral politics	Restricted	BJP
Gujarat Kshatriya Sangh	Ahmedabad	-do- and influential in electoral politics	Restricted	BJP
Patidar Mandal	Ahmedabad	-do-	Restricted	BJP
Kurmi Mahasabha	Lucknow	-do-	Restricted	SP
Kyastah Mahasabha	Lucknow	-do-	Restricted	BJP/Congress
Vaish Mahasabha	Lucknow	-do- and influential in electoral politics	Restricted	BJP
Yadav Mahasangh	Lucknow	-do-	Restricted	SP
Kanya Kubj Brahmin Sabha	Lucknow	-do-	Restricted	BJP
Ravidas Sabha	Lucknow	-do-	Restricted	Dalits

Table 3

Associations of Traders and Petty Business Associations

Name of social collective	*City*	*Agenda*	*Nature of member-ship*	*Political party to which they are ideologically/ functionally close*
CG Road Business Association	Ahmedabad	Protects and promotes business interests of the members and develops and maintains cordial relationship with local politicians and government officers	Restricted	BJP
Vastrapur Shop Owners Association	Ahmedabad	-do-	Restricted	BJP
Ahmedabad Chemist Association	Ahmedabad	-do-	Restricted	BJP
Ahmedabad Brick Manufacturing Association	Ahmedabad	-do-	Restricted	BJP
Aliganj Vyapar Mandal	Lucknow	-do-	Restricted	Primarily SP
Aminabad Traders Association	Lucknow	-do-	Restricted	BJP
Ganesh Ganj Iron Merchant Association	Lucknow	-do-	Restricted	Primarily BSP and SP
Lucknow Goldsmith Association	Lucknow	-do-	Restricted	Primarily BJP
Brick Kilns Associations	Lucknow	-do-	Restricted	Primarily BJP
Khatik Vypar Mandal	Lucknow	Promotes caste solidarity and acts as caste business interest group	Restricted	BSP
Dhobi Sangh (informal association of cloth washers involved in chikan garment trade)	Lucknow	Promotes caste solidarity and acts as caste business interest group	Restricted	BSP

Note: SP: Samajwadi Party and BSP: Bhujan Samaj Party, BJP: Bharatiya Janata Party.

cultural differences within the Hindu community. Further, it constructs an image of the Muslim community as polluting the Hindu social order. Hence, they are culturally and socially unacceptable and as a consequence become object of intense hatred. Mass hatred by its very nature just requires a trigger to inflame sentiments and flare up into physical violent demonstrations. The post-Godhra riots in Gujarat are apt examples of this hatred. Lucknow has not seen any explicit manifestation of hatred but bias against Muslims has grown.

Table 4

Religious Social Order

Name of social collective	*City*	*Agenda*	*Nature of membership*	*Political party to which they are ideologically/ functionally close*
Murari Bapu	Ahmedabad	Gives religious/spiritual discourse, preaches equality of human beings but does not question the fundamental principles of caste-based social hierarchy	Open	BJP
Sant Shri Asaramji	Ahmedabad	-do-	Open	BJP
Neeb Karori Baba	Lucknow	-do-	Open	BJP
Nami Sharan Ashram	Lucknow	-do-	Open	BJP

The caste associations invoke the loyalty of a group of men and women towards their ascriptive identity. They also try and organise people and communicate to them the potential benefits of a collective social front. Traditionally, the caste associations were used to settle intra-community disputes and mediate between inter-community disputes. This still holds true for rural India and also for urban India to some extent. However, caste associations have also converted themselves into interest groups where they bargain with the state and other social groups for the socio-economic interests of their members. They do not have sophisticated tools of mobilisation, in comparison to ethno-religious groups, but still they are able to command the loyalties of their community members. They operate independent of other similar associations but as and when required they come together either against the state or other caste associations. The latter implies that the fault line of purity and pollution unite them against each other. In other words, as and when required, the upper caste associations unite, notwithstanding the differences between them, against the lower caste associations. The same also holds true for lower caste associations. Caste associations, like the ethno-religious groups, are able to invoke loyalties of individuals beyond face-to-face interactions of individuals, on common socio-economic and political interests. Upper caste associations also try and *co-opt* lower caste associations to their own agenda, by promising fringe benefits as well as by coercion.

The membership of religious social orders cuts across caste, class, gender and vocation. Religious social orders, it was perceived, were able to blur the difference between various castes and communities. As discussed before, they do not question and mitigate the social hierarchy, but the members still perceive them as egalitarian. Leaders of caste associations and ethno-religious groups devote themselves in efforts to be recognised as important members of these social orders. Due to this status, the respect commanded by the religious order also transfers, to an extent, to them. This gives them far more legitimacy in the eyes of their community.

The business associations are a crucial source of funding for these social collectives as well for political donations. At times, some important and rich members also give large donations, which also increase their importance in the community. The important business associations are normally the ones, which belong to the upper castes. The lower caste business associations do not normally contribute to such activities of raising money for the rent seekers in order to ensure the smooth running of their business.

The memberships of these social collectives overlap. Individual(s) constituting one particular collective say that a trade association has social (ethno-religious groups) and religious (religious social order) stakes in other collectives; and by virtue of belonging to a particular caste, also have their presence in caste associations. The prominent members of the traders associations, caste associations and ethno-religious groups are more or less the same individuals. Moreover, many of the government officials not only belong to the caste associations but are also regular visitors to the religious discourses given at the religious order(s). Some of them are members of ethno-religious groups and numerous others support them from outside. We also documented through newspapers' reports as well as through the perception of many respondents that lucrative postings and transfer of officers are governed by their choice of membership of social collectives. This should not be read as if the important individuals only constitute the social collectives. There is also a presence of not-so-socially important individuals as well as the labouring class. This particular fact gives these social collectives a numeric strength. The numeric strength in combination with financial resources of the trading community helps these social collectives to become a social force to reckon with.

In the cosmopolitan setting of the two cities covered by the study, these associations also use other sophisticated means to enlist the support of the new members, especially from the lower castes. Celebrating important lower caste festivals and associating them with Hindu festivals is an important tactic. For instance, in Lucknow, even the apparently lower caste festival like *Vishwakarma Puja*[3] is celebrated with great fanfare by the *Hindu Jagran Manch*. The local political bosses of the Sangh preside over the function and also distribute gifts to the working class. The working class is mobilised in a manner that a majority of them mostly belonging to lower castes start supporting them. Similarly, all the caste Hindu festivals are celebrated with great enthusiasm. In the caste Hindu festivals too, the working class (read Dalits) is mobilised in both the cities, and gifts are distributed. The mobilisation of Dalits and the subsequent distribution of gifts is done through the ward level leaders and members. Other mobilisation techniques, which have religious or social significance through carving out extended social networks, ensure an ever-increasing mass base of these collectives. The ward level leaders are important cadres who can in turn politically guide the network during the time of electoral contest.

The social networks carved out with the help of social collectives try and satisfy different classes of people through different systems of patronage and benefits. The elite members of the social collective are able to extract different extralegal concessions or facilitation of their interests due to their proximity with the elites in the political and bureaucratic structures. The lower class/caste people are not only given gifts but they are also the ones to have a first claim on the development goods. The latter may be their right but they are bestowed like favours or as rewards for their membership of social collectives. This not only makes them more committed to the social collectives but also to the political regime supported by that particular social collective. This is also a mechanism where every class of people tries to form an alliance with people higher up the class ladder for perceived or real benefits. The lowest class/caste tries to form a social alliance with the leader of the social collective who in turn tries to forge an alliance with leaders up the hierarchy or important government officials and prominent professionals. This extended social network ensures the demise of horizontal caste/class solidarity and constructs a vertical caste/class alliance.

A collective articulation as well as entry of newer groups into the political and social processes is found. In one sense, it can be called 'deepening of democracy' but frankly we fail to perceive any democratisation of society, polity and economy. The so-called deepening of democracy has resulted in a readjustment of social, political, legal and administrative institutions in their attempt to maintain status quo. The status quo has meant the hegemony of the entrenched castes and classes operating in a dominant coalition at the local level. The dominant coalition is comprised of local politicians, including musclemen, bureaucrats and traders. The coalition, through the medium of social collectives, co-opts the dissenting worldviews with the help of the extended social network. The social identities of caste, religion and ethnicity, which fragment the working classes, become a source of unity between the dominant coalition partners in the interest of establishing their dominance, which, in practical terms, implies a blurring of the lines dividing the state, the civil society and the markets since the membership of these collectives, as explained earlier, may overlap. Individual(s), says a government official, constituting one particular collective, may have social and religious stakes in one or many social collectives. If the collectives and the executives managing the political regime understand society, politics and economics from the same vantage point, then, the strength of the former translates into the might of the latter and vice versa. Similarly, the market in some goods may be controlled by few or many traders who may have social and religious stakes, along with the government officials in one of the many collectives. Their social proximity in the social collectives also allows members to exploit this proximity to use the state's resources in their favour. This is particularly true when it comes to issues relating to taxation and use of coercion to discipline the labour force. The administrative and police departments invariably side with business interests. Thus, the social collectives mediate between traders, politicians and government officials to ensure a horizontal interaction between them and blur the dividing line between state and market and civil society.

Development Programmes, Social Conflicts and Role of Dominant Communities

This section is based on the study, which was carried out to look into the social conflicts that unfold with the execution of development programmes. It was primarily a case study of four large and known NGOs – Seva Mandir (South Rajasthan – bordering Gujarat), MARAG (South West Gujarat – Kutch), Manav Kalyan Trust (Northern Gujarat – Sabarkantha) and UMBVS (Western Rajasthan – Jaisalmer and Jodhpur) – in several districts of rural Rajasthan and Gujarat (see Appendix 3). All the NGOs work in partnership with the state (as community mobilisers and often as the executing agency of some specific part of the development programme), and are also funded by the national and international donors. The primary aim of the research was to analyse the role of NGOs in executing developmental programmes and their capacity to mitigate/resolve social conflicts. However, it was soon realised that NGOs work is embedded in the larger socio-economic dynamics of the society, and is also constrained by the social relations existing in their area of operation. Moreover, NGOs' programmes cannot be seen in isolation from other developmental schemes conceived and implemented by the state. In other words, the work is only a sub-set of the gamut of developmental schemes and their outcomes are influenced by the local social dynamics.

The field visits reveal that caste, class, ethnicity, gender and religion structure the local socio-economic and political environment of the study area. The various social identities operate in different permutations and combinations for maintaining the status quo in favour of the dominant social group of that particular area, which in turn results in social conflict. Social conflict can be understood as patterned behaviour between different social groups that results in a strained relationship between two or more individuals or between different social groups. The strained relationships are generally caused due to attempts on behalf of the social group(s) to maintain the socio-economic status quo in face of opposition/assertion from the other social group(s). Thus conflict exists where two or more sets of actors are keen to achieve apparently incompatible goals, and where the other party is perceived to stand in the way of these goals. Developmental resources always have the potency to give birth to newer social conflicts or exacerbate the existing/dormant ones. The different types of conflicts in the study area are enumerated in Table 5.

Narrative on the Social Conflicts

The conflicts are not always inter-class in nature but also acquire an intra-class dimension in our study area. For instance, the contest over the space in the labour market often results in conflict between migrant labour and local labour. This conflict is mostly triggered off when the local labour demand market rates for their work. In order to avoid the rightful demands of the labour, the owners of economic enterprises seek the help of a labour contractor and procure the required labour force from a different district or state. The influx of fresh labour force and consequent conflict between the migrant labour and the local labour over labour market space facilitates the owner of the capital to depress the wages. Similarly, there emerges a conflict between the organised labourers and contract informal labourers because the former get social security benefits as well as the prescribed official minimum wages. The contract labourers have to be content with market rates, which are mostly below the prescribed minimum wages, and they are not entitled to any social security benefits. Further, the intra-class rivalry is not only between the labouring classes but also between owners of the capital. In the study area, this conflict gets most prominently manifested over the sharing of canal irrigation water, local elections – cooperatives as well as panchayats – and over the control of skilled labourers.

Table 5

Typology of Social Conflicts

	Groups Involved	*Reason for Conflict*
	Class-based Social Conflicts	
Inter-class	Labour, small and marginal farmers versus landowners, sharecroppers versus landlords	Wage exploitation, violent guarding of land and privatised common property resources, issues pertaining to water, market, political contestation
	Mine owners versus mine workers	Over the issue of benefits, etc.
	Labour contractor versus labour	Wages
Intra-class	Contract labour versus organised labour	Benefits
	Local versus migrants	Labour market space
	Medium and small farmers versus big landowners	Canal water distribution, political contestations
	Big farmers versus big farmers	Over the control of cooperative, land disputes, political contestations
	Caste/Community-based Conflicts	
Inter-caste	Dalits versus upper caste	Purity and pollution, though now restructured, control over resources, political contestations
	Hindu male versus Dalit female	Sexual exploitation
Intra-caste/ community	Between different sub-castes of Dalits	Purity and pollution issues
	Adivasis versus Dalits	Purity and pollution issues
	Capture of Local State	
Inter-caste and inter-class	Entrenched/dominant versus socially/politically less powerful	Cornering of state's resources, especially on the question of livelihood diversification
	Gender-based Conflicts	
Inter- and intra-class as well as inter- and intra-caste	Male versus female Women versus women	Sexual exploitation, violence against women and control over sexuality Purity-pollution issues, religious issues, 'against natural social order'

Cont'd...

...Cont'd

Religion-based		
Inter- and intra-class and by establishment organic unity amongst different castes	Muslims versus Hindus	Stereotyping Muslims (terrorist, community which infringes the dignity of Hindu women), labour market issues, political contestations
Conflict between NGO Beneficiaries versus Other Villagers		
Inter-class and inter-caste		Perceived that they are left out of beneficiary lists

Notes: Usually governed (not always) by protection of class interests.
Inter-and intra-class conflicts also acquires inter-and intra-caste dimensions.

It may be noted that these seemingly secular conflicts over class interests, more often than not, acquire a communal dimension. In the absence of any secular platform to articulate the common interests, the poor find the community identity as the only source of airing their collective voice. It gets manifested and further concretised as conflicts between social group(s) with the flow of developmental goods as well the lack of them, as both lack of development as well as development itself can be the cause and consequence of social conflict. Lack of development may spur demands by the poor households for claiming their rights over developmental resources. The demand invariably affects the entrenched/dominant social group who tends to control and channelise the developmental benefits in its favour. Similarly, development initiatives trigger off such conflict because the poor households may perceive that they are discriminated against in resource distribution. In practice, if the discriminator and discriminated happen to be the members of different social groups (which they invariably are), the conflict takes the form of inter-social group conflicts.

The conflicts get more prone to articulation on community lines because of the intra-class clash of socio-economic and political interests. For instance, the rural social geography of the study areas ensures that each community not only stays in close proximity but also own land side by side. Due to this historical pattern of ownership of land, a conflict over sharing of water often emerges. The community owning land closest to the canal (entrenched social groups) not only extracts the maximum water but also stores it in small ponds on their fields. This withdrawal of water more than their share is at the expense of other dominant as well as marginalised communities down the line of water channel. The worst sufferers are the tail-end users who happen to be the Dalits and Adivasis. However, this nature of conflict did not result in a natural alliance of communities excluded from their rightful share of water but instead, resulted in a conflict between the two dominant communities – Darbars and Rajputs – who were placed first and second on the irrigation canal line. As a result of the conflict, an informal agreement between them emerged, facilitating some portion of water reaching the land owned by Rajputs. On the other hand, an alliance of all excluded communities would have been more beneficial since it might have facilitated the formation of institutions governing the sharing of water equitably. These kinds of institutions could not be ever formed in the present political economy of the study area because the extra water extracted from the canal is sold to tail-end users by members of the same marginalised community who were excluded from their rightful claim to water. The Darbars in the areas are entrenched castes dominating the political field as well as controlling the local economy.

Such instances are numerous even among the marginalised social groups, where their immediate material or social interest is a trigger for group solidarity, thereby ensuring some kind of conflict between different social groups. The most common source of conflict is the dispute over sharing the common property, especially fodder and water. The rampant illegal privatisation of these resources by the entrenched social groups has resulted in fierce conflict between the marginalised social groups over whatever is still left in the public domain. It has been documented by the study that Adivasis and Dalits as a group align with dominant communities for their short-term interest against each other.

The conflict becomes more intense if the developmental initiatives seek to diversify the livelihood opportunities in the face of dwindling income from agriculture produce and agriculture labour. For maximum benefit by the more powerful social groups, the new avenues have to be captured.

The differences between social groups and ensuing conflict over material resources get more intensified, especially between the dominant communities and marginalised social groups, with the invoking of stereotype construct of the latter (Adivasis are lazy, Adivasis and Dalits are pampered by politicians, Muslims support Pakistan, etc.). In the face of the growing assertion of marginalised social groups for claiming their rights over developmental resources, the dominant communities vehemently reinforce the cultural stereotypes in order to culturally and morally suppress them and thereby maintain the status quo in terms of their dominant status.

The construct of stereotype images also affects the social relationship between different communities drastically. As far as the social relationship between Dalits and other Hindu castes and Adivasis is concerned, it is marked by restructured rules of 'purity and pollution'. In some of the regions, even the Dalits are not allowed to wear slippers in the presence of the higher castes. The utensils are never shared. Almost every household has separate utensils for serving Dalits tea and refreshments on one hand, and on the other, a member of a higher caste rarely takes water or food in a Dalit household. Any inter-caste marriage is vehemently opposed and often results in violence. There may not be any explicit discrimination in school but Dalit students feel that they are not treated on equal terms by the teachers. The Dalits invariably have separate wells. When the government tankers supply the drinking water, they have to stand outside the queue and their turn comes when all other communities have filled their water pots. Such incidents of discrimination against Dalits are manifold, and could be found in scores in the study area.

It may be noted that discrimination of Dalits is not only at the hands of upper castes. The same practice has been culturally internalised by Adivasis and Muslims who consider themselves culturally superior to Dalits. Besides this, there is an internal hierarchy within Dalits too. They also invoke the upper caste norms of 'purity and pollution' for ensuring internal differentiation and consequent superior-inferior social status. Harijans, Bhangis and Chamars are considered to be on the lower rung of the hierarchy and they are met with same treatment by Dalit sub-castes like Balais, Meghwals and Paswans.

The collective strength of the different castes and communities comes from robust existence of *Jati Panchayats*. However, it is not to say that all such *Jati Panchayats* are equally powerful. The most powerful panchayats in the study area were the ones belonging to the upper castes, namely, Patels, Rajputs, Darbars and Jains. They are not only rich, but belong to the middle strata, better organised and have substantial influence in the local economy, polity and society. Many of the leaders of the panchayats have economic stakes both in the village as well as nearby urban areas.

The difference between the Upper Caste Panchayats, the Lower Caste Panchayats and Adivasi Panchayats is that the latter two are not as competent as the former in influencing the local administration and controlling the local economy. It has been observed that the lower caste and Adivasi Panchayats mostly meet on primordial issues like elopement of their community women with men of different community/caste.

Another prominent feature of the study area was the near absence of local state apparatus for mitigating these social conflicts. The researcher was repeatedly told that local officials and police choose not to interfere in the affairs of the *Jati Panchayats*. In other words, there seems be a parallel system of justice operating in the study area. *Jati Panchayats* seem to be an all-powerful body in deciding disputes over marriage, inter-caste violence, adultery, etc.

Thus caste and community most jealously make all efforts to control the sexuality of their women. Endogamy, though not historically observed, has become the norm of the present social order. Any violation of the same is met with the strictest punishment possible. The nature of punishment is always decided by the *Jati Panchayats*. However, there again exists a strain in this type of caste and community discourse. A relationship by consent between a man and women of different caste is despised and viewed with contempt but frequent infringement of modesty and dignity of lower castes and Adivasi women by upper caste men (invariably outside the marital boundaries) are taken as normal and often considered as the right of the rich and powerful. Moreover, *Jati Panchayats* have never reacted against the violence against women within the family.

It seems that the discourses of *Jati Panchayats* make a distinction between the private and the public. The former, implying marriage is considered as a private affair and it has to be confined within the caste or community, and violation of this boundary has to be punished. Moreover, the affairs within the family are strictly private and outsiders cannot or should not interfere. In the public domain where the *Jati Panchayats* of lower castes and Adivasis do not command similar power and status, there is not much chance of taking a belligerent stand against higher castes. Moreover, the public domain is the 'domain of the man'. The male fraternity, it has been observed, are usually united against women, irrespective of social location. The best manifestation of this is the practice of *Dakan* in Udaipur. *Dakan* is an oppressive practice against women. It is believed when an evil spirit possesses the woman, she has to be cured by the complex religious rites, which are preformed by the *Ojha*. Another explanation given of this social custom is that the woman is considered to be possessed by the evil spirit when she starts becoming assertive and reacts at times violently against the discrimination and oppression she faces within the family or outside. On such matters, the males of the village unite and force the woman to be taken to the *Ojha*. The symbol of such male unity is also reflected in the fact that all men contribute money as per their capacity towards the fee of the *Ojha*.

The violence against women, irrespective of their caste and class, is the most commonly observed phenomenon. It appears there is no specific reason for the violence. In the dominant social construct, the men are supposed to be the main breadwinners, even if the women of the household are contributing substantially to the income basket of the family (given the feminisation of the workforce and increasing casualisation of the male workforce). In this milieu, if the man of the family is not able to make an entry into the labour market, the women often face the brunt of his frustration, which is often expressed through frequent beatings. Moreover, if he makes an entry into the labour market, he usually comes back home tired and often drunk and again the woman cushions the brunt of his anger. Further, the women in the village are extremely discourteous to women of other religions and lower castes. Some women refer to grass roots NGO leaders as 'mislead and confused entities' under the influence of external agencies.

It was documented in the study area that the internal contradictions between upper castes and Dalits, between Adivasis and Dalits, between Adivasis and upper castes and between men and women wane in contrast to those with Muslims and Christians. The current dominant political discourse has managed to portray Muslims as 'culturally and socially alien', 'terrorists' and 'supporters of our enemy' – that is Pakistan. The Muslim men are considered to be sexual exploiters of Adivasi and Hindu women.

The discourse of right-wing communalism is not only limited to Muslims but also take a tough political stand against the Christians. The missionaries are considered to be luring away the innocent Adivasis to the fold of their religion. It is notable that the Adivasi is not considered as smart and capable of fooling the upper castes but an innocent person who falls prey to the trap of missionaries.

In the study area, there have been numerous instances of violence against Muslims and re-conversion of Adivasi Christians to the Hindu fold. The well-orchestrated political and social discourse against Muslims and Christians is to form an organic unity among the caste Hindus and Adivasis and Dalits. The upper caste *Jati Panchayats,* in association with right-wing political party and social collectives, organised few religious discourses in order to discipline the popular consciousness towards Hinduism. The main objective of all these attempts seems to maintain the current socio-economic and political status quo.

Even in the face of intense conflict, the dominance of middle-income strata, predominantly belonging to the upper castes, is able to dominate the local economy, polity and society. Again, the membership of social collective *(Jati Panchayats)* is an important medium through which domination is effected. There may be strains between different dominant castes but they still negotiate with each other with more or less equal strength where one group may acquire relative ascendancy at the expense of other and vice versa. Note, the articulation of historically deprived social groups is also through their collectives but they are mostly not in a position to negotiate with dominant groups at equal strength.

Conclusions

In the above discussion, we have indicated that the state cannot be seen as a homogenous block neatly tied at various levels into an organic whole. First of all, it is divided administratively into macro (national), meso (federal) and micro (local). Second, the state is segmented not only by differing economic interests but also by caste, religion, ethnicity and religion. Our own narrative as well as scores of other scholarly works point out that state is not autonomous. However, the autonomy of the state at each level is constrained by different set of socio-economic groups. The interests of the socio-economic groups present at different level of polity do not necessarily complement each other. The story of unevenness of economic reforms discussed before is the best testimony of this fact. However, the crucial fact is that the middle class articulates dominant interests at all levels. At the macro level, it is increasingly felt that the middle class has acquired the legitimacy to speak on behalf of the society. This is the class, which provides an ideological articulation and legitimacy to the present face of capitalist development under the overall domination of corporate capital in alliance with international capital.

Below the national level, the situation is quite complex. The same middle class (which is also the major beneficiary of the capitalist development) often articulates their interests with the help of their social identity – be it religion, caste or ethnicity. The use of social identity ruptures the boundaries between state and market and allows the permeation of dominant interests in the rank and file of the state. The argument that we are trying to put forth being: The identity of the middle class is predominantly an upper caste identity. There is relatively bigger middle class amongst the other backward classes but it is present amongst the Dalits, Adivasis and Muslims. In a scenario of segmented state, the role of middle class becomes crucial in the attempt to preservation of status quo.

Notes

1. Most of the foreign investments in India has an Indian partner. This symbiotic relationship allows the 'united' capital to manage their concern with the Indian state. There are instances, when national capital perceives an adverse inclusion/treatment at the hands of international collaborator. During such occurrences, they have sought the help of the state and the Indian state has come to the rescue because of their political outcry against foreign 'domination'. The same pattern is visible in the relationship between state-level capitalist vis-à-vis national-level capitalists. Hence, the national capital has acquired international dimension but it has still retained its Indian roots due to (a) economic reason – large markets; (b) political reason – seeking support of the state under 'adverse' inclusion in the international economic regime.
2. This is not true for Lucknow.
3. Vishwakarma puja is a day when the working class offers puja to the tools and implements of their trade from which they derive their livelihood.

References

Abrams, Philip (1988). 'Notes on the Difficulty of Studying the State', *Journal of Historical Sociology*, 1: 58–59.

Austin, Granville (2000). *Working a Democratic Constitution: The Indian Experience*, New Delhi: Oxford University Press.

Bailey, F.G. (1963). *Politics and Social Change: Orissa in 1959*, Berkeley: University of California Press.

Bardhan, Pranab (2003). *The Political Economy of Development in India*, Fourth Impression, New Delhi: Oxford University Press.

Chatterjee, Partha (1986). *Nationalist Thought and the Colonial World: A Derivative Discourse?*, London: Zed Books.

—— (1993). *The Nation and Its Fragments: Colonial and Postcolonial Histories*, Princeton: Princeton University Press.

—— (2000). 'Development Planning and the Indian State', in Zoya Hasan (ed.), *Politics and the State in India*, New Delhi: Sage Publications.

—— (2004). *The Politics of the Governed: Reflections on Political Society in Most of the World*, New York: Columbia University Press.

—— (2008). 'Democracy and Economic Transformation in India', *Economic and Political Weekly*, April 19: 53–62.

Gupta, Akhil (1995). 'Blurred Boundaries: The Discourse of Corruption, the Culture of Politics, and the Imagined State', *American Ethnologist*, Vol. 22, Issue 2, pp. 375–402.

Harriss-White, Barbara (2003). *India Working: Essays on Society and Economy*, Cambridge: Cambridge University Press.

Kaviraj, S. (1989). 'A Critique of Passive Revolution', *EPW*, 23 (45): 2429–44.

Khilnani, S. (1998). *The Idea of India*, Harmondsworth: Penguin Books.

Kohli, Atul (1987). *State and Poverty in India*, New Delhi: Cambridge in Association with Orient Longman.

—— (1990). *Democracy and Discontent: India's Growing Crisis of Governability*, Cambridge: Cambridge University Press.

Lerche, J. (1995). 'Is Bonded Labour a Bound Category? Reconceptualising Agrarian Conflict in India', *Journal of Peasant Studies*, 22 (3): 484–515.

Madan, T.N. (1997). 'Secularism in Its Place', in Sudipta Kaviraj (ed.), *Politics in India*, New Delhi: Oxford University Press.

Nandy, Ashis (1997). 'A Critique of Modern Secularism', in Sudipta Kaviraj (ed.), *Politics in India*, New Delhi: Oxford University Press.

—— (2000). 'The Political Culture of the Indian State', in Zoya Hasan (ed.), *Politics and State in India*, New Delhi: Oxford University Press.

Roy, Arundhati (2006). 'The Cost of Living: The Narmada Dam and the Indian State', in Lloyd I. Rudolph and John Curt Jacobsen (eds), *Experiencing the State*, New Delhi: Oxford University Press.

Rudolph, Lloyd I. and S.H. Rudolph (1987). *In Pursuit of Laxmi: The Political Economy of Indian State*, Chicago: Chicago University Press.

Saberwal, Satish (1996). *The Roots of Crisis: Interpreting Contemporary Indian Society*, New Delhi: Sage Publications.

Sengupta, Arjun et al. (2009). *The Challenge of Employment in India: An Informal Economy Perspective*, Volume 1 – Main Report, New Delhi: NCEUS, April.

Vanaik, Achin (1990). *The Painful Transition: Bourgeois Democracy in India*, London: Verso.

Varshney, Ashutosh (1995). *Democracy, Development and Countryside: Urban-Rural Struggles in India*, Cambridge: Cambridge University Press.

Yadav, Yogendra (1996). 'Reconfiguration in Indian Politics: State Assembly Elections, 1993–95', *EPW*, 31(2/3) (13 January): 95–104.

Appendix 1

Institutions Supporting Economics of Market and Politics of Democracy

Institutions Supporting Economics of Markets				*Institutions Mandated By Politics of Democracy*	
Market Creating		*Market Regulating Institutions*	*Market Legitimising Institutions*	*Institutions Giving a Call for Inclusive Development*	*Watch Dog Institutions*
Withdrawal of State	*To Attract new players*				National Integration Council/ National Judicial Council/ National Commission for Minority Educational Institutions/ National Minority Commission/ National Commission for Backward Classes Act/ National Commission for Women/ Bifurcation of National Schedule Caste and National Schedule Tribe Commission
Foreign Direct Investment Policy 2006 (started with Industrial Policy of 1991)	Foreign Investment Implementation Authority (FIIA)	The Central Electricity Regulatory Commission	National Investment Fund	National Advisory Council	
Board for Reconstruction of Public Sector Enterprise (Ministry of Dis-investment)	Committee on Infrastructure	The Telecom Regulatory Authority of India	National Commission for Enterprises in the Unorganised Sector	Panchayats and Urban Local Bodies	

Cont'd...

...Cont'd

The Fiscal Responsibility and the Budget Management Bill	Public Private Partnership	National Knowledge Commission	National Farmers Commission/Report of the Expert Group on Agricultural Indebtedness/Reconstituted National Rainfed Area Authority	National Rural Employment Guarantee Act	
				Right to Education Bill	
				National Rural health Mission	
				Proposed Food Security Act	Proposed Equal Opportunity Commission and Diversity Index
Special Economic Zones (New Model of Industrialisation)	Investment Commission of India	Security Exchange Board of India		The Scheduled Tribes and Other Traditional Forest Dwellers (Recognition of Forests Rights) Act, 2006	
	National Manufacturing Competitiveness Council and Investment Commission	Insurance Regulatory and Development Authority			Right to Information
	Jawaharlal Nehru Urban Renewal Mission	Prime Minister Economic Advisory Council		National Urban Street Vendor Policy	

Appendix 2

Deciles Average Monthly Per Capita Expenditure of Various Social Groups

Hindu	*Poorest 10 percentile*									*Richest 10 percentile*
	1	*2*	*3*	*4*	*5*	*6*	*7*	*8*	*9*	*10*
1999–00										
Scheduled tribe	167	218	249	280	311	345	383	432	513	863
Scheduled caste	192	249	284	316	349	385	430	489	583	937
Other backward castes	212	274	313	349	386	428	482	552	671	1107
General	258	339	396	452	512	583	674	807	1040	1862
Gap										
Gen-Scheduled tribe	91	120	147	172	201	238	291	375	527	999
Gen-Scheduled caste	67	90	112	136	163	198	244	318	456	925
Gen-Other backward castes	47	65	83	103	126	155	192	255	369	755
2004–05										
Scheduled tribe	191	258	298	334	371	412	462	526	631	1036
Scheduled caste	236	302	343	381	419	464	519	592	710	1180
Other backward castes	264	336	383	431	479	535	600	692	857	1519
General	319	428	504	577	662	768	911	1122	1497	2938
Gap										
Gen-Scheduled tribe	128	169	206	243	291	356	449	595	866	1902
Gen-Scheduled caste	84	125	161	196	243	304	392	529	787	1758
Gen-Other backward castes	55	92	121	146	183	233	311	430	640	1419
Difference over the period (Gap 2004–05 minus Gap 1999–00)										
Gen-Scheduled tribe	37	49	59	71	90	117	158	220	339	903
Gen-Scheduled caste	17	35	49	60	80	105	148	211	331	834
Gen-Other backward castes	9	27	38	43	57	78	119	175	271	664

Note: Gen: General.

Source: NSSO, various rounds.

Appendix 3

Field Area of Case Study on Social Conflict and Development

SEVA MANDIR: (South Rajasthan-Bordering Gujarat)	
Objective:	Empowerment of the least advantaged in society
Target Group and Area:	Rural population in Udaipur district in Rajasthan
Intervention:	Strengthening livelihood of village communities, Building local capabilities in areas of health, education and gender equality, creating autonomous village level institutions
MARAG (South West Gujarat-Kutch)	
Objective:	Empowerment of the disadvantaged, especially the Maldhari community in Kutch
Target Groups and Area:	Maldhari community in Bhuj and Rapar blocks in Kutchh and Chotila, Sayla and Patadi blocks of Surendranagar
Intervention:	Focus on natural resource development and human resource development while also trying to do away with age-old reactionary customs and traditions like bride purchase and child marriage.
MANAV KALYAN TRUST (Northern Gujarat-Sabarkantha)	
Objective:	Empowerment of the poor and tribal and rural people particularly the farmers, cattle rearing families and destitute women and provide them with common platform to voice their concerns and
Target Group:	Tribal localities in disaster prone districts of Northern Gujarat and Kutch region
Intervention:	Natural resource management, creating avenues for empowered livelihood opportunities, housing projects, forming micro-credit groups for women, health and education, riot victim rehabilitation programme, sexual health projects.
UMBVS (Western Rajasthan-Jaisalmer and Jodhpur)	
Objective:	Building up collectives of rural artisans and keeping alive the traditional craft of weaving communities.
Target Group:	Organising artisans in villages of Jaisalmer and Jodhpur, especially the Dalits and women
Intervention:	Organising weavers and facilitating them with market linkages with a focus of enabling the women of the family to get share in the economic activities.

7

The Indian Middle Class and Consumption Culture

Change and Continuity

N. RAJARAM

About two decades ago, India shifted gears in its path of development. From being a system where important economic institutions and enterprises were state controlled, India embraced the market and opened its economy in a big way to foreign capital and multinational companies, besides its own private players. The initial steps in this direction were taken around the mid-eighties, but the most important propulsion in this direction came in the year 1991, when India decided to liberalise and throw open its economy. Around this time, changes in information and communication technology became more widespread and reshaped human relations around the world. Globalisation as this process came to be known also affected the middle class.

In India it seems to be the accepted view amongst intelligentsia that the middle class was not responsible for liberalisation of the Indian economy[1] nor was it the one that ushered changes in information and communication technology.[2] However, the changes unleashed by liberalisation and globalisation affected the Indian middle class in a big way, shaping the direction in which the middle class grew. The Indian middle class embraced the new technology in a big way and made use of the opportunities of privatisation and liberalisation to grow and enhance. The potentially huge market no doubt attracted foreign capital in a big way. India started to grow rapidly as it used the path of low-wage cost service sector growth. The policy makers hoped that by utilising these opportunities they could lift people from poverty into the expanding middle stratum of society, called the middle class. Not only did the existing policies and the way economy was run undergo a change, but it also brought about a change in the social relations within India, especially amongst the middle class. This paper examines the continuities and discontinuities in this emerging middle class of India.

The emerging middle class has been referred to as the 'new' middle class;[3] and it has been contrasted with the middle class at the time of independence, which has been called 'old' middle class. This comparison between the middle classes at these two points of time is in terms of its consumption both economic and cultural. This will be seen in terms of how there is hype about the size of the middle class, the kinds of goods it consumes, and its attitude towards consumerism. As for social consumption it will be analysed in relation to issues of religion, transnational influence in lifestyle and the space given to women during this period. This comparison thus points out to the continuities and discontinuities of the present with that of the past and thus points to the direction that India is being shaped by this emerging middle class.

Meaning of Middle Class

Before examining these issues, let me first deal with what is meant by the term 'middle class'. Globally, there is no consensus about what constitutes the middle class. Erik Olin Wright (2007: 8), who has written extensively on the middle class, identifies three approaches to the understanding of middle classes, which he called 'individual attributes approach', 'opportunistic hoarding approach' and 'exploitation-domination approach'. He does not privilege any approach, but his preference is towards the exploitation-domination approach. Thus, he says, 'middle class is defined as those positions which are simultaneously in a position of both dominating and dominated, or exploiting and exploited'.

In India, Andre Beteille views the conceptualisation of the middle class as being 'composite' because 'it had proved impossible to dispense with either the property structure or occupational structure in defining it' (2007: 89). He goes on to say that 'any reasonable conception of the middle class must accommodate more than one kind of market situation, work situation and status situation' (Beteille, 2007: 296). Thus, it is not surprising that in the various writings on the middle class, this 'composite' approach is very visible. The criteria emphasised are income, education and non-agrarian occupations.

Economists' definition tends to differ. It emphasise on income. Banerjee and Duflo (2008: 4), for example, identify the middle class in India (and other developing countries studied by them) as those having income between \$2 and \$10 per capita per day. This seems close to the definition given by Mckinsey Global Institute (2007: 3), which for 2005 considered the middle class to be those having a household income between ₹ 2,00,000 and ₹ 10,00,000 per annum and comprised about 50 million people.

Martin Ravallion of the World Bank Policy Research Institute (2009) follows the economists' way of measuring the middle class, that is, in terms of income. However, his position is different from that of other economists. For him, the middle class would be that earns between $2 and $13. For the Asian Development Bank (2010: 5), the middle class would constitute those consuming between $2 and $20 per day per capita.

However, this definition would constantly change as incomes rise (or even fall) or the growth of economy rises or ebbs. During the last decade, the growth rate was considered to be 'high' for India as a whole, although there are inter-state variations. However, I must add that the recent global economic meltdown at the global level (in 2008) and the persistent high inflation has had its impact on the growth rate. In India, as stated above, there are inter-state variations. For instance, Gujarat is considered to be having a growth rate much higher than the national average and this growth rate (of Gujarat) is claimed to be comparable to that of China. However, whether this growth rate has had a beneficial impact on the society as a whole is in doubt, as a recent study on hunger puts Gujarat's situation as 'alarming' and along with other states not doing well economically. At the global level, it would rank 70th amongst a group of 88 (Menon et al., 2009: 9).

Middle Class in India

Misra (1961: 1–13) traces the emergence of the middle class in India to the onset of British rule, when there was a growth of new occupations in law and bureaucracy. This was also the period of industrialisation, and those who took to new occupations became the nucleus of the middle class. As occupations expanded, the middle class also expanded. These new occupations were in administration, law, bureaucracy, academia, engineering, health and medicine, and in other professions. These occupations were non-agrarian and required a certain level of educational skill for a person to get into. During the colonial period, these 'new' knowledge and skills were imparted in English. With time, English became the language, which united this newly emerging middle class (Scrase, 2004).[4] Initially, this class consisted mainly of the upper castes from various regions that were the first to take to higher education and consequently enter these new emerging occupations. Slowly persons from lower castes also entered this class. This class played a significant role in the independence movement of India.

Misra also traces the reactions of the middle class to changes in India in the late 19th and in the first half of 20th century. He mentions that 'the reformist character or revivalist character' (Misra, 1961: 368) in the reactions of the middle class to changes in late 18th century; and these reactions became more complex with the growth of nationalist movements (ibid.: 390–400). He states that the middle class that led the movement had two components: the 'radicals' with a socialist viewpoint and the 'conservatives' who had a revivalist fervour. As he says, 'India won freedom but was divided. Both freedom and division were the work of the middle classes' (ibid.: 400).

At the time when India gained independence in 1947, as Beteille (2007: 952) remarks, 'the educated and salaried middle class was a very small fraction of the Indian population'. According to one estimate, the middle class comprised about 10 per cent of the then population (Varma, 1998: 26). This was the era when the middle class dominated the administrative bureaucracy.[5] The bureaucracy controlled the economy in the name of taking care of balanced growth in society, as India was under the influence of 'socialistic' ideology advocated by Nehru, the first Prime Minister. Indian democracy, although patterned on the British electoral system, in the early years after independence was dominated and shaped by the Congress party and Nehru. This feature of the state controlling the leading sectors of the economy continued over the next four decades or so, when in 1991, the Indian economy, as mentioned earlier, India changed gears and threw open its economy to foreign capital and the market was given importance in the distribution of resources and services. This strategic change was influenced by developments both within the country and outside. The collapse of Soviet Union[6] and its model of development, the emergence of new technologies of information and communication and its quick spread the world over, including India (now referred to as the globalisation process), compounded by the failure of the then prevailing policies to bring about rapid economic and social development, all led to a paradigm shift by the decision-makers.

Since 1991, the economy has only got more liberalised and globalised in terms of integration to the market of the world economy. A new set of workers and work culture (more popularly known as the BPO – Business Process Outsourcing – or better known as the 'call centre' culture)[7] has developed. The developments in software industry, coupled with the cheap labour that India had, have resulted in the development of the service sector in India in what has been called the 'new' economy. The stories of the few young persons who have made 'millions' go round and round, spawning a dream of rags to riches and stories of quick success. Furthermore, the parental generation of these young rich successful persons could not dream of such wealth when they were young. All this has changed the entire scenario in India.

The quick adoption of the new technologies of information and communication by the urban middle class, along with the development of satellite TV channels in news and entertainment, has resulted in newer images being created and marketed in India. This has resulted in opening up the market to new goods and services; and the Indian middle class embraced it in a big way. This is perhaps captured best by the biggest symbolic shift in the sartorial attire of the Indian male politician. Many an Indian politician, who till early nineties would wear *khadi*[8], now started donning the tie and the suit considered symbols of corporate business managers. This symbolic change captured the shift in the dominant political and social value in India, because till then the emphasis was on simplicity, spartan living, and no ostentatious display of wealth. This symbolic shift was perhaps reinforced by global trends as well: China being a good example of this where the western managerial attire replaced old style Mao suits.

Today, in the second decade of the 21st century, another feature has been added to this scenario. Because of the speed at which newer sectors of the economy are being thrown open to market forces, the notion of 'permanent employment' – which was a euphemism of security of employment – is being replaced without any corresponding social security. Now, this worldview is even penetrating into the state sector. This is a radical shift of values and work culture for the Indian middle class. There are numerous cases of persons who have been laid off, or who have taken 'VRS'[9] from various enterprises. But, at the same time, there has not been any concerted and consistent protest to these changes taking place (Fernandes, 2000).[10]

But Beteille (2007: 948) considers that although privatisation and liberalisation have 'hurt some individuals with secure employment, but they have also created new opportunities for others with drive and initiative but with little prospect for paid employment'. Thus, it is not surprising to see that this changing worldview has not resulted in a reduction in consumption. In fact, the middle class has started consuming more – be it more of the same things or newer things that have now become easily available than before, as a way to gain social status. Material consumption of goods and services has increased as seen in the consumption of TVs, refrigerators, motor vehicles, computers and the like. Along with the changes in consumption of material goods, there has also been an increase in the emergence of newer lifestyles. The houses one lives in now have items from various regions of the world. The changes include not only in the way one commutes to work (now by latest models of vehicles, usually cars), or travels to other towns (thanks to the growth of cheaper airlines to newer destinations), and how people communicate (thanks to cell phones), but also how one spends his/her leisure time. Traditional cinema halls have been replaced by multiplexes, the places where one shops are in malls, and of course now more and more Indians go abroad for holidays. The packaged tours are very popular and there is a new breed of the Indian middle class, which is doing things completely different from what their parents did. This market-driven consumer culture is no more confined to metros but has also spread to smaller cities and towns and even rural areas as seen in the growth of the cell phones, multiplexes and internet to all regions of India.

Further, now, the middle class approaches matters of nepotism, corruption and ill-gotten wealth (called popularly as 'black money') in an amoral way. Although black money, nepotism and corruption have existed for long, there is no study to suggest that they have reduced or declined in the post-liberalisation phase. In fact, they only seem to have grown as the recent exposure of various scams in the last few years, especially by those who were at one time the icons of the middle class like senior army officers[11] and civil servants, seem to indicate. Throughout the post-independence era, the middle class has been a beneficiary of these practices.[12] In spite of regular exposures in the media and other attempts to control them, the attitude of the middle class towards these happenings is that of an established practice about which one has to co-exist, rather than attempt to do away with.

Scholars and others in the intelligentsia have noticed these changes and have commented on the distinction between 'old' middle class – the middle class at the time of independence – with the 'new' emerging middle class.[13] They were quick to point to the differential attitudes to wealth and ethics. While the 'old' middle class was discreet and perhaps reticent in displaying wealth, the 'new' middle class is brash and ostentatious in displaying wealth. The old middle class was more concerned with the role of ethics in social life and probity in public life, while this is less emphasised now.

How Big is the Middle Class in India Today?

The moment one asks how big this middle class is in the second decade of the 21st century, there is little clarity. Perhaps, it is because the size of the middle class is related to consumerism (and marketing of goods) there is a lot of hype about its size. The figures that are mentioned vary a lot depending upon which source one is quoting from. More often than not those who are from the world of business seem to paint a rosy picture,[14] while academics and others tend to be more sceptical.

All over the world, there is the hype of the 'huge' middle class in India (as it is about China). The middle class is supposed to be fuelling the rapid growth of the economies of India and China. Perhaps the best example of this is the McKinsey Global Institute and Asian Development Bank (ADB) reports. McKinsey's report on India (2007: 10) states:

> Our analysis shows that if India continues on its current high growth path, over the next two decades the Indian market will undergo a major

> transformation, income levels will almost triple and India will climb from its position as the 12th largest consumer market today to become the fifth-largest consumer market by 2025 ... Over 291 million people will move from desperate poverty to a more sustainable life and India's middle class will swell by over ten times from its current size of 50 million to 583 million people. By 2025 over 23 million Indians – more than the population of Australia today – will number among the country's wealthiest citizens.

On the other hand, the ADB's estimate is that the middle class constitutes anywhere between 274 million (2010: 8) and 418 million (2010: 11) in 2004–05, depending upon the source of data.

The answer about the size of the middle class reflects more of speculation than factual data. What is well known is the huge population of 1 billion plus in India (and China as well). This figure gets merged with the hype of the size of the 'growing middle class' to give an image and a picture of very huge market. So perhaps to mention vast figures is in fashion to drive the appetite of the market. Thus, for instance, is the following excerpt from *Business Week*[15] of April 2006, which states that 'in industries from telecom to cars, China and India are fast becoming the biggest markets in the world'. The same article goes on to state that 'these nations are the world's biggest pools of low-cost engineers, scientists, and service workers, [so] multinationals also must be good at hiring, retaining, and managing talent there. They (the multinational companies) must be adept at using these countries as sources of manufacturing, back-office processing, components, and new technologies.' There are a large number of articles in the print and visual media about the 'huge' market, which this 'big middle class' represents in these countries. Perhaps the state in India (and as much in China) has an interest to project and propagate this image so as to attract foreign capital to invest in their respective economies.

So it is not surprising that the debate about the size of the middle class differs. Thus, for instance, in the case of India, there have been statements that at present the Indian middle class is larger than the entire population of USA!

So what is the basis of such figures? It appears that the size is more an estimation; and the figures would keep changing, if the growth rate continues to be high.

In the case of India, the figures for the middle class vary from a low of 50 million (McKinsey Global Institute, 2007) or 62 million (Barnard, 2006) to that go up to as high as 400 million.[16] But the one that is mentioned most is a figure of 250 million (Das, 2006) while some others mention 300 million – a figure repeated by former President of USA, George Bush, in his speeches before and during his trip to India in March 2006.[17] Perhaps the figures mentioned by a committee set up by the Government of India,[18] called popularly as Arjun Sengupta Committee report, is about 23 per cent[19] or 253 millions. However, as a well-known journalist points out, this large figure is valid only if the middle class is defined 'loosely'.[20] Thus, as per this definition, not only the 'slum dwellers' of Mumbai but those living in other smaller cities would also constitute part of the Indian middle class, even though many of them may lack some of the basic civic amenities.

Ninan (2005) writes that despite the evident emergence of a strong middle class, barely 10 per cent of all households have life insurance cover – traditionally the first form of savings for anyone with a reliable income flow and with dependants. And medical insurance is available for barely 1 per cent of all households.

Even some of the reports put forward by private companies show the existing picture as not very rosy for the middle class. For instance, the study of Shukla (2007) for an insurance company points out that even among the self-employed category there are a large number who do not take insurance cover even though one would expect them to be the first to do so; and this is the category that is growing.[21] Perhaps, the analysis in the same study in terms of income categories reveals an interesting picture. It is only the wealthier income sections that have some form of insurance cover.[22]

If consumption were the only criterion to identify the middle class, then the phenomenal increase in number of cell phones would make the middle class very large. Now, there are in urban areas persons who are very poor and wage labourers[23] but keep cell phones. Such persons would resemble an aspiring middle class, but the possession of simply a cell phone would not make them a part of middle class.

Perhaps this kind of criteria of considering those who consume as middle class reflects the interest of those who put forth this create a kind of myth – the myth of a large middle class. It reflects more the desire of capital to squeeze every penny from every source more akin to the argument of management guru Prahlad's (2005) argument that fortune can be made at the bottom of the pyramid, although it is a matter of doubt as to whether these neo-liberals believe in Prahlad's argument that poverty can be eradicated by such efforts.

Whatever be the actual figures, there seems to be a general consensus that the size of the middle class is growing and increasing in India[24] (and China) although it may not be at the rate claimed by private multinational companies. However, at this moment, it is difficult to gauge the impact the downturn in global economy, which began in late 2008, had on the growth of the middle class.[25] But, at the same time, it is interesting to note that there is a lot of expectation that the middle class of India (along with that of China) would help the world economy to reverse this economic downturn! As far as India is concerned, although the economic downturn has resulted in jobs being lost, with fears of more being lost in the near future, there is no noticeable change in attitude to consumerism reflecting perhaps new 'cultural signs' of displaying status and emphasising social rank in a society characterised by social inequality and hierarchy.

Increasing Consumerism: Differential Perspectives

How has the middle class reacted to this increasing consumerism? There are different perspectives of the new trend of consumerism.

Today, Indian democracy is not characterised by dominance of one party nor is it ruled by one dominant ideology. Ideological views and opinions differ as do the interpretation about the middle class itself. The Indian middle class is heterogeneous because it comprises persons of different castes[26] and religious, linguistic and ethnic groups. What is common to them may be their consumption of material goods and the importance given to this consumption as a social marker of status and class, and which may be termed as the 'middle class lifestyle'. Today, English language is a significant, although not the only, marker for this class; and it is this language, which unites them across their divergent caste, religious, linguistic and ethnic backgrounds. Discussing the role of English amongst the middle class, Scrase (2004) argues that English was the language of the middle class and it is by the usage of English that they maintain their hegemony. Now, with globalisation, the middle class considers English as an important cultural resource to negotiate globalisation.[27]

Although the middle class emerged with those who were involved in non-agrarian occupations, today, it would also include those who have one foot in agriculture and another in non-agrarian source of income. Such persons would include the farmer-businessmen and those others who earn from investments in shares, bonds and the like, or by combining blue- or white-collar work with agriculture.[28] For them English has become an important cultural capital to negotiate the globalising world.[29] With the growth of modern technology, including information and communication technology, it has become easier to lead urban middle class lifestyle in rural areas.[30]

In this kind of globalised situation, the middle class is influenced about different lifestyles by media and also partly because of migration. Appadurai (1997) says that more and more people consider a wider set of life styles than what they could think of before.

Some scholars have welcomed the new trends of consumerism. One such scholar is Das (2001). He points out to the emergence of a confident new middle class and at the same time how uninhibited and amoral it is in its approach to matters of displaying wealth. Das thinks that the new middle class is a sign of success of the country and its policies; for him the future of India is bright as he expects the numbers of middle class to increase. Unlike the old middle class – whose principle virtue was education and merit – the emerging new middle class is more concerned with self, and is street smart. It is driven by desire to achieve success monetarily and get things done; and its politics is driven by this goal.

But there are others who have been more critical. Varma (1998) was the first to point out that the emerging middle class was self-centred and was abdicating its responsibility to the poor and the nation as a whole. Over the years, the commitment to democracy and electoral process has declined. Further, he makes a case for middle class intellectual dishonesty. Hindi was not made the official language, as the middle class was comfortable with English; it favoured industrialism over agriculture as it was professionally more qualified to benefit from it. Finally, he states if the middle class is insensitive to the need of the poor, it does so at considerable risk of political instability, which will go against the very prosperity it so desires.

At the same time, there are critiques that express their apprehension about the new middle class being concerned only with the self. Fernandes (2000) is one such scholar who explains how the middle class while accepting new consumerism is actually insecure and is facing a situation parallel to that of the working class. But this has not led to political opposition to this growing consumerism and the changes in work relations and work culture.

Then, there are others who point out to ambivalence in the attitude of the middle class. Van Wessel (2004), a Dutch scholar, analyses the specific interaction of the consuming public with the images that are produced for them. According to her, the nation is a non-entity in the imagining of the emerging middle class. For them they do not see themselves as individuals or as a class to work for the poor or for the greater good of the nation. For them there is a crisis, but it is a moral crisis and is not based on doing 'good' to the nation or the poor. According to her, the middle class culture provides for people to dissociate themselves from consumer practice, in that it allows speakers to construct and present themselves as being '*in* the world but not *of* it', and this imparts agency to the individual who can use it for self-affirmation.

There is weight in Van Wessel's argument that the middle class does not consider it necessary to work for the poor – an argument, which gets reinforced with the kind of inadequate response to the earthquake in Kashmir (October 2005). In contrast to this was the response, which the middle class displayed to the earthquake in Kutch (Gujarat) in January 2001. Some consider the 2001 earthquake and the response to it as a 'middle class earthquake', owing to the overwhelming response and outpouring of aid by the middle class. This is attributed to the first images of destruction of middle class localities and elite areas of Ahmedabad and Surat (two big cities of Gujarat) that were broadcast by TV and other media, perhaps making them wonder, 'what if it happened to us'. It touched a chord in a class, which was and is known for being self-centred!

In India, this emerging middle class is increasingly insecure. There is the new culture of 'hire and fire'. Further, whatever social security was offered by the state is getting eroded. Indeed some have pointed out to this aspect of persistent insecurities. The newly emerging middle class attitudes have however changed. Perhaps this is seen in the way it has embraced the forces of globalisation and has become transnational in lifestyle.

Middle Class and Globalisation

The Indian middle class has increasingly become transnational in taste and lifestyle in the post-liberalisation era. This is a contrast to the situation in the first decade after independence, when nationalist feelings and tastes seemed to be widespread.

The Indian middle class perhaps was western and global, owing to the process of westernisation (Srinivas, 1966). Certain regions of India, like Gujarat and Punjab, had a long tradition – dating back to the 19th century – of persons going abroad for study or for work.[31] This continued throughout the 20th century. When opportunities opened up in Europe and America in the latter half of 20th century, migration to these areas became the most preferred choice. However, the migration to the developed countries of West got more pronounced with liberalisation of the economy, as many of the former restrictions on foreign travel got relaxed. The period of liberalisation of Indian economy coincided with the onset of growth and expansion of changes in information and communication technology. And, with the growth of the Indian economy, conspicuous consumption by the middle class increased and its lifestyle increasingly reflected global tastes and touch. To add to this, they are subject to transnational influence because of NRI (non-resident Indian) relatives. The Indian middle class at the end of the first decade of the 21st century had an established network of kin and family relations across the globe. In many a case these NRIs are wooed by the Indian political leadership[32] not only for investments but also for votes!

Thus, in the last two decades, one not only sees the middle class travelling abroad for holidays, but also consuming items which were previously only available in the developed world. This transnational dimension is also seen in the way the middle class send their members to developed countries for studies and/or to work.[33] This migration is seen amongst both the salaried and self-employed sections of the middle class.

While increasingly open, the middle class has also shown continuity to certain features of the past. Perhaps this is seen in matters to do with religion.

Middle Class and Religion

The Indian middle class has perhaps always had an ambivalent attitude to matters of religion. During the independence movement, in the late 19th and early 20th century, religion was the backbone for many of the leaders of nationalist movement – be it Bal Gangadhar Tilak, Lala Lajpat Rai or Bipin Chandra Pal (Misra, 1961). There was similarly a religious revivalism amongst Muslims then. But, the success of Russian Revolution of 1917 had its impact on India and its middle classes, leading to the emergence of reformist/radical and secular leaders like Jawaharlal Nehru and others. So in the early years of independence and thereafter, perhaps owing to the dominating influence of radical left ideas, the middle class in India did not display it religious proclivities publicly in spheres and arenas considered secular, like institutions of learning. But, with the collapse of communism in Eastern Europe in late eighties and the decline of Soviet Union itself in 1991, and with China itself embracing capitalist market in a big way, leftist ideology, especially Marxism, has had a set back. Along with it the practice of secular lifestyle took a beating in general. The ideological vacuum thus created it appears has been filled by religion. The revival of religions in the countries of Eastern Europe has led to religious leaders coming to positions of influence once again. This has coincided with forces of globalisation. All these changes have had an impact on the Indian middle class as well.

The middle class is now socially diverse with persons belonging to different castes; but in matters of religion, the way it gets organised and displayed has changed. Now, there are a variety of religious sects (amongst Hindus) that have followers from different castes and linguistic groups.[34]

Another feature is the visible display of religion in areas, which were considered taboo.[35] It is this assertion of religiosity, especially by the Hindu middle class community, which is something new. This assertion is now seen more and more amongst the salaried section of the middle class. The self-employed sections perhaps did display their religiosity in the past as well just as they tend to do now. The business communities mostly follow the Hindu religious calendar. The day after the Hindu festival of 'Deepavali' is the beginning of the new year when accounts books used to be opened with a 'puja' (ceremony of worship) to Goddess Lakshmi (the goddess of wealth) for a fruitful and profitable year.

Now, what is seen is that, in institutions considered secular and patronised by the middle class, like colleges and universities, buildings and institutions would be named after some religious head of a Hindu sect.

Another feature seen more frequently is that the person nominated to a high office performs (Hindu) rituals in the chamber before assuming office.

Parallel to this assertion of religiosity, is the usage of modern technology and means of communication – be it internet, computer or mobile phone – by religious organisations to reach out to their followers world wide, including those belonging to the middle class. Thus, it is not surprising to see the usage of a modern assembly line approach in the production of CDs, DVDs, and sending them to various destinations just like that of a marketing network of multinational companies.[36] Religion and marketing of religious material has adapted to changes in technology fast, facilitating the Indian Hindu diaspora to their religious leaders back home.

Further, this modern technology has helped in establishing a trans-national religious market, linking middle class clients in villages (like seen in rural Gujarat) to their patrons in USA or UK.[37]

The expanding middle class is now comprised of persons belonging to diverse caste, ethnic and linguistic backgrounds. Those belonging to lower castes undergo a process of sanskritisation (Srinivas, 1966). This is seen in various upper caste rituals being practised by those castes, which hitherto did not practise them.[38] But this middle class has in the process also redefined the very process itself, as it has imbued this process with what may be called western influence and values. Amongst some of the religious sects of Hindus, women now do *havans,*[39] which they previously were not allowed to do. At the same time, there are certain practices and festivals[40] of lower castes, which are now celebrated with gusto by middle class persons belonging to lower castes. These two instances illustrate a new way of accommodating religious practices (of lower castes) and at the same time reinventing Hinduism so as to give more space to women. We now see the co-existence of elements of tradition and modern. Thus, there is continuity of traditional normative structure while at the same time embracing consumerism in a big way to assert ones 'modern' and 'higher' status.

Middle Class and Women

One of the interesting features of the emerging middle class in India is the visibility of women in spheres, which hitherto were dominated by men. One of India's pro-business weeklies *India Today*, brought out a special issue on women, where they write in a lauding manner how the urban Indian woman is 'doing it all' – be it the kind of work she does and the choices she is making[41] regarding her own lifestyle. Whether this visibility has made a difference to bring about a change in the patriarchal norms and usher in gender-just lives, or does it reflect an increased presence in the organised sector, could be a matter of debate. But, this visibility of woman in India amongst the middle class has increased or paralleled with the growth of the women's movement since the 1980s.

Women, especially from the middle class, took the initiative and have provided leadership to the women's movement. Today, the women's movement is diverse and has different ideological strands. Women's activists have started focusing on separate areas of interest. Thus, there are those who work on health concerns of women, others on developmental issues, while others on political aspects, and so on. All this has resulted in a robust NGO sector of women's organisations, a movement well spread and effective and which has been in the forefront of a variety of issues concerning women. This has had its impact in a number of spheres – be it business, bureaucracy, media, sports, armed forces, professions like law, medicine, management and so on. In the newly emerging service sector of BPOs, women have been recruited in large numbers. But they have to work in night shifts, as the working time in USA happens to be night time in India. This has led to redefining the family norms (of women having to work out late in the night). At the same time, during this period, cases of discrimination against women have come out more in the open. This has resulted in defining the boundaries of decent behaviour in the workplace, and attempting to make life for women better in general and especially for working women belonging to the middle class in particular.

However, along with these developments, there has been one very disturbing trend. There appears to be no change in the society regarding preference for sons. The strong preference for sons, reflecting the continuance of patriarchy, has resulted in using modern technology to determine the sex of the unborn child. This has in turn led to a decline in sex ratio in an alarming manner. Activists of women's movement brought this into relief during the last decade and half. However, the issue of declining sex ratio concerns more the newly emerging middle class than the poorer sections of society.

In India, strangely, the more developed states, like Punjab, Haryana, Gujarat and Maharashtra have a declining sex ratio. The ratio has declined sharply in the age group 0–6 during the last two decades! These are the states, which have developed economically[42] and are held out as models for others! Further, in these states, the developed urban regions have a much lower sex ratio as compared to the rural areas. The sex ratio amongst the upper social strata is lower (Edlund, 1999) than those lower in the social hierarchy. Further, 'discrimination against girls has found to increase with prosperity and education level of mothers in India'.[43] The abuse of modern medical technology has affected the middle class sections most.

The medical fraternity, especially doctors, who are considered the icon of the middle class, has been hand in glove in this nefarious activity of sex-selective abortion, well known now as 'female foeticide'. It is often justified by those in the medical fraternity saying, 'If the people want it, why should we not give it. Do they not have a right to decide the sex of the child they want?' The greed for money seems to be distorting the values of some doctors; and the extent to which these doctors violate medical ethics, rules and regulations, is now coming out in the open. Women's organisations were the first to take the initiative to point to this issue. Now, the media has also started exposing the role of doctors and their nefarious activities.[44] The attempt by such exposures is to bring about a change in attitudes in society to the issue of female foeticide and also force the authorities to take action against the doctors who connive in this practice and violate the law.

Women's organisations have also pointed out that in the Indian context the shortage of women would have shocking and disastrous consequences.[45] In Haryana, this has already led to cases of kidnapping of women and forcing such women into marriage. In some cases, a woman has been married to a group of brothers! In some villages, no '*barat*'[46] has been seen for a long time. In states like Gujarat, there are reports of tribal women being brought as brides amongst certain 'high' communities. The shortage of women does not follow the rules of market. Instead of raising their status (as women are in short supply), it has only resulted in making their life more miserable!

Conclusions

In the above analysis, we have tried to trace the continuity and changes in Indian middle class. The old middle class exhibited probity in public and showed concern for others; now, the new middle class is brash in lifestyle exhibiting self-centred consumerism. This increasing consumerism is accompanied by increasing insecurity in the conditions of employment and insecurity. This ambivalence in attitude is visible to the increasing consumerism.

Another feature is the increasing religiosity of the middle class, and this is visible especially among the Hindu component. While religiosity has increased, there is also attempt to reinvent it, where women have been given more roles in rituals and practices.

The middle class has become global in taste, lifestyle and consumption. Women belonging to the middle class have got more and more opportunities to take to new occupations emerging in the new economy like BPO sector. However, in some regions of India, especially in the north and western states, there is also a worrying phenomenon – the sex ratio has been declining amongst the middle classes, indicating still a strong 'son preference' in spite of increase in wealth and education. All this portends to a difficult future for the middle class, which shows that while consumerism has become the status marker of having arrived to show off rank and status, the reinventing of religion and the declining sex ratio in the states in which the middle class is growing, seems to reflect the continuance of traditional hierarchical normative structure.

Notes

1. There is a widespread view that liberalisation of Indian economy in 1991 took place because of pressures of IMF and World Bank, called neo-liberal agenda. The structural adjustment policies advocated by 'Washington Consensus' put forward by economist John Williamson (2004) for countries of Latin America were those to which countries like India accepted in 1991, when faced with an economic crisis in balance of payments.
2. Changes in information and communication technology took place in the western world, specifically USA first before coming to India.
3. The terms 'new' and 'old' are used heuristically; Singh (1985) uses this distinction as well.
4. Another argument is that English got entrenched because of the bureaucracy. See Stevenson (2005).
5. Beteille (2007: 952) says that this middle class 'had a very great influence in creating and sustaining the open and secular institutions which carried forward the modernization of India. The middle class was not only small in size, it was also socially exclusive. Hindus belonging to a handful of upper castes predominated in it and the backward castes and religious minorities were disproportionately few in number, particularly in superior professional, managerial and administrative positions'.
6. Beteille (2007: 48) says 'the polarization thesis, or the thesis of increasing antagonism between the bourgeoisie and the proletariat, which was the fulcrum of the Marxian approach to class, appeared to be increasingly at odds with the reality of industrial societies as they moved from the 19th to the 20th century'.
7. Some persons consider this work as the equivalent work of physical labourers, as they are at the lowest end of the social prestige spectrum.
8. 'Khadi' is the Hindi word for homespun cotton. Mahatma Gandhi popularised Khadi.
9. VRS refers to 'voluntary retirement scheme' introduced by some companies. It is a way to lay of employees by offering them a lump sum financial amount as compensation for retrenching them. Although called 'voluntary', there is an element of coercion as the employee has very little choice. He is cornered to accept this 'lump sum' compensation package or work on terms which are difficult, like lower wages, usually at a different place, and the like. Even for those who have accepted the compensation package, there are stories of persons who have been paid only a part of what they have been promised! In some cases, the amount promised is released in installments and usually after pressure is

brought upon the management. This involves expenditure and very often the person fighting the legal battle loses a good chunk of the compensation amount in the process.

10. Fernandes (2000) makes this point effectively. She points out how there is acceptance of the change without much protest.
11. The senior army officers involved include the Adarsh housing society scam, the Sukhna land scam in the Darjeeling area, and the civil servants include the IAS officer couple in MP from whose house huge amount of money was found. To add to this list are the allegations against senior members of the judiciary.
12. Perhaps this was and is still seen in the world of real estate, where there is a 'white' component and a 'black' component when one purchases real estate. It has now expanded to more sectors in the last decade.
13. See Singh (1985), Rajaram (2007) and Bose (2007).
14. This rosy picture is more often to do with the image of India becoming 'big' consumer society for what would be considered 'luxurious' or 'iconic' of higher status. For instance, see the following report *India to be world's 3rd Biggest Car Market by 2020*, put forward by Market Research Firm (http://autos.in.msn.com/autonews/article.aspx?cp-documentid=4947542), accessed on 17 March 2011. Another report by McKinsey *Next Big Spenders: India's Middle Class* (http://www.mckinsey.com/mgi/mginews/bigspenders.asp), accessed on 10 March 2011.
15. 'What Firms Need to Succeed in India, China', *Business Week*, 7 April 2006 (http://in.rediff.com/money/2006/apr/07bspec.htm), retrieved on 7 April 2006. On the other hand, Van Wessel (2004) mentions that the middle class is usually estimated at 100 to 350 million people, depending on the criteria employed.
16. The figures vary according to the criteria employed. The figure of 400 million is from *Himalayan Trade Travel Journal* (http://www.httj.com.np/feb_2005/pata.htm), retrieved on 21 February 2006. On the other hand, Van Wessel (2004) mentions that the middle class is usually estimated at 100 to 350 million people, depending on the criteria employed. (Repetition)
17. This figure is also high. The NCAER study took household annual income of 1800 dollars as the minimum for middle-income families; at this income level, Indian families can purchase motorbikes, televisions and refrigerator.
18. This report is titled *Report on the Conditions of Work and Promotion of Livelihoods in the Unorganised Sector* and was set up by the National Commission for Enterprises in the Unorganised Sector, New Delhi (Chairman: Dr Arjun Sengupta). The report was submitted in August 2007 (www.nceus.nic.in: *Report on the Conditions of Work and Promotion of Livelihoods in the Unorganised Sector*).

19. See *Report on the Conditions of Work and Promotion of Livelihoods in the Unorganised Sector*, Table 1.2, p. 6.
20. T.N. Ninan, editor of *Business Standard*, quotes this figure of 300 million (see Ninan 2005). *Business Standard* along with the National Council of Applied Economic Research collaborated in a market survey in India of 300,000 households. The Arjun Sengupta Committee Report considers those who earn an amount as low as ` 20 per capita per day in 2004–05, as belonging to middle income group!
21. Shukla (2007: 61) points out in Table 5.1 that only 36.3 per cent of the self-employed category in their survey had an insurance policy.
22. See Shukla (2007: 60). In Figure 5.4, he shows that in terms of his income categorization, the insurance ownership amongst those who would be considered lower categories of 'middle income' has a low insurance ownership.
23. In urban areas, I have seen rag pickers using cell phones to collect garbage in the recent past; while in rural areas, as my students pointed out in early March 2011 for a tribal district Narmada (in Gujarat), tribal wage labourers had cell phones even in villages where there was no network coverage. They used the phone to listen to music.
24. The Arjun Sengupta Committee found that the middle-income category grew from 18 to 23 per cent! (See *Report on the Conditions of Work and Promotion of Livelihoods in the Unorganised Sector*, paragraph 1.30, p. 7).
25. Media reports tend to be contradictory and conflicting. Thus, when President Obama decided not to give tax breaks to companies which outsourced jobs, one Gujarati newspaper (*The Gujarat Samachar*, Vadodara, 6 May 2009) published on its front page in an eight column headline – 10 lakh Indian professionals struck by Obama! On the same day, *The Times of India* (Ahmedabad edition, 6 May 2009) carried a news item that nearly 50,000 employees in India could be handed pink slips (i.e., euphemism for job loss).
26. For the emergence amongst the Dalits, see Ram (1988). See Sheth (1999) for another perspective.
27. For an interesting discussion of the changing role of English in India and how different sections have been reacting to it, see Prasad (2006). For an interesting account in Bengal, see Roy (1994).
28. This kind of situation is seen in various regions of India like Gujarat, Punjab, Haryana, Maharashtra, Tamil Nadu, Andhra Pradesh, Karnataka and Kerala.
29. There is mushrooming of schools called 'English' medium schools in big villages and towns. Many of them tend to have names, which appear Christian, owing to the association of missionaries with imparting of education in English. Thus, there would be a name like 'St. Kabir'! Some ignoramus would pronounce it as 'Sant Kabir' school! A recent media report mentions that English as a medium of instruction in primary

schools occupies second position by 2007; and the growth has been remarkable in most states, increasing in some by threefold in some states. (http://epaper.timesofindia.com/Default/Scripting/ArticleWin.asp?From=Archive&Source=Page&Skin=TOINEW&BaseHref=TOIA/2009/12/05&PageLabel=1&EntityId=Ar00102&ViewMode=HTML&GZ=T), accessed on 5 December 2009.

30. Income from agriculture is not taxable; and thus there are a number of middle-class entrepreneurs who are using modern technology in agriculture to do business across the world.
31. Gandhi and Sardar Patel are two names from Gujarat who went to UK to study. Migration to East Africa, Southern Africa and countries like Fiji had persons from Gujarat going in late nineteenth century.
32. NRIs being wooed for investment is not uncommon; and there are regular conclaves held for this purpose in various states. But in the 2009 elections to the Lok Sabha, the Chief Minister of Gujarat who is a leading light of BJP was seen in a video release addressing specifically NRIs and asking these NRIs to tell their relatives in India to vote for BJP. Many groups working and promoting Hinduism in other countries exist in various countries of the world. The largest number of websites on Hinduism exists outside India.
33. Many middle-class students take loans either from private sources or from institutional sources to go and study and/or work abroad.
34. To mention a few from western India, there are groups like Swaminarayan who have followers from different castes – although Patels predominate, or Vaishanavs (where Banias predominate) or Art of Living of Sai Baba and Art of Living or Asa Ram Bapu where the followers cut across linguistic boundaries and castes. Thus, the situation seems to have changed for Swaminarayan from what Hardiman found in 1988. Today, there are persons from other castes – although not in significant numbers as well, as we found while interviewing Swaminarayan leaders for another study. This is true for other religious sects amongst Hindus and groups. They all seem to be competing between themselves to attract more and more followers by using modern technology by organising huge gatherings regularly.
35. The minority religious communities like Muslims, Christians, Sikhs and others did enjoy certain benefits under the constitution to run institutions to serve and preserve their community identity. Now they have started carrying their religious identity by emphasizing on markers to distinguish them from others. It may be wearing the burqa to the college; and I have found that burqa-wearing girls mixing with opposite sex in ways no different from non-burqa wearing girls. But it is the assertion by the majority Hindu community – that is new; so now middle-class Hindu men come with tilak on their forehead to the class; or the officials in universities performing Hindu pooja before beginning their duties. On one occasion, while taking a viva voce exam in a room in a university in

Maharashtra, the person concerned in whose room we were made to take the exam, came and disrupted the examination as the pooja had to be performed. The examiner was asked to vacate the chair, as the person sat and completed the pooja.

36. Thus, in a study on how Swadhyaya, Swaminarayan sects, in which I was associated during 2000 to 2003, I saw the way these sects produce and send their literature and other material to various corners of the world.
37. During a fieldwork in rural areas of Kheda and Anand district, I have come across instances where internet was used to get orders to print religious material, calendars and so on from clients in USA/UK.
38. This includes upper-caste ceremonies like 'seemanth', performed in the seventh month of pregnancy of first child. In addition, the middle case and lower caste wear the cross thread while performing havans.
39. Havan is the ritual prayer in which offerings are made to sacred fire. 'Gayatri parivaar', a Hindu sect, now allow Hindu women to do the offerings along with their husbands.
40. One example of this is the celebration of '*dasha maata*' (literally meaning goddess of condition) celebrated by the lower castes that at one time were poor, continue to do so with gusto. Usually this festival involves the immersion of goddess in a pond late in the night.
41. 'Women's Special Issue', *India Today* (2006), April 24. One article even mentions that India has 15 million working women across 25 cities. This workforce has increased by 10 per cent between 1993 and 2003, which the study claims is based on a survey of 10,150 women, across 28 locations ('She Buys to Conquer', pp. 34–35). Traditionally, there has been asymmetrical structural relationship between male and female workers. Women's participation in organised employment is low; it was as low as '22 per cent'; but in unorganised sector occupations, majority of them are women (see Venkataratnam and Jain 2002).
42. See (a) *Census of India 2001, Provisional Population Totals*, Chapter 6: Sex Composition of the Population (www.censusindia.net/data/chapter6); (b) Patel (2003); (c) Retherford and Roy (2003).
43. Edlund (1999: 280) quotes from other studies to substantiate this claim. This is supported by NFHS data as well (see note 23).
44. The first case was in the state of Haryana in March 2006. This made headlines. On 7 April 2006, another news channel, Sahara Samay, has been exposing the role of doctors (including lady doctors) in Rajasthan (Chittaurgarh, Jaipur, Hanumangardh, Ajmer, Dhaulpur districts), Madhya Pradesh (Gwalior) Uttar Pradesh (Agra), Gujarat (Palanpur). These sting operations perhaps hope to shame the medical fraternity to give up this practice of abetting in this crime. The news channel claims that they have caught 100 doctors involved in this crime!
45. The recent release of provisional population totals for 2011 indicates that the overall sex ratio for the 0–6 age category has further declined to

914 in 2011 from 920 in 2011 (http://www.thehindu.com/news/national/article1587153.ece?homepage=true&css=print) accessed on 31 March 2011.

46. *Barat* is the wedding procession of the groom; the groom comes to the bride's place for wedding. The expenditure of the wedding is borne by the bride's family.

References

Appadurai, Arjun (1997). *Modernity at Large: Cultural Dimensions of Globalization*, Delhi: Oxford University Press.

Banerjee, Abhijit V. and Esther Duflo (2008). 'What is Middle Class about the Middle Classes around the World?', *The Journal of Economic Perspectives*, 22 (2), Spring: 3–28 (http://www.jstor.org/stable/27648239), accessed on 22 March 2011.

Barnard, Patrick (2006). 'When it Comes to China and India, Technology Companies Must Be Patient' (http://news.tmcnet.com/news/2006/jan/1278146.htm), retrieved on 11 March 2006.

Beteille, Andre (2007). *Marxism and Class Analysis*, Delhi: Oxford University Press.

Bose, Pradip (2007). 'Emerging Middle Class in India and China', in Chumling Li (ed.), *International Forum Middle Class Research with Comparative Perspective*, Conference Papers, Beijing: Sociology Institute, Chinese Academy of Social Sciences, pp. 154–60.

Census of India (2001). *Provisional Population Totals*, Chapter 6: Sex Composition of the Population (retrieved from www.censusindia.net/data/chapter 6).

—— (2011). *Provisional Population Totals*, Office of the Registrar General, March (http://www.censusindia.gov.in/2011-prov-results/data_files/pov_popu_total_ppt_2011.pdf).

Das, Gurcharan (2001). *India Unbound*, New York: Knopf.

—— (2006). 'The India Model', *Foreign Affairs*, July/August (http://www.foreignaffairs.org/20060701faessay85401/gurcharan-das/the-india-model.html), retrieved on 1 June 2007.

Edlund, Lena (1999). 'Son Preference, Sex Ratios, and Marriage Patterns', *Journal of Political Economy*, 107 (6), Part 1, December: 1275–1304 (http://www.jstor.org), retrieved on 8 April 2006.

Fernandes, Leela (2000). 'Restructuring the New Middle Class in Liberalizing India', *Comparative Studies of South Asia, Africa and Middle East*, 20 (1 and 2): 1–25.

Government of India (2007). *Report on the Conditions of Work and Promotion of Livelihoods in the Unorganised Sector*, National Commission for Enterprises in the Unorganised Sector (Chairman: Arjun Sengupta), New Delhi.

Hardiman, David (1988). 'Class Base of Swaminarayan Sect', *Economic and Political Weekly*, 23 (37), September 10: 1907–12 (http://www.jstor.org/stable/4379024), accessed on 22 March 2011.

McKinsey Global Institute (2007). *The Bird of Golad: The Rise of India's Consumer Market*, San Francisco.

Menon, Purnima, Anil Deolalikar and Anjor Bhaskar (2009). *Comparison of Hunger Across States: India State Hunger Index*, Washington, DC: International Food Policy Research Institute, Welt Hunger Hilfe, University of California, Riverside.

Misra, B.B. (1961). *The Indian Middle Class*, London: Oxford University Press.

Ninan, T.N. (2005). 'Middle Class has Arrived', *Business Standard*, July 2.

Osella, Fillipo and Caroline Osella (1999). 'From Transience to Immanence: Consumption, Life-Cycle and Social Mobility in Kerala, South India', *Asian Studies*, 33 (4), October: 989–1020 (http://www.jstor.org/stable/313107), accessed on 22 March 2011.

Patel, Vibhuti (2003). 'Political Economy of Missing Girls', paper presented in the Seminar on Missing Girls in India: Science, Gender Relations, and the Political Economy of Emotions, Delhi: Department of Sociology, University of Delhi, October (http://www.feministagenda.org.au/Missing%20girls1.htm), retrieved on 7 April 2006.

Prahlad, C.K. (2005). *The Fortune at the Bottom of the Pyramid: Eradicating Poverty through Profits*, New Jersey: Pearson.

Prasad, G.J.V.P. (2006). 'A Minute Stretching into Centuries: Macaulay, English, and India', *Nineteenth Century Prose*, 33 (2), Fall: 175–96.

Rajagopal, Arvind (2001). *Politics after Television*, Cambridge: Cambridge University Press.

Rajaram, N. (2007). 'The Emerging Middle Class in India and China: Issues and Concerns', in Chumling Li (ed.), *International Forum Middle Class Research with Comparative Perspective*, Conference Papers, Beijing: Sociology Institute, Chinese Academy of Social Sciences, pp. 161–77.

Ram, Nandu (1988). *The Mobile Scheduled Castes: Rise of a New Middle Class*, Delhi: Hindustan Publishing Corporation.

Retherford, Robert and T.K. Roy (2003). 'Factors Affecting Sex-Selective Abortion in India and 17 Major States', *National Family Health Survey Reports*, No. 21, New Delhi (http://pdf.dec.org/pdf_docs/PNACR987.pdf#search=%27declining%20sex%20ratio%20in%20India), retrieved on 1 December 2009.

Roy, Madhumita (1994). 'Englishing India': Reinstituting Class and Social Privilege', *Social Text*, 39, Summer: 83–109.

Scrase, Timothy J. (2004). 'The Hegemony of English in India', paper presented in the 15th Biennial Conference of Asian Studies Association of Australia in Canberra, 29 June to 2 July (http://coombs.anu.edu.au/SpecialProj/ASAA/biennial-conference/2004/Scrase-T1–ASAA2004.pdf), retrieved on 20 April 2006.

Shah, Ghanshyam (1987). 'Middle Class Politics: Case of Anti-Reservation Agitations in Gujarat', *Economic and Political Weekly*, 22 (19/21), May: AN157– AN172 (http://www.jstor.org/stable/4377019), accessed on 22 March 2011.

Sheth, D.L. (1999). 'Secularisation of Caste and Making of New Middle Class', *Economic and Political Weekly*, 34 (34/35), August 21–September 3: 2502–10.

Shukla, Rajesh (2007). 'How India Earns, Spends and Saves Results from The Max New York', *NCAER India Financial Protection Survey* (http://www.maxnewyorklife.com/pdf/MNYL-NCAER%20Book%20–%20How%20India%20Earns,%20Spends%20and%20Saves.pdf), accessed on 1 March 2011.

Singh, Gurcharan (1985). *The New Middle Class in India*, Jaipur: Rawat Publications.

Singh, Yogendra (ed.) (1978). 'Traditional Cultural Values and Contemporary Challenges', in *Essays on Modernization in India*, Delhi: Manohar, pp. 176–89.

Srinivas, M.N. (1996). *Social Change in Modern India*, Bombay: Allied Publishers.

Stevenson, Jane (2005). 'Take My Word for It', Review of *Empires of the World: Language History of the World* by Nicholas Ostler, *The Observer*, March 13 (http://books.guardian.co.uk/reviews/history/0,,1436277,00.html), retrieved on 1 November 2009.

Van Wessel, Margit (2004). 'How an Indian Middle Class Dissociates from Middle Class Life', *Cultural Dynamics*, 16 (1): 93–116.

Varma, Pavan K. (1998). *The Great Indian Middle Class*, New Delhi: Viking.

Venkataratnam, C.S. and Harish C. Jain (2002). 'Women in Trade Unions in India', *International Journal of Manpower*, 23 (3): 277–92.

Williamson, John (2004). 'The Washington Consensus as Policy Prescription for Development', a lecture in the series *Practitioners of Development* delivered at World Bank, 13 January 2004 (http://www.iie.com/publications/papers/williamson0204.pdf), retrieved on 26 December 2009.

Wright, Erik Olin (2007). 'Three Logics of Class Analysis', in Chumling Li (ed.), *International Forum Middle Class Research with Comparative Perspective*, Conference Papers, Beijing: Sociology Institute, Chinese Academy of Social Sciences, pp. 1–9.

8

Emerging Patterns of Income and Consumption in China

Some Evidence on Rural-Urban Gaps

SURJIT SINGH

China has transformed itself during the last 30 odd years, posting extraordinary rates of growth and increasing the living standards of nearly all its citizens. At the same time, it has become a far less equal nation, with vast differences emerging between those living in rural and urban areas, inland and coastal areas, and globally-oriented and more insular areas. High growth, coupled with rising inequality, has fostered social tension, raising question about the sustainability of the country's economic transformation. In the face of increasing income inequality among Chinese provinces over the past two decades, three important facts emerge. First, economic growth has lifted living standards throughout China, with all provinces gaining in absolute terms. Second, economic growth has benefited some provinces more than others, increasing regional income inequality. Third, no single explanation can account for the steady increase in inequality among provinces over time.[1] These observations suggest that China, like many other industrialised nations, will continue to struggle to meet its growth goals while distributing the benefits of an expanding economy more equally. In this context, one of the top priorities of current Chinese economic policy is the increasing disparity in income, which is rightly perceived as the stumbling block in the path to a 'harmonious society'.[2] There is an almost universal consensus that economic disparities have grown relentlessly since the mid-nineties, and the issue is also related to big challenges in Chinese nation-building, in particular with respect to the so-called western development issue (Goodman, 2004). There is no doubt that now rural development is the centre stage of economic policies of China.[3] China had set a growth target of 7 per cent for 2011–15 which is lower than it had in the previous plan, suggesting that the pattern of growth now matters as much as the speed. As per China's Prime Minister Wen Jiabao's speech in the National Peoples' Congress (NPC) held on 15 March 2011, the country's development is neither balanced or coordinated nor sustainable. It relies too heavily on investment and on swallowing natural resources and too little on consumer spending. The income generated is unevenly divided: between profits and wages, rich and poor households, coastal provinces and inland regions, the cities and the countryside (see, Tao and Fang, 2000). He squarely blamed the state-owned enterprises' (SOEs) hunger for cheap credit from state banks and recycling of outsized profits as a cause of unbalanced development (*The Economist*, 2011: 29). Also, the central government's spending on education, health care and social security was to increase by more than 16 per cent and on subsidised housing by more than a third (*The Economist*, 2011a: 28).[4] It is against this backdrop that this paper looks at the emerging patterns in income and consumption in China.

Income Inequalities

China's high growth rates have allowed it to become the second largest economy in the world since 2010. However, high growth rates have also been accompanied by an unprecedented rise in income inequality. The Gini index of income inequality increased from 31 in 1981 to 44.73 in 2002 (Ravallion and Chen, 2004). Besides this, the calculation by the International Institute for Urban Development in Beijing had put China's Gini coefficient at 0.438 in 2010, which meant China was fractionally more unequal than in 2005, when the Gini coefficient was 0.425 (World Bank, 2005). China's wealth gap raises concerns about its development path as the National Bureau of Statistics data show that the top 10 per cent of households control around 32 per cent of income. The 2011 CHIP survey, of 8,000 households across China, suggests a much greater level of inequality, with the top 10 per cent controlling 56 per cent of income and 86 per cent of wealth.[5] It is considerably higher share of income than one suggested by the official National Bureau of Statistics and points to a worrying level of inequality. Similar surveys in 1995 and 2002 found that China's top 10 per cent controlled just 30 per cent and 41 per cent of wealth, respectively. Concentrating wealth in the hands of China's few has implications for both financial and social stability. According to Naughton (2007: 218), 'There may be no other case where a society's income distribution has deteriorated so much, so fast'. Not surprisingly, 'In the course of two decades China has gone from being one of the most egalitarian societies about as equal as Japan, to being more unequal than the United States' (ibid.). This increase in income inequality has attracted wide attention in recent decades. Ravallion and Chen (2004) also point out that the pattern of growth matters and inequality has emerged as a concern for both growth and poverty reduction. They also found that inequality has been rising, though not continuously and more so in some periods and provinces. China no doubt has made strong strides to eradicate poverty, but the progress has been uneven.[6] Rural economic growth reduced inequality in both urban and rural areas, as well as between them. It is also found that provinces with rapid growth did not bring more rapid increases in inequality. In fact, during 1981–2001, the provinces that saw a more rapid rise in inequality saw less progress against poverty. CHIP 2011 survey also found that 55 per cent of China's households had little or no savings for the year. This is against the perception that the farmers and migrant workers save to pay for education, health care and pensions.[7] Further, the Gini coefficient was 0.56 in urban households and 0.60 in rural households, compared with a global average of 0.44 in 2010 (CHIP survey, 2011).[8] Fan and Sun (2006) find that there are three distinct phases in the trend in regional inequality in China: in the 1980s inter-provincial inequality declined, in the 1990s the eastern region grew rapidly and inter-regional inequality surged and in the late 1990s and 2006 across provinces, regions growth rates of per capita GDP exhibited some convergence while Wu (2006) showed that regional economies have experienced different rates of convergence during 1978–1997 and it was fast in the late 1970s and early 1980s. The two non-coastal regions converged faster than the coastal economies.

Many studies attribute rising inequality to varying general factors, mainly related to urban-rural inequality (see Shi, Zhao and Zhang, 1998; Wu and Perloff, 2005; Wang et al., 2007; Xueliang, 2010). In fact, the relationship between urban-rural income differences and overall inequality can be easily contrasted by reference to the parallel evolution of the urban-rural gap[9] and the Gini index (Figures 1 and 2).

Causes of the Emerging Inequalities

China started out in 1978 with everyone equally poor but later as incomes started rising it was natural that inequality would also rise. This inequality was accentuated by policies that benefited factory owners, and not the mass of workers. A growing divide between have and have-nots has far-reaching implications for China's future growth.[10] The redistribution of income is the key to raising China's consumption because low-income households spend a higher share of their income than rich households. Household consumption in China came down from 46 per cent of its GDP in 2000 to just 34.9 per cent in 2011 and substantially below the 70 per cent rate in the US. With investment producing diminishing returns and export growth falling,

Figure 1

China's Urban-Rural Inequality and Gini Index (1978–2007)

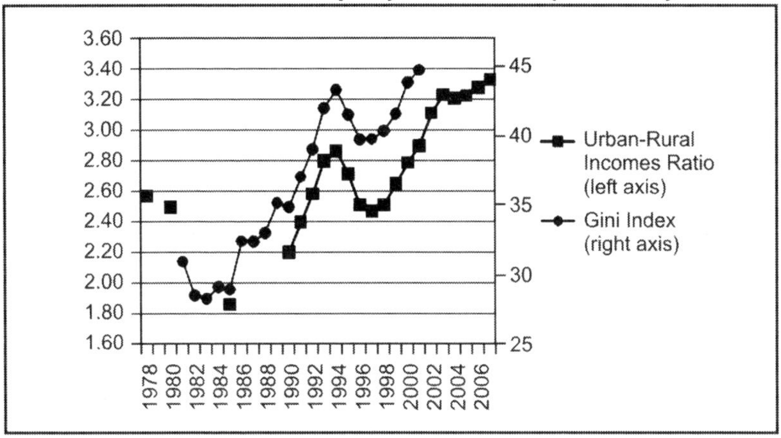

Source: Simarro (2012).

Figure 2

Top Incomes and Gini Index

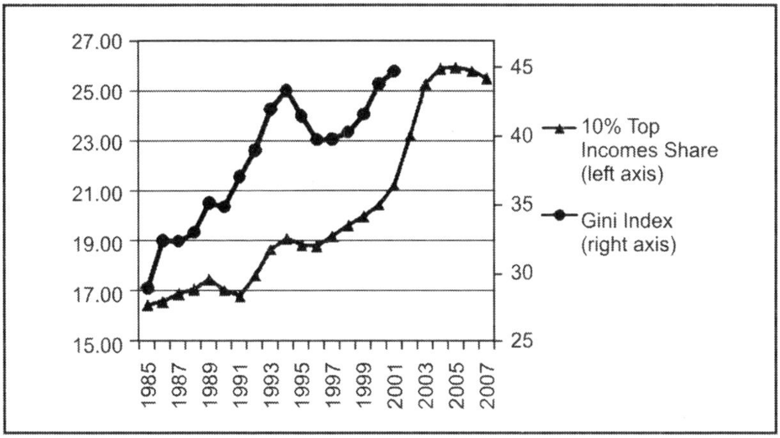

Source: Simarro (2012).

raising consumption has become crucial to keeping growth on track. Inequality in the distribution of income also raises fears of social instability. It is also argued that the link is not straightforward; it is a subjective popular perception of fairness or unfairness, not objective income and wealth trends that contribute to instability. Thus, causes of rising unequal income distribution are related to many factors, including the impact of reforms and effectiveness of government policies to deal with emerging inequalities.

- Since the 1980s, ownership system in China has witnessed significant changes. The public sector's share has been declining since 1978, whereas the share of non-public sector has been growing. In this transformation of ownership, some people have accumulated a huge sum of wealth. Even the workers in the non-public sector earn more than those in the public sector.
- International evidence has proved that education has important influence upon income inequality in the medium and long run. Education plays a vital role in explaining the widening income gap in China today.[11]
- The reform process of the SOEs in China has also influenced the pattern of income distribution. While some SOEs have made great achievements in terms of raising productivity and efficiency, thus making it possible to raise wages/bonus for workers, others, however, have been slow or even unable to make adjustment to adapt to the changing market conditions and failed to provide the workers with higher wages/bonus. Many SOEs were closed leading to retrenchment of workers and thus no income.
- Some workers are afraid of being laid off; others are lucky enough to gain wealth through all means – legal or illegal. For example, some could acquire state assets by 'buying' or 'leasing' an SOE at a low price and runs it as a family business; others enriched themselves by smuggling, making faked goods, obtaining funds through bribery, monopolising the market, evading taxes, etc. This leads to resentment and anger against such rich and voices are loud to call upon the government to take effective measures to stop them from accumulating more wealth.
- Some experts blame the tax regime in China, which is not effective at improving income distribution.[12]
- As China had joined the WTO in January 2002, its tariffs for more than 5,300 items of imports were lowered, and the average rate cut being 15.3 per cent to 12 per cent. With its economy more integrated with the globalisation, China is facing new challenges in many areas, including the prospects of income distribution.[13]
- On the whole, WTO membership is positive for its economic development, but the distribution of benefits is not even across sectors and regions. Thus, some segments of the society are getting much than others, thus causing inequality of income distribution more conspicuous.[14]
- It is also argued that the widening income gap is being caused by restricting small- and medium-sized companies from entering high-profit sectors, as well as by employment discrimination. The

wage gap between finance and agriculture, earning the highest and lowest wages respectively, has widened to a ratio of 4.2 in 2010 from 2.24 in 1997. Low standards for labour and environmental protection have increased the wealth of the rich at the cost of the health and income of the poor.

- Urban housing privatisation and the development of urban residential real estate markets, expansion of stock and capital markets, the growth of private enterprise and other property right reforms are also cited as reasons for rising inequalities (see Shi, Chuliang and Sicular, 2001).

Trends in Income in China

This section looks at urban-rural income patterns in detail. China's rapid growth has produced remarkable improvements in the living standards of its citizens. Various international agencies point to three decades of extraordinary increases in income and consumption, vast reductions in poverty rates in both rural and urban areas, and improvements in adult literacy, infant mortality and adult life expectancy. While such data clearly show that all provinces have benefited from growth, some provinces have fared better than others. Perhaps the most obvious divergence in incomes across China is between rural and urban areas. Incomes in China's cities have grown faster than income outside urban centres, opening a rural-urban income gap that has widened continuously.[15] Although scholars have spent considerable time in studying China's rural-urban income gap, until recently the public showed little concern about the phenomenon. Several things have kept public dissatisfaction in check. First, rural residents had access to self-produced consumption goods, primarily food, which boosted their living standards but were not included in official income measures. Second, the Chinese government used several policy measures to reduce the rural-urban gap, including subsidising rural workers and providing price supports for agricultural commodities. Third, the gap between rural and urban incomes created an incentive for people who lived in the countryside to move to cities, which helped fuel China's growth. Finally, the gap was considered a short-run phenomenon associated with economic transformation and not something that would permanently leave rural residents behind (Candelaria, Daly and Hale, 2009).

Urban Incomes

Table 1 shows that per capita annual disposable income of urban households increased from 343.4 yuan in 1978 to 15,780.8 yuan in 2008 (46 times increase) while the rural per capita net income increased from 133.6 yuan to 4,140.6 yuan during the same period (31 times increase). In 1978, the urban per capita income was 2.57 times the rural per capita income and this ratio reduced to 1.86 in 1985, but then it increased till 1994 (2.863) and declined again till 1997 (2.469). The next peak emerged in

2003 (3.231) and then another at 3.330 in 2007. Table 1 and Figure 3 also shows that rural-urban per capita income gap is widening over time. In 1978, the absolute income gap (per capita) was 209.8 yuan between urban and rural areas, which increased to 11,020.2 yuan by 2008. Thus, economic reforms over the years have widened the income gaps in China. This means income inequality is on an increase. Besides, the average size of the urban households has gone down from 3.5 in 1990 to 2.91 in 2008 – the result of single child policy. The average number of persons employed per household has also observed a decline since 1990 and stood at 1.48 persons in 2008. The proportion of employment per household too declined from 56.6 per cent in 1990 to 50.9 per cent in 2008. This would have extenuated the rural poverty in China in the recent times.

Figure 3

Urban-Rural per Capita Incomes

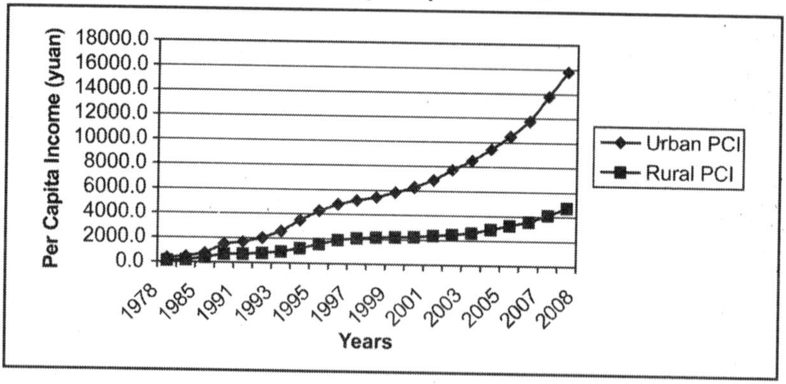

Further, in 2008, 60 per cent of households were lower middle-income households, middle-income households and upper-income households (Urban Household Survey, 2008). About 10 per cent households were lowest-income households and among them half were poor households. The average household size is slightly higher among lower poor. And, among all income classes, the average number of employed persons per household is below 2 and it is lower among poor households. As one moves up the income deciles, the proportion of employment per household goes up – 38.14 per cent in the 1st decile group compared to 62.55 per cent in the 10th decile group. However, the number of dependents per employee reduces as one moves up the income deciles. The ratio of per capita income between the lowest income household (1st decile) and the highest income household (10th decile) is 1:9.11. In case of per capita disposable income, the ratio of per capita disposable income between the lowest income household (1st decile) and the highest income households (10th decile) is 1:9.17. Excess income over expenditure per capita significantly goes up as one moves up the income deciles.

Table 1

Per Capita Annual Income and Engel's Coefficient of Urban and Rural Households

Year	*Per capita annual disposable income of urban households*		*Per capita annual net income of rural households*		*Urban-rural income gap (yuan)*	*Ratio of urban to rural income*	*Engel's coefficient of urban households (%)*	*Engel's coefficient of rural households (%)*
	Value (yuan)	*Index*	*Value (yuan)*	*Index*				
1978	343.4	100.0	133.6	100.0	209.8	2.570	57.5	67.7
1980	477.6	127.0	191.3	139.0	286.3	2.497	56.9	61.8
1985	739.1	160.4	397.6	268.9	341.5	1.859	53.3	57.8
1990	1510.2	198.1	686.3	311.2	823.9	2.200	54.2	58.8
1991	1700.6	212.4	708.6	317.4	992.0	2.400	53.8	57.6
1992	2026.6	232.9	784.0	336.2	1242.6	2.585	53.0	57.6
1993	2577.4	255.1	921.6	346.9	1655.8	2.797	50.3	58.1
1994	3496.2	276.8	1221.0	364.3	2275.2	2.863	50.0	58.9
1995	4283.0	290.3	1577.7	383.6	2705.3	2.715	50.1	58.6
1996	4838.9	301.6	1926.1	418.1	2912.8	2.512	48.8	56.3
1997	5160.3	311.9	2090.1	437.3	3070.2	2.469	46.6	55.1
1998	5425.1	329.9	2162.0	456.1	3263.1	2.509	44.7	53.4
1999	5854.0	360.6	2210.3	473.5	3643.7	2.649	42.1	52.6
2000	6280.0	383.7	2253.4	483.4	4026.6	2.787	39.4	49.1
2001	6859.6	416.3	2366.4	503.7	4493.2	2.899	38.2	47.7
2002	7702.8	472.1	2475.6	527.9	5227.2	3.111	37.7	46.2
2003	8472.2	514.6	2622.2	550.6	5850.0	3.231	37.1	45.6
2004	9421.6	554.2	2936.4	588.0	6485.2	3.209	37.7	47.2
2005	10493.0	607.4	3254.9	624.5	7238.1	3.224	36.7	45.5
2006	11759.5	670.7	3587.0	670.7	8172.5	3.278	35.8	43.0
2007	13785.8	752.5	4140.4	734.4	9645.4	3.330	36.3	43.1
2008	15780.8	815.7	4760.6	793.2	11020.2	3.315	37.9	43.7

Source: Statistical Yearbook of China, various years.

Again, Table 2 reveals that the annual per capita urban disposable income has gone up by more than 10 times since 1990 and this growth has been more prominent during the nineties compared to the first decade of this century whereas the annual per capita rural disposable income has grown at a slower rate during the nineties and almost halved during the first decade of this century. Besides, the income ratio in 1990 between urban-rural areas was little more than 2 while it almost touched 3 in 2000. Per capita annual disposable income in urban and rural areas has increased by almost eight times though slightly at a lower rate in rural areas. However, urban per capita income has multiplied 46 times between 1978 and 2008 while rural per capita income has multiplied only 36 times. Thus, there is slower change in rural disposable incomes.

Table 2

Per Capita Annual Income

(in yuan)

Item	*1990*	*1995*	*2000*	*2005*	*2008*	*Times change in 2008 over 1990*
Per Capita Urban Annual Income (yuan)	1516.21	4279.02	6295.91		17067.78	
Distribution (%)	100.00	100.00	100.00		100.00	
Income from wages and salaries	75.83	79.23	71.17		66.20	9.8
Net business income	1.48	1.70	3.91		8.52	64.8
Income from properties	1.03	2.11	2.04		2.27	24.8
Income from transfer	21.66	16.96	22.88		23.01	12.0
Disposable income (yuan)	1510.16	4282.95	6279.98		15780.76	
% change over the previous year		183.61	46.63		14.47	
Per Capita Annual Net Income of Rural Households (yuan)						
Net income (by source)	686.31	1577.74	2253.42	3254.93	4760.62	6.9
Distribution (%)	100.00	100.00	100.00	100.00	100.00	
Wage income	20.22	22.42	31.17	36.08	38.94	13.4
Property income	0.00	2.60	2.00	2.72	3.11	3.6
Transfer income	4.22	3.63	3.50	4.53	6.79	11.2
Net income from household operations	75.56	71.35	63.34	56.67	51.16	4.7
Net income from household operations (yuan)	*518.55*	*1125.79*	*1427.27*	*1844.53*	*2435.56*	*4.7*

Source: Same as in Table 1.

Contribution to urban income: It is interesting to observe a changing of sources to urban per capita income over the period: in 1990, the contribution of income from wages and salaries reduced from 75.83 per cent in 1990 to 66.2 per cent in 2008 while the contribution of business income improved from 1.48 per cent to 8.52 per cent during the same period. This reflects on changing occupational profile of urban population in China. The two other sources of income, viz., incomes from properties and transfers, have maintained their share, though incomes from transfers is significantly better at 23.02 per cent in 2008 from 21.66 per cent in 1990.

Regional incomes: As regards the per capita urban annual income across regions is concerned, it was 20,965.49 yuan in the eastern region compared to 13,917.01 yuan in the western region and the gap between the highest and lowest per capita income is 1.51 in 2008. The highest disposable income of 19,203.46 yuan is in the eastern region and the lowest of 12971.18 yuan in the western region and the gap between the highest and lowest disposable income is 1.48 (Table 3).

Table 3

Regional Differences in Per Capita Urban Annual Income: 2008

(in yuan)

Item	*Eastern*	*Central*	*Western*	*North-eastern*
Per capita annual income	20965.49	14061.73	13917.01	14162.02
Disposable income	19203.46	13225.88	12971.18	13119.67

Source: Same as Table 1.

Table 4

Percentage of Rural Households Grouped by Per Capita Annual Net Income

(in yuan)

	Percentage of households				
	1990	*1995*	*2000*	*2005*	*2008*
< 400	20.68	2.82	1.63	1.27	0.96
400–600	28.31	5.67	2.38	0.98	0.44
600–800	34.74	12.91	5.81	2.45	1.06
800–1000	12.49	11.63	5.72	2.84	1.23
1000–1500	12.25	26.95	17.92	9.9	4.53
1500–2000	3.48	17.31	17.93	12.56	6.58
2000+	1.99	26.08	49.99	70.56	85.45
or					
2000–2500		10.29	14.54	12.49	7.95
2500–3000		5.89	10.29	11.42	8.63
3000–3500		3.49	7.11	9.55	8.13
3500–4000	1.99	1.95	4.76	7.57	7.93
4000–4500		1.34	3.44	5.93	7.06
4500–5000		0.86	2.40	4.64	6.46
or 5000 +		2.26	7.45	18.96	39.29

Source: Same as in Table 1.

Rural Incomes

Incomes of rural households are changing, but there are still some households with meagre incomes. As shown in Table 4, in 1990, there were 20.68 per cent households with net per capita income of below 400 yuan, but this proportion went down to 2.82 per cent in just five years (in 1995) and further reduced to 0.96 per cent by 2008. However, there are still households with below 100 yuan per capita income (0.61% in 2008). There were 28.31 per cent households with per capita net income of 400–600 yuan in 1990 while this percentage reduced to 5.67 in 1995 and further to 2.38 per cent in 2000 and was just 0.44 in 2008. Further, 34.74 per cent households in 1990 had per capita income of 600–800 yuan and this proportion went down to 1.06 per cent in 2008 while another 12.49 per cent households had per capita income of 800–1,000 yuan in 1990 and this percentage was 1.23 per cent by 2008. At the other extreme, there were mere 1.99 per cent households with per capita income of yuan 2000 or more in 1990 and this proportion went up to 26.08 per cent in 1995 and then to 49.99 per cent in 2000 and to 70.56 per cent in 2005 and finally touched 85.45 per cent in 2008. It may also be noted that in 1995, there were 2.26 per cent households with per capita income of 5,000 yuan or more and steadily this proportion rose to 39.29 in 2008 (also see Figure 4). One can argue that some of these changes may have been affected by the efforts made during the reforms, especially the national '8–7' programme designed to lift 80 million people out of absolute poverty during 1994 to 2000.

Similarly, according to the Outline for Poverty Alleviation and Development of China's Rural Areas (2001–2010), at the end of 2007, the number of rural residents in the absolute poverty was 14.79 million, averaging 8 million annual decline in number of poor since 1978. The impoverishment rate dropped by 29.1 percentage points from 30.7 per cent in 1978 to 1.6 per cent in 2007. Besides, in 2007, there were 28.41 million rural residents in the low-income bracket, which had just enough to eat and wear. This figure represents a decline by 33.72 million from the 62.13 million in 2000, or an annual average decrease of over 4 million. The proportion of low-income people in the rural areas had decreased to 3 per cent in 2007 from 6.7 per cent in 2000. The number of rural residents who lived in poverty and thus were provided with a minimum standard of living increased from 3.002 million in 2000 to 35.66 million in 2007. In the recent years, the National Bureau of Statistics has been monitoring the progress made in building a well-off society in an all-round way in six aspects including economic development, social harmony, life quality, democracy and law, education, and resources and environment. The results show that between 2000 and 2007, China enjoyed a fairly rapid economic growth, the quality of people's life noticeably improved, construction of social undertakings accelerated, and efforts made to 'Build up a Well-off Society in an All-Round Way' paid off. The index of 'Building

Figure 4

Percentage of Households with Per Capita Income (yuan)

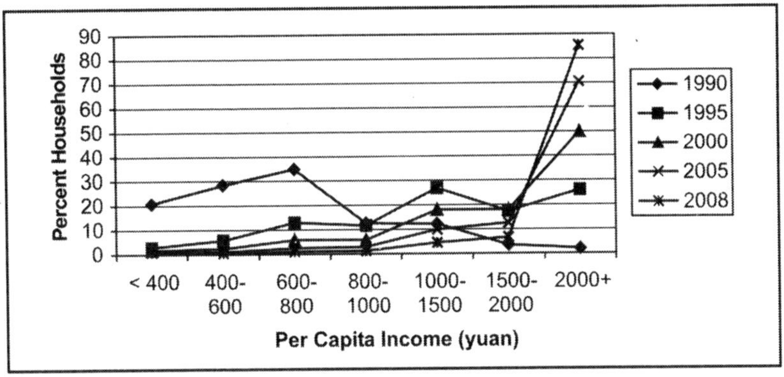

up a Well-off Society in an All-Round Way' was 72.9 in 2007, up 13.6 percentage points from 2000, or an annual average increase of 1.93 percentage points. It can be predicted that by 2020, China will successfully build up a well-off society in an all-round way.

Structural changes in rural incomes: Table 5 and Figure 5 presents rural incomes over the years. In 1990, per capita annual net income of rural households stood at 686.31 yuan, which increased to 4760.62 yuan in 2008, i.e., 6.9 times increase. This has four components, viz., wage income, property income, transfer income, and income from household operations. It is found that in 1990, 75.56 per cent rural income accrued from household operations while 20.22 per cent from wage income and the remaining was transfer income. The contribution of property income

Figure 5

Per Capita Rural Income

(in Yuan)

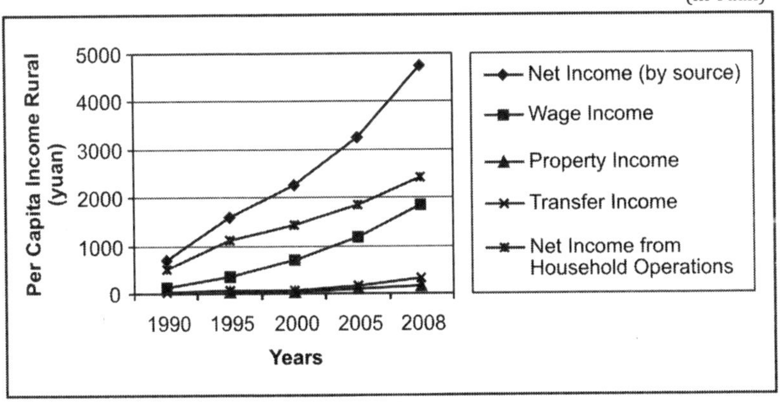

was non-existent. Significant gradual changes have taken place since then as in 2008, 51.16 per cent of rural income accrued from household operations while 38.94 per cent from wage income and the remaining was transfer income (6.79%) and property income (3.11%). Wage income increased more than 13 times since 1990 while transfer income by 11 times and property income by just 3.6 times whereas household operations income went up by 4.7 times only. These changes are more significant since 2000. Table 5 further shows that the contribution of farming to per capita income from household operations was 66.45 per cent in 1990, which declined to 58.59 per cent in 2008 though it increased four times.

Table 5

Contribution to Per Capita Annual Net Income of Rural Households

(in %)

Item	*1990*	*1995*	*2000*	*2005*	*2008*	*Times change in 2008 over 1990*
Net income (by source) (yuan)	686.31	1577.74	2253.42	3254.93	4760.62	6.9
Distribution in (%)	100.00	100.00	100.00	100.00	100.00	
Wage income	20.22	22.42	31.17	36.08	38.94	13.4
Property income	0.00	2.60	2.00	2.72	3.11	3.6
Transfer income	4.22	3.63	3.50	4.53	6.79	11.2
Net income from household operations	75.56	71.35	63.34	56.67	51.16	4.7
Net income from household operations (yuan)	518.55	1125.79	1427.27	1844.53	2435.56	4.7
Distribution in (%)	100.00	100.00	100.00	100.00	100.00	
Farming	66.45	71.01	58.43	59.51	58.59	4.1
Forestry	1.45	1.20	1.57	2.48	2.72	8.8
Animal husbandry	18.67	11.35	14.53	15.38	16.32	4.1
Fishery	1.37	1.39	1.89	2.31	2.27	7.8
Industry	1.76	1.21	3.69	3.31	3.35	8.9
Construction	2.35	3.07	3.27	2.55	2.77	5.5
Transport, postal and telecommunication services	2.59	2.47	4.46	4.56	4.26	7.7
Wholesale and retail trades and catering services	2.45	3.04	5.50	5.88	5.83	11.2
Social services	1.26	1.53	1.97	1.77	1.72	6.4
Culture, education and health care			0.48	0.55	0.69	2.5
Others	1.64	3.73	4.21	1.69	1.48	4.2

Source: Same as in Table 1.

In 1990 the second most important source of household income was animal husbandry (18.67%), which declined to 16.32 per cent in 2008, though it had touched 11.35 per cent in 1995 and increased thereafter continuously. It however, quadrupled between 1990 and 2008. The other sources of household income were ranging between 1.26 per cent (social services) and 2.59 per cent (transport, postal and telecommunication services) in 1990. In 2008, the other sources of household income were ranging between 0.69 per cent (culture, education and health care) and 5.83 per cent (wholesale and retail trades and catering services). This shows that income from household operations still is dominated by farming and animal husbandry activities, though the decline in farming has marginally led to increase in contribution of other activities. The fastest growing activity is wholesale and retail trades and catering services which grew 11 times over 1990. Industry, forestry and fisheries follow it.

Regional rural income gap: There are also wide regional differences in per capita net income in rural China. As Table 6 reveals, the top five regions that had per capita net income of more than 1,000 yuan in 1990 were Shanghai, Beijing, Zhejiang, Tianjin and Guangdong while the bottom five regions were Gansu, Guizhou, Henan, Shaanxi and Anhui (below 539 yuan). The gap between Gansu and Shanghai is 1,476.34 yuan. In 2008, Shanghai, Beijing, Zhejiang, Tianjin and Jiangsu were the top five regions in terms of per capita income while the bottom five regions were Gansu, Guizhou, Qinghai, Yunnan and Shaanxi. The gap between Gansu and Shanghai is 8,716.47 yuan. During the intermediate years, similar picture emerges with slight changes in bottom five regions. This shows that not only relatively positions of the regions have changed every five-year period, but also the gap between the top and the bottom regions has widened. This is indicative of widening inequalities across rural regions.

Inter-provincial Real Wage Inequality

Income inequality is reinforced by wage differentials too. Though the gap between cities and the countryside has continued to widen, more recent studies have shown that Chinese inequality is not limited to the rural-urban divide. There is also an increase in urban wage inequality among Chinese provinces (Candelaria, Daly and Hale, 2009). Several facts are worth noting. Both average nominal wages and average real wages are rising in China and are growing even in the provinces at the bottom of the distribution. At the same time, though nominal wages are rising fastest at the top of the distribution, reflecting more rapid growth in higher-wage than in lower-wage provinces. As a result, differences in average urban wages among provinces are increasing. To be sure, cost-of-living differences do offset somewhat the average wage differences. The gap between

Table 6

Per Capita Net Income of Rural Households by Region

Region	*1990*	*Rank 1990*	*1995*	*2000*	*2005*	*2008*	*Rank 2008*	*Times change in 2008 over 1990*
National Average	686.31		1577.74	2253.42	3254.93	4760.62		6.9
Beijing	1297.05	2	3223.65	4604.55	7346.26	10561.92	2	8.2
Tianjin	1069.04	4	2406.38	3622.39	5579.87	7910.78	4	7.4
Hebei	621.67	19	1668.73	2478.86	3481.64	4795.46	12	7.7
Shanxi	603.51	21	1208.30	1905.61	2890.66	4097.24	22	6.8
Inner-Mongolia	607.15	20	1208.38	2038.21	2988.87	4656.18	15	7.7
Liaoning	836.17	7	1756.50	2355.58	3690.21	5576.48	9	6.7
Jilin	803.52	8	1609.60	2022.50	3263.99	4932.74	10	6.1
Heilongjiang	759.86	10	1766.27	2148.22	3221.27	4855.59	11	6.4
Shanghai	1907.32	1	4245.61	5596.37	8247.77	11440.26	1	6.0
Jiangsu	959.06	6	2456.86	3595.09	5276.29	7356.47	5	7.7
Zhejiang	1099.04	3	2966.19	4253.67	6659.95	9257.93	3	8.4
Anhui	539.16	26	1302.82	1934.57	2640.96	4202.49	19	7.8
Fujian	764.41	9	2048.59	3230.49	4450.36	6196.07	7	8.1
Jiangxi	669.90	15	1537.36	2135.30	3128.89	4697.19	13	7.0
Shandong	680.18	13	1715.09	2659.20	3930.55	5641.43	8	8.3
Henan	526.95	28	1231.97	1985.82	2870.58	4454.24	17	8.5
Hubei	670.80	14	1511.22	2268.59	3099.20	4656.38	14	6.9
Hunan	664.24	16	1425.16	2197.16	3117.74	4512.46	16	6.8
Guangdong	1043.03	5	2699.24	3654.48	4690.49	6399.79	6	6.1
Guangxi	639.45	18	1446.14	1864.51	2494.67	3690.34	23	5.8
Hainan	696.22	11	1519.71	2182.26	3004.03	4389.97	18	6.3
Chongqing				1892.44	2809.32	4126.21	20	2.2
Sichuan	557.76	24	1158.29	1903.60	2802.78	4121.21	21	7.4
Guizhou	435.14	29	1086.62	1374.16	1876.96	2796.93	30	6.4
Yunnan	540.86	25	1010.97	1478.60	2041.79	3102.60	28	5.7
Tibet	649.71	17	1200.31	1330.81	2077.90	3175.82	26	4.9
Shaanxi	530.80	27	962.89	1443.86	2052.63	3136.46	27	5.9
Gansu	430.98	30	880.34	1428.68	1979.88	2723.79	31	6.3
Qinghai	559.78	23	1029.77	1490.49	2151.46	3061.24	29	5.5
Ningxia	578.13	22	998.75	1724.30	2508.89	3681.42	24	6.4
Xinjiang	683.47	12	1136.45	1618.08	2482.15	3502.90	25	6.9

Source: Same as in Table 1.

the highest-wage province and the lowest-wage province is half as large when measured in terms of real wages instead of nominal wages. Still, these increases in inter-provincial real wage inequality among urban residents suggest that structural and long-term drivers of wages and incomes may be at work.

One plausible explanation for regional disparity is that coastal provinces have had a growth advantage over inland ones. Coastal areas have posted faster wage growth than inland provinces (Ravallion and Chen, 2004). This pattern is not especially surprising given that much of China's recent economic development was led by rapidly expanding exports, financed to a considerable extent by foreign direct investment. China established 15 free trade zones (FTZs) in coastal areas, most of which are located near cities with major ports. In addition, 15 export processing zones (EPZs) were established, mostly in coastal areas. Foreign companies, which often pay higher wages than domestic enterprises, quickly moved into these zones, perhaps pushing wage levels up throughout the coastal regions. The real wage difference between inland and coastal regions is high and rising.

A more surprising observation is that the difference between inland and coastal provinces is less pronounced than that across coastal provinces. In fact, the highest average real wage among the coastal provinces increased dramatically, while the lowest average real wage among coastal provinces remained similar to the average real wage in inland provinces. It appears, therefore, that the benefits of China's economic growth have been concentrated in a sub-group of all coastal provinces. Yao and Zhang (2001) also observe that groups of Chinese provinces diverge in terms of real per capita gross domestic product (GDP).

Another plausible reason is that China's economic growth is largely driven by exports, and the access of a province to shipping facilities could be important in determining its performance in general and its wage level in particular. It is observed that the gap between the highest and the lowest average real wage for two sub-groups of provinces – one including those with large commercial port capacity (defined as having more than 10 berths of 10,000 tons class) and the other without such capacity – is substantial. Just looking at coastal provinces excluding Shanghai and Tianjin (the provincial-level cities), the category with substantial port capacity includes six provinces, while the category without such capacity includes three, viz., Fujian, Guangxi, and Hainan. In support of the port hypothesis, it is found that the coastal provinces without large commercial ports have a similar average real wage close to the average real wage in inland provinces. This lends support to the idea that access to the coast boosts wages more in those provinces that have large commercial ports. However, there remain large differences in average real income among the provinces with large ports, indicating that increasing export activity is not the sole explanation for growing regional income inequality. This needs to be further investigated. Wan, Lu and Chen (2007) show that while globalisation is a contributor to regional inequality in China, differences in physical capital, as well as speed of economic reform such as privatisation, play an increasing role in fuelling regional inequality. Moreover, Candelaria, Daly and Hale (2009a) find that cross-provincial differences in industry composition and availability of skilled and unskilled labour also account for some of the inequality.

Thus, there is an increasing trend towards wage inequality among cities in different regions of China. This likely reflects structural factors and therefore could be persistent. The Chinese government has taken the problem of rising income inequality seriously, responding with regional income redistribution. Still, the persistent nature of the rise suggests that more steps are required. One possible area of change would be to allow greater labour mobility. Such mobility in China remains relatively low given regional income disparities and is not sufficient to prevent regional wage differences from rising (ibid.). Thus, removing formal barriers to labour mobility, providing skill training in low-income regions, and also social services to workers who relocate may be useful in stemming regional inequality.

Inequalities and Duality

There are four types of dualities noted in the Chinese economy, viz., in household registration system, in employment system, in system of income distribution and in education system.

(i) *Dual Household Registration System:* For a long time, China has implemented an urban-rural division of the duality in household registration system. This household registration system was set up under the planned economic system, which is the product of urban-rural dual structure.

(ii) *Dual Employment System:* In the planned economy era, in order to tackle the problem of unemployment simultaneously in rural and urban areas, while the peasants were employed in the rural production teams, the jobs in urban were first offered to urban residents and then to rural residents if urban labour supply was not able to meet the needs, and thus only a small number of peasants were fortunate enough to find a job in urban area. In addition to the planned recruitment and enrolment, the government thus strictly controlled the peasants' entry into the urban centres for employment purposes.

(iii) *Dual System of Income Distribution:* The city's industrial workers income comes from wages, while the income of peasants is mainly derived from agriculture. Compared to urban industrial sector with a capital of a large scale, high level of accumulation, following the rules of increasing returns to scale, advanced production methods, fast technological progress, high production efficiency, high economic efficiency, structure and other characteristics to change rapidly and so on, agricultural development has been remarkably in a weak position. This is because the farmers engaged in agriculture have inherent weak nature: get the relatively large natural environment and climate influence, small-scale capital, per capita cultivated lands are few, low levels of accumulation, backward mode of production, slow technological progress, sale prices of agricultural products are lower than its value, etc. Therefore, the income level of farmers is often lower than urban workers, and has forced many farmers to abandon agricultural work to work in cities. The related aspect is that the households are incurring debt to meet expenses and living standards.

The 2011 CHFS survey[16] reveals that household debt includes debts incurred through the agricultural, industrial or commercial undertakings, real estate mortgages, car loans, education loans, credit card debts, and other debts. Table 7 shows that the average total debt of the 8,000 sample households was 62,576 yuan. The figure is 1,00,816 yuan for urban households and 36,504 for rural households. It is also observed that in rural areas, 46.43 per cent debt is due to housing followed by business while in urban areas, the corresponding percentages are 41.55 and 50.96 per cent respectively. There still appears to be a limited tendency to incur debt for purchase of cars, education, credit cards and other durables in both the areas, though urban household debt on these items is higher than the rural areas in absolute terms.

Table 7

Average Household Debt Structure

(in yuan)

Area	*Housing*	*Business*	*Cars*	*Education*	*Credit Cards*	*Others*	*Total*
Rural	16950	15344	1702	717	57	1733	36503
%	46.43	42.03	4.66	1.96	0.16	4.75	100
Urban	41889	51377	2665	1262	351	3271	100815
%	41.55	50.96	2.64	1.25	0.35	3.24	100
Total	27060	29952	2092	938	176	2357	62575
%	43.24	47.87	3.34	1.50	0.28	3.77	100

Source: CHFS survey 2011.

(iv) *Dual Education System:* In this duality system, most of China's spending on education has focused on the urban education, specially the higher education. The 2011 (China Household Financial Survey) CHFS survey shows that there is still a relatively large group of people with elementary or under degree education (Table 8). Meanwhile, there exists a huge education disparity between the rural and urban populations and across regions. People living in cities tend to have a higher level of education than those in rural areas, resulting in a higher literacy rate in cities. Those in the more economically developed eastern region also have a higher level of education than those in less developed western region. Vocational education is much lower in rural areas, which means capacity to have greater employability is not there. The same is the case with higher education – junior college and bachelor degrees – in rural areas. These educational achievements render rural population less capable to have higher incomes.

Table 8

Structure of Education Degree in Urban and Rural Areas

(in %)

Education Degree	*Urban*	*Rural*
Illiterate and semi-illiterate	4.23	14.51
Elementary school	9.88	28.81
Middle school	25.86	37.98
High school	18.84	11.07
Vocational school	10.27	3.09
Junior college	13.77	2.75
Bachelor	15.09	1.76
Graduated school	2.07	0.03

Source: CHFS survey 2011.

Consumption Differentials

As income gaps are widening, it would reflect on consumption pattern of rural and urban areas and regions. The average China's per capita living expenditure in 2008 stood at 11,242.85 yuan and 37.89 per cent was spent on food. The lowest income households expend 48.14 per cent on food and this proportion declines continuously as one moves up the income deciles (29.18% in case of tenth decile, CHIP survey 2011). Table 9 shows that per capita urban household expenditure multiplied four times in the nineties but grew two times since 2000 while rural per capita living expenditure grew three times in the nineties but two times since 2000.[17]

Table 9

Ownership of Major Durable Consumer Goods per 100 Urban Households at Year-end

Item	*1990*	*1995*	*2000*	*2008*
Motorcycle (unit)	1.94	6.29	18.80	21.39
Washing machine (set)	78.41	88.97	90.50	94.65
Refrigerator (set)	42.33	66.22	80.10	93.63
Colour television set (set)	59.04	89.79	116.60	132.89
Hi-fi stereo component system (set)		10.52	22.20	27.43
Camera (set)	19.22	30.56	38.40	39.11
Air-conditioner (unit)	0.34	8.09	30.80	100.28
Water heater for shower (unit)		30.05	49.10	80.65
Computer (set)			9.70	59.26
Video camera (set)			1.30	7.12
Microwave oven (unit)			17.60	54.57
Mobile telephone (unit)	0.002		19.50	172.02
Telephone (set)				82.01
Automobile (unit)			0.50	8.83

Source: Same as in Table 1.

Urban Consumption Expenditure

Food consumption: The Engel coefficient (food expenses in consumption outlay) is generally used to evaluate people's living standard and when the Engel coefficient is above 60 per cent, people are in poverty; a society is having enough to eat and wear when it is 50–60 per cent, and below 40 per cent means a well-off society (Carter and Zhong, 1999). The Engel coefficient of China's urban residents remained over 57 per cent until the early years of the reform programme. This means they had just shaken off poverty and were still struggling for 'having enough to eat and wear'. This lasted until the Sixth Five-Year Plan (1981–1985), when China enjoyed economic development and a booming market. People were making more money and the coupon was no longer in need for the purchase of commodities. Engel coefficient saw a sudden fall to 53.3 per cent in 1985 from 57.5 per cent in 1978. The figure indicates that the Chinese people gained a secured life with enough food and clothes, and started to accomplish the goal of living a well-off life in 2000. In the 1990s, Engel coefficient decreased every year. It fell to 50 per cent in 1994 for the first time and was 44.7 per cent in 1998. Engel coefficient of the rural people was 43.7 per cent in 2008 and has observed sharper decline from 67.7 per cent in 1978 (40 percentage point fall) and that of urban people stood at 37.9 per cent (19.6 percentage point fall between 1978 and 2008). This does indicate improvement in standard of living but at a faster rate in rural areas. However, the standard of living is better in urban areas than in rural areas and is resultant of policy interventions like tax withdrawal on agriculture. This index indicates that urban people in China are living a comparatively better-off life (see also Ravallion and Chen, 2004).

Over the past 63 years since 1949, especially during the last 34 years, food available to urban residents gradually became great in variety and rich in terms of nutrition. In the early days of the 1950s, China worked hard for economic recovery and people's life improved greatly. However, political movements launched one after another after 1958 seriously undermining China's economic development and resulted in the decline in people's standard of living. The 'cultural revolution' (1966 to 1976) pushed the Chinese economy to the verge of collapse and people's standard of living continuously declined. In 1957, urban per capita expenditure stood at 222 yuan. Of these, 130 yuan went to food and 27 yuan to clothes; these two items accounted for 70 per cent of the total expenses. Remaining 30 per cent was spent on other items. In 1964, urban per capita expenditure marginally declined to 221 yuan. However, if prices are accounted for, the decline amounts to 10.4 per cent. Of these, 131 yuan was spent on food and 24 yuan on clothes; together again accounted for 70 per cent share. In 1978, the urban per capita expenditure was 311 yuan. Allowing for inflation, this meant a real increase of 22.6 per cent. Of these, 179 yuan were spent on food and 42 yuan on clothes. These two items combined to take up 71 per cent – a slight increase from 1957. In 1990, the per capita urban expenditure stood at 1,279 yuan (694 yuan on food and 257 yuan on clothes), which significantly increased to 11,243 yuan in 2008 (4,250 yuan on food and 1,166 yuan on clothes). The above indicates that, from the founding of the PRC in 1949 to the introduction of reform and opening up in late 1978, the expenses of urban people were mostly paid to 'having food to eat and clothes to wear'. Commodities were in so short supply that coupons were issued for what was considered fair distribution. Over the past 34 years of reform and opening up, the urban residents have been enjoying an increasingly improved standard of living. The problem of food and clothing, which remained a big headache for 30 years before 1978, was completely solved during the 1981–1985. No coupon is issued for the supply of commodities. And, the urban residents had begun to move into a well-off society.[18] Besides, the per capita living space in rural areas has almost doubled.

Health care: The proportion of expenditure on health care in urban areas increased from 2 per cent in 1990 to 6.4 per cent in 2000 to go up to 7 per cent in 2008. In absolute terms this expenditure went up by more than 30 times. The jump is significant between 1995 and 2000, but since then it has stagnated more or less. On the other hand, the expenditure on health care in rural areas increased from 3.3 per cent in 1990 to 5.2 per cent in 2000 to go up to 6.7 per cent in 2008. This shows that rural households tend to spend a higher proportion on health compared to urban areas in 1990 but fell short of urban proportion in 2000 and thereafter.

Housing expenditure: Housing expenditure (residence and household facilities, articles and services) is going down in percentage terms (17.12% in 1990 to 16.34% in 2008), though expenditure share on residence has marginally gone up.

Education, cultural and recreation services expenditure: Education, cultural and recreation services expenditure share has only marginally improved over the period, though in absolute terms the increase has been 12 times between 1990 and 2008. This also shows that as the incomes have gone up there is diversification observed in expenditure pattern of urban households.

Durable consumer goods: The past 64 years have witnessed changes in urban life – changes that find expression in the increasing demand of the people for better quality durables. Before 1978, people not only strove to own bicycles, sewing machines, wristwatches and radios, but also took pride in owning these. In the early days of the reform and opening up, owning refrigerators, washing machines, colour TV sets and tape recorders were in vogue. Nowadays, air-conditioners, home-computers and cars have begun to move into urban families. Per capita urban incomes have gone up over the years and expenditure on durable goods should a prior go up. In urban areas, in 1981, every 100 urban families owned an average of 0.6 colour TV sets, six washing machines, 0.2 refrigerators, and 13 tape recorders; and in the rural areas the durables were rarely seen then. In 1990, 1.94 motorcycles were owned per 100 urban households and this number rose to 21.39 in 2008. In 1990, 78.41 washing machines were owned per 100 urban households and in 2008 this number was 94.65 – almost every household having a washing machine. With regard to refrigerators, 42.33 refrigerators per 100 households were owned in 1990 that went up to 93.63 in 2008. Besides, some families started to buy hi-tech household electrical appliances for the purpose of study and entertainment. Colour televisions per 100 urban households stood at 59.04 in 1990 but rose to 132.89 in 2008 – more than one colour television per household. Hi-fi stereo component system were 10.52 per 100 households in 1995 (none in 1990) and this number stood at 27.43 in 2008 while cameras per 100 households were 19.22 in 1990 and in 2008 the number was 39.11. Air-conditioners were 0.34 per 100 households in 1990 and this number stood at 100.28 in 2008 (every household has one AC at least) while water heaters for shower were 30.05 in 1995 (none in 1990) per 100 households and in 2008 the number was 80.65.

In the 21st century, urban households turned to buy mobile phones, computers and cars. Computer ownership is of recent origin; there were 9.7 computers per 100 households in 2000 but rose to 59.26 in 2008. Video camera is still not part of the household assets, as just 1.30 per 100 households in 2000 and 7.12 in 2008. Microwave ovens were 17.6 per 100 households in 2000 and 54.26 in 2008. Mobile phone possession stood at 19.5 per 100 households in 2000 and 172.02 in 2008. Since 1949, China has been enjoying fast economic development and so modern transportation and telecommunication take a part of the public consumption expenditures in China. In 1981, per capita annual expenditure on traffic and communication in the urban areas was only 6.6 yuan, of which 6.12 yuan went to traffic and 0.48 yuan to communication (postal service). In 1998, the public expenditure in this regard rose sharply to 257 yuan – a 38-fold increase. A significant rise in share of expenditure on transport and communication has been witnessed from 1.2 per cent in 1990 to 12.6 per cent in 2008 – a 35 times increase since 1990 in absolute terms. The Chinese government invested heavily in the construction of transportation and communication facilities and strong networks have taken initial shape in the country. In the past, people used to contact their relatives and friends by means of telegrams and letters, which today have been replaced with telephones, mobile phones and emails. The national penetration rate of telephones was 1.11 per 100 persons in 1990. Transportation tools used include not only bicycles but also motorcycles, electrical motor cars and cars. To travel, people ride not only buses and trains but also taxis and aircrafts. Statistics shows that national passenger transport volume reached 22.28 billion people in 2007, a 7.8-fold increase from 1978, up 7.8 per cent annually on average. National passenger turnover totalled 2,159.3 billion passenger kms, 11.4-fold increase, up by 9.1 per cent annually on average. In 2011, approximately 14.53 per cent of the households in the CHIP survey own cars, buses or trucks. The car ownership of rural households is about 10.26 per cent, i.e., 452 out of 4,405 rural households. Comparatively, 19.23 per cent of urban households own a vehicle, i.e., 758 out of 3,914 urban households. Communication network improved significantly over time. There were 82.01 telephones per 100 households in 2008, which were almost not there prior to that. Automobile ownership is marginal only, i.e., 0.5 per 100 households in 2000 and 8.83 in 2008.[19] This shows that asset ownership has improved in urban households but still not all households have all these durables.

Income and expenditure nexus: The per capita income of urban households increased from 1,516.21 yuan in 1990 to 4,279.02 in 1995 (182.22% increase) but the growth slowed down significantly to 47.13 per cent between 1995 and 2000 to go up again during 2000 and 2008. The per capita income of urban households stood at 17,067.78 yuan in 2008, which is more than 11 times the 1990 figure. On the other hand, the disposable income of urban households increased from 1,510.16 yuan in 1990 to 15,780.76 yuan in 2008, which is 10.5 times the 1990 figure. Besides, per capita annual consumption expenditure as percentage of disposable income declined from 84.69 per cent in 1990 to 71.24 per cent in 2008 while that of per capita income declined from 84.35 per cent in 1990 to 65.87 per cent in 2008. In absolute terms, per capita annual consumption expenditure increased from 1,278.99 yuan in 1990 to 11,242.85 yuan in 2008, which is 8.8 times the 1990 figure (Table 10). Though as the per capita income and disposable income have been going up, the share of expenditure on food have been declining from 54.25 per cent in 1990 to 37.89 per cent in 2008, but expenditure expended on clothing has also observed a declining trend and stood at 10.37 per cent in 2008. This has stood around 10 per cent since 2000, however.

Table 10

Per Capita Annual Consumption Expenditure of Urban Households

Item	*1990*	*1995*	*2000*	*2008*
No. of households surveyed	35660	35520	42220	64675
Per capita annual consumption expenditure (yuan)	1278.89	3537.57	4998.00	11242.85
Distribution (%)	100.00	100.00	100.00	100.00
Food	54.25	20.09	39.44	37.89
Clothing	13.36	13.55	10.01	10.37
Residence	6.98	8.02	11.31	10.19
Household facilities, articles and services	10.14	7.44	7.49	6.15
Health care and medical services	2.01	3.11	6.66	6.99
Transport and communication	1.20	5.18	8.54	12.60
Education, cultural and recreation services	11.12	9.66	13.40	12.08
Miscellaneous goods and services	0.94	3.25	3.44	3.72

Source: Same as in Table 1.

Before 1978, the urban residents were told to 'lead a simple life' and the slogan was that a new garment should be used for three years; when it becomes 'old', it be worn for another three years; and when it is worn out, one should refrain from buying new ones and instead patch it to wear for the next three years. In 1957, people bought 0.7 readymade clothes and 7.3 metres of clothes (not enough to make a quilt which the Chinese usually made themselves) on average. In 1964, a citizen bought an average of one readymade clothes and 4 metres of cloth. After 1978, a dazzling variety of clothes were available in the market, and people were better dressed. In the past, they bought cloth and hired tailors to make clothes for them. Today, however, they purchase readymade clothes in supermarkets. Almost no one is doing what individuals used to do decades ago. In the urban area, the per capita clothing expenditure in 1990 was 71 yuan, which went up to 479 yuan in 1995 and then up to 500 yuan in 2000 and to 1166 yuan in 2008.[20]

Rural Consumption Expenditure

Table 11 shows that in rural areas of China, in 1990 expenditure on food constituted 58.80 per cent of per capita consumption expenditure and this went down to 43.67 per cent in 2008 and share of clothing also has declined marginally since 1990. In the rural areas, the per capita clothing expenditure increased from less than 6 yuan in 1983 to 130 yuan in 2007, rising 21.8 times, and the number of clothes purchased increased from 0.7 per person to 2.4 per person, a rise of 2.3 times. However, the share of expenditure on residence has marginally improved from 17.34 per cent in 1990 to 18.54 per cent in 2008 and it is the second most important item of rural consumption expenditure. The share of household facilities, articles and services has declined from 5.29 per cent in 1990 to 4.75 per cent in 2008 while the share of transport and communications has improved from 1.44 per cent in 1990 to 9.84 per cent in 2008 and that of education, cultural and recreation and services has also gone up from 5.37 per cent to 8.59 per cent during the same period. Education expenditure has some rigidity, meaning a certain amount of money has to be spent to meet minimum requirements. This rigidity in education expenditure therefore implies a heavier burden for low-income households. Households do borrow for education and, thus, education expenditure is a serious financial burden for low-income groups. Health care and medical services expenditure constituted 6.72 per cent in 2008 up from 3.25 per cent in 1990. This shows that with changing incomes in rural areas, consumption basket has also undergone changes and people are spending more on education, health, transport and communications. Telecom service is relatively underdeveloped in the rural areas. In 2007, however, the administrative villages with access to the postal service accounted for 98.5 per cent of the total. Some 99.5 per cent of the administrative villages have been installed with home phones. But still housing expenditure is significant because of expansion in floor area with time.

Table 11

Composition of Per Capita Annual Consumption Expenditure of Rural Households

(in %)

Item	*1990*	*1995*	*2000*	*2005*	*2007*	*2008*
Consumption expenditure	100.00	100.00	100.00	100.00	100.00	100.00
Food	58.80	58.62	49.13	45.48	43.08	43.67
Clothing	7.77	6.85	5.75	5.81	6.00	5.79
Residence	17.34	13.91	15.47	14.49	17.80	18.54
Household facilities, articles and services	5.29	5.23	4.52	4.36	4.63	4.75
Transport and communications	1.44	2.58	5.58	9.59	10.19	9.84
Education, cultural and recreation and services	5.37	7.81	11.18	11.56	9.48	8.59
Health care and medical services	3.25	3.24	5.24	6.58	6.52	6.72
Miscellaneous goods and services	0.74	1.76	3.14	2.13	2.30	2.09

Source: Same as in Table 1.

Table 12 shows that as one moves up the income quintiles, the per capita consumption expenditure goes up – it is 1,088.41 yuan for the lowest income quintile and 2,521.54 yuan for high income quintile. The same happens for clothing expenditure across quintiles of income. Food expenditure gap difference between low and high income households is 2.3 times in 2008 while that for clothing it is 3.3 times, 4.4 times for residence, 2.9 for household facilities, articles and services, 4.8 times for transport and communications, 4.2 times for education, cultural and recreation and services, 3.1 times for health care and medical services and 4.2 times for miscellaneous goods and services.

Table 12

Per Capita Consumption Expenditure of Rural Households by Income Quintile (2008)

(in yuan)

Item	*Type of households*						
	Low income	*Lower-middle income*	*Middle-income*	*Upper-Middle income*	*High income*	*Gap between low and high income*	*Times difference between low and high quintile*
Consumption expenditure (yuan)	2144.78	2652.77	3286.44	4191.25	6853.69	4708.91	3.2
Food	1088.41	1293.70	1526.96	1815.70	2521.54	1433.13	2.3
Clothing	121.64	149.34	192.20	247.56	397.04	275.40	3.3
Residence	348.24	428.34	538.77	764.25	1518.67	1170.43	4.4
Household facilities, articles and services	88.24	122.55	155.31	205.27	342.96	254.72	2.9
Transport and communications	168.35	224.25	302.35	410.75	806.13	637.78	4.8
Education, cultural and recreation and services	147.00	194.58	277.07	383.47	662.17	515.17	4.2
Health care and medical services	145.93	187.27	224.18	273.53	451.47	305.54	3.1
Miscellaneous goods and services	36.96	52.74	69.60	90.72	153.71	116.75	4.2

Source: Same as in Table 1.

Other Features of Rural Living Standard

Housing conditions: There are various indicators in existence to understand rural household living standards. The per capita floor space of newly-built rural houses this year was 0.82 square metre per person and this has marginally improved to 0.99 square metre per person (Table 13). However, the value of houses had gone up from 92.32 yuan per square metre in 1990 to 533.66 yuan per square metre in 2008. This means cost of housing has gone up. On the other hand, if we consider per capita floor space of rural houses at year-end, it was 17.83 square metre per person and this has improved to 32.42 square metre per person. However, the value of houses had gone up from 44.60 yuan per square metre in 1990 to 332.83 yuan per square metre.

Table 13

Housing Conditions of Rural Households

Items.	*1990*	*1995*	*2000*	*2005*	*2008*
Houses newly built this year					
Per capita floor space of houses (sq. m/person)	0.82	0.78	0.87	0.83	0.99
Value of houses (yuan/sq. m)	92.32	200.30	260.23	373.31	533.66
Structure of houses (sq. m/person)					
Reinforced concrete structure	0.23	0.33	0.47	0.51	0.66
Brick and wood structure	0.47	0.37	0.36	0.29	0.28
Houses at year-end					
Per capita floor space of houses (sq. m/person)	17.83	21.01	24.82	29.68	32.42
Value of houses (yuan/sq. m)	44.60	101.64	187.41	267.76	332.83
Structure of houses (sq. m/person)					
Reinforced concrete structure	1.22	3.10	6.15	11.17	13.40
Brick and wood structure	9.84	11.91	13.61	14.12	14.89

Source: Same as in Table 1.

Further, in case of houses newly built this year, reinforced concrete structure was 0.23 square metre per person in 1990 that increased to 0.66 square metre per person in 2008 while brick and wood structure was 0.47 square metre per person in 1990 and it was lower at 0.28 square metre per person in 2008. In case of houses at year-end, reinforced concrete structure was 1.22 square metre per person in 1990 that increased to 13.40 square metre per person in 2008 while brick and wood structure was 9.84 square metre per person in 1990 and it was higher at 14.89 square metre per person in 2008. This shows that older houses have lower value in 2008 compared to such houses in 1990 and per capita floor space improved in older houses. Households have been making modification during the year.

Rural-urban comparison: In recent years, there has been a popular saying to the effect that whether the China has entered a well-off society and it depends on whether the Chinese have a good housing to live. Housing is one of the most complicated problems, which has yet to be solved. Before 1949, families with 3–5 persons sharing the same title-roofed accounted for 70 per cent of the total population in urban areas. The rent was extremely high for those who had no houses. Since 1978, people's living standard has improved significantly. In 1981, there were only 13.5 per cent of the total urban households with a living space averaging eight square metres per capita, which rose to 48.1 per cent in 1988 and 76.8 per cent in 1998. Before 1978, most of the urban residents lived in the houses, which belonged to the leasing units or the housing authority, and only a small number of people had their own houses. In a populous country, it is common to see people enjoy small living space and, in many cases, three generations of the same family had to live under the same roof. That was a true of the housing situation at that time. After 1978, the state attached great importance to improving living conditions in the urban areas, and has been investing in construction of apartment buildings. In recent years, the state has tried all possible means to solve the housing problems through construction of low-rent houses and economically affordable houses. Many apartment buildings have been built, making it possible for large numbers of urban households to staying in low-lying, shabby houses and move to the spacious ones with large windows and bright kitchens and toilets. In 2008, the living space of the urban residents reached 22.6 square metre per capita, as against 4.2 square metre in 1978. Meanwhile, there is great improvement in the surroundings of the dwelling quarters in the urban area.

The rural residents also enjoy better living conditions and environment. The per capita share of the living space in the rural areas increased from 8.1 square metre in 1978 to 31.6 square metre in 2007 – a 2.9–fold increase. So far as the type of buildings are concerned, the brick and wood houses and those of the reinforced concrete structure account for 86.4 per cent – an increase of 37.8 percentage points from that of 48.6 per cent in 1981. In 2008, the living conditions have also improved remarkably. In 2007, for instance, 16.4 per cent of the rural residents had houses equipped with the flush toilets, 25.7 per cent had access to electricity, clean fuel, and fuel gas, and 41.3 per cent had access to tap water.

Quality of life: People are spending more on travel in China today. As the government allows its people to work five days a week and enjoy long holidays on 1 May and 1 October, started in 1998, the people not only have

Table 14

Floor Space of Newly-Built Residential Buildings and Housing Conditions of Urban and Rural Residents

Year	Floor space of newly built residential buildings in urban areas (100 million sq. m)	Floor space of newly built residential buildings in rural areas (100 million sq. m)	Urban-rural diff. (%)	Per capita floor space of residential buildings in urban areas (sq. m)	Per capita floor space of residential buildings in rural areas (sq. m)	Urban-rural diff. (%)
1978	0.38	1.00	–163.2	6.70	8.10	-20.9
1980	0.92	5.00	–443.5	7.18	9.40	-30.9
1985	1.88	7.22	–284.0	10.02	14.70	-46.7
1986	2.22	9.84	–343.2	12.44	15.30	-23.0
1987	2.23	8.84	–296.4	12.74	16.00	-25.6
1988	2.40	8.45	–252.1	13.00	16.60	-27.7
1989	1.97	6.76	–243.1	13.45	17.20	-27.9
1990	1.73	6.91	–299.4	13.65	17.80	-30.4
1991	1.92	7.54	–292.7	14.17	18.50	-30.6
1992	2.40	6.19	–157.9	14.79	18.90	-27.8
1993	3.08	4.81	–56.2	15.23	20.70	-35.9
1994	3.57	6.18	–73.1	15.69	20.20	-28.7
1995	3.75	6.99	–86.4	16.29	21.00	-28.9
1996	3.95	8.28	–109.6	17.03	21.70	-27.4
1997	4.06	8.06	–98.5	17.78	22.50	-26.5
1998	4.76	8.00	–68.1	18.66	23.31	-24.9
1999	5.59	8.34	–49.2	19.42	24.20	-24.6
2000	5.49	7.97	–45.2	20.25	24.80	-22.5
2001	5.75	7.29	–26.8	20.80	25.70	-23.6
2002	5.98	7.42	–24.1	22.79	26.50	-16.3
2003	5.50	7.52	–36.7	23.70	27.20	-14.8
2004	5.69	6.80	–19.5	25.00	27.90	-11.6
2005	6.61	6.67	–0.9	26.10	29.70	-13.8
2006	6.30	6.84	–8.6	27.10	30.65	-13.1
2007	6.88	7.75	–12.6		31.63	
2008	7.60	8.34	–9.7		32.40	

Source: Same as in Table 1.

money but also time to spend on travelling. In response, the travel services are organising weekend tours of the surrounding scenic spots, and also of such spots in other provinces. Overseas visits are also available to the

Chinese. The year 2007 saw 1.61 billion domestic tourists, which is 2.1 times over the figure of 1994. Also, in 2007, some 34.924 million people made overseas visits, a figure which is 2.5 times more than in 2002 and an annual average increase of 28.3 per cent.

More cultural facilities have been set up to cope with the growing needs for diversified cultural activities. With improved life, people who used to watch TV at home now go to cinemas, visit teahouses, bars, cafe bars, reading rooms and holiday resorts. In public places nearby communities, fitness facilities have been added for the public use. There is mushrooming of many sports centres, such as stadiums, natatoriums, gyms and yoga houses. In the face of the sharp market competition, many adults, young students and even children attend knowledge enhancement training classes. The per capita expenditure on entertainment and education in the rural areas was only 10.1 yuan in 1981 that touched 305.7 yuan in 2007 – an annual average increase of 14 per cent. The figure was 35.8 yuan in 1981 in the urban areas and 1,329.2 yuan in 2007 – an annual average increase of 14.9 per cent.

Regional situation: Table 15 presents regional information on basic conditions of urban households in 2008. The average household size is

Table 15

Regional Basic Conditions of Urban Households (2008)

Item	*Eastern region*	*Central region*	*Western region*	*North-eastern region*
Number of households surveyed	28417.58	10989.08	17268.42	8000.00
Per capita annual living expenditure for consumption (yuan)	13434.72	9249.02	9604.04	10038.24
Distribution (%)	100.00	100.00	100.00	100.00
Food	36.68	38.89	40.75	37.11
Clothing	9.21	11.72	11.32	12.09
Residence	10.08	10.56	9.29	11.63
Household facilities, articles and services	6.21	6.57	6.13	5.02
Health care and medical services	6.41	7.64	6.92	8.94
Transport and communications	14.48	9.92	11.35	10.36
Education, cultural and recreation services	13.11	11.33	10.78	10.47
Miscellaneous goods and services	3.82	3.38	3.47	4.38

Source: Same as in Table 1.

highest in western region (2.92) and the lowest in north-eastern region (2.77). Average number of employed persons per household is 1.37 in north-eastern region while it is 1.53 in eastern region. Thus, the percentage of employment per household is 51.86 in eastern region and 49.46 per cent in north-eastern region. Number of dependents per employee (including the employee himself or herself) stood at 2.02 persons in north-eastern region while it was 1.93 persons in eastern region. Per capita annual living expenditure for consumption is highest in the eastern region and the lowest of 9,249.02 yuan in the central region and the gap between the highest and lowest per capita annual living expenditure for consumption is 1.45. Across regions the per capita annual expenditure on consumption as proportion of per capita income varies between a low of 64.1 per cent in the eastern region and a high of 70.9 per cent in the north-eastern region while per capita annual expenditure on consumption as proportion of per capita disposable income varies between a low of 69.9 per cent in the central region and a high of 76.5 per cent in the north-eastern region. Across regions the share of food expenditure in per capita annual expenditure varies between 36.68 per cent in the eastern region and 40.75 per cent in the western region. Across regions again the share of clothing expenditure in per capita annual expenditure varies between 9.21 per cent in the eastern region and 12.09 per cent in the north-eastern region.

The share of residence expenditure in per capita annual expenditure varies between 9.29 per cent in the western region and 11.63 per cent in the north-eastern region while in case of share of household facilities, articles and services expenditure in per capita annual expenditure varies between 5.02 per cent in the north-eastern region and 6.57 per cent in the central region. The share of health care and medical services expenditure in per capita annual expenditure varies between 6.41 per cent in the eastern region and 8.94 per cent in the north-eastern region when the share of transport and communications expenditure in per capita annual expenditure varies between 9.92 per cent in the central region and 14.48 per cent in the eastern region. Further, the share of education, cultural and recreation services expenditure in per capita annual expenditure varies between 10.47 per cent in the north-eastern region and 13.11 per cent in the eastern region. This shows that variations are found across regions as far as distribution of per capita annual expenditure on different items is concerned, though relative differences are not significant.

Social Security Coverage

The CHFS survey 2011 shows that 44.2 per cent of the residents do not have any retirement insurance. The data also shows social welfare coverage is higher in the cities than in the rural areas. Among rural residents, 65.51 per cent do not have any retirement insurance, 32.09 per cent have social retirement insurance, and only 2.4 per cent have a retirement salary (Table 16). In contrast, among urban residents, only 13.05 per cent of them do not have any form of retirement benefits, 43.33 per cent have social retirement insurance, and 43.62 per cent have a retirement salary. Among the rural residents who purchased commercial health insurance, 63.91 per cent bought it for themselves and 28.73 per cent for their family members. For the urban residents, the figures are 75.91 and 17.46 per cent respectively.[21]

Table 16

Distribution of Social Welfare, 2011

(in %)

Items	*Rural*	*Urban*	*Eastern*	*Central*	*Western*
Without retirement insurance	65.51	13.05	30.60	63.36	61.32
With retirement insurance	34.49	86.95	69.40	36.64	38.68
Social retirement insurance	32.09	43.33	48.05	22.62	22.85
Retirement salary	2.40	43.62	21.35	14.02	15.83

Source: CHFS survey 2011.

Table 17 shows that the number of employees joining urban basic pension insurance stood at 616.6 million and this increased to 2,189.1 million by 2008. Besides, another 520.1 million employees joined basic endowment insurance in 1990 and this number rose to 1,658.8 million in 2008. In case of retirees joining basic endowment insurance, the number

Table 17

Social Security

(10,000 persons)

Items	*1990*	*2000*	*2008*
Number of employees joining urban basic pension insurance	6166	13617	21891
Number of employees joining basic endowment insurance	5201	10447	16588
Number of retirees joining basic endowment insurance	965	3170	5304
Number of persons and retirees joining urban basic medical care system		3787	19996
Number of employees joining unemployment insurance		10408	12400
Number of employees joining injury insurance		4350	13787
Number of persons joining maternity insurance		3002	9254
Revenue of social insurance fund (100 million yuan)	187	2645	13696

Source: Same as in Table 1.

increased from 96.5 million in 1990 to 530.4 million in 2008. Further, persons and retirees joining urban basic improved from 378.7 million in 2000 to 1,999.6 million in 2008. In 2000 the number of employees joined unemployment insurance was 1,040.8 million that increased to 1,240 million by 2008. Number of employees that joined injury insurance in 2000 stood at 435 million, which increased to 1,378.7 million in 2008. Another 300.2 million persons joined maternity insurance in 2000 and this number improved to 925.4 million. Finally, the revenue of social insurance fund stood at 18,700 million yuan in 1990 that significantly went up to 13,69,600 million yuan by 2008.

Conclusions

The paper reveals that since the initiation of reforms and especially after 1990 not only China has witnessed high growth rates but these have also been accompanied by rising inequalities and significant changes in per capita income, its sources and consumption levels and its structure. Rural China has also observed upward improvement in per capita incomes and consumption pattern. However, still the two major sources of rural income are farming and animal husbandry activities. The importance of food in total consumption expenditure is going down, as expected, with increasing incomes across areas and regions. There are still laggard regions and even within coastal regions some provinces are performing better than others. Rural areas are behind urban areas in terms of educational achievements and vocational training. Quality of life has improved, especially in urban areas, with increasing per capita floor area increasing. There are four types of dualities found in China that reinforce what is being observed and they are: dual household registration system, dual employment system, dual system of income distribution and dual education system. The common notion that households are increasingly using savings to incur expenditure is not observed as in both rural and urban areas households are borrowing for housing and business mainly. There are various factors that have fuelled the income and consumption gaps in China. These range from policy restrictions, taxation regime, international trade (WTO), reform process itself as it has led to development of urban real estate interests and corruption, education, health and social security development problems, SOEs reforms and many such factors. However, growth has led to poverty reduction across areas and provinces with varying effects. Rural growth reduces inequality in both urban and rural areas, as well as between them. Wages are lagging behind profits in the recent times too. Not all are covered by social security.

Given the above, the government needs to protect the property rights of low-income people and create equal opportunities for smaller companies to enter all sectors. It is articulated that greater urbanisation may help ease the income gap. China needs to boost economic transformation and improve social security. China's poor have acquiesced in an iniquitous system because their income is also rising; if that stops, they might not be so tolerant of entrenched privilege. The state has to address China's consumption-light growth model. The government's efforts have been focused on extending public health, education and pension services to reduce the need for household precautionary saving and to free up income to enhance expenditure, but it may not be enough. The reason the mass of China's households are not spending is not because they save too much, it is because the incomes are too low. The reason the rich are saving is not because they want to, it is because they have too much money to spend all of it. The best way to boost consumption in China is not through extending public services but through a more equitable distribution of income. A high Gini coefficient is not disastrous and is commonly seen in the process of rapid economic growth. In the short term, the government can narrow the wealth gap through transfer payments including welfare, social security and government subsidies, and in the long term, better education can effectively equalise opportunity. Tax increases are not necessary to increase social security and welfare. Increased consumption and the retained profits of state-owned enterprises can provide the means for income redistribution, which means 3.8 trillion yuan each year and transfer payments can help ease a widening income gap while expanding domestic demand. Need would be to restructure expenditures to focus on increasing social welfare instead of building roads and bridges.

Notes

1. These changes were originally a series of progressive political reform-driven. The late 1970s observed the agricultural sector reconstruct known as the 'agricultural reform' that lasted for eight years. The subsequent second period known is known as the 'urban reform' beginning 1985 and still continuing. The rapid development of industrialisation, restructuring of state-owned enterprises, trade openness increased export tax rebates and financial assistance links, as well as the gradual liberalisation of the financial markets are the characteristics of this period. The urban reform also brought the negative impact: it caused the inequalities between urban and rural increased again. The causes of inequality caused by urban and rural China is multifaceted, but the main reason is the 'duality system'.
2. Carstern Herrmann-Pillath and the China Center for Monitoring Regional Development (2006). Also see, Hertel and Zhai (2004).
3. Rural population is to be paid back for the forced accumulation in favour of industry (the *gongye fan bu nongye* formula, Chi 2005).
4. A survey revealed that only 6 per cent of citizens felt happy.

5. China is more unequal than the United States and even more unequal than African societies. The CIA also publishes a calculation of the Gini coefficient, which it puts at 0.48 in China in 2009 – substantially higher than the institute's calculation for 2010. The CIA puts the Gini coefficient for the US at 0.45 in 2007 (*The Wall Street Journal*, 'China's Inequality Gini Out of the Bottle', 17 September 2012).
6. The percentage of population living below new poverty line declined from 53 per cent in 1981 to 8 per cent in 2001, but some provinces made greater progress against poverty than others (Ravallion and Chen 2004).
7. Ibid.
8. China's official Gini coefficient was 0.412 for both rural and urban residents in 2000. Since then only the Gini data for rural areas had been released, standing at 0.3897 in 2011 (http://www.chinadaily.com.cn/cndy/2012-12/11/content_16004398.htm).
9. The income gap between urban and rural, between communities, and lack of middle class are factors that could affect social stability (*China Daily*, 11 December 2012).
10. Pan Jiancheng, Deputy Director-General of the China Economic Monitoring and Analysis Center points out that the country would steadily push forward its urbanisation process and economic transformation in an effort to tackle the disparity. But, China must continue to raise the educational level to improve the income level and employment rate, *China Daily*, 12 November 2012, p. 16 (weitian@chinadaily.com.cn).
11. Generally speaking, a worker with higher education background is much less likely to 'leave the workplace' than a worker with less education. In the countryside, a farmer who has completed high school education (12 years of schooling) is much easier to locate sources of income from non-agricultural activities than his illiterate counterpart, whereas a closer look at the poor households shows that their members have had little education.
12. For instance, taxes on wages and salaries are levied progressively at rates between 5 per cent and 45 per cent, and private business at rates between 5 per cent and 35 per cent; but savings interests, returns from stocks exchanges, dividends and profits from property leasing or transferring, among others, are taxed at a fixed rate of 20 per cent. That is to say, tax rate for incomes from work are the highest (45%), then comes the incomes from semi-work (35%), and the lowest rate is for incomes from non-work (20%).
13. For instance, while the urban consumers will enjoy more varieties of imported agricultural products, some of the Chinese farmers will face more fierce competition, which will worsen the ongoing tendency of declining incomes.
14. The government is determined to minimise the social costs of WTO membership by speeding up reforms of the social security system and improving the social welfare safety net.

15. A factor that played a role was the State Council that promulgated the Regulations on Guaranteeing Urban Residents' Minimum Standard of Living in 1999. A system has since been introduced to ensure a minimum standard of living for the urban residents. A total of 4.026 million urban residents were benefited in 2000 and 22.72 million in 2007.
16. China Household Financial Survey 2011 was overseen by Gan Li of Texas A&M University and Southwestern University of Finance & Economics in Chengdu. It covers 8,438 households excluding Tibet, Xinjiang, Inner Mangolia, Hong Kong and Macau (http://www.chfsdate.org/introduction.aspx?cid=8).
17. It can be due to average number of persons employed in an urban household which has continuously declined since 1990; average number of persons employed in a rural household is higher than the urban household, though declined during the nineties to rise again; number of dependents per employee of urban household has been rising since 1990 while it has been declining in rural households; urban unemployment rate has been rising and; registered job seekers having multiplied almost 3 times.
18. The same period also saw improvement in terms of the variety and nutrition of the food consumed. From 1978 to 2007, for example, food consumption of the rural residents reduced from 248 kg to 199 kg, while that of the urban residents experienced a decrease from 205.3 kg to 77.6 kg. In the aspect of nutrition, meat, poultry, egg and milk consumed are on the increase. The pork consumption of the rural residents per capita rose from 5.2 kg in 1978 to 13.4 kg, and that of egg from 0.8 kg to 4.7 kg. As for the urban residents, there was a rise in pork and egg consumption from 13.7 kg and 1.97 kg in 1978 to 18.2 kg and 10.3 kg (China Statistical Yearbook 2012).
19. In 2007, every 100 urban households owned an average of 6.1 cars, a 9.1 fold increase from that in 2001 (ibid.).
20. Of these, expenditure on readymade clothes was 748–yuan per-capita, accounting for 71.8 per cent of the total in 2007. The number of readymade clothes bought by the urban residents rose from 3.13 in 1978 to 7.82 in 2007. Fashions in vogue among the public serve as a window on modern life in China (ibid.).
21. In case of total retail sales of consumer goods, it reached 8921 billion yuan in 2007, an increase of 56.2 fold compared to 1978, or an annual average increase of 15 per cent. As far as the balance of bank savings is concerned, the year-end balance of savings deposits of the urban and rural residents was 17253.42 billion yuan in 2007, or 818.3 times more than the figure of 1978, or an annual average increase of 26 per cent (ibid.).

References

Bai-Fang (undated). 'Urban-Rural Income Gap between the Impact on Household Consumption Empirical Analysis', *The Northern Economy* (available at http://eng.hi138.com/?i158309_China#39s_urbanrural_income_gap_caused_by_effects_on_consumption_analysis_and_counter-measure_selection) accessed on 12 January 2012.

Candelaria, Christopher, Mary Daly and Galina Hale (2009). 'Interprovincial Inequality in China', *FRBSF Economic Letter*, April 10 (available at http://www.frbsf.org/publications/economics/letter/2009/el2009-13.pdf) accessed on 12 January 2012.

—— (2009a). 'Beyond Kuznets: Persistent Regional Inequality in China', FRBSF Working Paper 09–07 (available at http://www.frbsf.org/publications/economics/papers/2009/wp09-07bk.pdf) accessed on 30 January 2012.

Carter, Colin A. and Funing Zhong (1999). 'Rural Wheat Consumption in China', *American Journal of Agricultural Economics*, 81 (3) August: 582–92.

Chi, Fulin (ed.) (2005). *Zhongguo gaige pinggu baogao* (Evaluation Report on China's Reform), Beijing: Waiwen chubanshe (Foreign Language Press).

Fan, C. Cindy and Mingjie Sun (2008). 'Regional Inequality in China, 1978–2006', *Eurasian Geography and Economics*, 49 (1): 1–20.

Fuller, Frank, Francis Tuan and Eric Wailes (2010). 'Rising Demand for Meat: Who will Feed China's Hogs?', *China's Food and Agriculture: Issues for the 21st Century*, AIB-775, Economic Research Service, USDA (available at http://sciencetimes.com.cn/upload/blog/file/2010/9/2010913214830915615.pdf) accessed on 13 February 2012.

Gale, Fred, Ping Tang, Xianhong Bai and Huijun Xu (2005). 'Commercialization of Food: Consumption in Rural China', ERS Report Summary, July (available at www.ers.usda.gov) accessed on 2 March 2012.

Goodman, David S.G. (2004). 'The Campaign to "Open Up the West": National Provincial and Local Perspectives', *China Quarterly*, 178: 317–35.

Herrmann-Pillath, Carstern and China Center for Monitoring Regional Development (2006). 'Rural-Urban Inequality in China: Spatial or Sectoral' (available at http://www.giga-hamburg.de/ifa/premium-content/ca/0606/2006/201.ca-studi-herrmann-pillarth.pdf) accessed on 2 March 2012.

Hertel, Thomas W. and Fan Zhai (2004). 'Labor Market Distortions, Rural-Urban Inequality and the Opening of China's Economy', World Bank Research Policy Working Paper No. 3455, November (available at http://papers.ssrn.com/sol3/papers.cfm?625332(1).pdf) accessed on 2 March 2012.

Naughton, Barry (2007). *The Chinese Economy: Transitions and Growth*, London: MIT Press.

Ravallion, Martin and Shaohua Chen (2004). 'China's (Uneven) Progress against Poverty', World Bank Policy Research Working Paper 3408, Washington, DC: World Bank, September (also published in *Journal of Development Economics*, 2007).

Shen, Chunli (2005). 'Regional Disparities in China: A Poverty Perspective', *Chinese Public Affairs Quarterly*, 2 (1): 38 (available at http://www.chinaipa.org/cpaq/v2i1/Chunli%20Shen.pdf) accessed on 8 January 2013.

Shi, Li Luo Chuliang and Terry Sicular (2001). 'Overview: Income Inequality and Poverty in China, 2002–2007' (available at http://www.iza.org/conference_files/CIER2011/li_s1.pdf) accessed on 16 January 2012.

Shi, Li Renwei Zhao and Ping Zhang (1998). 'China's Economic Transition and the Change in Income Distribution', *Economic Research Journal*, April: 42–52.

Simarro, Ricardo Molero (2012). 'Primary Distribution, Top Incomes and Inequality in China, 1978–2007', Working Paper Series No. 301, November, Amherst: Political Economy Research Institute, University of Massachusetts.

Tao, Dennis and Cai Fang (2000). 'The Political Economy of China's Rural-Urban Divide', Working Paper No. 62, August, Stanford, CA: Center for Research on Economic Development and Policy Reforms, Stanford University.

The Economist (2011). 'Take Five', March 12: 29.

—— (2011a). 'The Truncheon Budget', March 12: 28.

—— (2012). 'For Richer, for Poorer', October 13: 3–28.

Wan, Guanghua, Ming Lu and Zhoa Chen (2007). 'Globalization and Regional Income Inequality: Empirical Evidence from within China', *Review of Income and Wealth*, 53 (1): 35–59.

Wang, Sangui, Dwayne Benjamin, Loren Brandt, John Giles, Yingxing Li and Yun Li (2007). 'Inequality and Poverty in China during Reform', PMMA Working Paper 2007-07, PEP-PMMA.

World Bank (2005). *World Development Report 2006: Equity and Development*, New York: Oxford University Press.

Wu, Yanrui (2006). 'Income Disparity and Convergence in China's Regional Economics', in P.J. Lloyd and Xio-guang Zhang (eds), *China in the Global Economy*, Cheltenham, UK: Edward Elgar, 261–81 (also available at http:www.econs.ecel.uwa.edu.au/econos/staff/wu.htm).

Wu, Ximing and Jeffrey M. Perloff (2005). 'China's Income Distribution, 1985–2001', *Review of Economics and Statistics*, 87 (4), November: 763–75.

Xueliang, Liu (2010). 'Decomposition of China's Income Inequality, 1995–2006', *Chinese Economy*, 43 (4): 49–72.

Yao, Shujie and Zongyi Zhang (2001). 'On Regional Inequality and Diverging Clubs: A Case Study of Contemporary China', *Journal of Comparative Economics*, 29 (3): 466–84.

Yusuf, Farhat and Ping Zhao (2006). 'Consumption Patterns of Urban Households in China: 1990–2003' (available at http://smib.vuw.ac.nz:8081/www/anzmac2006/documents/yusuf-farhat/pdf) accessed on 8 January 2013.

Appendix

Basic Statistics on People's Living Conditions

Item	*1990*	*2000*	*2008*
Per Capita Balance of Saving Deposit (yuan)	623	5076	16407
Residence Condition			
Per Capita Building Space in Urban Areas (sq. metres)	13.7	20.3	
Per Capita Living Space in Rural Areas (sq. metres)	17.8	24.8	32.40
Traffic Condition			
Number of Automobile Per 100 Urban Households (unit)		0.50	8.83
Number of Motor Cycles Per 100 Rural Households (unit)	0.89	21.94	52.45
Communication Condition			
Telephone Popularisation Rate (including Mobile Telephone) (set/100 persons)	1.11	20.1	74.29
Mobile Telephone Popularisation Rate (set/100 persons)	0.002	6.77	48.53
Per Capita Domestic Expenditure on Tour (yuan)		427	511
Urban		679	849
Rural		227	275
Culture, Education and Health Care			
Number of Colour TVs per 100 Households (set)			
Urban	59.0	116.6	132.9
Rural	4.7	48.7	99.2
Number of Computers per 100 Households (set)			
Urban		9.7	59.3
Rural		0.5	5.4
Percentage of Household Expenditure on Education, Culture and Entertainment (%).			
Urban	11.1	13.4	12.1
Rural	5.4	11.2	8.6
Rate of Radio Broadcast Coverage of the Population (%)	74.7	92.5	96.0
Health Care (Percentage of Resident Expenditure on Health Care (%))			
Urban	2.0	6.4	7.0
Rural	3.3	5.2	6.7

Source: Statistical Yearbook of China, various years.

9

Towards a Civic-minded Civil Society

Religious Giving in Contemporary China

HE RONG

Given that compassion, altruism and charity are core tenants of the main world religions (Wuthnow, 1991), it is understandable that religion and the giving of time, talent and treasure are inextricably linked. Charitable giving is institutionalised in different world religions, e.g., Christian tithe (10% of one's income), Islam's zakat ('alms-tax' on roughly 2.5% of an individual's wealth). In the US, religious giving has been a strong tradition from the early beginning (Weber, 1948); total church contributions appear to have remained around one per cent of gross national product (GNP) since at least 1955, religious giving consistently accounts for about half of all charitable giving, which is 64 billion dollars in 1995 (Iannaccone, 1990).

Moreover, a strong connection between religiosity and charity has been shown, which makes religious giving an indicator other than competitor of non-religious giving. Religious monetary giving, as a positive externality of religiosity, not only functions as the primary source of financial supports for religious organisation, but also represents a significant part of charity. Researchers have found that churchgoers who contribute more to their church are also more generous to other charitable organisations (Clain and Zech, 1999). Brooks (2006) (quoted from Lincoln, Morrissey and Mundey, 2008) claims that religious persons are generally more likely to give to all types of charity than their secular counterparts. Evidence of such connection among American youths suggests that religion may serve as the seedbed of philanthropic giving in

America. Since 1990s, religious giving has been a significant issue in the area of religious studies, which nowadays is addressed in research across many academic fields and has drawn global interest (Lincoln, Morrissey and Mundey, 2008). While most of the Western literature focuses on the Christian practice of religious giving, only Chang (2006) investigates religious giving in Taiwan, with over 70 per cent of its total population affiliating with Eastern religions that are mainly formed by folk beliefs, Buddhism and Taoism. Only 4.8 per cent and 2.4 per cent of its total population are Protestant and Catholic, respectively.

Giving or donation to religious organisations is not institutionalised in traditional Chinese religions. On certain occasions, the competition over the control of economic resources was the cause of the outburst of church-state conflicts during imperial China. Since 9th century, Chinese Buddhism turned to self-support pattern, i.e., to farm rather than be supported by givings from the laity or profits from monastic economy. With the Imperial government's strict regulations in Ming dynasty, temples' property was used to set up public school. In the early 20th century, religious organisations in China were always under an unstable economic situation. Since 1980s, state policy of religion in Mainland China has been changed, but self-support is still encouraged, though different economic policies direct towards different religions. For example, Buddhist temples are treated like state-owned, Islamic mosques as community-owned and Christian church as private-owned. Till now, the lack of effective management has hampered the growing of voluntary giving in China. Social donation is in certain degree the consequence of motivation from *Danwei* (work unit) (Liu, 2004; Bi et al., 2010). Due to these historical and institutional contexts, it is difficult to research religious giving from the angle of religious organisation. This paper focuses on religious monetary giving at individual level in contemporary China: firstly, to find the determinants of religious giving based on the Western scholar's research, and then test the connections using the data of empirical study of values in China (ESVIC, 2007). It will be helpful to get the basic of religious giving and also an overview of religious life in China.

Literature Review

The basic question in Western literature on religious giving is: 'Who gives and who gives more?' Two approaches can be adopted in the study of religious giving: one is economic and the other is sociological.

Azzi and Ehrenberg (1975) were the first to analyse religious behaviours through an economic approach based on an individual's rational choice. According to Azzi and Ehrenberg's multi-period utility-maximisation model of household allocation of time and goods, religious participation is treated as 'afterlife consumption', and the relationship between religious participation and religious giving is substitutive, because individuals allocate time and money among religious and secular commodities so as to maximise their lifetime and afterlife utilities. There is also an age effect and gender difference in religious behaviour, i.e., religious activity increases with age, households with lower income participate more in time-consuming religious activity and within a given household, members with lower wages (typically wives) put more time into religious activity, which partly explains the gender difference in religious participation.

In the subsequent studies, Ehrenberg (1977) investigated gender difference in the form of age/participation profiles; the here-and-now benefits or meaning of religious participation is emphasised. Religious participation can be seen as human capital investment (Iannaccone, 1990; Hollander, Kahana and Lecker, 2003). From the sociologist's point of view, Hoge (1994) shows that both individual and sociological factors influence the amounts church members give to churches. Besides two individual factors, i.e., the person's religious faith and the amount of discretionary income, there exist many other influences, such as personal relationship within the church, leader-follower relationship, family and kinship factors, church institutional definitions and practices, perceptions of needs, etc.

To sum up, researchers use two groups of factors to answer the question 'who gives?'. At the individual level, religious affiliations, the frequency of church attendance, certain beliefs (e.g., the concept of God) and demographic factors (income, age, education, etc.) are included. At the group level, the type, size, tenet, programme, etc., of religious groups are believed having certain connections with religious giving.

Religious Giving in the Perspective of Religious Practice in China

In the Western Christian tradition, according to Hart (1990) (quoted from Lincoln, Morrissey and Mundey, 2008), although it may not be that religious participation 'makes' religious giving, but it is congregational religious life which weaves these two together. About Chinese religion, some widespread impressions appear to be interesting dichotomies, either as the 'Virtuosen' vs 'Massen' religion, i.e., the traditional, adaptational Confuciusm and the so-called 'magic garden' ... folk religions (Weber, 1964), or the 'Institutionalised' vs 'Diffused' religion (Yang, 1961). An important judgement beneath these observations is the lack of congregational religious life.

To learn more about the religious life in China, the paper uses data from empirical studies of values in China (ESVIC, 2007). This is a national probability sample of 7,021 adults in China. The survey rendered a total of 88 questions about religious beliefs and practices. Horizon Information and Consulting Co., Ltd. administered the survey between May 2007 and

July 2007. With two pre-tests, the survey was formally carried out in 56 locales in China, including three metropolitan cities, six province-level capital cities, 11 region-level (*diji*) cities, 16 small towns and 20 administrative villages. The multi-stage probability sampling method was employed to select metropolitan cities and towns. In rural regions, 1–2 administrative villages for each town and 1–2 'natural units' for each village were selected. In addition, the KISH grid was adopted to randomly select one respondent from each household for a face-to-face interview. To ensure data quality, a post-survey team was formed to cross-check via telephone over 20 per cent of the interviews (Zhai, Huang and Wei, 2008). According to ESVIC, 77.1 per cent of the 7,021 respondents claimed believing in nothing, 18.1 per cent said they believed in Buddhism, and the other two traditional Chinese religions, Taoism and Confuciusm, have 0.6 per cent and 0.2 per cent of believers respectively. With 2.5 per cent Protestants and 0.2 per cent Catholics, Christians represent a significant component of religious people. And, only 0.2 per cent respondents were believers of Islam.

Though the non-believers compose the main part of the population, people tend to believe in certain religious tenets without any religious affiliation. For example, those who hold the belief in the existence of Buddha and 'karma' are 17.6 per cent and 22 per cent respectively. There were 2.7 per cent Christian respondents who claim the belief in the existence of God is 8.8 per cent, while the percentage for the belief in Jesus is 5.5 per cent.

In terms of religious involvement, 35.2 per cent of the total respondents claimed to have never been involved, but compared to the 77.1 per cent non-believers, we may say that possibly more than 40 per cent of them participate in some religious activity without clear religious affiliation. During the 12 months prior to the survey, 17.4 per cent of the respondents had worshipped in temple, church, mosque, etc., and 43.2 per cent of them had participated in weeping-grave or burning incense around the tomb. From these basic measures, the impression may be that in China, people may get involved in religious activity or believe in certain things without belonging to any religion. This may be the evidence of the lack of congregational religious life. But what will the religious giving be? ESVIC tells us that 20.6 per cent of respondents claimed they had donated during the past 12 months which include 23 per cent females and 18 per cent males. But 62.7 per cent of them donated three times or below ranging between 1 yuan and 10,000 yuan. Religious giving did not happen very often or regularly: only 7.6 per cent of the respondents donated regularly, 30 per cent made a will when giving and 20 per cent of the donations happened while travelling. Giving may have connections with certain beliefs, as of the 449 respondents believed in afterlife, 237 (53%) had ever donated, and 496 (34%) of the 1,140 respondents believed in the theory of 'karma' donated.

Hypotheses and Test

Based on the 'believe or practice without belonging' pattern shown by ESVIC, this paper investigates religious giving and its determinants in China. The question is who gives? Here, religious giving is defined as monetary donation to temples, churches, mosques, etc. Giving in kind is also included after converting into monetary values. Religious involvement or participation can be measured by inner belief or observable activity. Belief in afterlife is concerned with the benefit after the end of this life, while belief in 'karma' focuses more on the this-world effects, personal salvation and self-made ideal (He and Mencken, 2010). The two hypotheses are: (1) since lack of congregational religious life, religious participation does not have significant influence on religious giving; and (2) those who believe in the existence of afterlife tend to donate, while belief in the existence of 'karma' has no effect on deciding to give. This paper uses logistic regression to test the hypotheses. Since there is a significant disparity in income between urban and rural China, the cost of living is also significantly different between these two contexts. The ESVIC measures income separately in urban and rural settings, so this paper must split the analysis into two contexts.

Table 1

Logistic Regression of Religious Giving

Variables	*Urban: N=3749*		*Rural: N=1308*	
	B	*exp (B)*	*B*	*exp (B)*
Gender		−0.095	−0.058	
Age		−0.011	0.001	
Marriage		0.574	−0.305	
Occupation		0.030	0.048	
Income	0.006		0.000	
Education	0.075		−0.141	0.869*
Buddhist	1.940	6.960*	1.824	6.195*
Protestant	1.107	3.024*	1.705	5.499*
Afterlife	0.879	2.408*	0.862	2.367*
Karma	0.352	1.422*	0.147	
Worship	1.590	4.903*	1.087	2.964*
Constant	−3.378	0.024*	−3.378	0.024*

*p<0.05 or less.

The dependent variable is religious giving (dummy variable, giving=1), independent variables are: (1) demographic variables, i.e., age, gender (dummy variable, male=1), marriage (dummy variable, married=1), occupation (dummy variable, paid job=1), household income (urban household income monthly 1=less than 500 yuan to 15=20,000 yuan and more; rural household income yearly 1=less than 500 yuan to 20=1,00,000 yuan and more), education (1=below primary school to 7= master's degree and above); (2) belief in the existence of afterlife (dummy variable, believing=1); belief in the existence of 'karma' (dummy variable, believing=1); (3) religious affiliation (Buddhist, Protestant); worship (dummy variable, worship=1).

Conclusions

In both urban area and the countryside, religious giving has significant link with religious involvement, participation and belief, the only exception is belief in the existence of 'karma' held by countrymen. Similarly, in both urban area and the countryside, religious giving has no strong link with all the demographic variables, the only exception is that countrymen with more education slightly tend to give more. The data support rural part of the hypothesis, i.e., since belief in 'karma' focuses more on this-world effect, and good deed-good effect causation, in some way a self-made ideal, it has no significant effect on religious giving. This survey was conducted in the end of 2007, when the earthquake in Sichuan happened, religious organisations' participation in salvation became visible and voluntary giving began to spread widely. The contribution of this paper is to show the basic pattern of religious involvement and giving. Compared to the more institutionalised and continual religious giving in Christian tradition, the China data shows that religious giving is small in amount, situational and discretionary than being a fix part of the household expenditure. But, it is strongly related to religiosity, whether or not there is a congregational religious life. For policy consideration, it means that religious activity will encourage voluntary giving and can be a way to foster altruism, cooperation and other civic virtues in contemporary Chinese society. Chang (2006) studies Taiwan around 2000, where traditional Chinese folk religions prevail. Religious giving is the most important category among the contributions made to all types of non-profit organisations. About 54 per cent of all donors had given money to religious organisations, with an average amount of NT$6000 (US$189) yearly. Taiwan's Tax Code allows taxpayers to list their religious giving as itemised deductions to encourage contributions. From the experience in Taiwan, certain changes in the institutional context will have effects in encouraging charity and concerns for other people as a way towards an inclusive civil society.

References

Azzi, Cory and Ronald G. Ehrenberg (1975). 'Household Allocation of Time and Church Attendance', *The Journal of Political Economy*, 83 (1), February: 27–56.

Bi, Xiangyang, Jun Jin, Mingjie Ma and Jiangsui He (2010). 'The Reach of Danwei Mobilization: An Analysis on Urban Resident's Charitable Giving to Project Hope', *Sociological Studies*, 6: 149–77.

Brooks, Arthur (2006). *Who Really Cares: The Surprising Truth About Compassionate Conservativsm*, New York: Basic Books.

Chang, Wen-chun (2006). 'Determinants of Religious Giving in an Eastern-Culture Economy: Empirical Evidence from Taiwan', *Review of Religious Research*, 47 (4), June: 363–79.

Clain, S.H. and C.E. Zech (1999). 'A Household Production Analysis of Religious and Charitable Activity', *American Journal of Economics and Sociology*, 58 (4), October.

Ehrenberg, Ronald G. (1977). 'Household Allocation of Time and Religiosity: Replication and Extension', *The Journal of Political Economy*, 85 (2): 415–23.

ESVIC (2007). *Empirical Studies of Values in China,* Institute for Studies in Religion, Waco, TX: Baylor University.

Hart, Stephen (1990). 'Religious Giving: Patterns and Variations', paper presented at the Annual Meeting of the Religious Research Association and Society for the Scientific Study of Religion, Virginia Beach, November 9.

He, Rong and F. Carson Mencken (2010). 'Judged by Karma: Belief in Karma and the Socio-Economic Status in Contemporary China', *Religious Cultures in the World*, 65, December: 14–21.

Hoge, D.R. (1994). 'Introduction: The Problem of Understanding Church Giving', *Review of Religious Research*, 36 (2): December.

Hollander, G., Nava Kahana and Tikva Lecker (2003). 'Religious and Secular Human Capital: An Economic Model', *Journal of Socio-Economics*, 32: 489–98.

Iannaccone, Laurence R. (1990). 'Religious Practice: A Human Capital Approach', *Journal for the Scientific Study of Religion*, 29 (3): 297–314.

—— (1998). 'Introduction to the Economics of Religion', *Journal of Economic Literature*, 36 (3), September: 1465–95.

Lincoln, Ryan, Christopher A. Morrissey and Peter Mundey (2008). 'Religious Giving: A Comprehensive Review of the Literature', Report for the John Templeton Foundation Generosity Planning Project (http://generosityresearch.nd.edu).

Liu, Neng (2004). 'The Willingness of Ordinary Urban Citizens Toward Participating in Social Donation Activities and their Behavioural Preferences', *Sociological Research,* 2: 68–78.

Weber, Max (1948). 'The Protestant Sects and the Spirit of Capitalism', in H.H. Gerth and C.W. Mills (eds), *From Max Weber: Essays in Sociology*, London: Routledge, pp. 302–22.

—— (1964). *The Religion of China* (translated and edited by H.H. Gerth), New York: Collier and Macmillan.

Wuthnow, Robert (1991). *Acts of Compassion: Caring for Ourselves and Helping Others*, Princeton: Princeton University Press.

Yang, C.K. (1961). *Religion in Chinese Society: A Study of Contemporary Social Functions of Religion and Some of Their Historical Factors*, Berkeley: University of California Press.

Zhai, J.E., Jianbo Huang and Dedong Wei (2008). *White Paper: An Introduction to the Empirical Study of Values in China*, ISR: Taylor University.

10

Religious Diversity and Nation-State

Development, Democracy and the 'Minority Question' in India

SURINDER S. JODHKA

Independence from colonial rule in 1947 was an important turning point in the history of contemporary India. Together with some other parts of South Asia, India became a sovereign nation-state. This also marked the end of 'autonomous' princely states in most of the subcontinent. The emergence of sovereign nation-states was accompanied by adoption of a constitutional democracy. The initial impetus to the adoption of democratic systems of governance had come from the experience of political mobilisation against colonial rule preceding the independence. Though the newly emergent middle class elites articulated the ideas of independence and nationalism, the nationalist movement attracted diverse social classes and communities, who responded enthusiastically to the promise of a better social and economic life.

At the time of its independence India was confronted with many challenges. Division of the subcontinent into Pakistan and India resulted in large-scale migrations and bloodshed. While a large number of Muslims living on the Indian side of the newly-drawn international border left for Pakistan, Hindu and Sikh populations of 'East' and 'West' Pakistan fled their homes for India. Partition of the subcontinent remains the single largest episode of uprooting of people in modern history. According to available estimates, as many as 12 to 14 million people left their homes to take refuge across the newly-drawn international borders. The estimates of people who died in the 'communal' violence during this period vary immensely, generally hovering in the range of 0.5 to 1.5 million.[1]

Apart from the immediate challenge of dealing with a large number of refugees, providing them with shelter and viable sources of livelihood, the partition and violence that accompanied India's independence had many other long-term implications for the new state. Notwithstanding India's espousal of secularism as a state ideology, partition established a mode of defining territorial identities along communal lines.

Further, communal violence and influx of refugees were not the only problems that the new state of India was confronted with at 'birth'. Unlike the nation-states of Western Europe, India had not evolved as a homogenous 'political community'. It was primarily the experience of participation in the freedom movement against colonial rule that had brought people from different walks of life together. The new institutions of governance and communication introduced by colonial rulers had also helped to make Indian nationalism possible (Desai, 1947). On the ground, however, India was still characterised by a large number of diversities. Writing on the *Idea of India*, Khilnani describes this rather well:

> The possibility that India could be united into a single political community was the wager of India's modern, educated, urban elite, whose intellectual horizons were extended by ... modern ideas and whose sphere was expanded by ... modern agencies .... The nationalist elite itself had no single, clear definition of this idea, and one of the remarkable facts about the nationalist movement that brought India to independence was its capacity to entertain diverse, often contending visions of India. (1998: 5–6)

The political elite which acquired the reins of power in 1947 also had a rather narrow social base. They were mostly from the traditional upper castes of Indian society, who had acquired Western education in schools and colleges opened in India by the colonial rulers. Some of them had also studied further in British universities and had returned to join modern professions in colonial India.

The diversity was not confined to the visions of India's selves and futures held by its elite. Diversities also had some concrete social and historical dimensions. Culturally and linguistically, Indian people differed quite significantly. There were more than a dozen well-developed linguistic regions and languages with a sense of independent identity and culture. India also had a substantial population of groups and communities whom the British had classified as 'Scheduled Tribes'. Though they constituted little more than 6 per cent of the total population of India at that time, a large majority were concentrated in certain pockets where they were invariably the largest communities. They spoke several different dialects and had diverse ways of life. The question of bringing them into the national mainstream became a serious issue of contention among academics and the political elite around the time of independence. Caste was yet another factor that made Indian society complex. Ideas of hierarchy and pollution were common to caste everywhere. However, the actual structures of caste varied considerably from region to region. From a local level institution that organised social life typically in the rural setting, with growing integration of Indian society, caste identities began to acquire a pan-regional and pan-Indian character. Right from the days of colonial censuses, caste groups had begun to consolidate themselves into regional blocs and were to play an important role in democratic politics in the days to come.

Perhaps the most challenging was the diversity of religions. Mobilisation of communities around religious passion has produced immense amount of violence in the 20th century in India and in other parts of the subcontinent. Though a large number of Muslims moved from the Indian side of the subcontinent to the new state of Pakistan, the number of those who stayed behind was substantial. The proportion of Muslims in India was around 10 per cent at the time of partition, and has marginally increased since. At the levels of cultural mores, social/kinship networks and language, there have always been diverse communities among the followers of Islam in India. Christians (around 2%) and Sikhs (around 2%) too were important minority groups in independent India, with significant presence in certain parts of the country. India also had several other religious communities such as Buddhists, Jains, Zoroastrians and Jews.

Apart from these cultural and political challenges, India was also confronted with several material/economic difficulties. In the language of development, India at the time of independence was largely a backward country, with low levels of national income and a stagnant economy. In terms of demographic distributions only around 15 per cent of its population lived in urban centres. Of the 85 per cent or so who lived in rural India most were dependent, directly or indirectly, on agriculture. As a consequence of colonial policies and the historically evolved structures of social hierarchy and dependency, the prevailing state of affairs in rural India was rather dismal.

Several economists, such as Daniel Thorner (1956), Krishna Bharadwaj (1974) and Amit Bhaduri (1984), pointed to the implications of the inherently backward-looking and rigid nature of prevailing economic structures. Such 'traditional institutions', they argued, were directly responsible for the apparently perpetual stagnation of Indian agriculture. The real producers – the peasants and labourers – not only did not possess ownership rights over the land they cultivated, they were also tied to local landlords. Their indebtedness made them participate involuntarily in markets that were nearly completely controlled and manipulated by these dominant landlord-moneylenders. Such 'interlocking' of land, labour and product markets produced stagnant agriculture and an authoritarian power structure. No viable democratic institutions, they argued, could work in the context of such semi-feudal social relations of production.

Nation, Development and Secularism

It was in context of the challenges posed by partition and the existence of significant diversities that India under the leadership of Jawaharlal Nehru evolved a 'national philosophy' that could help it succeed as a nation-state. In the global political environment of the time, Nehru chose a specific brand of 'modernisation', which despite its novelty had much in common with the classical evolutionary view of social change, in line with what had happened in the West and was being advocated by the modernisation/development theories popular at that time. According to Bhikhu Parekh (1991), Nehru's articulation of modernisation as the national philosophy had seven interlinked goals. These were the national unity, parliamentary democracy, industrialisation, socialism, development of scientific temper, secularism and non-alignment.

This philosophy found its resonance in the Indian Constitution. After prolonged deliberations, the Constituent Assembly, under the leadership of Dr B.R. Ambedkar, framed a Constitution for independent India. The Indian Constitution made a clear and unambiguous statement that the vision of India was to modernise itself within the framework of democratic politics. This is perhaps best reflected in the Preamble. India was to be a 'sovereign, socialist, secular, democratic republic', and the new nation promised social, economic and political justice to its entire citizenry. It also granted them freedom of thought, expression and faith. It promised to work for equality of status and opportunity that would enable every individual citizen to live a life of dignity and self-respect. It was in one of his speeches delivered in the Constituent Assembly in 1946 that Pandit Nehru spelt out this promise, explicating the path of development India proposed to pursue after independence. He said:

> The first task of this Assembly is to free India through a new Constitution, to feed the starving people, and to clothe the naked masses, and to give every Indian the fullest opportunity to develop himself according to his capacity. (as quoted in Harriss, 1998: 289)

Thus, apart from making legal provisions and installing an autonomous judicial system, the independent Indian state initiated a process of planning for development. Inspired by the erstwhile Soviet Union, and without compromising on the liberal form of democratic polity, India chose 'mixed economy' as its path to economic development. The state was not only to provide a regulatory mechanism for the economy and markets to function in a manner that would bring growth and prosperity, but was also to invest in building economic infrastructure and industrial production. The

Indian philosophy of planning was best summarised in the second chapter of the Second Five-Year Plan document in the following words:

> Economic development is intended to expand community's (sic.) productive power and to provide the environment in which there is scope for the expression and application of diverse faculties and urges .... The task before an underdeveloped country is not merely to get better results within the existing framework of economic and social institutions but to mould and refashion those so that they contribute effectively to the realization of wider and deeper social values .... These values have been summed-up in the phrase 'socialist pattern of society'. Essentially, this means that ... the benefits of economic benefits must accrue more and more to the relatively less privileged classes of society and there should be a progressive reduction of the concentration of income, wealth and economic power.[2]

As is evident, there are three different agendas that are spelt out in this statement. First and foremost was to evolve an institutional framework for democratic politics. Second was to raise the basic standard of living by increasing incomes and improving distribution. The third was to expand the capability of the Indian population by providing social security and opportunities, which would include education, health and a general atmosphere that would encourage a culture and institutionalisation of equal opportunities for all citizens of independent India.

Religious Diversity and the Challenges of Development

Development and modernisation of a country, with not only a stagnant economy, but also divided culturally and socially, was indeed a difficult task. Apart from the political orientation of the nationalist leadership and the new political elite that took over the reins of power from the British colonial rulers, India was also faced with historical and demographic compulsions that made it necessary for the new leadership to choose the path of secularism. The experience of partition and the widespread communal riots that followed in its wake in the subcontinent convinced the new leaders of the indispensability of secularism. Further, despite 'partition' and the large scale transfer of populations, independent India continued to be a nation with enormous demographic diversities. Also, the influence of the Soviet Union and the socialistic path of development, from which Nehru had borrowed the idea of planning, made the new political elite suspicious of religious organisations and their place in a modern India.

Though a modern system of education had emerged in India during the colonial period, the social sciences acquired an identity of their own only after independence. Even while they continued to use the theoretical paradigms and conceptual systems developed in western universities, the social sciences in India began to engage very closely with the task of nation

-building. Apart from giving them a sense of legitimacy, this engagement also set out a research agenda that was close to the ground realities of Indian society. Historians in the post-independence period, for example, framed their research questions directly around the struggle for national autonomy and independence from colonial rule. Similarly, economists soon became closely involved with the project of planning for development. Political scientists had a vast and exciting arena for studying the working of parliamentary democracy in a country like India, which was not only economically poor but was also marked by the kind of cultural diversities that had never been present in a single nation-state before. Sociologists/social anthropologists, though not directly involved with questions of nation-building, allowed their interests to be shaped by the larger agenda of modernisation and development.

Although everyone recognised the centrality of religion, it did not acquire centrality in the research agenda of any of the social science disciplines. To the historian preoccupied with the question of nation-building against the backdrop of partition, questions of 'religion' were reminders of the 'two-nation theory' and communal violence. The economists simply had nothing to do with religion. In fact, in most cases, their approach to religion was negative, as it was seen as part of tradition, which was regarded as a hindrance to economic growth. Though for the sociologists and social anthropologists, religion had always been an important area of inquiry, they too invariably searched for the legitimation of their disciplines in the larger project of development and treated religion as being a part and parcel of traditional culture. Modernisation, they expected, would inevitably lead to secularisation, where religion would be relevant only in the personal lives of India's citizens. In his vastly influential study *Becoming Modern: Individual Change in Six Developing Countries*, Alex Inkeles (1974) had promoted secularisation as an imperative for the process of modernisation to advance in developing countries. Inkeles was perhaps echoing what had earlier been argued, albeit indirectly, by Max Weber about the other-worldly attitudes of Hindus, which he regarded as the major impediments to the growth of capitalist ethics in societies like India.

However, there were some who argued against such simplistic assumptions about religion and development and contested the modernisation theory approach to religion and culture (Singer, 1966; Dube, 1974). Perhaps the most obvious criticism of Western-style modernisation had come from Mahatma Gandhi, who had emphasised the need for integrating spiritual aspects of human existence with material development. In the Western paradigm the two tended to be negatively correlated. Material development was invariably expected to bring about spiritual and moral degeneration (Iyengar, 2005). Thus, Gandhi was often in disagreement on the subject of development with Nehru. However, it was Nehru's version of development that emerged as the official philosophy of social change in independent India.

Interestingly, despite many criticisms of the grand theses on modernisation and development, religion, or even culture, rarely became a serious candidate for public policy debate until the 1980s. Religious communities and traditions were studied by scholars, mostly for academic reasons. Even the question of ethnic minorities and their socio-economic status was rarely taken seriously by planners and those engaged with the implementation of development projects. Programmes were designed almost exclusively by economists, keeping economic criteria in mind.

This approach to religion and secularism had many problems. Even when operationally secularism acquired a local touch in India, it was essentially derived from the western notion of modernity. It was rarely seen as a political process or an ideological system. Rather it was seen as a natural process, an inevitable outcome of evolutionary change (Jodhka, 2001). The continued presence of religion only meant distortion. Communal mobilisations or communalism was regarded as one such example of distortion. As a conceptual framework, the influence of communalism has been so extensive in the Indian social sciences that it virtually became 'a gate-keeping concept', one that limits theorising about a place or process (Appadurai, 1986).

In this context, religion could not become a part of the development discourse in India. Though some social scientists had continued to work on various aspects of religion, it was seen primarily as an aspect of tradition. Religion as a value system, as well as a source of social organisation/communal identities, was mostly seen as a hindrance in the path of development.

The Crisis of Development and the Cultural Turn

The decade of the 1980s was an important turning point in the history of contemporary India. Apart from a wider consolidation of democratic political processes at social and cultural levels, the decade of the 1980s also saw some interesting new trends, including the rise of several 'new' social movements. These new mobilisations questioned the wisdom of the developmental agenda being pursued with much enthusiasm by the post-colonial state. The following decade saw the beginning of liberalisation policies and a gradual withdrawal of the state from the economic sphere. This was an important ideological shift, a decline of the Nehruvian framework of development and social transformation (Jodhka, 2001). This change is well summarised in the following words by Veena Das:

> The goals of rational organization of life, the scientific management of society, modernization and development, to which great energies had

> been devoted in the sixties and early seventies, now seem like signposts to cities that are abandoned and empty. (1994: 1)

Critiques of the dominant development paradigms came from a variety of actors. Local private capital that had initially grown with the help from the state increasingly began to feel uncomfortable with the license/quota raj and began to lobby for state withdrawal from the economy (see, for example, Kohli, 2006). While India's model of development had promised a better life to those on the margins, four decades of planning had not solved many of the basic problems faced by the historically deprived. The poverty studies of the 1970s clearly showed that a substantial population of India (nearly 50%) continued to live below the officially drawn poverty line. Autonomous movements by farmers, women, tribals and above all, ethnic groups, also began to criticise the dominant statist paradigm of development.

Popular mobilisations on religious and communal lines during the decade of the 1980s produced an acute sense of anxiety among the 'secular' elite of India. Though the Indian state was eventually able to restore normalcy in these states, the question of ethnic identity acquired a new dimension during the post-1980s period. The old Nehruvian idea of secularism became a contentious issue. Its advocates and critics raised many fundamental questions concerning the specific historical context of India and the implications of secularism/secularisation policies for a culturally diverse society like India.

The questions of community identities (particularly of the minority cultures) and their place in building a democratic national society were raised as core issues in this debate (see, for example, Bhargava, 1998). Madan, for example, went to the extent of describing secularism as an elite ideology that reflected members' 'moral arrogance and worse' (1992: 395). 'Secularism', he argued, 'was the dream of a minority which wants to shape the majority in its own image' (ibid.). However, this dream was not going to come true because, unlike the western religions,

> ... South Asia's major religious traditions – Buddhism, Hinduism, Islam and Sikhism – are totalising in character, claiming all of a follower's life, so that religion is constitutive of society ... they do not recognize the distinction between the terms 'religious' and 'secular'. (ibid.: 399)

The ideas of development and modernity were criticised on moral ground as well. Nandy, for example, offered a rather aggressive critique of the dominant paradigm of development and secularism which, according to him, had only produced violence and misery. He advocated the recovery of ethnic and religious tolerance, from 'the hegemonic language of secularism popularised by the westernised intellectuals and middle classes exposed to the globally dominant language of the nation-state'

(Nandy, 1994: 69). It was around this time that Gandhi was rediscovered by scholars and popular movements in India and in the West. Gandhi's ideas on development had been ignored by Nehru and others who took charge of the independent Indian state. Some revisited his notions of tradition and reform in the changed context of the 1980s, while others found his suspicion of western modernity useful in dealing with the contentious questions of environment and sustainability or growing violence and deprivation (Parekh, 1987, 1991; Nandy, 1987; Rudolph and Rudolph, 2006).

Rudolph and Rudolph (2006), for example, described Gandhi as one of the first postmodern thinkers who developed a serious critique of western modernity. His emphasis on human capital, decentralised production and 'appropriate technology' challenged modernity's emphasis on physical capital and its efficiency when deployed in Fordist mass production assembly lines.

Changes in the geopolitics of the world following the collapse of Soviet Union, the end of the Cold War, and the unleashing of new technologies of telecommunications, all meant the beginning of a new phase in the reach of the global capital. This process of 'globalisation', as it has come to be known, was not confined to the economy alone. It has also influenced culture and politics everywhere and has opened up new possibilities for social action and networking. Growing migration and the expanding population of Indian diasporas have unleashed new kinds of social processes. The inability of people of Indian origin to assimilate in their host societies produced a cultural anxiety about identity and cultural continuity among them. This has given birth to new global networks of religious resources (Williams, 1988; Vertovec and Peach, 1997; van der Veer, 1995; Appadurai, 1996; Werbner, 1999), the focus of which is on the family, for fear that children will lose touch with their parents' cultural traditions (Blank, 2001). van der Veer has summarised this process quite well in the following words:

> The globalisation of production and consumption, including flexibility and mobility of their labour, is addressed by religious movements and is a major element in their politics of belonging. The idea that migrants are rootless because they are highly mobile misunderstands the imaginary nature of roots. To have roots requires a lot of work for the imagination (dream-work). One element of that dream-work is that pride in one's nation of origin is important in the construction of self-esteem in the place of immigration. (2002: 183)

Apart from the changing global context of religion, during the decades of the 1980s and 1990s, India also witnessed the rise of several 'new' social and political movements around questions of environment, ethnicity, gender, urban bias in development and human rights. Some of these questions arose almost simultaneously in different parts of the world. Networking across national boundaries gave them a different kind of legitimacy and strength from earlier movements. For example, the movement against the construction of a dam across the Narmada river invested considerable energy in mobilising not only internal public opinion but also the global funding agencies against the project, with some degree of success. Similarly, the questions of human rights violations are critically observed and commented upon by global agencies. The question of gender rights is articulated more or less similarly at the global level and women's organisations working in India actively network with their counterparts in other parts of the world. Even the Dalit movement, which rediscovered itself during the 1980s and 1990s, has tried to take the question of caste to international platforms by linking it to the question of race (see Thorat and Umakant, 2004).

The growing significance of 'vote banks' also gave impetus to minority groups to make demands from the political elite and use pressure group politics. The Muslim communities of India underwent an interesting transformation during this period. Many of them shifted their loyalty from Muslim communal parties and the Indian National Congress to smaller and local level parties. The ethnic minorities also began to articulate their grievances through the newly available discourse of human rights and social justice.

Another important trend that took off during this period was the growing involvement of non-governmental organisations (NGOs) with development. The advocates argued that voluntary action could be a viable alternative to state-sponsored poverty alleviation programmes like the Integrated Rural Development Programme (IRDP), which had been unable to help the rural poor. The NGO sector, they argued, had become a 'potent instrument for bringing about social transformation and building an egalitarian and humane society. It may be only a protest forum in the short run, but over time, it had considerable potential for effective social change' (Dantwala et al., 1998: 9).

Though it was Mahatma Gandhi who had advocated voluntarism long ago and some Gandhians had been practising it throughout, the NGO movement took off in India only with the growing interest of international funding agencies in issues of rural poverty. The paradigm shift from state-oriented development to a market-driven economy also helped in giving legitimacy to the NGO movement. With NGOs came a new language of development: empowerment, participation, participatory rural appraisal (PRA), social capital, etc. One of the most popular and effective programmes initiated by NGOs has been the promotion of thrift societies (Dantwala et al., 1998; Rajasekhar, 1998; Khan and Thomas, 1989; Srivastava, 1999). These shifts during the 1980s towards civil society interventions also created a new space for faith-based organisations (FBOs) to participate in the process of development.

These changes have also brought about a significant shift in the Indian discourse of development. Religion is no longer seen as necessarily being anti-developmental. Similarly, development is not seen as being anti-religion. Though at one level, this shift has produced space for right-wing religious and majoritarian politics, religious idiom is also being used quite extensively by those on the margins of the Indian society.

Minority Question and Development: Recent Trends

After assuming power at the national level in 2004, one of the most interesting new initiatives by the government of the United Progressive Alliance (UPA) under the prime ministership of Manmohan Singh was its decision to appoint a committee of experts to look into the development concerns of the Muslim minority population of India. This 'high level' committee headed by Justice Rajinder Sachar interrogated the social, economic and educational status of the Muslim community of India and submitted its report to the Prime Minister in November 2006. As could have been expected, the report generated a good deal of interest and debate in the media and academic circles. The report has also been widely discussed and debated within the Muslim communities in different parts of the country with much enthusiasm and hope.

Even though the leaders of the Muslim communities did not expect anything radical to emerge out of it, they were nearly unanimous on the point that there was something very constructive in the report and that it 'articulated for the first time what the common masses of Indian Muslims had always wanted to say about themselves'.[3] Scholars working on India's religious minorities too found it to be a valuable document, 'unparalleled in terms of data collation and putting together all these in one single volume'.[4] The pro-minorities popular media acclaimed it as an important turning point in the history of the Muslim community and minority studies in India.[5] Even the 'Hindu right' could hardly put together an argument against the report even when it criticised the recommendations made by the Sachar Committee as being yet another instance of 'minority appeasement'.

Equally interesting and important has been the response of the Indian secular-left to the report. Leaders of the left-wing political parties not only overwhelmingly welcomed the report, but they also were in the forefront of demanding an appropriate policy response from the Indian state to address the issues raised by the Sachar Committee. While it is certainly true that it was for the first time that facts about the 'development deficit' among the Indian Muslims were presented with the support of such a comprehensive data, it was certainly not something completely unknown, either to the scholars working on the subject or to political activists working with a leftist ideology.[6] However, Muslim deprivation could not become a politically important issue with them because the Indian left always advocated the need for a class-based understanding of deprivation. They have been among the most vocal opponents to the use of 'caste' and 'communitarian' identities as sources of mobilising in a democratic society. Such identities, they have been arguing, were the potential sources of division and fragmentation among the working classes and thus serve the interests of 'ruling classes' by dividing the oppressed and exploited.

Why then did they not find anything objectionable in the tenor and substance of the report even when the framework in which its 'terms of reference' were set by the Government of India was clearly communitarian in nature? Indeed, the proposals put forward by the Sachar Committee for amelioration of the Muslim population are premised on the assumption that religious identity be treated as a relevant category in the state policy and perspective on development. If taken seriously, the recommendations of the Sachar Committee's report can certainly have far-reaching implications for the Indian discourse on development. How do we understand such responses to the Sachar Committee's report? What is new and different in the report that has made it so widely acceptable to different sets of political opinions in the country? Is there a larger trajectory of these shifts?

For classical colonial historiography and anthropology, India was a land of 'tradition', organised through the norms of village community, caste and religious belief. The characteristic feature of the Indian village was its hierarchical social order that both united and divided different *jatis*. Louis Dumont was to later theorise this in terms of the dialectical unity of the pure and impure that produced the ideology of inequality and the hierarchical structure of caste. While caste was a local-level social reality, the differences of religion mattered more at the macro political level. Put together they produced a social order, which in the colonial/western thinking, compared well with pre-modern Europe. India was thus placed in an evolutionary schema where the form of social organisation prevalent in modern Europe reflected the future of 'traditional' societies like India. The communities in this universalistic grand theoretical framework had something enduring about them, stable and generally resistant to outside influence. Their continuity 'was ensured by passing down of shared traditions, customs, language and social norms – in short, culture – from generation to generation' (Upadhya, 2001: 33).

This kind of social organisation was opposed, implicitly or explicitly, to the individualism of the modern West where identity of individuals was not derived from the ascriptive community of their birth but from their personal achievements, which placed them in an open and mobile occupational structure. As societies developed, the kinship-based communities gave way to associational social groupings and interest-based coming together of individuals. In other words, the significance of kinship and culture declined and that of class and 'market situation' went up. It was not only the colonial regime that used such categories to place pre-colonial India in such an evolutionary schema, post-independence Indian social sciences also continued to work with a similar conception of social change. For example, mainstream Indian sociology for a long time looked at caste from such an evolutionary perspective, expecting it to change into a class-like phenomenon with the processes of industrialisation and urbanisation.

Religion too was to 'wither away' from the public sphere with the processes of modernisation and secularisation. Mainstream secular-left politics too worked with a similar framework. Talking about religious communities in the discourses on public policy or development was giving space to 'communalism', a reminder of the two-nation theory that led to partition of the subcontinent and the gory violence that killed and uprooted millions. Despite some fundamental ideological differences, the Indian left shared the vision of Jawaharlal Nehru that India needed to focus on economic development to overcome poverty and deprivation. They also agreed on the point that development and secularism went hand in hand. Though the founding fathers of Indian democracy recognised the significance of 'caste' for building a viable democratic polity in the country and a quota of seats was reserved for the scheduled castes and scheduled tribes in legislative bodies, government jobs and education, the stated objective of the policy was to annihilate caste and not to preserve it. Similarly, religious minorities were given some special rights so that they could have a more level playing field that would eventually help them in getting over their sense of insecurity. But when it came to hard policy and planning for development, economists worked with 'hard data' generated through the use of 'secular' economic and demographic variables. Thus poverty was defined through caloric intake, disparities through income and assets and mobility through growth rates.

However, the democratic political process as it began to unfold over the years changed the grammar of Indian politics in a manner that did not seem to go along with the expectations of those evolutionary models of development and social change. Even while democratic polity became popular, its outcomes were not always 'secular' as understood classically. The new political elite that emerged from the 'grassroots' of Indian politics also brought with it a new idiom of doing politics, which was different from the one that the urban middle class/upper caste elite wished to work with. However, given the demographics of popular democratic process, their presence continued to grow. Also, the new social movements that arose from 'below' articulated aspirations of India's marginal citizens in a language that sounded more communitarian than secular. While the 1980s saw these processes of 'churning' becoming evident, they began to translate into a new form of politics during the 1990s. It was around this time that a new form of pan-Indian autonomous Dalit politics began to consolidate itself.

The Muslim minority politics also experienced some important shifts during this time. Like other religious communities, the Indian Muslims too are internally diverse and differentiated. Apart from cultural and denominational differences, they are also divided on caste and class lines. Though the caste structures of the Muslim communities differ considerably across regions of India, they are popularly classified into three categories, viz., *ashrafs, ajlafs* and *arzals*. Historically, the Muslim politics in the subcontinent had been a monopoly of the ashraf elites. However, the 1990s witnessed an interesting differentiation within the community politics of the Muslims, at least in some pockets of India. This process has been well-documented by T.B. Hansen for Maharashtra (Hansen, 2000). Although communal riots affect all Muslims negatively, their impact is certainly felt more by the poor and marginalised sections of Muslim communities. The poor, living in urban slums, are always more vulnerable. Notwithstanding these differences, communal riots and violence invariably end up strengthening the traditional communitarian politics/identities among the minority groups, making the upper caste leadership of the community more powerful within Muslim politics. However, beginning with early 1990s, the so-called backward Muslims across different regions of India began to use different strategies of dealing with their social and political exclusion. In Mumbai, for example, Hansen found two different modes of Muslim response to such a situation: one was a largely conservative quest for internal purification and unity of the Muslim community and return to the basics of Koran and a withdrawal from political, legal and economic dependence on the larger society; and the other was a more pragmatic strategy of 'plebeian assertion' that evolved from the entrepreneurial spirit and milieus of small industry and informal businesses (ibid.: 261). Both these trends were present among the Muslims of Mumbai city. However, it was the second trend that was new. The ajlaf Muslims began to move away from traditional Muslim organisations and no longer identified with communitarian formations, invariably controlled by conservative mullahs. They also stopped sending their children to Urdu-medium schools. Instead, they sent them to English-medium private schools. This process also made them realise that they were socially and educationally backward in the larger framework of development. As one of his respondents told Hansen:

> We have to look at ourselves, see who we really are. We are no longer rajas or big people, we are as poor as the backwards [i.e., lower-caste Hindus], and even worse. (ibid.: 268)

This shift has also led to a new set of mobilisations for recognition as 'other backward classes' (OBCs) by the state, at par with the Hindu OBCs, which made them entitled to jobs reserved under the OBC quota.

This also had implications for their political loyalties. Many of them moved away from the traditional Muslim-only parties and have been looking for secular alternatives. Their disillusionment with the Congress turned them to the Samajwadi Party during the 1990s. Though the strategy has not been of much help to them in the case of Maharashtra, their representation in the state assembly has grown significantly in Uttar Pradesh through their growing alignment with the Samajwadi Party and Bahujan Samaj Party.

It is in this larger context of the changing nature of the political process in India that we need to locate the real significance of the Sachar Committee's report and the kind of response it has received from different political formations, including the secular left. Perhaps more important than the data that it has been able to marshal in support of its formulations on the development deficit among the Indian Muslims is the manner in which it has dealt with the subject.

As I have tried to argue above, during the first four decades of independence, the 'Muslim question' remained trapped in the past, in memories of partition and communal violence. The Muslim aspirations were always articulated in terms of their religious identity, as if that was all they needed and asked for. Such an articulation only fed into the communal politics of the right-wing Hindutva parties. Against this, the Sachar Committee analysed and articulated the Muslim question in a very different language – a language that has reinforced the shift already underway in the discourse on Indian Muslims, viz., from 'identity' to 'development' and 'participation'. In its opening chapter, the report identifies three major concerns of all minorities in the modern nation-states, viz., security, identity and equity. However, it foregrounds the concern for equity while recognising that the three could not always be seen independently of each other.

Using another innovative strategy, it divides the Indian Muslims on caste and class lines, using their socio-economic attributes, and compares them with other 'socio-religious categories' (SRCs) on similar criteria. Using the recent data-sets like NSSO, census and the National Family Health Survey, it classifies Muslims into 'general' and OBC categories. Elsewhere also it underlines the need to recognise the three-fold caste-like division among the Indian Muslims – the ashrafs, the ajlafs and the arzals – and advocates for the listing of arzals, the 'ex-untouchables' communities among them, as scheduled castes along with similar categories from Hindus, Sikhs and neo-Buddhists. Such a classificatory system thus changes the discourse of the Indian state towards Muslims in a fundamental way. From 'communities' with specific cultural histories and self-identities with clearly marked out boundaries, the Muslims of India are transformed into a 'population', identified and described through a language that primarily belongs to the state. This language of classification then also makes them available to the development agencies for an engagement which is different from the language of identity and recognition.

Such an engagement of the state eventually also becomes available to the communities and populations of the Indian Muslims and other minorities. And thus, in the long run, this process has the potential of generating new kinds of mobilisation among them, in a language through which they can articulate their demands and aspirations in a manner that the state and the secular political opinion will find difficult to dismiss. In other words, the question of citizenship begins to take priority over the questions of identity and cultural distinctiveness.

While not everyone will be happy with this relegation of the identity question, the shift is certainly going to have an appeal for the large mass of Indian Muslims for whom struggles of everyday life have always been paramount. Questions of cultural identity are indeed very critical, but they will have to be articulated through the language of citizenship and democratic rights. The Sachar Committee's report opened up this possibility and help in further accelerating a process that has already been underway. For the Indian left, the Muslim question finally became a matter of social justice, human rights and development of the marginalised and excluded.

Notes

1. A good amount of literature is now available on the partition, ranging from historical and demographic aspects to cultural and literary aspects (see Pandey 2001; Mahajan 2000; Nanda 2003; Prasad 1999; Bhalla 1999; Hassan 1994).
2. From Chapter II of the Second Five-Year Plan document reproduced in Wadhwa (1977: 10–11).
3. Asghar Ali Engineer speaking at a seminar in Jawaharlal Nehru University, New Delhi on 26 March 2007.
4. See, for example, Kalam 2007; Robinson 2007; Shah 2007 and others in the special issue of *Economic and Political Weekly*, 42 (10).
5. See, for example, pieces by Venkitesh Ramakrishnan, Yoginder Sikand, Javed Alam, T.K. Rajalakshmi and Praveen Swami in the special issue of *Frontline* (2006) on 'Community of the Margin', December 15.
6. The Gopal Singh Committee's Report on Minorities submitted to the government of India in 1983 too had pointed to the growing marginalisation of Muslims during the post-independence period. It said: There is a common belief that Muslims in India have remained largely unaffected by the economic development in the country ... further, that their general economic condition is becoming worse than before ... (p. 14). Similarly, we also have some other reports and writings that have

been indicating to Muslim marginalisation, see, for example, *India Development Report* published by National Council of Applied Economic Research, New Delhi in 1999. For a qualitative account on the subject, see Breman (1999).

References

Appadurai, A. (1986). 'Is Homo Hierarchicus?', *American Ethnologist*, 13 (4): 745–61.

—— (1996). *Modernity at Large: Cultural Dimensions of Globalisation*, Delhi: Oxford University Press.

Bhaduri, A. (1984). *The Economic Structure of Backward Agriculture*, Delhi: Macmillan.

Bhalla, Alok (1999). 'Memory, History and Fictional Representations of the Partition', *Economic and Political Weekly*, 34 (44), October 30.

Bharadwaj, K. (1974). *Production Conditions in Indian Agriculture*, Cambridge: Cambridge University Press.

Bhargava, Rajiv (ed.) (1998). *Secularism and Its Critics*, Delhi: Oxford University Press.

Blank, J. (2001). *Mullah and the Mainframe: Islam and Modernity among the Daudi Bohras*, Chicago: Chicago University Press.

Breman, Jan (1999). 'Ghettoisation and Communal Politics: The Dynamics of Inclusion and Exclusion in Hindutva Landscape', in R. Guha and J.P. Parry (eds), *Institutions and Inequalities: Essays in Honour of Andre Beteille*, Delhi: Oxford University Press, pp. 259–83.

Dantwala, M.L., H. Sethi and P. Visaria (eds) (1998). *Social Change through Voluntary Action*, New Delhi: Sage Publications.

Das, Veena (ed.) (1994). 'Introduction', in *Mirrors of Violence: Communities, Riots and Survivors in South Asia*, Delhi: Oxford University Press.

Desai, A.R. (1947). *Social Background of Indian Nationalism*, Bombay: Oxford University Press.

Dube, S.C. (1974). 'Sociology of Economic Development: A Trend Report', in *ICSSR: A Survey of Research in Sociology and Social Anthropology*, Vol. II, Bombay: Popular Prakashan.

Hansen, T.B. (2000). 'Predicaments of Secularism: Muslim Identities and Politics in Mumbai', *Journal of Royal Anthropological Institute*, (6) 2: 255–72.

Harriss, J. (1998). 'Development Studies and Development of India: An Awkward Case?', *Oxford Development Studies* (formerly *Oxford Agrarian Studies*), 26 (3): 287–309.

Hassan, M. (ed.) (1994). *India's Partition: Process, Strategy and Mobilization*, Delhi: Oxford University Press.

Inkeles, A. (1974). *Becoming Modern: Individual Change in Six Developing Countries*, Harvard: Harvard University Press.

Iyengar, Sudarshan (2005). *Gandhian Economic Thought and Modern Economic Development: Some Reflections*, Surat: Centre for Social Studies.

Jodhka, S.S. (ed.) (2001). *Community and Identities: Contemporary Discourses on Culture and Politics in India*, New Delhi: Sage Publications.

Kalam, M.A. (2007). 'Conditioned Lives?', *Economic and Political Weekly*, 42 (10): 843–45.

Khan, M.Z. and M.E. Thomas (1989). 'Role of Voluntary Agencies in Rural Development', *Social Change*, 19 (1): 3–12.

Khilnani, S. (1998). *The Idea of India*, New Delhi: Penguin Books.

Kohli, Atul (2006). 'Politics of Economic Growth in India, 1980–2005', *Economic and Political Weekly*, 41 (13), April 1: 1251–60.

Madan, T.N. (ed.) (1992). 'Secularism in its Place', in *Religion in India*, Delhi: Oxford University Press.

Mahajan, S. (2000). *Independence and Partition: The Erosion of Colonial Power in India*, New Delhi: Sage Publications, India.

Nanda, B.R. (2003). *Witness to Partition: A Memoir*, Delhi: Manohar Publishers.

Nandy, Ashis (1987). *Traditions, Tyrannies and Utopias: Essays in Political Awareness*, Delhi: Oxford University Press.

—— (1994). 'The Politics of Secularisms and the Recovery of Religious Tolerance', in Veena Das (ed.), *Mirrors of Violence: Communities, Riots and Survivors in South Asia*, Delhi: Oxford University Press.

Pandey, G. (2001). *Remembering Partition: Violence, Nationalism and History in India*, Cambridge: Cambridge University Press.

Parekh, Bhikhu (1987). *Colonialism, Tradition and Reform: An Analysis of Gandhi's Political Discourse*, New Delhi: Sage Publications.

—— (1991). 'Nehru and the National Philosophy of India', *Economic and Political Weekly*, 26 (1 and 2), January 5: 35–48.

Prasad, B. (1999). *Pathway to India's Partition: The Foundations of Muslim Nationalism*, New Delhi: Manohar Publishers.

Rajasekhar, D. (1998). 'Rural Development Strategies of NGOs', *Journal of Social and Economic Development*, 1 (2): 306–27.

Robinson, Rowena (2007). 'Indian Muslims: The Varied Dimensions of Marginality', *Economic and Political Weekly*, 42 (10): 839–43.

Rudolph, L.I. and S.H. Rudolph (2006). *Postmodern Gandhi and Other Essays: Gandhi in the World and at Home*, Delhi: Oxford University Press.

Shah, Ghanshyam (2007). 'The Conditions of Muslims', *Economic and Political Weekly*, 42 (10): 843–45.

Singer, M. (1966). 'Religion and Social Change in India: The Max Weber Thesis, Phase Three', *Economic Development and Cultural Change*, 14 (4): 497–505.

Srivastava, Alka (1999). 'Non-Governmental Organizations and Rural Development', *Social Action*, 49 (1): 27–44.

Thorat, Sukhadeo and Umakant (eds) (2004). *Race, Caste and Discrimination: Discourses in International Context*, Jaipur: Rawat Publications.

Thorner, D. (1956). *The Agrarian Prospects of India*, Delhi: Oxford University Press.

Upadhya, Carol (2001). 'The Concept of Community in Indian Social Sciences: An Anthropological Perspective', in S.S. Jodhka (ed.), *Community and Identities: Contemporary Discourses on Culture and Politics in India*, Delhi: Sage Publications, pp. 32–58.

van der Veer, Peter (1994). *Religious Nationalism: Hindus and Muslims in India*, Berkeley: University of California Press.

—— (1995). *Nation and Migration: The Politics of Space in the South Asian Diaspora*, Philadelphia: University of Pennsylvania Press.

—— (2002). 'Religion in South Asia', *Annual Reviews of Anthropology*, 31: 173–87.

Vertovec, S. and C. Peach (1997). *Islam in Europe: The Politics of Religion and Community*, London: Macmillan.

Wadhwa, C.D. (1977). *Some Problems of India's Economic Policy: Selected Reading on Planning, Agriculture and Foreign Trade*, New Delhi: Tata McGraw Hill.

Werbner, Pnina (1999). 'Global Pathways: Working Class Compositions and the Creation of Transnational Ethnic Worlds', *Social Anthropology*, 7 (1), February: 17–35.

Williams, Raymond (1988). *Religions of Immigrants from India and Pakistan: New Trends in the American Tapestry*, Cambridge: Cambridge University Press.

11

From State to Market

The Transformative Impact of Globalisation on the Gender Discourse for Chinese Working Women

WU XIAOYING

This paper is within the framework of the UNESCO programme on 'Gender Equality and Development', whose topic during 2006–07 was the socio-economic rights and conditions faced by working women in times of globalisation. But the core of the paper is not the Chinese working women's gain and loss in a globalised era, but the transformation in gender discourse and its impact on women themselves. There are two fundamental hypotheses the paper looks at: one is relative to the Maoist era before the opening of the economy, i.e., in the past 20 plus years, in China there has been a big change in gender discourse; another is that the transformation of gender discourse in globalisation has made significant effect on working women's situations and choices in contemporary Chinese society. The former is sponsored by the state and the latter is dominated by the market.

The research data for this paper is collected from two sources: one is the data on the relevant gender policies and important gender events in Maoist and post-Maoist times, mainly from the contemporary media, internet and some academic articles, mostly through the method of literature review and comparative analysis; another is the data obtained through interviews with 21 working women in different occupations, ages, strata and marriage states, and also their oral history. Through the analysis of the data from two sources, I try to explore how the gender discourse in two different periods is constructed and transformed, how the collaboration and balance among the state, market and traditional culture affect the transformation, and how the transformation influence working women's individual fate. The data of oral history and interviews of women gave an alternative explanation and evaluation different from the official one on the questions such as gender equality as a socialist heritage, and the relationship between globalisation and Chinese women's development.

The methodology used, is qualitative. Either for the official policy texts, gender event texts in pop culture, or for the personal narrative texts, it adopts a method and standpoint of critical discourse analysis other than the methods mentioned above. It believes that 'the discourse is a kind of social practice making effect on knowledge structure and the formation of people's identity and relationship' (Talbot, 2004: 173). At the same time, the discourse is restrained by the social structure: 'social discourse formation does not resulted from the freely dancing of thinking in people's minds, but from the social practice which is rooted deeply in and also oriented by the real substantial social structure' (Fairclough, 2004: 61). Therefore, we may find the implying social institution, structure and power relationship behind through the daily narratives and experiences people are accustomed to.

A View from Literature

There are both domestic and international researches on the formation of gender discourse and its change. For example, domestic researches such as 'The double function of the state and market on women' (Lin, 1998), 'Which discourse do we think of women?' (Li, 1998), 'Gender in discourse formation' (Tong, 2005), and 'Rethinking on "iron girls": gender and labour during the "cultural revolution" in China' (Yihong, 2006) – all discuss this issue. Overseas researches such as *Other Maternities: Gendered Yearnings in China after Socialism* (Rofel, 2006); 'Theorizing Woman: Chinese Woman, Chinese State, Chinese Family' (Barlow, 1994), *Changing Identities of Chinese Women: Rhetoric, Experience and Self-perception in Twentieth-century China* (Croll, 1995), and *Rural Women in Urban China: Gender, Migration, and Social Change* (Tamara, 2006) also talk about the change of gender discourse in the process of modernisation.

The formation of Chinese gender discourse and its change can be summed up as under:

1. Acknowledging that in Maoist and post-Maoist periods, the content and way of gender discourse formation in China has changed. On the content, researchers agree that in the Maoist period, the main idea behind the gender discourse was that 'women are the equal to men' and 'women can hold half the sky'. It was supported by the labour institution and woman protection policies, and with obvious 'de-gendered' characteristic, i.e., no-sex culture of gendered

sameness modelled on man. At the same time, it is an attaching discourse and represents the interests of the state and nation, so it appeared as a style of revolutionary discourse. It originates from the Marxist theory on women's liberation, and brings with it strong state will and political colour.

On the content of gender discourse in the post-Maoist period, researchers mention the effect of marketisation and the weakening of the state political forces, and also the enlarging of gender difference and inequality. But talking about the definition of the dominant gender discourse, they have different focuses. Some focus on the modernity rule centred on efficiency and rationality, some focus on the body politics in consumerist era, some emphasise to go back to the 'natural' gender, and some emphasise the construction of quality and ability in basis of individualism.

From the viewpoint of gender discourse formation, researchers have basically consistent opinions. They argue that the Maoist gender discourse was implemented compulsively politically from top to bottom, and attached a long-time guarantee in institution and was supported highly by propaganda, which shaped a myth of gender equality. This kind of equality is often at a discount in reality because of the need of national interests or social production. For example, even when woman's participation in socio-economic activities was highly encouraged, woman labourer still existed as a reservoir, drifting between the home and society with the changing social employment situation.

In the post-Maoist period, researchers basically have two judgements on the formation of gender discourse: one is considering that in the period, gender discourse is market-oriented and the state has retreated from its position. In fact, it is dominated by different interest groups in the market, so it is hard to define in a single narrative, and its construction is changed from one voice to plural voices. Another is considering that the state is still playing a significant function in the formation of gender discourse, but it absorbs more ideas of modernity, and often becomes accomplice of market and consumerist culture.

2. For the gender discourse in Maoist and post-Maoist periods, researchers have different perspectives, and can be divided basically into positive and negative ones. The positive affirmations on the Maoist gender discourse are as follows: firstly, since the advocation in ideology and arrangement in institution by the state, gender equality was accepted generally as a political fashion, and women's liberation was brought into the process of modernisation to be one of the important heritages of socialism; secondly, under the banner of

gender equality and women's liberation, women were allowed to go outside the home to involve in social activities, whose living conditions and participating abilities improved and enhanced greatly; and thirdly, this revolutionary discourse stroke to some extent the traditional style of gender division and the patriarchal culture of taking man as superior and woman as inferior.

The negative criticism of the Maoist gender discourse is mainly from the following aspects: firstly, gender equality is actually a kind of gendered sameness modelled on man, which erases the gender differences between man and woman, and recognises the superior position of the man; secondly, women's participation in work has not changed the traditional arrangement of gender role, but brought them double burden. Gender equality has not been implemented completely in practice, and women's liberation always served the interests of state and has become an 'unfinished' or 'delayed' revolution; and thirdly, since gender equality was implemented through top down approach, as a 'bestowed' equality it may accustom women to a dependent mentality. Without a subject consciousness, it cannot be regarded as real women's liberation.

In the post-Maoist gender discourse, positive affirmations from researchers are very seldom. Firstly, recognising the existence of gender difference is a kind of resistance to the political discourse in revolutionary period, which provides justification for the construction of women's experience and subject consciousness; secondly, emphasizing on the market rule of efficiency and rationality and modernity discourse on the basis of individualism brings women more opportunities of self-development, and also brings them multiple spaces of individual choice.

In contrast, negative criticisms of post-Maoist gender discourse are much more varied. Firstly, overemphasis on the 'natural' difference between man and woman is essentialist, that leads to the revival of the traditional gender culture and the prevalence of body politics, pleading for women's commercialisation in consumerist culture; secondly, the overspread of marketisation and the retreat of the state makes women face discrimination in public and become one of the marginal groups. The notion of 'women going back home' is suggested again and again, and the traditional style of gender division is admired, and the state to some extent plays the role of an ally; thirdly, efficiency-oriented and individualist narratives of modernity discourse appear constantly in the media, which represents power relationship among different interest groups. The 'quality' discourse advocated by the state strengthens the fragility of women, and slides over the issues of gender inequality institutionally and structurally.

Based on the researches mentioned above, this paper explores the disputing issues of gender discourse formation in the Maoist and post-Maoist eras, and tries to figure out the relationship between the globalisation and the transformation of gender discourse using the official and the media gender texts in two different periods and from the oral history texts from working women themselves. On the ground, this paper discusses how working women are restrained by and negotiate the transformation of gender discourse.

Analysis of Elements of Gender Discourse Formation

There are various meanings of the term 'discourse'. This paper uses Foucault's terminology. It represents different ways of constructing fields of knowledge and social practice, and is formed in history and society, implying a kind of power relationship, prescribing a social order, and shaping people's social identities and subject positions. 'It is the social effects of the discourse that become the centre of discourse analysis' (Fairclough, 2004: 3). The critical discourse analysis 'is to inspect how the language makes influence on the social reproduction and social change', to recognise 'how the current discursive habits become the effects of power relationship and power fight', and 'to reveal the social and historical mechanism naturalising these habits' (Talbot, 2004: 161). So the critical examination of gender discourse is actually to examine how gender is constructed socially, how it has become a natural part of daily life, and how it could continuously change and advance.

Among the elements of gender discourse formation, the state, market and traditional culture are three fundamental forces. Sometimes they fight, sometimes separate and sometimes unite, playing different roles in the construction of gender discourse in different eras. The traditional culture is the basic element of gender discourse formation. It has longest history, broadest effect, and plays important roles both in Maoist and post-Maoist times. But it is also most ambiguous and disputing element, because different agents holding the banner of traditional culture usually agitate for variable ideas. It is the variability that identifies its special long position either in the folk or in the official discourse: You can never stand it aside, either canonise or denounce. The state is unquestionably in the dominant official status among the three elements, especially in Maoist time, it played a role of all-powerful creator of gender discourse, and strangled any other alternatives. Even the traditional culture had to be a property of the arena. Nevertheless, it still meets unavoidably challenge from the market, and adjusts its narrative and position it in the modernity. Market is the latest one within the three elements but not the least one. In post-Maoist era, the influence of market has grown and impacted the other two elements. It has become an internalised dominant element that people have followed actively both in the folk and officially. Although in China the gender discourse in different periods is not constructed simply by a single element, for analysing the complicated mechanisms behind it clearly, the discourses are dominated by three different elements, viz., state discourse, market discourse and traditional discourse.[1] They are decomposed one by one and analysis is made.

Traditional Discourse

The core of the traditional discourse is patriarchy, which maintains male centralism and the mastering relationship on women from the cultural opinion, institutional arrangement and identification. Its basic premise is the stress on the biological differences between man and woman, and the rationality in the gender division of role. For example, in the family, it adheres to the relationship mode of 'man is in charge of outside and woman is in charge of inside' or 'husband singing and wife accompanying'; in the social division it adheres to the public-private mode of man aiming for career and woman aiming for family; and in the gender relationship it adheres to the hierarchical mode of taking man as superior and woman as inferior, man as strong and woman as weak, man dominating and woman subordinating. Accordingly, a set of gender-related social habits and institutional customs have been formed, such as the man is the breadwinner of the family, and performs the task of rearing up the kin. He holds the heritage of the family property, and also takes the responsibility of supporting the elders of the family. A woman's responsibility in the family is to support children, look after husband, elders and children, and not to be involved in social activity. So, as per tradition, a woman has to live with her husband's family together after getting married and become a virtuous wife and good mother. And, they have usually no right to share the ancestral property, and also have no obligation of supporting their parents.

This set of gender discourse not only prescribes the running mechanism of social order and power relationship in traditional kindred society, but also prescribes the subject position, and identification of man and woman, constructs the knowledge about who is man and who is woman, and what is the difference between masculinity and femininity. The construction of the knowledge is grounded on the traditional dualism, where man and woman are corresponded respectively with *yang* and *yin*, heaven and earth, strong and weak, hard and soft, tough and tender, rational and emotional, master and subservient, and so on. It establishes an evaluation system in which a good man's criterion is successful and firm, and a good woman's criterion is pretty and virtuous. This traditional discourse system comes through thousands of years and stands as of old. Undergoing the May Fourth enlightenment, women's liberation movement of Communist Party and the impact of the market rule in globalisation, it is just the same as putting on different coats in different situations.

In the Maoist period, gender equality was advocated all over the country, and women were encouraged to go outside the home to get involved in socialist construction. At that time the traditional discourse was a villain in the official discourse, representing 'feudalist' harmful influence of taking man as superior and woman as inferior. And women must go outside the home to work if they would like to achieve liberation. But, in fact, it is greatly determined by the practical situation of the nation and society if women could work outside or not indeed. Professor Jin's study indicates that woman plays 'a role of supporting labour and important reservoir of industry'. That is to say, in the condition of lack of social labour, women become 'a great human resource' and are encouraged to participate in social work, and to establish the idea that working is glorious. But, in the situation of economic contraction, women usually are the first ones to quit, 'to go back home to engage in housework securely' (Yihong, 2006). The norm of gender role in traditional discourse did not suffer substantial refuse in the Maoist period, but was changed into 'traditional virtue of women' or 'special demand of women'. And, although the state advocated and promoted the notion of equal pay for equal work between man and woman, at least in the rural area, man and woman participating in the same work still had differential Gong Fen treatment. And, this kind of situation has been verified in my interviews by middle-aged rural women. For example, a 55 years old woman, working now as a maidservant in the city, talked about her life in the countryside when she was young and used the term 'feudalist' 11 times in negative sense. From her narrative we can easily find the influence of official discourse on the general people, and also find that the idealism dominant discourse promoted was discounted in reality.

In contrast, in post-Maoist period, the role of traditional discourse in the mainstream is mainly positive though relatively complicated. Its revival and flourish has got people's admiration and admission. For example, in 1980s, the national fashionable trend of 'looking for a man with masculinity' and 'going back to be a woman with femininity' could be regarded as a typical return of traditional discourse. This return appears in a way of protest about the institution of oppressing and distorting human nature in the Maoist period, and is a rectification of the no-sex culture of gendered sameness. So at that time the term 'female consciousness' arose in high frequency in the discussions of media and the writings. As Professor Wang Zheng said, the discursive practice, replacing 'man and woman is the same' by 'man and woman is the different', is a challenge to Maoist official dominant discourse. That's why it could be resounded widely, whose goal is 'to criticise and throw off the absolute control of the state on the individual, and to exploit women's own space' (Zheng, 1997). But Zheng reviewed that this construction strategy of 'naturalising women' has not challenged the traditional gender institution, because it focuses on returning to women's biological nature, and seldom examines the male centralism within the traditional discourse. 'This explains to a large extent why the appearance of "female consciousness" not only didn't confront big resistance, but also got widely resound including drive from the male in short time. Furthermore, since the "female consciousness" only has the force of destructing the state discourse "man and woman is the same", and has no challenge to the traditional culture of taking man as superior and woman as inferior, the market economy can accept, absorb and utilise the "female consciousness" undoubtedly' (ibid.).

The return of the traditional discourse in the post-Maoist period is also embodied in the narratives of my interviewees. *Xym*, a 36 years old woman, is a manager in a company. Born in an intellectual family, she was taught from childhood by her parents that 'girls should be independent'; 'they shouldn't be dependent on somebody else'. But when she graduated from college and was introduced to dating boys, she felt frustrated more than once. And, she said most unbearable is the reason of her failure: 'You know what? It is the reason why people wouldn't like to date me provokes me. They all feel that the girl is too strong to rein in. They introduce a Ph.D. to me, who after talking to me, said no to the matchmaker, fearing that I am too capable. He hoped to find a wife who would help the husband and educate the children. Sometimes I'm really disappointed' (13 July 2006). Two points emerge from the narrative: the traditional discourse of man being in charge of outside and woman in charge of inside is still rooted deeply even in the well educated group; it represents the women as a villain with independent consciousness. But talking about the return of the traditional discourse in the post-Maoist period, *Xym* acknowledged frankly that in her own mind there exists similar idea. She emphasised that she will give her daughter not only good education, but also good femininity. I asked her what femininity means to her, she replied: 'My understanding of femininity is broader. It is first in your appearance; another is in life, as a woman you should be able to do something, right? It seems to merge into some traditional things. For example, is it right that a man shouldn't learn cooking? I feel subconsciously that it is really this kind of idea' (ibid.). From the narrative what we see is a positive acceptance and recognition of traditional discourse, but it is more like a strategic thinking. So we can say that the traditional discourse has different styles with different fashionable coats, and has become a usable resource of choice life for different individuals. It is understandable why working women often have ambivalent attitudes towards the traditional discourse.

State Discourse

The state discourse in the Maoist period could be generalised as *state feminism.*[2] Institutionally, in 1950s the state promulgated a set of regulations and laws on gender equality, including ones on liberal marriage, equal pay for equal work, and women's participation in politics, and so on, prescribing in constitutional meaning 'women's equal rights with men in political, economic, cultural and educational, and all aspects of social lives' (*Conjunct Creed,* 1950). These regulations include marriage law, land law, election law, provision of labour protection, policies of employment and retirement, and so on. *Wsm*, a senior specialist of women's studies, also a high official of ACWF (All-China Women's Federation), used the words like 'radical' and 'perfect' to review the Chinese policy framework on women issues in the early period of revolution. She argued that this policy framework reflects the 'plain thought of gender equality' of the leaders like Mao Zedong and also their idealist belief of 'building up an egalitarian new society'; on the other hand, it was a need of the complicated social reality of that time. The state must mobilise women as a valuable human resource to participate in the socialist construction, so even the men then supported women's policies very much. But, as *Wsm* said, 'Gender equality is not generated naturally, but achieved through the edification of democracy and advocation. It is necessary to have a process like that' (26 May 2006). Therefore, the state discourse embodied in ideology is to make propaganda of idealism and an atmosphere of gender equality in various ways. It includes the speech of the well-known leader, such as 'The time is different; woman is the equal of man. So anything a man can do, a woman can do better', 'Women can hold half the sky', 'Chinese woman is a kind of great human resource', and so on. It also includes the women's images in revolution and construction standing by men shown in contemporary newspapers, media and literary works. Furthermore, the state established a special institute – ACWF – in 1949 as the bridge connecting the party and government with the women at large. Its goal is to unite the women from various strata and ethnicities all over the country, with the national people together, and organise them to fight against imperialism, destroy feudalism and bureaucratic capitalism, and for constructing a united people's democracy republic, to strive for abolishing all the feudalist traditional customs, and to protect women's rights and children's welfare, carrying out gender equality and women's liberation. From the ACWF constitution we can conclude at least two points: (1) women's liberation is covered and submitted to the undertaking of national liberation and construction of the country; and (2) abolishing the feudalist traditional custom and to take part in socialist construction is the premise of achieving gender equality. So, the knowledge construction on gender equality and women's liberation has a special political meaning in the Maoist period.

Exploring the knowledge construction of women in 1950s China, Professor Jiping Zuo finds that this liberation 'was served the national and class liberation and socialist practice, so it took a strong instrumental colour'. But, she argues, 'that's it is not to say the instrumental liberation does not contain the nature of individual liberation', but 'the instrumentality and multiplicity of Chinese women's liberation destines the compatibility of right and obligation of women in the process of struggle, and also the limitation to carry out completely the individual liberation' (Zuo, 2005). Therefore, she argues that 'this multiple, instrumental and top-down women's liberation' determines that Chinese gender equality is different from the western 'equality of opportunity and right between man and woman grounded on the individual liberation', but all the more means 'equality of individual obligation for the nation and class liberation and for the country' (ibid.). This equality in obligation was solidified in the form of working unit system in the city. Urban women workers get identification and 'a mentality of host' from the unit system and, at the same time, it constrains their personal and familial space of development. It is because 'the implementing of equality in obligation changes the traditional values of work and gives a political meaning to work. Attending work means attending revolution, and stand or fall in work is becoming one of important symbols to measure the individual's faith or not with the country, and the couple is also becoming "revolutionary comrades" of co-constructing the great undertaking from the partner of "man is in charge of outside and woman in charge of inside". Employment for women means not only freeing from the home, but also "no longer idling about in the home" and "adding tiles for the socialism"' (ibid.). So, in Zuo's perspective, 'when liberation and obligation are compatible, the mode of women's liberation is not just imitating the male standard, but both use a standard as a "state person"'. In this meaning, 'neither man nor woman has ever gained complete liberation in individual meaning' (ibid.).

Accordingly, the nature of the state feminism is the basis of the state's will and need. This kind of women's liberation and gender equality sponsored by the state is too confined to the public fields of social lives, and is still far away from the goal of real equality and liberation in individual meaning. Liu Bohong emphasises that women's equality with men is a different concept from gender equality. In China women's equality with men has been misinterpreted by the traditional culture. It has two tendencies: one is taking man as the criteria; another is actually taking 'man is in charge of outside and woman is in charge of inside' as equality, neglecting the basic request of breaking gender division between man and woman in gender equality (Workshop Records, 2007). In my interviews, I have asked some elders about their personal feeling of gender equality in the Maoist period, and the answers are unusually identical:

almost negative. For example, previously mentioned *Aj*, when talked about the lifestyle in village, emphasised over and over again that 'in countryside woman's life is especially hard, where is any equality?'

Wu	In post-Maoist period, wasn't gender equality popular?
Aj	But in my village it didn't carry out.
Wu	Why?
Aj	Because the old force of feudalism was still working.
Wu	Which aspect does it embody? You mean man and woman do the same work?
Aj	They do the same, but going back home; you have to do heavy work. Everything in the home and house, man has never minded.
Wu	That's to say woman always does more housework.
Aj	They do much more, and very hard.
Wu	And then they have to take care of the mother-in-law, the old and the young, all is their business.
Aj	You're right. All those are woman's business.

(14 April 2006)

The narrative indicates that even in the powerful state, the traditional discourse is still working in some range, especially in a field like family which is usually ignored by the state discourse and the equality of gender relationship within it is restricted largely. And, since the state discourse in Maoist period focuses on the equality between man and woman in obligation and contribution to the country and the society, which means women perform some part of function belonging to men and without lightening their own role and obligation as the traditional discourse required, it must bring the women then unprecedented double burden.

Talking about the woman-related labour policy in the Maoist period, Wsm acknowledged that actually 'there existed a big contradiction between policy and practice'. On the one hand, the state had a wide range of propaganda for activating people's passion, and mobilising women to go outside to work; on the other hand, the low-level of industrialisation and the lack of working positions brought heavy pressure in the city. So housewives were a very large group at that time. And, the government just declared 'housework is also a social work, so it is glorious'. That is to say, woman's employment was unstable during that period and was determined by the state situation and policy. Somebody even describes it as 'moving women' but not 'women's movement' (26 May 2006). Nevertheless, as Zuo's study indicates, women in that period 'were absolutely not passive group being manipulated in the process of construction of "liberation" and "equality", but the main force creating equality in obligation. Their involvement not only reflects the desire of the party for women's liberation and contribution, but also represents women's activity to the construction and identification of their subject position' (Zuo, 2005). And, this subject identity to a large extent profits from the 'most significant technical strategy' during the construction of knowledge on women's employment, that is to equate employment or not with revolution or progress or not, and also with whether 'women in new China' would like to 'keel over for liberation' (Tong, 2005: 77). Attached with such a label, women's employment holds some special political meanings, and has a host stance entering into the dominant discourse and feeling of self-liberation. This stance and feeling keeps women's employment down as a unique tradition, and makes it work even when the state discourse is inflexuous in post-Maoist era.[3]

After reforms and openness in the 1980s, Chinese government's basic attitude and general idea in gender issues has not changed. But, the narrative of state discourse has some new content and approach. Gender equality is regarded as a fundamental national policy, and the status of women as half the sky is affirmed adequately. In the working report on the 6th Women Representatives Conference in 1988, the general mission of women's movement was described as: 'under the guidance of the party's fundamental line, women from various ethnicities and circles should unite together, being self-esteem, self-confidence, self-independence and self-strength, and to raise the quality as a whole, to involve actively in the reforms and construction, for getting the victory during the main stage of reforms, and promoting the gender equality.' And, the 'basic social responsibility of ACWF is to represent and to protect women's interests, and to promote equality between men and women'. In 1992, the state promulgated the law on the protection of rights and interests of women to declare that 'women shall enjoy equal rights with men in all aspects of political, economic, cultural, social and family life. The state shall protect the special rights and interests enjoyed by women according to law and gradually perfect its social security system with respect to women. Discrimination against, maltreatment of, or cruel treatment in any manner causing injury to women shall be prohibited'. The Programme for the Development of Chinese Women, promulgated by the State Council in 1995, raised explicitly that 'by the end of the century, the general mission of women's development in our country is: women's quality as a whole should be raised obviously, and in the process of participating in economic construction and social development completely, and participating in the management of the state and social issues, women's equal rights imbibed legally in political, economic, cultural, social and family lives should be implemented further'.

In these texts women's liberation was connected with national reforms and openness and the undertaking of modernisation. But, the different thing is added in new articulations about raising the women's quality, advocating the four-self spirits, and maintaining women's rights and interests. This transformation in articulations is related to the new recognition of the modernity by the state, which follows the logic as follows: The realisation of modernisation needs the promotion of all people's quality. And, the market economy is to break the traditional egalitarian big pot rice, to change the psychology of waiting, relying and wanting for the country, through enhancing the individual quality and striving constantly to achieve the individual self-development. Therefore, this new narrative includes two underlying transformations of the relationship between a general person (including woman) and the country: (i) is to transform from the collectivism underlining individual submission unconditionally to the need of the country, to the individual the modernity of the state must presuppose the promotion and development of individual ability; (ii) an individual has become an autonomous subject of market choice from the passive object of protection and manipulation by the state, and the personal identity has also been measured from the simplified label of innate class to the acquired ability comparison. So, though the quality discourse has the flaw as the western scholars criticise that 'focus on only the overcoming of the personal disadvantage but not the fundamental inequality structurally' (Tamara, 2006: 67), since quality is relative to the acquired study and ability, being dynamic and changeable, it at least destroys the discourse according to the born status in the Maoist period, and provides the individual explicit direction of striving and larger space of choice. This has an irresistible positive meaning for Chinese people, especially who experienced the all-controlled close society in the Maoist era.

Aside from this, the new state discourse specifically highlights the maintenance of women's rights and interests. It is because the problem of women's rights and interests has gradually become severe since the 1980s. For example, more and more people are leaving their working positions with the advance of reforms and the increase of employment pressure, and amongst which women are usually the first group. More and more women have been driven out from the formal labour market. They are forced to engage in informal work or be unemployed, being the marginalised group in the labour market. In the process of rural modernisation, the labour division has presented a phenomenon of 'polarizing gender' (Yihong, 2000). As large number of men leave the agriculture for the non-agriculture jobs in urban area, it leads to the 'feminisation of agriculture'. The sexual segregation in occupation is more serious. Men get priority in the labour market, and women are marginalised in the processes of industrialisation and urbanisation, leading to the 'feminisation of poverty'. Thus, there appears the phenomenon of discrimination, deprivation of women in various aspects of the social lives and the differentiation between man and woman is representing a severe trend (The Project Group of the Second Survey on Chinese Women's Social Status, 2001). Therefore, maintaining rights becomes an indispensable task for mobilising women to enter into the process of modernisation in the post-Maoist era. The ACWF takes the 'development on the one hand, while maintaining rights on another hand' as its working guideline:

> The 16th People's Representative Conference underlines that the development must be the first mission of reign and prosperity. We must 'resolve the problems as the development progresses', must 'deploy all positive factors widely and adequately', to make 'the people's political, economic and cultural rights and interests gain substantial respect and safeguards'. It has important meaning for us to recognise and deal correctly with the relationship between 'development' and 'maintenance of rights'.

To mobilise and organise the women to take part actively in the construction of socialist modernisation, and to realise their own development in pushing economic and social development, is the essential way of maintaining women's rights and interests. But we cannot say once economy grows, women's problems will be resolved naturally. While paying attention to the development, we must also try to maintain the equal position and legal rights of women in political, economic, cultural, social and family spheres, to struggle with the phenomenon of discriminating and hurting women, so that we can create a good social environment for the women's development. Accordingly, development and maintenance of rights are interlinked. Only adhering to the guideline of 'development on the one hand, while maintaining rights on another hand', can we deploy the activity and creativity of women involved in the construction of socialist modernisation, and the equality of women with men can be promoted further (Peiyun, 2002).

In this narrative text, we can see that gender equality is imbibed in a new content. It does not focus on the equality in obligation between man and woman as in the Maoist period, but highlights much more than the equal right and opportunity between them; it does not argue to promote social development on the ground of static equality as in the Maoist period, but asserts to push the dynamic realisation of equality in the way of women's development. In the meantime, it identifies explicitly that it does not mean that women's problem will be settled with the growing economy. That means it acknowledges the unmatched situation between economic development and gender equality in the post-Maoist period, and points out the role the government should play in balancing the relationship.

But, in the institution and regulation, this idea of equality highlighting the empowerment sense has not been embodied adequately. Discussing the current situation of gender equality, *Wsm* criticised the state gender policy during the reforms and its openness. She described the conflict in the word 'heart quake' on the issues of 'women's going back home' and 'irregular employment' between the ACWF and the related of decision-making departments in the 1970s, 1980s and 1990s and the early 21st century. She said that the most breathtaking time was 2001 when the government had put the sentence 'building a system of employment brokenly, and developing a form of flexible employment' into the Development Programme of the Tenth Five-Year Plan. The ACWF decided to resist it by pointing out that so far there has not been a country that puts the irregular employment into a regulation, and this kind of policy will provide a bad model internationally. This policy violates the Constitution, Labour Law and the Law on Protection of Women's Rights and Interests. As a consequence it orders women to go back home justifiably resulting in wasting the efforts made in achieving gender equality for years, and is a big reserve. The resolution of the employment issue can never be at the cost of women's interests (26 May 2006). The shift in the official position on women's employment issue under the pressure of employment in market economy implies that the state has greatly impacted the market discourse. Li Huiying criticised that the responsibility of promoting the gender equality has been laid aside or relegated into the background by the state under the market economy, and it is a big dereliction of duty for the government (Workshop Records, 2007).

Market Discourse

Market discourse was initiated in the context of market economy. Its core is the quality and ability theory based on individualism, which presupposes that the market can provide a fair competitive platform for both men and women, with high quality and ability, to make great advancement. This discourse recognises the differences and traits between man and woman, and believes that it is these differences and traits which determine the different resources and abilities man and woman hold, and make them face different sufferings and situations. So, the quality discourse advocated by the state in the post-Maoist period is a typical market discourse. The quality is different from the biological character. It can be shaped by the acquired education and endeavour. According to the discourse, women's liberation is not an issue of changing their biological character, but an issue of improving their competitive abilities and resources to adapt to the mainstream society. Here market discourse is completely identical with the state discourse. Both do not consider the issue of inequality socially structured and institutionalised, focusing on only the cultivation and improvement of modern quality of woman as individual. But, the definition of and judgement on qualified quality needed by modernity is absolutely controlled by the male-dominated society. It takes the pursuit of efficiency as the first principle, and the egalitarian discourse advocated in the Maoist era loosing support unconsciously.

For example, in the debate on 'women going back home' amongst media, scholars and the public, the reasons given by the supporters are as follows: in the social perspective, it can lightened the pressure of employment, guarantee a fair social competitive order, and enhance the social efficiency; in the familial perspective, maintaining the natural division of gender is also most efficient in economy, and simultaneously it benefits the growing-up and education of the children. The reasons given by the opponents are as follows: from the practical consequence, letting the women go back home or employ irregularly equates to depriving women the right to work and employment. It may lead to women's marginalisation and going down the social and familial position; from the social angle, it cannot resolve the unemployment problem. We can thus see that the supporters regard women as innately of low-quality and low-efficiency, and replace the familial and social interests as personal interest of women, ignoring women's demand as subject; whereas the opponents distinguish the interests of individual woman from the familial and social interests, considering women's demand as subject, but they have not criticised the equation of women to the low-quality and low-efficiency, and that is the core of male centralism in market discourse.

The other meaning related to the market discourse is the gendered orientation in consumeritic culture. The marketism presupposes the existence of division and difference, and the traditional gender discourse gains a large developing space in this context. Comparing with the Maoist period, the 'naturalisation' of gender division and difference between man and woman is underlined unprecedentedly during the period, and woman's body, appearances and roles are valued highly as an irreplaceable resource which may get efficiency and opportunity in the market. This has justified to some extent the commercialisation and bodilisation of women. So, at this point, market discourse absorbed entirely the norm on gender role advocated in traditional discourse, and pushes the traditional orientation of women to an extreme, just packing in a style of modern fashionable discourse. Therefore, women's quality discourse is divided into two aspects: one is the modern competitive ability based on individualism; another is the symbol of body consumption based on the orientation of women's special role in the relationship to gender. The first aspect is related to the pursuit of modernity, which gets strong mobilisation and support from the state discourse; while the second aspect gains quickly the recognition from the public and women themselves in the globalised consumptive fashion helping the traditional discourse, while in summary, only holding the first aspect of the quality discourse can make woman 'doing well'; and only holding the second aspect of the discourse can make her 'marrying well'.

Actually, the most disputing issue on the women's situation in post-Maoist era is the issue of relationship between 'doing well' and 'marrying well'. The second national survey on Chinese women's social status in 2001 indicate that the traditional stereotypes on gender generate visible influences in the context of market economy. For instance, 53.9 per cent of males and 50.4 per cent of females agree with the saying 'man is in charge of outside and woman is in charge of inside', and 34.1 per cent of respondents agree with the saying 'rather marrying well than doing well', and females within this group are 37.3 per cent, 7.1 per cent higher than males (The Project Group of the Second Survey on Chinese Women's Social Status, 2001). A survey on Contemporary Gender Expectation in China conducted by the First Asian Women Forum also shows that 46.1 per cent of participants agree with 'rather marrying well than doing well', and female percentage is much higher than the percentage of males (*The Beijing News*, 2004). A letter from a female college student published in *China Youth Daily* also expresses the confused emotion facing the phenomenon that girls concern marriage more than individual striving:

> As a female student, I have been longing for success through my own efforts, but the reality is far away from the idealism. Female students are frustrated in looking for a job, and some super-women succeed in career at the cost of personal marriage. The society is advancing today. Women have got liberation and can participate in the social competition. But they face many difficulties in various aspects. Even they want to get the same success but have to face more hardship than men. Nowadays more and more better-educated female students are inclined to look for a successful man to get a better life. And furthermore, their choices are perfect and happy either in their own and other's eyes, or from the interest and traditional angles. Does woman really have to be appendage of man and 'rather marrying well than doing well'? I'm confused and have no idea how to make my choice. (*China Youth Daily*, 2006)

A review in sina.com concludes the relationship of 'doing well' and 'marrying well' as below: 'For a woman, what is more important, "marrying well" or "doing well"? Let me tell you the truth ... if you can't achieve "doing well", then you can try "marrying well"; if you have no chance of "marrying well", then you can try "doing well"; but if you can achieve neither "doing well" nor "marrying well", then you have to discuss ... "doing well" or "marrying well"!' (Geng, 2003). This description represents the meaningful relationship between 'doing well' and 'marrying well' in the post-Maoist period from the perspective of woman's choice as an individual. The two aspects of the market discourse construct two basic lines of the choices, and the contrast between them implies another perspective of examining the relationship of 'doing well' and 'marrying well' – perspective of social structure and cultural norm. Firstly, in perspective of social structure, women cannot get equal opportunity of 'doing well' with men. Since the market itself has not provided real fair competitive platform, and in the context of competition of ability based on individualism women face greater frustration. They have to suffer more difficulties than men to achieve 'doing well'. Secondly, in perspective of cultural norm, women 'doing well' must not achieve 'marrying well', sometimes they even have to face the embarrassment of marrying nobody. And, the symbol of body consumption based on women's orientation of special role in the gender relationship is approved in the market, which brings women back to the traditional discourse aimed for 'marrying well'. So 'rather marrying well than doing well' has become a popular slogan among the working women, including good-educated working women, in the post-Maoist period. And it is also one of the hotly debated issue in the media and on the internet.

The prevailing debates on 'rather marrying well than doing well' actually imply such an assumption, that is, regard the two kinds of quality discourses as opposite and separate aspects, as an alternative lifestyle for women. But for many of my interviewees, especially in case of women below 40 years, the two quality discourses are simultaneously accepted. In their opinion, it is not contradictory to do well and to marry well, and the most significant is to realise their own autonomous choices. *Clh* is a 29 years old graduate student. In her oral history narrative, she mentioned many a time the importance of doing well for herself. At the same time, she surprisingly confirmed the traditional orientation of women's role in family. In her view, the criteria of an excellent woman should be 'excellent in multiple fields'. She should be 'outstanding both in guestroom and in kitchen, being capable in career, and can play her social role perfectly either in the work place or at home. She should know what is her responsibility? I think the most important is that you should be content with your own life (11 July 2006). And excellent women are those who can make use of the resources and advantages from both the aspects of quality discourse to achieve their own goals, doing well and marrying well. So, the market discourse for *Clh* has a positive meaning than the female college student mentioned above. Because what she values is the freedom of autonomous choice, and it is only market that can provide such a platform.

Nevertheless, the negative effect of market discourse is obvious to all. Women to a large extent become a passive object of consumption due to overadmiration of body, appearance and role. This kind of consumptive fashion enlarges the natural difference between man and woman, guiding women's body towards commercialisation and objectification, and the quality discourse is simplified to be a market orientation of body's price. At this point, the tradition and the market unite to become an alliance, building together a sexist commercial discourse world. In my interviews, almost everyone realises the importance of body and appearance of a woman, and many claim that she has, is or is going to lose weight. They are very sensitive to the changes in their bodies and appearances, especially the white-collar workers in companies. *Zca* works for a foreign company, whose diet is a cup of coffee as lunch every day. When I asked her why she wouldn't have lunch, she answered: 'I'm just used to. Because my absorbing capability is extraordinary strong, and whatever I eat works.' Then I asked her if she hoped to keep slim, she answered implicitly: 'It's because girls always hope that they can feel good in front of the other people', and many girls in her company just want to keep a young and energetic state as her (15 June 2006).

Apart from this, the growing beauty industry and sex industry, and also the appearance of more and more professional housewives and 'second wife', has formed a landscape unique of this era. It implies that in post-Maoist market context the opportunity to get the two kinds of quality discourses is not equal for women. And it is obviously easier by a way of women's body and role than by individual's ability to enter into the market and get higher remuneration. Therefore, an interesting phenomenon is that 'superwoman' in this era is usually a negative term naming the women with high personal ability and 'doing well'. For instance, the girl mentioned above, 34 years old *Zca* is in a very high position in her company, but she said frankly that she does not like the word 'superwoman'. In fact, the most classical saying prevailing on campuses and internet is calling the female Ph.D. with high-level knowledge and strong independence as 'the third category of human being' other than man and woman. They are described as unsocial strangers and hard to find partner in marriage market. In various discussions about female Ph.D., participants usually concentrate on how to remove the 'misunderstanding' about female Ph.D. and recover their reputation. A female Ph.D. even wrote a book called *I'm a Female Ph.D., Whom Will I Marry* to correct people's biases. 'In fact, the female Ph.Ds are not monsters. They also have pretty appearance, slim figure and tender nature. Compared with general women, they are more knowledgeable, a little more rational, and face little more difficulty in finding a partner ...' (Caiyun, 2005). But few participants question the gender discourse behind these 'misunderstandings' and 'biases'. Jin Yihong's 'Talking about Female Ph.D. among Five Persons' may be the few exceptions: 'Contemporary society requires women to have much higher quality and some extent of freedom and independent personality. But the premise is women can't go too far away, can't threaten men's position as authority ... If the chains put on women is steel-made in the past, now they are changed to flexible one' (Yihong, 2003). This implies that even for the successful women like a female Ph.D. and superwoman, their traditional identity and character as a woman is always more important than their identity as an independent person, and so gets more concern from the male-dominated society. That is to say, the first aspect of the quality discourse cannot replace the special meaning of the second aspect in the market of appreciation of women. In gender issues, modernity and tradition in market discourse have weirdly united.

From State to Market: Globalisation and the Transformation of Gender Discourse

According to the above analysis, the gender discourse in Chinese society from Maoist to post-Maoist era has a great transformation: from a discourse model dominated by the state to one oriented by the market. But the transformation is not simply from state discourse to market discourse, because the traditional discourse has played an important role in both the periods, and the state discourse her not retreated completely in market era, but is changed in both content and way of narrative. This complication constructs very different models of gender discourse in two periods.

I will call the gender discourse in Maoist era as a 'Yo-Yo Model'. The elements constructing the model are the state discourse and traditional discourse, which are bound in the two poles of a spring. And, the state is the hand which is at the position of control, and the traditional discourse is the yo-yo hanged up by the spring (see Figure 1). On the one hand, the state discourse takes an exclusionary attitude on the traditional discourse, determining its going up or down through flapping. And, even the traditional discourse is rebounded; it will be grasped tight in the state's hand. By this way, the state discourse establishes its own authority, and changes the appearance of the traditional discourse as it desires. On the other hand, the traditional discourse as yo-yo has a very tenacious life force. Especially once it touches the ground reality, it will rebound highly, sometimes even slipping the leash of the state discourse and showing its own force. Therefore, in this model, the state discourse manipulates the traditional discourse only through a flexible force, tight or loose, over and over again. So, this kind of women's liberation and gender equality will come under limitations. And, the traditional discourse suffers greatly in the public political fields, while it finds wide existing space in the daily life. The conflict between the two discourse forces is not face-to-face and firm. Many a times there are flexible and countless ties between them. Its main attribute is: women as subjects are usually submerged in the conflicts and blends between the two forces, attending to one thing and losing another, without real freedom of choice.

Figure 1

Yo-Yo Model

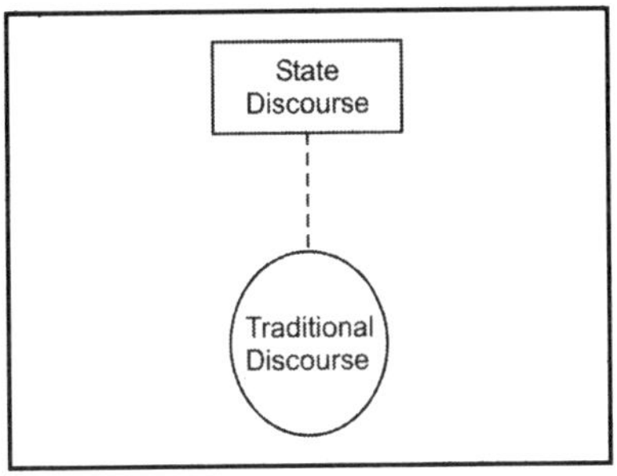

Figure 2

Three-Circle Overlapping Model

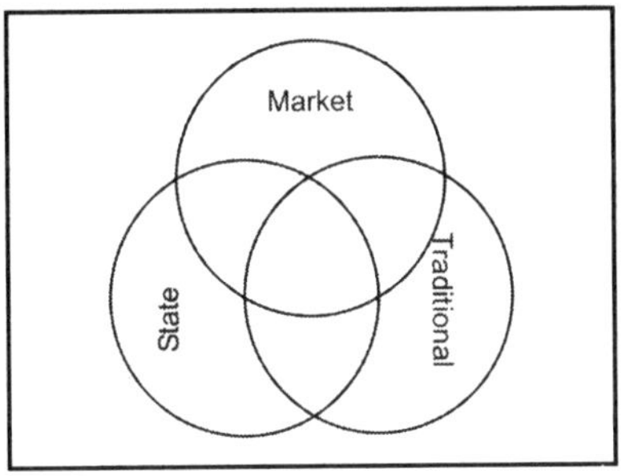

The elements of gender discourse in post-Maoist era add market discourse aside from state and traditional one, so its structure is more complicated. I will call it as 'Three-Circle-Overlapping Model' (see Figure 2). Each circle represents a discourse element. They overlap each other to construct a dynamic balance and collaboration. For example, centred on the market discourse, on the one hand, it highlights the individual ability and quality, which is corresponded with the quality discourse and 'Four Selfs' advocated by the state discourse; on the other hand, it highlights the women's body and role as resource, which is corresponded with the cultural norm of gender declared in the traditional discourse. From the standpoint of state discourse, although it calls for 'development on one hand, while maintaining right on other hand', it raises quality and ability theory equated with market discourse to recluse itself from duty on women's frustration in development; and when women's maintenance of rights encounters difficulty, it often surrenders to gender norm such as 'man is in charge of outside and woman in charge of inside' declared in the traditional discourse to deconstruct the problem it face. This means, that the state discourse in the post-Maoist period relies largely on and submits to the market discourse. And, the traditional discourse appears as the collaborator of the state and market discourse. It has a more positive role, becoming a part of new fashion in the consumerist period. Therefore, the gender discourse in the post-Maoist period takes a strong attribute of de-politicalised, generally from a 'pan-politicalisation' in the past to a present-day 'pan-marketism'. Women in this period face various opportunities of choice and freedom. But, it also makes them lose the direction of choice, getting into a dilemma between gender and development, independence and ease.

A significant background shaping the transformation of gender discourse is the impact of globalisation on China since 1990s initiated through the reforms. As demonstrated above, in the pursuit of 'development is a firm truth' and 'joining tracks with the world', modern quality discourse based on individualism has become official dominant discourse. The 4th World Women's Conference (WWC) held in Beijing in 1995 introduced the concepts such as NGO and human rights into gender fields in China. So globalisation first changes the content and approach of narrative of the state discourse. As Liu Bohong from the Institute of Women's Studies in ACWF said, 'The impact of international society including globalisation has direct effect on the policy enactment of gender equality in China. For example, the holding of the 4th WWC promoted the advancement of Chinese gender equality policy in two aspects: Firstly, the Programme of Action passed in the WWC tries to bring gender perspective into the mainstream decision-making, i.e., it mainstreamed the gender perspective. Governments of 186 countries, including China, made commitment to this action programme. As the host country, China had made a specific commitment, making the Programme for the Development of Chinese Women from 1995 to 2000 as an action programme before the conference. Secondly, Jiang Zemin declared in his opening remarks that the Chinese government will put women's equality with men into a national fundamental policy of promoting social development ... . The national fundamental policy is basic regulation and policy of the country. I think it's probably a narrative of mainstreaming gender perspective with Chinese character' (Bohong, 2001). Accordingly, even as Li Huiying pointed out, 'In the process of marketism of Chinese society, the original policy of gender equality is weakening, the traditional model of gender division is rising, and the growing of gender sensitive policy is very hard' (Li, 2006). At the same time, international premise has forced the government to bring gender into the mainstream decision-making, and also gave fillip to civilian forces to spread gender consciousness. For example, the well-known NGOs in Beijing such as 'The Migrant Women's Club' and 'The Maple Women's Psychological Counselling Centre' were all established and developed gradually under the globalisation. Therefore, Liu Bohong emphasises that the positive influences from globalisation should not be neglected. The global democratic politics greatly influenced and exerted premise on Chinese government to be responsible and provide social justice, and impelled the Chinese society to increase the democratic demands and human rights and the forces of civil society, including the transformation of women from objectivity to subjectivity. Tan Shen thinks that globalisation itself can be regarded as a unique discourse. It brings not only the exploitation of the capitalism, but also the consciousness of human rights, feminist thoughts and new gender discourse in the forefront (Workshop Record, 2007). This background forces the states to connect gradually the gender discourse to the global system, and simultaneously provides fillip to growth of civilian organisations and the promotion of women's consciousness of human rights.[4]

The most direct influence of globalisation is the reassembling of the power and status of different strata and the prevailing of consumerist culture. Women as a fragile group suffer the marginalised fate provided by the market. A great number of working women are forced to quit or laid off. Female students face frustration in search for a job. Many women engage in occupations related to body and appearance, and the media is full with commercials and activities that take women as consumed object. The market discourse is formed in the background. On the one hand, it highlights the competition of modern ability based on personal quality; on the other hand, it highlights the importance of naturalisation and bodilisation, and aggrandises the traditional difference in biology and role of gender, taking as an aspect of personal quality in market competition. So, the alliance of the market and the traditional culture is a characteristic of gender discourse in globalisation. The saying 'man is in charge of outside and woman in charge of inside' is popular again. Even some well-known scholars advocating 'going back home and learning to live', criticise that 'so-called women's equality with men breaks the gender division in Chinese family, and creates confusions', because it 'misguides the minds on both sides', affects the efficiency of the family, and also breaks the existing order (Yefu, 2004). Zheng emphasises that 'women's equality with men should follow such a rule: no bottom and no ceiling. As a woman, if her capability is fit to be a premier, she should be. And, the society shouldn't discriminate her, saying that she's a woman and can't be competent. There shouldn't be an ideology that prevents her rise to any high position. But simultaneously, he suggests no affirmative action to protect women. If you can't find a job in the competitive market, the society must not provide a job for you just as in the period before reform and opening. What the society offers is your right, but not your job' (ibid.). He concludes in the end: 'Facing the rising of market economy and the end of official bestow, every Chinese woman should re-orient herself. She should no longer take masculine character as the symbol of women's liberation. Woman is a pole of human group. She should present her unique potential and find her own fitting way of living, working and aesthetic style' (ibid.).

In the paragraph of self-contradictory narratives, we see the two aspects of typical market discourse: one is the blind faith in marketism and unconditional maintenance to the quality discourse, believing that in the market context both man and woman can find their job and opportunity only if they hold some ability and quality. But this is a hypothesis under an idealist state, without that the inequality in Chinese social structure will offer diverse chances to man and woman. Therefore, it is hard to realise the equality between man and woman only by the rule of 'no bottom and no ceiling'. Another is the maintenance of the traditional division of gender role. It assumes that 'man is in charge of outside and woman in charge of inside' is efficient both for the society and the family. And, the 'reorientation' or 'new choices' he emphasised time and again is just letting women go back home and take the glorious task of helping husband and raising children. Yet, this discourse's combined marketism and sexism has a broad market in globalised China.

In my interviews, most of the women approve of the saying 'man is in charge of outside and woman in charge of inside'. But when the question, 'would you go back home to be a professional housewife on your conditions' was asked, most answered in the negative. *Lh* has been a professional housewife since she gave birth to twin sons ten years ago. She worked for a foreign company with her husband before her pregnancy. And, now her husband has reached very high position, and her twin sons have gone to school. Reflecting on her life these years, she has various feelings:

Lh	I think it depends. If your economic condition allows it, then it's idealist. In this situation, it's of great benefit to the children, and the husband is free from the housework. But it's not easy to live well in this model. You see the social pressure on the housewife is heavy.
Wu	Really?
Lh	Of course I'm mother of two children. My colleagues envy me. But if I'm a stranger woman, they may discriminate.
Wu	Have you faced a situation like that?
Lh	Yes, saying that working women are most beautiful. It seems people staying at home are ugly.
Wu	They talked like that deliberately in front of you?
Lh	I can feel that they would say it to me. But for my friends I know, they may feel that it's nice to be like me. But not every person is thorough bred in the society. It's a good thing itself, but it's not easy to do well. Once women outside have common language with men, they may play tricks more or less, and the woman staying at home may worry more or less. In fact, mother's job is great, but it's not easy too. The country seems not to recognise it.
Wu	You think so? In which aspects does it not recognise?
Lh	For example, talking about housewives, people always regard their positions as low. But actually if you indeed want to do it well, it is more difficult than working outside in my perspective.

(7 June 2006)

During the whole interview, *Lh* was repeatedly talking about her pride as a mother; but she was complaining the disrespect and discrimination the work of professional housewife and mother in the country and society gets. Eventually her conclusion is 'women should have space of her own'. Another interviewee *Zyf* is a pretty saleswoman working for a big national distributor. She came from a small village to a county after junior high school and then married a boy from a rural area. Reflecting on her experience of living with her parents-in-law and nurturing her baby at home, she said with a sigh: 'In that environment I really felt depressive. During the period of getting married and having a child, I've never went outside the home', 'I had little self-confidence then'. When the baby was 18 months old, she insisted on going out of home to look for a job. Finally, she found a job in a upholstering and dressing of automobile shop with assistance of her classmate.

Zyf	You know what? I feel I am ... I have been really depressed in my husband's family for too long. When I fled away from there, once I left that cage, I feel I can no longer go back to the cage. I feel I should adopt a life of modern woman.
Wu	What's the lifestyle of a modern woman like you said? How do you imagine it?
Zyf	It should be freedom in money, and freedom in mind.
Wu	Freedom in money you mentioned means economic independence and with good condition, then freedom in mind means good spiritual space and with your own friends, is that right?
Zyf	Yes.
Wu	It's actually very high aspiration.
Zyf	But my husband couldn't understand it at that time.
Wu	Maybe he felt frustrated too. He might have felt that you would change after going out to work, didn't he?
Zyf	He has been against me. He cited various reasons such as I would exert too much strength, or he can feed me even if I don't work, and something like that. But I myself stick to nothing, because I feel I no longer want to go back to that environment.

(10 September 2006)

From *Lh's* pride and complaining of her professional housewife's life, to *Zyh's* endeavour to struggle for a free space as a woman, we can figure out the inconsistent influence of the variety and complexity of gender discourse on the working women under the globalisation era. It not only embodies the spirit of self-esteem, self-confidence, self-independence and self-strength emphasised by the state discourse, but also includes the respect on the personal quality and ability, freedom and independence emphasised by the market discourse, and simultaneously integrates active or passive following on the gender role division and cultural norm stressed in the traditional discourse. In the diversity of choices, the biggest impact of globalisation on the working women could be described as the transformation: from passively following the state-dominant discourse on gender equality in the Maoist period, to actively making use of the balance and collaboration of three market-oriented gender discourses in the post-Maoist period. In this manner they might look for maximising the available resources to face various probable disadvantaged situations in globalisation. Therefore, the gender discourse in globalised China represents no longer a myth of equality ideologically constructed of the state and discounted in reality, but a calculated negotiating strategy on utilising the balance of various forces among the state, market and traditional culture to make a autonomous choice in the process of pursuing modernity and individual freedom.

Crisis and Negotiating Strategy of the Working Women

Anthony Giddens (1998) takes risk and uncertainty as the basic characteristics in globalisation. The insecurity and crisis brought by it have adequate embodiment in the tranformative era in Chinese society. Among my interviewees, there exists a universal sense of crisis. It is embodied not only in their attitudes to work and family life, but also in their self-identity as a woman. The co-existence of complicated and multiple gender discourses brings Chinese women various possibilities of gender identity, and also makes them wander and lost between the alternative of 'doing well' and 'marrying well'.

In fact, the market discourse itself delivers such a sense that in the competitive labour market, you may be washed out at any moment, so the basic premise for women to keep their bearings in modern society is to promote quality and ability. *Zca*, a white-collar working for a foreign company mentioned above, referred to 'when I was young' more than 10 times during the two-hour interview, such as when she was young it's no problem working over time at night, she's not feeling bad in comparing herself with boys, she's eager to do well in everything, she's passionate, and so on. It seems she's an aged person now, full of crisis sense in her narrative. This crisis sense is also embodied in her family life situation. She is married for eight years but insists on no children. When I asked her why she chose this family style of 'Dink', she just replied, 'It may be because of my character. I am a person who is eager to do well in everything from my childhood. At that time I was always thinking to do something. By now I'm not emulative as before, and my personality is much softer. But I still want to do what I wanted to do, and hope not to spend my energy on a child. I understand it's unavoidable whether good or bad. Once a woman has a child, her life is centred around the child inevitably, everything encircling her child. It's normal in my opinion, but I just hope not. I hope my life is running true to form' (15 June 2006). Obviously, *Zca* can be categorised as having high identification with both aspects of market discourse, emphasising individual independence and holding basically negative attitude to the traditional norm of gender role.

Another 22 years old girl *Xz*, coming from a village of Shanxi province, has worked in Beijing for six years. She has worked in game-playing room and park, and then worked as a cleaner in a school.

During that time, she joined a computer-education short-term class and learned to use computer skilfully. Then, she got a chance to work at the lodging house office. Now, she has a relatively stable job and salary, with apparel like a city girl. But during the interview, her narrative disclosed a sense of crisis. She kept on saying that 'if one day I cannot muddle along here', fearing some day she would really quit and would go back to her village with no street lamp'. The fear has resulted from two aspects: one is 'I have stayed here for six years after all. I'm very happy in the big city. I feel reluctant if I couldn't muddle along after I stayed in Beijing for so many years'; another is usually 'girls have to go back home to get married after a couple of years', but she has not or would not adapt to the environment in her hometown. *Xz* is very clear about not only the uncertainty of her job and life in the urban, but also the probable risk she faces if she hopes to get a life she desired by a way of 'marrying well'.

Wu	What kind of boyfriend you are looking for?
Xz	At least he should be aspirant.
Wu	What does that mean? Does that mean he earn enough money?
Xz	Being aspirant mean he will make effort to find a job.
Wu	If he works hard but makes no money, would you say he's not an aspirant?
Xz	(smiling) Only even if he made effort that would be okay.
Wu	Would you like to find a handsome man?
Xz	If I had stayed back in my hometown, I would have to. But now I'd like to stay in Beijing, then I can't desire that.
Wu	So you want to find a boyfriend with Beijing Hukou? Probably you need to find a circle to associate with them.
Xz	But there isn't a circle like that.
Wu	It's hard to let other people know you if you just stay here the whole day. Would you choose a boyfriend who is also a rural migrant working here in Beijing?
Xz	If he is capable to stay in Beijing, I would.
Wu	But the housing in Beijing is too expensive. It's not easy to establish a home here.
Xz	We can rent an apartment, and save money slowly.

(8 June 2006)

From the dialogue we can figure out the double crisis in her identity as a rural migrant girl: one is the crisis of identification as either a rural or an urban, another is the crisis of choice in depending on either the quality discourse of marketism or the traditional discourse of sexism, i.e., the crisis of identification as either 'doing well' or 'marrying well'. Obviously, *Xz* accepts both the discourse resources, and also considers the risks accompanying in any kind of choice. So, what globalisation brings her is much more opportunities of attempt and choice, and the worst for her is just going back home one day if she cannot muddled along any more in the city.

Yet for the middle-aged women such as those more than 50 years old and not well educated, what globalisation brings is the crisis of their whole state of making a living. For example, *Dsf* is a lay-off worker of a state-owned factory. After suffering many frustrations and pains during the process of re-employment, finally she found a temporary work in an Institute as a cleaner. Talking about the situation in this period when she and her husband were laid off and stayed at home a couple of years ago, she was full of tears in her eyes:

Dsf	I found female comrade has to pay for herself out if she wants to take up responsibility. And then she will have little time to play or have fun for her family. But you can also do nothing. You can just follow the trend, and live a life of unconstraint and enjoyment. That's okay. But I think you have to finish the task the society gives you. For example, you can leave the child alone. But if you bear a child, you must take the responsibility.
Wu	You appear to be in charge of your family more than your husband.
Dsf	It's true.
Wu	Has he any suggestions on your working outside home?
Dsf	Sometimes he says, you are too bitter living with me the whole life. I say it depends on how you value it. I say I'm still working now, which means I have some ability. Sometimes if I compare my economic condition with others, I would say I'm the weak. But if you compare the responsibility to the family, I would say I am doing my best, and my life is not meaningless. That is, I feel I'm terrific measuring myself from the spirit. Talking about the issue of the child, I feel female comrade is really bitter (crying). It's true. I stayed at home during the two lay off years to be re-employed. That time the pressure on my family was almost unbearable .... That time I even regreted having the child. I said I was incapable of bringing him up. I said I could choose to run away, or divorce my husband. But I thought over later and felt it's not a good idea. If I run away and one day my child would face problems, I will feel sorry. And furthermore, if every person in the society behaved like me ...

(17 May 2006)

The text of *Dsf's* narrative is full of official discourse, merging within the state discourses of Maoist and post-Maoist times. While the individualism grounded in the market discourse and the natural division of gender role renewed with the trend is not emerging obviously. This double crisis of work and family brought by globalisation leads to a more passive negotiating situation for the middle-aged and less-educated women. Since the gender discourse under globalisation characterised the alliance of the market and traditional culture plays greater negative role for them. That is to say, the transformative gender discourse has not become their available resource, or the official discourse is still the most direct force affecting them even in market era. This case indicates that the formation and transformation of gender discourse exerts different influences on women with different ages and strata in extent and direction. On the contrary, the negotiating strategy for them to face the crisis is respectively different.

The trend of marketism and sexism of Chinese gender discourse under globalisation is criticised by feminists, and the state is accused to retreat from the intervening action on gender inequality and doing nothing, and even often becoming the accomplice of consumerism and marketism, attaching importance to the development and ignoring the equality issue, and so on. Nevertheless, the standpoint of the working women themselves can be divided into four different categories from my interviews. The first category is completely positive and affirmative. They argue that the state of gender equality now is much better than in the Maoist era, because the economic status of women has improved, and they have much more freedom than before. The rural migrant women working in the urban area basically approve this standpoint. For example, *Xh* and *Xc* are two hour-maidservants working in a high-level community in Beijing. They emphasise 'women are really equal now with men', 'they are holding not only half the sky, but almost the whole sky.' In the rural area, 'women are entirely in charge of the family', and they are 'more free now', because 'they earn much more money than before' (11 June 2006).

The second category is less positive although it is most affirmative. They acknowledge that there is still inequality in reality, but generally the society nowadays is better than the one in Maoist era, and women master to some extent the freedom of active choice. Many of the women with high education approve this standpoint. In a tea party, I talked with three 40 year old professors *T, H* and *X*. They all affirmed the importance of gender equality. When I asked them to compare the state of gender equality in Maoist and post-Maoist periods, their answer is 'more equal now than before', because women's economic status has improved now, and their 'feeling consciousness is raised also', although their 'mental pressure' is much heavier now than before.

Wu	But how do you think about the saying 'rather marrying well than doing well'? It seems to go back to the trend in pre-Maoist time.
H	The trend of pre-Maoist time is marrying well and completely obeying the man. Now it's different. She wants to marry well, and in the mean time she desires equality with the man. She is not only in pursuit of a good marriage and just following him completely. It's not like the 'marrying well' she wanted.

From this text we can see the impact of formation and transformation of gender discourse on the working women: the improvement of women's economic status and the raising of individual consciousness and the insistence on the independence during the process of alternative between 'doing well' and 'marrying well'. This implies that the market discourse has been rooted deeply in people's heart, and has become one of the most important resources for women in choosing their lifestyle.

The third category quits the old question of gender equality completely, and turns to concern the possibility of individual independence and autonomous choice as modern women. These working women do not regard the equality between man and woman as an important thing; some even think it is not a good thing for women. So it does not matter for them to choose working outside or staying at home as a housewife. But they explicitly understand the risk which is available resource of discourse for them, and they are manifested what kind of strategy should be used to deal with various possible pressures they face. The younger generation of women approve more of this standpoint. For example, the female graduate student *Clh* mentioned above wishes herself to be 'outstanding both in guestroom and in kitchen', and her goal is to be an 'independent modern woman'.

Wu — How do you think the different roles as men and women today? Which one is more comfortable, and which are more difficult? For example, as a woman in which aspects you would feel comfortable and easy, and what kinds of difficulties you may meet? Have you thought about this issue?

Clh — Yes I have. I think as a women we have both advantages and disadvantages. For the former, since you are the weak in other's eyes, you may get help from them; for the latter, since you are weaker than others, it may be more difficult for you to communicate with other people and get their trust. In career, you may be uneasy because of the constrains your family face. So many enterprises would rather employ male. Of course some girls are delicate, that may be one of the reasons. I think as men their advantages are also bi-directional. In employment they have more opportunities and higher salaries. Concerning the disadvantage aspects, I think the competition between the men is full of power. And then their pressure of life is from the society, family and friends.

Wu — So you feel that pressure on men is bigger than on women?

Clh — It depends. In career women's pressure is smaller. They are desired to be independent only, but not successful or performing like men. Being self-independent, that's enough. But the demands on the men in career is much higher. The emphasised aspects for men are their career, for women is their family. And then there is an aspect of taking care of the parents of both sides and the education on the children, they may face different pressure.

(11 July 2006)

In the narrative, *Clh* analysed intensively the relationship of overlapping, balance and collaboration among the three discourses in globalisation. Women's various possible inequality is just attributed to involuntary gender differences. It is determined by the advantages and disadvantages of men and women, and not by the social structure problem.

The fourth category does not care for the issue of gender equality, or it is not sensitive to the old question. But from the perspective of dual responsibility working women took in the society and family, it recognises that women's situation under the market economy has gotten worse than before, and they take much heavier burden than in the Maoist period. Many of the middle-aged women who had been laid-off and losing competence in the labour market approve this standpoint. For example, the laid-off woman worker *Dsf* mentioned above compared the experiences of two periods as woman and concluded, 'In the past, man worked outside. Generally male comrade was in charge of outside, and female comrade was in charge of inside. But now female comrade has to be in charge of both outside and inside'. Since the competition of working outside is more drastic now, she said women nowadays are more tired than those in the 'old society' before revolution. But she argued that they are the generation that accepted the 'old education' in Maoist era, so 'it does not matter' to live such a life full of hardship and less of enjoyment (17 May 2006).

Although *Dsf* complains the state that creates the embarrassment in her life, she generally does not express her dissatisfaction with the market discourse. She acknowledges that in the environment of market economy the opportunities of earning money have increased, and people make much more money than before, and the living standard has also improved. She just sighs that she does not have the right time because of her disadvantage in her age and quality. On the gender discourse, she still adheres to the 'old education' acquired in the Maoist period: that is sharing the equal obligation with men and holding half the sky of working and living. But, during the process, even she recognises the personal quality and ability theory admired in the market discourse; she does not establish the individual consciousness as a subject constructed by the market discourse. The basic point of her choice is still the family admired in traditional discourse but not individual. At this point, it is very different from the younger generation. For the latter, even holding a banner of the traditional culture is on the basis of the personal interest choice and negotiating strategy. So for the generation like *Dsf*, the lack of subject consciousness is one of the most important reasons to become a fragile group in the process of reassembling of globalisation. It is especially significant for them to build an equal and loose context in the social structure and also provide adequate support in policy by the state.

Conclusion

Through the comparative analysis on the texts of the related state policies and gender events or discussions in media in Maoist and post-Maoist eras, based on the categorisation and analysis on the oral narrative data of 21 working women from different occupations, age, strata and marital status, this paper explored the impact of globalisation on the construction and transformation of gender discourse, and also the influence of this transformation on the situation of working women. It concludes as follows:

1. The construction of gender discourse in the Chinese society has an obvious transformation from Maoist to post-Maoist period. This transformation is not simply from a state discourse to another market discourse, but from a gender discourse of state-dominant 'pan-politicalisation' to a market-oriented 'pan-marketism'.
2. The gender discourse in the Maoist period can be called as 'Yo-Yo Model'. Its constructing elements are the state discourse and the traditional discourse, which are respectively bound in the two poles of a spring. Through exclusion and rebound it establishes the authoritative position of the state discourse, and also determines the existing space of the traditional discourse. This kind of gender equality on the part of the state has a very strong rallying point and practical consequence. But since it is limited in the equality of gender obligation and ignores the subject demands of women, consequently women gain the name of half the sky, but they lose the freedom of choice under the dual burden of the reality.
3. The gender discourse in the post-Maoist era can be called as 'Three-Circle-Overlapping Model'. Its constructing elements are dominant market discourse different from the state discourse and traditional discourse. They overlap each other, forming a dynamic balance and collaboration. Among them the state discourse to a large extent relies on the market discourse, and the market discourse gets support from the traditional discourse. Facing the complicated state of overlapping of the three discourses, women have various opportunities and freedom of choice, but simultaneously they often lose the direction of choice in contradictory gender discourses.
4. The market discourse in globalised era is just a quality discourse. It has two aspects: one is the modern competitive ability based on the principle of individualism; another is the symbol of body consumption based on the orientation of women's special role in the relationship of gender. The first aspect gets the strong mobilisation and support from the state, and the second aspect gains the assistance from the traditional discourse and becomes a part of consumptive fashion. In summary, the core of the market discourse is

the relationship of alternative between 'doing well' and 'marrying well' for women.

5. On the one hand, globalisation has changed the narrative content and approach of the state discourse; on the other hand, it has led to the alliance of the market and the traditional discourse. The combination of marketism and sexism is the main feature of gender discourse in globalisation. It represents no longer a myth of gender equality ideologically constructed by the state and discounted in reality, but a calculated negotiating strategy of utilising the balance of various forces among the state, market and traditional culture to make subject choice in the process of pursuing the modernity and individual freedom. The feminist thoughts and consciousness of human rights entering into China along with the globalisation will destroy to some extent the characteristic of the gender discourse.
6. In the risk of globalisation, there exists a universal sense of crisis among the Chinese working women. The different understandings and evaluations of the state of gender equality and the situation of women themselves during this period indicate that the transformation of gender discourse has different impact on the working women with different ages and strata both in extent and direction. On the contrary, their negotiating strategies facing the crisis are respectively different. In Giddens' words, 'Women today hold the nominal chances to pursue over-all possibilities and opportunities: yet in the masculinity culture, many of this kind of paths are closed actually. Furthermore, for getting the existing possibilities and opportunities, women have to abandon the old "stereotyped" identity more thoroughly than men. In other words, they experience the opening of the late modernity as more perfect and contradictory' (Giddens, 1998: 120).

Acknowledgement

My heartfelt thanks go to Genevieve Domenach, Karin Czermak, Li Huiying, Liu Bohong, Tong Xin, Li Yinhe, Tan Shen, Bu Wei, Meng Xianfan and Yang Yiyin who gave comments on my report, of which this paper is a part.

Notes

1. Tan Shen argues that along with globalisation there appears a new gender discourse which is different from state, market and traditional one and can be regarded as the fourth discourse. It is pushed by some international and domestic NGOs, and also some feminist researchers and activists, through ways and forces of developing programmes, providing training and service to impose on the government and exert

influence on the mass. It has become an unneglectable discourse in China (see Workshop Records, 2007).

2. Bohong thinks that there has never been real state feminism in China. But Wang argues that state feminism has various meanings in its transnational usage, early referring to feminists employed as bureaucrats in positions of power or women politicians who promoted gender equality policies, then being conceptualised to enable scholarly examinations of the institutionalisation of feminism in state agencies in a variety of political and economic systems. When used in the discussions on Chinese socialist state's gender policies, it often portrays a paradoxical image of a state patriarch championing women's liberation. Wang finds that existing studies have enabled dissection of patriarchal state power; however, it is never clear how pro-women laws and policies got to be initiated and passed by a patriarchal centralized power structure. They haven't excavated women's role in the policymaking process in the socialist state (Wang, 2005). In this meaning, I still adopt the term to name the state discourse in Maoist China.
3. Bohong suggests that the state discourse after 1949 can be regarded as a 'new tradition'. It is built on the standpoint of the Marxist opinions of women and on the ground of planning economy. Li also emphasizes that the state discourse in Maoist period includes some positive function which should be affirmed adequately. It represents a duty of the government (see Workshop Records, 2007).
4. Tong even argues that the transformation of discourse in globalisation should cover the shift from class discourse to human rights one. Since it's hard to find a solidarity or union of gender or class based on common interests, the only outlet may be to advocate the agency and civil society, to call for the appearance of a new subject in basis of respecting the differences and rights (see Workshop Records, 2007).

References

ACWF Constitution, 1949; Conjunct Creed, 1950; Working Report on the 2nd Women Representatives Conference, 1953; Working Report on the 6th Women Representatives Conference, 1988; Law on the Protection of Rights and Interests of Women, 1992; The Program for the Development of Chinese Women, 1995. For all these documents, please see the official website of ACWF: The Network of Chinese Women.

Barlow, Tani E. (1994). 'Theorizing Woman: Funu, Guojia, Jiating (Chinese Woman, Chinese State, Chinese Family)', in Angela Zito and Tani E. Barlow (eds), *Body, Subject and Power in China*, Chicago: The University of Chicago Press, Chapter 10.

Bohong, Liu (2001). 'Looking Back on the Chinese Social Policies and Gender Issues', Social Policy Forum sponsored by the College of Public

Management and the Institute of Social Policy in Tsinghua University, August 5.

Caiyun, Yutian (2005). *I'm a Female PhD, Whom Will I Marry*, Wuhan: Hubei People's Press.

China Youth Daily (Zhongguo Qingnian Bao) (2006). 'The Confusion in a Female Student's Mind', February 21.

Croll, Elisabeth (1995). *Changing Identities of Chinese Women: Rhetoric, Experience and Self-perception in Twentieth-century China*, Hong Kong: Hong Kong University Press.

Fairclough, Norman (2004). *Discourse and Social Change*, Beijing: Huaxia Press.

Geng, Wang (2003). 'On Doing Well and Marrying Well' (Sina Culture at sina.com), April 30.

Giddens, Anthony (1998). *Modernity and Self-Identity*, Beijing: Sanlian Shu Dian.

Li, Huiying (2005). 'Checking on Contemporary Chinese Social Policies in Perspective of Gender', in Huang Lin (ed.), *Feminism in China 3*, Spring, Nanning: Guangxi Normal University Press.

Li, Xiaojiang (1998). 'Which Discourse Do We Think of Women and Who Makes Discourse and Gives it Meaning?', in Qiu Renzong, Jin Yihong and Wang Yanguang bain (eds), *Chinese Women and Feminist Thought*, Beijing: Chinese Social Sciences Press.

Lin, Chun (1998). 'Gender Equality: Between State and Market', in Qiu Renzong Jin Yihong and Wang Yan'guang bain (eds.), *Chinese Women and Feminist Thought*, Beijing: Chinese Social Sciences Press.

Peiyun, Peng (2002). Summary of the Speach in the 5th meeting of the Executive of the ACWF of the 8th Natioinal Women's Congress, December 12.

Rofel, Lisa (2006). *Other Maternities: Gendered Yearnings in China after Socialism*, Nanjing: Jiangsu People's Press (also published in 1999 by University of California Press).

Talbot, Mary (2004). *Language and Gender: An Introduction*, Wuhan: Central China Normal University Press.

Tamara, Jacka (2006). *Rural Women in Urban China: Gender, Migration, and Social Change*, Nanjing: Jiangsu People's Press.

The Beijing News (Xin Jing Bao) (2004). 'Poll Implies that 40 Per Cent of Women Approve 'Rather Marrying Well Than Doing Well'', November 10.

The Project Group of the Second Survey on Chinese Women's Social Status (2001). 'The Primary Data Report on the Second Survey on Chinese Women's Social Status', *Collection on Women's Studies*, No. 5.

Tong, Xin (2005). *Introduction to the Gender Studies: Analysis to Dynamics of Gender Inequalities*, Beijing: Beijing University Press.

Workshop Records (2007). 'Working Women between the State and Market in a Globalized China', February 8.

Yefu, Zheng (2004). 'Going Back Home and Learning to Live', Speech China Women's College, November 7 (website on Sociology, Forum among Three Universities, Academic Debates).

Yihong, Jin (2003). 'Talking about Female PhD among Five Persons' (Sohu Women at sohu.com), November 14.

Zheng, Wang (1997). 'Explanation of 'Female Consciousness' and 'Gender Consciousness'', *Collection on Women's Studies,* 1: 14–20 (in Chinese).

—— (2000). *The Wane of the Patriarchy: Gender Studies on the Process of Rural Modernization in South of Changjiang River*, Chengdu: Sichuan People's Press.

—— (2005). 'State Feminism?' Gender and Socialist State Formation in Maoist China', *Feminist Studies*, 31 (3), Fall: 519–51.

—— (2006). 'Rethinking the 'Iron Girls': Gender and Labor during the Cultural Revolution in China', *Sociological Studies*, 21 (1): January.

Zuo, Jiping (2005). 'Women's Liberation and Gender Obligation Equality in Urban China: Work/Family Experience of Married Individuals in the 1950s', *Society,* 1 (in Chinese).

12

Son or Daughter?

Son Preference in a Southwest Community of China

ZHANG LIPING

After three decades of reforms and opening up in China, the proportion of ethnic minority (56 groups) population in the total population increased from 6.6 per cent in 1982 to 8.4 per cent in 2000. China's fertility policy (single child policy) did not affect the ethnic minorities but affected significantly the Han Chinese who constitute more than 91 per cent of the population. Ethnic minorities have different customs, marriage rituals and family and reproductive behaviour. Even among the minority, these are vastly different. Though the development of minority population is unique, but to achieve healthy development of minority population is related to national prosperity and social harmony. In order to ensure that the 56 Chinese ethnic groups live together in harmony, the government introduced a series of policies including ones to secure the equality and unity of ethnic groups, give regional autonomy to ethnic minorities and promote respect for the faith and customs of ethnic groups. Among these the policy of regional autonomy for minorities is the most fundamental. Under this policy, five autonomous regions, namely, Inner Mongolia, Xinjiang, Guangxi, Ningxia and Tibet, as well as numerous autonomous prefectures, counties, nationality townships and towns have been set up. With guidance from the Chinese government, the minorities in areas that have been given regional autonomy are entitled to deal with their own affairs. Together with the Han people, the Chinese minorities are making great efforts to build a prosperous China. Since the eighties of the last century, China's sex ratio at birth is more imbalanced than the global average, and it has become a serious population problem today. There are about 113 boys born in China for every 100 girls. While some reasons of this ratio might be biological, there is evidence of sex-selective abortion, neglect, abandonment, and even infanticide of infant females. With the fertility level of ethnic minorities declining, the sex ratio at birth is rising. Most ethnic minorities live in relatively remote areas and to cope with sex ratio situation, the nature and coping strategies become complex. There is lack of research in this area, which should be strengthened.

Gender Preference and Sex Ratio at Birth

The increase in the sex ratio at birth is caused by many factors and gender preference is the final outcome. Studies suggest that besides sustaining family lineage, increase in family's labour, support of elders, factors such as mental solace from the traditional culture, families, retirement, and psychological needs, etc., are also important. Therefore, the analysis of gender preference as the cause of sex ratio at birth is the focus of this paper.

Gender preference theory emphasises the environment's role in the formation of preferences, including marriage and inheritance of the family system. Gender preference has a decisive role in the formation of the family system that is a very important environmental factor (Lavely, Li and Li, 2001). Skinner (1997) points out that gender preference is embedded in the internal logic of the family system. Family system is both a customary and normative. Patrilineal joint family system, preferred form of marriage, family continuity, inheritance, housing arrangements, gender and age are at the centre of the family power structure and influence preference for boys. Patrilineal family system exists in many of the world communities, but the son preference exists in some communities only with different degrees of flexibility. China, Korea, India and other places in northwest have very strict patrilineal family system, which is the root cause of son preference (Dasgupta et al., 2003). The paper is based on an ethnic minority in Guizhou Miao village (hereinafter referred to as 'Miao' village) and analyses the above issues.

Participant Observation

Anthropological research is closely related with the fieldwork. Since Malinowski began participant observation, fieldwork has become the most important anthropological method. Zhuang Kongshao had argued that anthropology should not be wasted. In this fieldwork, the processes of research have not been lost track off. I was alien to the research site and experienced different culture and the research shocks, but the fieldwork provided deeper understanding of issues. Many problems were faced in the field. First was how to enter the field. A use of administrative resources was made which integrated with the local resources to get rid of the negative impacts. I relied on the family planning department at all levels to enter the Miao village. All this helped in gaining information from the respondents as very personal questions were involved in the interviews. The best efforts were made to keep the identity neutral. The field visits to the Miao village were made three times during 2007 to 2010. The fieldwork was a great experience with the emotions attached, new learnings, and challenges of language barriers, resource constraints, perspectives, and even the dress. The theory of gender preference behaviour, without exception, stressed the social and cultural background in understanding their role in gender preference.

Miao Village

Miao village has a population of 741 constituting 172 families. The history of village reveals that they have been living in this village for six generations. Village has an area of 371.63 acres. There are terraces and sloping land and meagre per capita arable land, only 0.51 acre. Village land contract was signed in 1984 and no change has taken place since then. The nd is very unevenly distributed across different families. Village is cated on the mountains and forest coverage rate is more than 72 cent.

trilineal Family System and Gender Preference

atrilineal Family System

he son preference is determined by its own characteristics. Patriarchal system (patrilineality) means men inherit property, living arrangements, family continuity and family dominance on the power structure: the main productive asset passes on through the male line tradition. Women only get the dowry or movable items as inheritance. Couples live with husband's family (the parent living system, patrilocality). In a social order constructed by men, only boys continue the family name, women are only a tool for reproduction, and children obtain their social identity and integration into the social order through the father. Women are valued mainly by the value of their ability to produce children, especially the ability to produce a son. Men have authority in the family and women's participation is limited to economic activities outside the home and for external communication, women have to depend on men.

In the Hmong family, the son of the family inherits the property. It is a tribe with a certain degree of common inheritance of property so as to ensure that the property remains in the hands of direct blood relatives. The clan enforces firmly the control of family property management within the right of inheritance of property in order to avoid the disintegration of clan.[1]

Research in Miao village focused on patrilineal family system o inheritance, living arrangements and other aspects of specific perfo mance. For the definition of family property, I did not communicate directly with the villagers, but found that there were property disputes including housing, land, forests, livestock, rice, jewellery, money, and so on. Parents pass over the property to children of the family, which they inherited from their parents. But at times it is not a complete succession. The eldest son, or the daughter, inherits property but the content and the amount of inheritance and the obligations are different. The terms of succession for the son are separate from the beginning, but for the daughter, it is through marriage. On analysing inheritance issue, I did not focus on the mechanism of separation, but on inheritance of sons and daughters and obligation differences and internal gender preferences.

In Miao village, most ancestral houses are old and crowded. With the child's birth, there is often a need for new house as the old house is not enough. As per the custom, grown up children do not sleep with the parents on the same bed; father has a separate bed while the mo children sleep in one bed. Separation of the kitchen is usual point of separation. When the son gets married, he has his own a sub-stove as a fire pit cooking. However, for this separation certain ceremony. For construction of the house, the brothers consulted. There is a negotiation and if two agree, the younger to help his elder brother build a house. The consultation is main as the elder brother leaves, the original old house will be ow younger brother, so he has the responsibility to help the elder construction of the house. In general, in case of two brothers, th will remain in the old house with the parents. He will also inherit the property, but there are exceptions. But in most separations, the younger brother lives in the old house. However, the elder brother would have slightly greater share of the fields/land. When parents live with the younger son, the other son's help is only moral, but not a responsibility. Property is the old age pension. But if the younger son does not take care of the parents, then the other son can take care of them.

Daughter Inheritance is Dowry

In Miao village marriage among couples with the same surname is banned, as they are exogamous. When women marry, they get dowry from their parents and there is no real estate and land involved which belongs to her family. Her dowry is the form of inheritance of family property. Thus, daughters do not have any inheritance right in the property from the house. Dowry varies across times and families.

Daughter has no Right to Inherit Land

In the household responsibility system, the land is divided as per the number of members in the household, and the daughter also has a share in land. However, in an interview, *BG* said, that an old couple had three daughters and the family consisted of five people. Three daughters got married. He did not give land to daughters but gave the ancestral home as dowry. In fact, land cannot be given to the daughter as dowry because it would go to her husband's family. If she is married in the same village, it cannot be given to the in-laws, as the field/land is small. The father may however share rice with the daughter. So, from her parents' home she only gets a dowry under normal circumstances, no inheritance of land. In case of residential real estate, it is rarely shared with the daughter because the demand for housing is high and due to scarcity of resources, the family wealth is not to be lost.

Inheritance with Limited Resources

Deeply rooted in the local concepts of family, property, inheritance and othe[illegible]lls is the family unit. According to Fei Xiaotong, the family [illegible]es for inheritance limitations of a relative following the system. [illegible] times when these provisions are difficult to follow, as vacancies [illegible]asy to fill. There are many suitable characteristics to follow such [illegible]eration arrangement. Differentiations between men and women [illegible]ily on a single system, which is affinity level.

[illegible]rited the Family Property

[illegible] property, both land and house, belongs to the family. Family [illegible]tions are ordered from near to far and in case no heir, inheritance [illegible]rst of the family room then extended to other family assets. Under the 'not married surname' principle, women married into other families are not eligible to inherit property. As property, fields and forests are a scarce resource, it is kept within the family and not given to anyone outside the family.

In an interview, BG reported about just occurred property dispute where a woman remarried after her husband's dead. She with her new husband wanted to live in the same room with the family of the brother of the deceased husband. The brother did not agree to their marriage and did not want her to take his brother's room, which is considered as family property. She went to Murakami town to complain where her marriage was declared legitimate and the appeal of the brother was termed as unreasonable.

In case of remarriage (without certificates) after a man's death, the families do fight over the estate. In such a case, before the death of the man, both husband and wife lived together to raise children as old age pension. The brother of the deceased husband claimed the barn, some fields and forest owned by the deceased husband, as it is their family property and does not want the woman inherit the property.

However, the final result is that the woman and her new husband should inherit all the property.

(b) *The Skills of the Family Heritage*
Moreover, not only property, the transmission techniques are also limited within the family. Skills are passed on within the family, such as Lusheng master in the village who are three brothers and learnt skills from their father, a silver craft master. This skill was passed on to three nephews. Ghost Master *YG* was aged fifteen when his father taught him. Families keep secret the skills of family as heritage.

(c) *Limited Resources and Inheritance*
Houses, mountains, fields are scarce local resources. Infrastructure, social and cultural systems are the constraints. These determine the relationship between families and relatives. The main line is the male line. Male-biasness is towards the guidelines, which become the basic rules. An elderly called *YGZ* had two daughters; one married into the village, and the other outside the village. The house was rundown and very old. The second floor had one room. The elderly was relatively stiff, when I went to his house with his nephew. He let me listen to his problems. He stated that the field was in poor shape and income was low. The property is too little and not cost-effective. He relies on his nephew for support. He said he couldn't allow his nephew and the daughter-law to stay with him, as it would create more problems.

The Inheritance of Family with No Son

Households without Children or Unmarried Person's Property Inheritance and Pension

Hmong community has a commitment to the common inheritance of property. Clan elders together decide on the separation wherein the patriarch presides over the ceremony. Clan elders together protect the inheritance and family's wealth. On the other hand, in dealing with the property without son, the rules are clearly defined. In Miao village, generally, non-sub-family within the family members gets the endowment. Family not having children adopt a child from within the sub-family. A son may be adopted from a brother. Mostly nephew of the family gets the family pension and fields as inheritance. These measures prevent the outflow of the property. As a general rule, if there is no son within the family, then elderly can find an old-age son. All this is done in the context of limited resources such as land and real estate. In few cases, the daughter is not married off to ensure that a family member inherits the property from the family room to fields. Cases are also there when the nephew inherits the property and the elderly are not cared for properly.

Heavy Burden of Dowry

Currently there is increasing demand for dowry and many people can no longer afford it. The ghost *YG* described it an act of 'lawlessness' to demand huge dowry. Though at the local level, *BG* says that economic conditions are better, but even for ordinary families, the cost of a daughter's marriage in 2000 required at least five or six thousand dollars. Given the low per capita income in the local conditions, it is not a small burden. When I investigated this in 2010, the cost of a daughter's marriage in general had touched nearly a million. When I tried to solicit information on this in Miao village, the response was regrettably not there. Thus, dowry required to marry off their daughters can be brought in by daughter-in-laws, so the economic costs of raising sons and daughters is self-evident. Dowry has become an economic burden on poor families and villagers who do not have field, land are worst off.

Ideal Child Number and the Family Simple Reproduction

In the social and cultural systems, values, ideas, symbols and rituals are the ideological content of the superstructure. Based on Harris technology that underlines environmental and techno-economic determinism, the social life is the basis of the causal sequence of structure – as the social life of the upper structure of the causal sequence; namely, the production and reproduction are ways to meet the most important human needs and infrastructure. These not only provide advantages to the family in terms of political and economic base but also lead to different types of values, concepts, symbols and rituals of the establishment. These things explain the ideological and political economy to strengthen family and status. Fertility is not only the ideological content of social and cultural system of the superstructure, but also is closely related with the gender preference.

Ideal Child Number and Gender Composition

When I first came to Miao village in 2007, I asked about the ideal number of children and preferred sex of the child. I found that more than 65 per cent respondents wanted two children and that too the boys.

The Reproduction of Family

As ethnic minorities, local fertility policy is of two children. According to the fertility level, the population size has remained unchanged. As per Marxian theory of population reproduction, it is the simple reproduction of population size. There is, however, need for some structure corresponding to the gender and family size in order to ensure the simple reproduction.

In a family of six people that include grandparents, parents and two children – one daughter and one son. But, according to patrilineal inheritance, the daughter no longer belongs to the family. After the marriage and birth of a child to the son, family size increases to eight. But when the grandparents die, the family reduces to six again, the population size remains unchanged, which is a simple reproduction.

In another case a family of six comprising grandparents, parents and the two sons and when two sons get married two daughter-in-laws come, the family of six becomes the family of eight. Further, two children are born each to two daughter-in-laws, the family size goes up to twelve. When grandparents die, the family becomes of ten people; thus, family size is an expansion in terms of reproduction.

In another case a family of six comprising grandparents, parents and the two daughters. Daughters when married off they are no longer member of the family, thus six-member family becomes family of four, and when grandparents die, only parents are left behind, reducing population size within the family to two.

Now, similarly, when we look at the real estate and per capita land, similar changes occur. In Miao village, in a family comprising a woman and her daughter, daughter is married, had a son, who lived with the elderly in old house. If you feel that the house is old, then reconstruct the house. If you have two sons, the room is very small. So son separation takes place. The son needs to go out and has to build a house. Given the father's financial ability, father will bear the cost of construction, but in general the sons bear the cost themselves, brothers help each other. But regardless of who is going to build a house, it is a heavy burden. A new house may require one hundred thousand yuan and so many people go out to work to earn money. The house is constructed bit by bit in four or five years as the money flows in. First, they take up the framework of house on stilts, and when more money comes, the house is completed. Therefore, from this perspective, the birth of the son is a heavy burden. The house has to be passed down from generation to generation which is mostly refurbished.

A two-children family is the ideal family model and that too a son and a daughter. This family of six has farmland and a house. Daughter gets married and goes out and did not take farmland while the son gets married, brings in daughter-in-law who did not bring farmland. Thus property is not divided. Daughter-in-law gives birth to a son and a daughter and the family becomes of eight people. When two elderly people die, six people are left with the farmland.

In another case, if there are two sons in the family, six people share the farmland. But when the sons get married, two daughter-in-laws come into the family to increase the family size to eight people. The daughter-in-laws produce two children each and family size goes up to twelve. Even with the death of grandparents, the family is still the poor. Twelve people living in a big old house and children have farmland. The children have a room; a large family of four children might get two or three individual farmlands/fields. With reproduction the family size has increased, but the farmland is a fixed resource and can only lead to a decline in per capita level. To maintain the family size, the replacement level of fertility in the families is important. Otherwise, per capita farmland would go down.

Look at the woman who gives birth to two children, parents have a house, six people depend on the farmland, and this is a very attractive resource in patrilineal inheritance system. If the resources are to be shared with the daughter, it means outflow of the family property, which is unacceptable to the family. According to the order of succession, family housing, surname of the family and patrilineal descent system, the assets belong to the family, within the family inheritance is valid, then the inheritance is the overall family room, and the fields.

If marriage is not permitted within the same surname, then the daughter is not part of the family and so cannot inherit her parents' house and also participate in care of the parents in the old age. Who settles their pension then? If the father does not have a son, then his brother is happy to offer his son for adoption to him. This is a great resource for the son of the tribe to agree to house more families, the family can resolve their problem of insufficient internal resources, but to protect the wealth of parents, the successor is the nephew and not the daughter.

From the cultural point of view the existence of the patrilineal inheritance system ensures the continuation of a family. From the child's gender structure, a son and a daughter is a very good model. For a family, if the resources permit, would like to expand its size, but with limited resources it becomes important to maintain a replacement level of children and a woman plays a role to maintain constant size of per capita resources. As an ideal model, not every family can follow the premise of a natural birth, and have to artificially alter the natural reproductive choice. It is bound to change the law of nature, i.e., changing the natural distribution of sex ratio at birth.

Effect of Decrease in Gender Preferences by Government

The daughter is excluded from the succession system in the village and the existing pension system. Thus, families go for son. In order to have girls, in the country 'care for girls' and 'girls are same as boys' were preached for generations. The daughter can be preferred becasuse in the old age of the parents, she can help obtain family pension.

Interest-oriented Mechanism

The current one-child family planning policy, female in households and two couples over sixty years with the national pension, the families can afford to give priority to girl for guaranteeing such care. Many of these families on the basis of field experience can get state subsidies or subsistence allowances, better household economic status than families with boys. In recent years, two-female households in the family planning policy leaned toward them with financial support, especially in the Miao village in low-income areas; a few hundred dollars in cash not only improved their standard of living, but also reduced the pension worries. For example, *ZJK* has two married girls. Meanwhile, in one girl's family daughter is married off, who does not get the farmland and the family is better off. However, when there are sons, such as two brothers, together with their parents, are four members at the farmland. When two brothers get married and have two children, the family size raises to eight and now eight people have the same farmland. The life becomes difficult, but because of the implementation of policies guaranteeing financial assistance due to birth of girls, the household becomes better off.

Interest-oriented mechanism leads to birth of females because of economic advantage in the old age. This could reverse the desire for boys. In fact, family with two girls gets subsidies from the state is indeed an envy. It is suggested that two-female households state preferential policies can increase income of such households and parents can get some protection in old age.

In short, the promotion of daughter for old age has emerged among the villagers. It would led to breakage of male line of succession in case of real estate and land inheritance. This needs to be publicized, especially through government propaganda. The example of *YSL* that built a new house using financial support of two-girl family pension or a pension is good experience. Daughters can also look after their elderly parents.

Notes

1. The Hmong ethnic groups: They live in their own clan, and in each clan there is a head master of the clan. The head master would be the one who is the wisest and the one who has been in the clan the longest. He would be the one to watch and take care of the whole tribe. Whenever problems arouses they would come to the head master to seek out answers. Also the ways of living is surrounded by guys being the dominant one's to the clans and girls are more likely to be outcast. For after the girls run off and get married she is no longer her parents' clan, but taken part of her husband's clan. According to scholars, 'Few Hmong know for long the close ties of the nuclear family as an isolated unit. As soon as a son marries and brings his wife to live in his father's house, the family

becomes an extended household. Firstly, therefore, we have a nuclear family, and then the male siblings bring in their wives and children under the same roof, giving the fullest expression to their relationship in the form of the extended household. This cluster of classificatory brothers may later separate into different households; but they, together with their spouses and offspring, can become a lineage. Lineal ties will be remembered. If it is forgotten, the sharing of common ancestral rituals will be evoked in reckoning the lineage membership with other people.' As today this kind of living is still practiced around the Hmong communities. It's been passed on down from many generations ago, so many must keep their heritage. Clanship has not been changed also.

References

Banister, J. (2004), 'Shortage of Girls in China Today', *Journal of Population Research,* 21(1): 19–45.

Dasgupta, M., Jiang Zhenghua, Li Bohua, Xie Zhenming, Woojin Chung and Bae Hwa-Ok (2003), 'Why is Son Preference so Persistent in East and South Asia? Cross Country Study of China, India, and the Republic of Korea', *The Journal of Development Studies,* 40 (2): 153–187.

Hull, T.H. (1990), 'Recent Trends in Sex Ratios at Birth in China', *Population and Development Review,* 16 (1): 63–83.

Lavely, William Li Jianke and Li Juanghong (2001), 'Sex of Children in a Meifu Li Community of Hainan China', *Population Studies,* (55): 319–329.

Skinner, G.W. (1997), 'Family Systems and Demographic Processes', *Anthropological Demography: Toward A Synthesis,* Chicago, Illinois: University of Chicago Press, pp. 53–95.

Index